THE EUROPEAN ROOTS OF THE *LEX SPORTIVA*

This open access book explores the complexity of the *lex sportiva*, the transnational legal regime governing international sports.

Pioneering in its approach, it maps out the many entanglements of the transnational governance of sports with European legal processes and norms. The contributors trace the embeddedness of the *lex sportiva* within national law, European Union law and the European Convention on Human Rights. While the volume emphasizes the capacity of sports governing bodies to leverage the resources of national law to spread the *lex sportiva* globally, it also points at the fact that European legal processes are central when challenging the status quo as illustrated recently in the *Semenya* and *Superleague* cases. Ultimately, the book is also a vantage point to start critically investigating the Eurocentricity and the complex materiality underpinning the *lex sportiva*.

The European Roots of the *Lex Sportiva*

How Europe Rules Global Sport

Swedish Studies in European Law
Volume 18

Edited by
Antoine Duval
Alexander Krüger
and
Johan Lindholm

•HART•
OXFORD • LONDON • NEW YORK • NEW DELHI • SYDNEY

HART PUBLISHING

Bloomsbury Publishing Plc

Kemp House, Chawley Park, Cumnor Hill, Oxford, OX2 9PH, UK

1385 Broadway, New York, NY 10018, USA

29 Earlsfort Terrace, Dublin 2, Ireland

First published in Great Britain 2024

A catalogue record for this book is available from the British Library.

A catalogue record for this book is available from the Library of Congress.

Library of Congress Control Number: 2023950827

ISBN: HB: 978-1-50997-144-2
ePDF: 978-1-50997-146-6
ePub: 978-1-50997-145-9

Typeset by Compuscript Ltd, Shannon

Contents

1

Made in Europe: Lex Sportiva *as Embedded Transnational Law*

ANTOINE DUVAL, ALEXANDER KRÜGER AND JOHAN LINDHOLM*

I. WHY TRACE *LEX SPORTIVA'S* EUROPEAN ROOTS?

WHEN WE WATCH the final of the FIFA World Cup or the opening ceremony of the Olympic Games, we, inhabitants of this globe, all experience the same spectacle, a globally shared moment (though presented and narrated differently by local media). This ideal of universality, embodied by international sporting competitions organised on a level playing field, lies at the heart of the Olympic Movement and is invoked to justify the need for the transnational governance and regulation of sports by sports governing bodies (SGBs). In practice, international sporting competitions are primarily shaped by an ensemble of private rules and processes produced and enforced by the SGBs. This transnational legal regime governing international sports, commonly referred to as the *lex sportiva*, has been characterised as one of the premier examples of private law-making on a global or transnational scale.[1] Like other so-called transnational legal orders, the *lex sportiva* is frequently described as anational, that is, not based on, developed by or legitimised by nation states. This conception of transnational legal orders as 'global law without a state'[2] challenges traditionalist, state-based concepts of law or, to speak with Teubner, 'breaks frames'.[3]

Undoubtedly, international SGBs, such as the World Anti-Doping Agency (WADA), the *Fédération internationale de football association* (FIFA) and the

* Antoine Duval is a Senior Researcher at TMC Asser Instituut, Alexander Krüger is a doctoral student at Umeå University and Johan Lindholm is a Professor of Law at Umeå University.

[1] F Latty, *La Lex Sportiva : Recherche Sur Le Droit Transnational* (Martinus Nijhoff Publishers, 2007); A Duval, 'Lex Sportiva: A Playground for Transnational Law' (2013) 19 *European Law Journal* 21.

[2] G Teubner (ed) *Global Law Without a State* (Dartmouth Publishing Company, 1997).

[3] G Teubner, 'Breaking Frames: Economic Globalization and the Emergence of Lex Mercatoria' (2002) 5 *European Journal of Social Theory* 199.

International Olympic Committee (IOC) engage in transnational governance through their private regulations.[4] Furthermore, specialised private dispute resolution bodies, primarily the Court of Arbitration for Sport (CAS), enjoy the quasi-exclusive competence to resolve the disputes that arise out of this private governance.[5] In doing so, they establish authoritative interpretations of the SGBs' rules and 'discover' general principles of sports law. As Foster has helped explain, this story is part of a more general ideology of sports as not only being capable of self-regulation but also, and strategically more importantly, as claiming autonomy from state interference.[6] The latter places the governance of international sports outside the reach of the state and its law and within its own self-governed social system.

There is no denying that private SGBs make significant normative and institutional contributions to the rules and principles governing international sports and their enforcement. However, we believe that the idea that the *lex sportiva* was born and developed independently of state-based, national and supranational, law cannot be supported empirically. Although some may for romantic or ideological reasons seek to claim otherwise, there is in practice no such thing as anational transnational law,[7] at least not in sports. Previous studies, as well as many of those presented in this volume, have demonstrated that even in such an extensively globalised, privatised and institutionalised sector as sports, 'law *without* a state' is a misnomer and that it is more appropriate to speak about transnational law as 'law *beyond* the states'[8] or as forming a transnational legal assemblage.[9]

The importance of this distinction lies in the focus on the intimate connections between (the) *lex sportiva* and state-based law: although the *lex sportiva's* connections to national and supranational law are subtle and complex, they are both real and substantial. What we do not wish to suggest, however, is that the *lex sportiva* is another form of international law dominated ultimately by nation states. Such a state-centric position would be equally wrong on empirical grounds. Instead, this volume is a call to dive into the complexity and enmeshment that characterises *lex sportiva* as a transnational legal assemblage and to explore the difficulties and paradoxes that its radically pluralist nature might pose for our traditional legal and political thinking.

[4] A Duval, 'Transnational Sports Law: The Living Lex Sportiva' in P Zumbansen (ed), *The Oxford Handbook of Transnational Law* (Oxford University Press, 2021).

[5] J Lindholm, *The Court of Arbitration for Sport and Its Jurisprudence: An Empirical Inquiry into Lex Sportiva* (TMC Asser Press, 2019).

[6] K Foster, 'Global Sports Law Revisited' (2019) 17 *Entertainment and Sports Law Journal*. On this autonomy, see J-L Chappelet, *Autonomy of Sport in Europe* (Council of Europe Publishing, 2010).

[7] R Michaels, 'The True Lex Mercatoria: Law Beyond the State' (2007) 14 *Indiana Journal of Global Legal Studies* 447.

[8] ibid.

[9] A Duval, 'Seamstress of Transnational Law: How the Court of Arbitration for Sport Weaves the Lex Sportiva' in N Krisch (ed), *Entangled Legalities Beyond the State* (Cambridge University Press, 2021).

The main hypothesis that drove the project and the conference behind this volume was that European laws, widely understood as covering national and supranational legal norms and processes stemming from the European continent, play a unique and significant role in defining the operation and substance of the *lex sportiva*. In other words, our intuition was that despite its global reach and its ambition to provide a universal level playing field for international sporting competitions, the *lex sportiva* is primarily embedded in legal institutions which are European in terms of their origins in social, cultural and geographical terms. In the literature, the *lex sportiva* is often pitched against other European legal orders and described as neatly separated from them. It is our ambition to go against this grain and to document instead the inter-legality – some would say the messiness – of a *lex sportiva* forged out of many legal components borrowed from Europe's legal heritage.

The centrality of Europe in our project is linked, on the one hand, to our own bias towards the legal contexts that we know best and where our expertise mainly lies and, on the other hand, our empirical hunch that Europeans (and European ideas) have a disproportionate influence on the *lex sportiva*. Indeed, it is a fact that most of the international SGBs' members of the Olympic Movement have their seat in European states, mostly Switzerland but not exclusively. Moreover, the CAS, as the central body where fundamental legal questions related to international sports are being debated and decided, is based in Lausanne and its awards can only be appealed directly to the Swiss Federal Tribunal (SFT). Finally, most of the other key judicial decisions discussed in the literature and seen as central to the current shape of the *lex sportiva*, such as the decisions in *Bosman*[10] and *Mutu and Pechstein*,[11] stem from supranational courts (located) in Europe. Thus, there are many indices that point at a eurocentrism of the *lex sportiva* and that justify our desire to dig further in this direction.

Furthermore, our research is also inspired by the growing scholarship on the extraterritorial reach of EU law,[12] which Bradford famously coined as the Brussels effect.[13] As the contributions to this volume illustrate, European laws are travelling the world on the back of the *lex sportiva*, shaping the way non-Europeans experience sports. This raises difficult questions linked to the legitimacy of such legal imperialism through the back door. Our ambition was not to tackle them head-on in this book, as they would deserve a separate volume with a more diverse group of contributors including non-European authors. However, as

[10] Case C-415/93 *Union royale belge des sociétés de football association ASBL v Jean-Marc Bosman, Royal club liégeois SA v Jean-Marc Bosman and others and Union des associations européennes de football (UEFA) v Jean-Marc Bosman*, ECLI:EU:C:1995:463.

[11] *Mutu and Pechstein v Switzerland* (2018) App no 40575/10 & 67474/10 (ECtHR, 2 October 2018).

[12] J Scott, 'Extraterritoriality and Territorial Extension in EU Law' (2014) 62 *American Journal of Comparative Law* 87–125; M Cremona and J Scott (eds), *EU Law Beyond EU Borders: The Extraterritorial Reach of EU Law* (Oxford University Press, 2019).

[13] A Bradford, *The Brussels Effect* (Oxford University Press, 2020).

expanded on in the final section of this introductory chapter, we do hope that this project triggers an interest in these issues. Indeed, we believe that one of the core contributions of this volume lies in showing how Europeans through a variety of legal interventions (or non-interventions) shaped (and still shape) the transnational governance of international sports, with little accountability vis-à-vis the many (non-European) people that are ultimately affected by them.

Our contributors were invited to engage in this tracing exercise in a variety of empirical contexts based on their expertise and interests. They explored the complex entanglements between the *lex sportiva* and European laws with both descriptive and normative ambitions and exposed how a multiplicity of European legal concepts and idea(l)s travel through the bloodstream of transnational sports law. As expanded on below, these entanglements can be separated into two types, where the first concerns how European laws (both legal rules and processes) are reflected in the institutional structure and normative substance of the *lex sportiva* and the second how European laws act as a form of constitutional check inside the *lex sportiva* on the exercise of legislative, executive and judicial power by the SGBs.

Draft versions of the chapters included in this volume were presented and discussed at a conference co-organised by Umeå University and the T.M.C. Asser Institute, which took place on 18–19 November 2021 in Umeå, Sweden. The conference and this volume were made possible through the generous financial support of the Swedish Network for European Legal Studies (SNELS), for which we are extremely grateful. We are also grateful for the participation of the keynote speakers, Professors Hellen Keller, Miguel Maduro and Stephen Weatherill, who through their presentations and comments greatly contributed to this project.

II. THE EUROPEAN ROOTS OF THE *LEX SPORTIVA*

One of the main objectives of this volume is to trace the European roots of the *lex sportiva*. Formulated differently, we set out to broadly identify some of the various contributions made by European laws to the constitution and substance of the transnational governance and regulation of sports. In this regard, we have collected contributions that study how different components of the *lex sportiva*, be they institutional or normative, are grounded in or influenced by European legal rules, processes and institutions. In so doing, the chapters of this volume highlight the manifold ways in which *lex sportiva* is embedded in a variety of European laws.

Firstly, it is well known that Switzerland is host to many international SGBs, such as the IOC, FIFA and the CAS.[14] It is thus not particularly surprising that

[14] J-L Chappelet, 'Switzerland's Century-Long Rise as the Hub of Global Sport Administration' (2021) 38(6) *The International Journal of the History of Sport* 569–90; RR Ruiz, 'Swiss City Is "the Silicon Valley of Sports"' *The New York Times* (22 April 2016).

Swiss law makes a fundamental contribution to the emergence and operation of the *lex sportiva*.[15] Duval argues in his chapter that Swiss law underpins the entire institutional architecture of the *lex sportiva* and constitutes it as a transnational governance regime. Indeed, without the support of Swiss law, most of the main international SGBs would not be able to operate as they do. It is Swiss law that confers on them their legal personality and allows them to autonomously regulate their members (and their members' members). Furthermore, the SFT has proven a key institution in bringing into existence the CAS and in endowing it with the legitimacy necessary to confer authority and finality to its awards. Hence, he suggests that the *lex sportiva* must be understood as a transnational legal regime deeply embedded in the Swiss legal and political context and fundamentally dependent on Switzerland's steady endorsement for its smooth transnational operation.

A further interesting example of the importance of Swiss law can be found in a specific area of the *lex sportiva*: the *lex olympica*, ie the transnational sports rules governing the Olympic Games. The value of universalism is particularly present and strong in Olympic sports and at the Olympic Games, as the symbolism of the Olympic rings clearly communicates. However, as *Chernyk* demonstrates through her historical review of past Host City Contracts (HCCs), the HCCs' 'legal gravity has been and still is located in Switzerland'.[16] HCCs are IOC-drafted standard and effectively mandatory contracts that host cities and host states must agree to in order to organise the Olympic Games. In addition to setting out the central terms governing the relationship between the IOC and the organisers of the Olympic Games, the HCCs contain provisions that require host countries to adopt specific Olympic laws that apply beyond the activities in the stadiums. Through archival research, *Chernyk* retraces at the core of the HCCs the longstanding presence of Swiss private law: it is Swiss law, as the governing law of the contract, that defines the limits of party autonomy, governs adjudication of disputes and provides many of the central concepts forming the substantive obligations under the HCCs.

In his chapter, *Lindholm* explores the European influence on the emergence and interpretation at the CAS of the principle of legality, which acts as a check on the SGBs. After mapping out different variants of legality found in the *lex sportiva*, the author demonstrates how the presence and content of this important principle can in part be seen as an externally-imposed requirement of Swiss law that in terms of content is directly inspired from Swiss law and European human rights law. However, the conception of legality in the *lex sportiva* also extends beyond such requirements. Since no legal order can exist without

[15] A Rigozzi, 'L'importance du droit suisse de l'arbitrage dans la résolution des litiges sportifs internationaux' (2013) 132 *Revue de droit suisse* 301; Duval (n 9).

[16] See Chernyk, 'Europeanisation of the Olympic Host City Contracts' in chapter four of this volume.

legality,[17] the principle is of existential importance to the *lex sportiva* as a legal order. Seen from his perspective, the CAS has, in its jurisprudence, drawn from state-based conceptions of legality to develop the *lex sportiva's* claim for status vis-à-vis state-based legal orders.

The embeddedness of the *lex sportiva* in Swiss law evidenced by these three chapters raises several important questions about the global implications and influence of a set of fundamentally local norms, processes, institutions and culture. Thus, this volume puts a spotlight on the complex local/global dynamic underlying the operation of the *lex sportiva*, which is to some extent characteristic of globalisation.

Swiss law is, however, not the only European national or supranational law that has found its way into the *lex sportiva* and through it regulates how the world experiences international sporting competitions. *James and Osborn* also focus on the *lex olympica* and HCCs with an emphasis on the phenomenon of legal transplants. An interesting aspect of the *lex olympica* is its particularly strong impact on state-based law. In particular, *James and Osborn* present the HCCs as powerful vehicles to transplant European legal concepts related to intellectual property rights into the legal orders of host states throughout the world. The authors show in their chapter how Anglo-European notions of contract law and intellectual property law are transplanted into host jurisdictions through Olympic law. Using the example of the law on ambush marketing for the 2012 London Olympic Games and its enforcement, the authors chart how the European influence on Olympic law 'is not only substantive, but procedural and cultural'.[18]

Similarly, *Flanagan* and *Exner*[19] highlight in their respective chapters the interpenetration of European supranational law, such as European Union (EU) law and the European Convention of Human Rights (ECHR), with the *lex sportiva*. *Flanagan*, in an extensive review of FIFA's data protection rules and its introduction of a FIFA Clearing House, traces empirically the influence of EU data protection law and EU financial services regulations on FIFA's private regulations and institutional designs. In doing so, *Flanagan* argues that FIFA enables EU data protection and financial rules to travel worldwide, far beyond their intended territorial or personal scope. Consequently, in this example, EU law is not only transposed and integrated by FIFA in its *lex FIFA*, it also becomes part and parcel of a worldwide standard that applies to the entire football community,

[17] See Lindholm, 'Putting the Lex into *Lex Sportiva*: The Principle of Legality in Sports' in chapter three of this volume.

[18] See James and Osborn, 'The Influence of European Legal Culture on the Evolution of *Lex Olympica* and Olympic Law' in chapter five of this volume.

[19] See Flanagan, 'Who Regulates the Regulators? How European Union Regulation and Regulatory Institutions May Shape the Regulation of the Football Industry Globally' in chapter six of this volume and Exner, 'The Europeanisation of Clean Sport: How the Council of Europe and the European Union Shape the Proportionality of Ineligibility in the World Anti-Doping Code' in chapter seven of this volume.

and in particular to national football federations and the actors active in the transfer market. In this situation, the *lex sportiva* is thus not only perceived as a receptor (or translator) of EU law but becomes a vector of the so-called Brussels effect.

The role of European institutions and processes also lies at the heart of *Exner's* analysis of the drafting process of the World Anti-Doping Code (WADC). In his chapter, he identifies the influence of the Council of Europe and the EU in the definition of the proportionality of ineligibility sanctions under the WADC and shows that both were able to influence at least in part the outcome of the revision process of the WADC 2021. The chapter highlights the political influence of European states and organisations in the drafting of the inherently global WADC. In doing so, European representatives are able to embed into the WADC concerns and concepts based on interpretations of the principle of proportionality which stem both from EU law and the European Court of Human Rights' (ECtHR) interpretation of the ECHR.

In sum, the first contribution of this book is in evidencing the integration of various European legal concepts, norms and processes in the transnational legal assemblage that constitutes the *lex sportiva*. Unlike its abstract image as a global legal regime detached from any locality, the *lex sportiva* is shown as being weaved from a variety of legal threads or constructed from a diverse set of legal components, many of which are grounded in different types of European laws. While it is evident that Swiss law plays a central role in the constitution and maintenance of the *lex sportiva*, it is not the only source of European influence identified by our contributors. The image that emerges of the *lex sportiva* is one of a complex legal tapestry made mostly in Europe's legal workshops but exported throughout the world to govern international sporting competitions and their many participants.

III. THE INTEGRATION OF EUROPEAN CHECKS INTO THE *LEX SPORTIVA*

European legal institutions are not only essential to the constitution of the transnational governance of sports by the SGBs, they also constitute the primary checks on the rules and decisions stemming from it. Thus, various European courts (and administrative agencies, such as the DG Competition of the European Commission) become part and parcel of the *lex sportiva* through their role as independent judicial review mechanisms where decisions of the SGBs (and in particular awards of the Court of Arbitration for Sport) can be challenged. These national and supra-national interventions are relatively rare and of a case-by-case nature, thus they do not deprive the SGBs of their central governance and regulatory power. Instead, they operate primarily as counter-powers taking the form of a proportionality test imposed on the SGBs' regulations and decisions. In sum, what the volume shows is that the SGBs are required to justify their regulatory approaches before a range of judicial and administrative institutions that are located on the European continent.

In theory, national courts throughout the world have the potential to review the decisions or regulations of the international SGBs. However, they rarely do so effectively in practice. As highlighted in *Duval's* chapter,[20] the SFT has a potentially central role to play in this regard, as it is directly competent to review CAS awards under the Swiss Private International Law Act. In fact, many national courts point at the possibility of such a review before the Swiss court as justification for their own unwillingness to entertain challenges against CAS awards. Yet, thus far, the SFT has exercised a very hands-off review of the awards submitted to it, leading in practice to a very deferential stance vis-à-vis the CAS. In general, the same is true of other national courts in Europe, which have been very reluctant to challenge decisions of international SGBs. In short, if European national courts play a role in the operation of the *lex sportiva*, it is more often than not by strongly limiting their own interventionism and in reinforcing the authority of the international SGBs that they do so.

National courts, while unwilling to shoulder the responsibility to challenge the SGBs, have been more inclined to refer this responsibility to the Court of Justice of the European Union (CJEU), which has been regularly issuing decisions related to the compliances of the SGBs' rules and decisions with EU law since the 1970s.[21] As we write these lines, the judges of the CJEU are deliberating on a number of high-profile preliminary references concerning the governance of football by FIFA and UEFA.[22] Furthermore, the CJEU, unlike most national courts, showed in its renowned *Bosman* ruling its willingness to challenge the regulations of the most powerful SGBs.[23] Since then, the Court has proven more accommodating to the SGBs, but it may very well be the case that it will again find them wanting in the near future. While the supervisory

[20] See Duval, 'Embedded *Lex Sportiva*: The Swiss Roots of Transnational Sports Law and Governance' in chapter two of this volume.

[21] Case 36/74 BNO Walrave and LJN Koch v Association Union cycliste internationale, Koninklijke Nederlandsche Wielren Unie and Federación Española Ciclismo (1974) ECLI:EU:C:1974:140; Case C-415/93 (n 10); Joined cases C-51/96 and C-191/97 *Deliège v Ligue francophone de judo et disciplines associées ASBL, Ligue belge de judo ASBL, Union européenne de judo and François Pacquée* (2000) ECLI:EU:C:2000:199; Case C-265/03 *Igor Simutenkov v Ministerio de Educación y Cultura and Real Federación Española de Fútbol* (2005) ECLI:EU:C:2005:213; Case C-325/08 *Olympique Lyonnais SASP v Olivier Bernard and Newcastle UFC* (2010) ECLI:EU:C:2010:143; Case C-22/18 *TopFit eV and Daniele Biffi v Deutscher Leichtathletikverband eV* (2019) ECLI:EU:C:2019:497.

[22] Two cases have already been heard and are in the process of being decided: Case C-333/21 *European Super League Company, S.L. v Union of European Football Associations (UEFA) and Fédération Internationale de Football Association (FIFA)*; Case C-680/21 *SA Royal Antwerp Football Club v Union royale belge des sociétés de football association ASBL*. While two additional requests for preliminary rulings have also been received: Case C-650/22 *Federation Internationale de Football Association (FIFA) v BZ* and Case C-209/23 *FT and RRC Sports GmbH v Fédération Internationale de Football Association (FIFA)*.

[23] On the legacy of the *Bosman* ruling, see A Duval and B Van Rompuy (eds), *The Legacy of Bosman: Revisiting the Relationship Between EU Law and Sport* (T.M.C Asser Press, 2016).

role played by the CJEU is now well recognised in the literature,[24] its resulting impact on the transnational regulation and governance of sports remains largely uncharted.

The chapter by *Mataija*[25] offers a critical take on the capacity of the SGBs to adapt to the challenge posed by the exercise of review power by the CJEU (and the EC). In a nutshell, the author argues that the EU's interventions have led to institutional changes inside the SGBs, in the form of so-called good governance reforms, but surmises that these are mostly cosmetic changes aimed at warding off further EU scrutiny. On the one hand, the chapter illustrates well the importance of the proportionality review exercised by EU institutions over the SGBs in determining the internal political and legal processes of the SGBs. On the other, it shines a light on the responsibility of the EU institutions in defining what they mean by good governance when engaging with the SGBs. In another contribution to this volume, *Villanueva* looks at the potential for the EU institutions, and in particular the CJEU, to contribute through their supervisory role to the decommodification of sports. She argues in particular that 'the EU is developing a societal narrative which has the potential to counterbalance the hyper-commodification of sport'.[26] *Villanueva* proposes to harness the supervisory competences of the EU to promote a deeper re-orientation of the fundamental goals of the *lex sportiva*. Jointly, both chapters illustrate the fact that over the years the CJEU has gained, with the complicity of national courts, an increasingly important role within the *lex sportiva*, which can be summed up as a form of transnational constitutional review of the executive and legislative powers of the SGBs.

The CJEU is not the only EU institution that has been engaging regularly in the review of the SGBs' governance activities. Indeed, DG Competition of the European Commission (EC) is regularly seized with complaints against international SGBs and their decisions. The private structure of the SGBs and their reliance on their monopoly control over a particular sport makes them particularly well-suited to the application of competition law.[27] Accordingly, the EC has had to deal with a number of disputes concerning the transnational governance of a variety of sports,[28] leading to a negative decision issued by the EC only in one case, the *ISU* case.[29] This does not mean that all the other

[24] In general, see S Weatherill, *Principles and Practice in EU Sports Law* (Oxford University Press, 2017).

[25] See Mataija, 'False Friends: Proportionality and Good Governance in Sports Regulation' in chapter eight of this volume.

[26] See Villanueva, 'Sport Beyond the Market? Sport, Law and Society in the European Union' in chapter nine of this volume.

[27] B Van Rompuy, 'The Role of EU Competition Law in Tackling Abuse of Regulatory Power by Sports Associations' (2015) 22 *Maastricht Journal of European and Comparative Law* 179.

[28] The sports governance cases considered by DG Competition are listed on the European Commission's website at https://competition-policy.ec.europa.eu/sectors/sports/cases_en.

[29] European Commission, *International Skating Union's Eligibility rules* (Case AT.40208), 8 December 2017.

cases did not affect the content of the *lex sportiva*, but it implies that most were settled informally through agreements providing for specific amendments of the SGBs' regulations.[30] The *ISU* case stands apart as the only instance in which the EC issued a finding of non-compliance with EU competition law, while exceptionally refraining from issuing a fine. This case, which is now under appeal before the Grand Chamber of the CJEU, highlights the potential for the EC to act as a counter-power to the SGBs and to force fundamental change to their regulatory approaches to alternative competitions. As pointed out by *Agafonova* in her contribution to this volume,[31] EU competition law offers many entry points to challenge the existing transnational regulation of sports, and can also be mobilised before national courts or the CAS.

The specific role played by EU (competition) law as a counter-power to the SGBs can be traced back at least in part to the limited economic or social leverage of the SGBs over EU institutions. Unlike nation states, against which the SGBs can (and regularly) threaten exclusion from their competitions,[32] the EU cannot be excluded from international sporting competitions because it is not represented in them. Moreover, excluding the national teams of all the EU Member States would be very damaging in terms of marketing and viewership for the SGBs. In short, the EU's strengths vis-à-vis the SGBs lie in its transnational structure, which counterweights the transnational exit power of the SGBs. This, as well as the centrality of the EU's Member States to the economic and social appeal of most international SGBs, has positioned EU institutions as key contributors to the *lex sportiva* through their function as administrative/constitutional review mechanisms. This position, however, should not be confused with the one of legislator or administrative regulator; the EU has neither the administrative capacity nor the political will to take over from the SGBs when it comes to the governance of transnational sports.

The final European court which is increasingly being integrated into the *lex sportiva* is the ECtHR. Not only is the ECHR and its interpretation by the ECtHR's jurisprudence being progressively (and selectively) integrated in its awards by the CAS,[33] but the ECtHR is increasingly called upon to rule on the compatibility of the decisions and regulations of the SGBs with the ECHR.[34] In procedural terms, the submissions are directed against Switzerland, due to its passive review of CAS awards, but in practice they target the decisions and

[30] For a detailed study of such an informal transnational law-making process, see A Duval, 'The FIFA Regulations on the Status and Transfer of Players: Transnational Law-Making in the Shadow of Bosman' in Duval and Van Rompuy (n 23).

[31] See Agafonova, 'EU Competition Law and Sport: Checks and Balances "à l'européenne"' in chapter 10 of this volume.

[32] HE Meier and B Gacria, 'Protecting Private Transnational Authority against Public Intervention: FIFA's Power Over National Governments' (2015) 93 *Public Administration* 890.

[33] A Duval, 'Lost in translation? The European Convention on Human Rights at the Court of Arbitration for Sport' (2022) 22 *The International Sports Law Journal* 132.

[34] *Mutu and Pechstein v Switzerland* (n 11); *Semenya v Switzerland* (2023) App no 10934/21 (ECtHR, 11 July 2023); *Platini v Switzerland* (2020) App no 526/18 (ECtHR, 11 February 2020).

regulations of SGBs and their compatibility with the ECHR. For example, in the *Pechstein and Mutu* case, the Strasbourg judges were called upon to assess the compatibility of the CAS arbitration proceedings undergone by Claudia Pechstein and Adrian Mutu with Article 6(1) ECHR. Importantly, the Court concluded in Pechstein's case that she was forced to submit to CAS arbitration and that, therefore, the arbitral process needed to be fully compliant with Article 6(1) ECHR.[35] The judges went on to find that the CAS could not refuse her request to a public hearing without violating the Convention, while controversially endorsing the independence of the CAS.[36] Thus, the ECtHR has shown its willingness to review the compatibility of the private processes fundamental to the deployment of the *lex sportiva* in light of the ECHR. This willingness will be tested again soon with the upcoming decision in the *Semenya* case. The chapter by *Boisgontier*[37] in this volume reviews the details of the case and provides an in-depth analysis of how the ECtHR's case law could (and should) influence its outcome. The author urges the ECtHR to stand by its jurisprudence and to adopt an interventionist stance against the decisions of World Athletics and the CAS. This case illustrates the way in which the ECtHR is shaping up as a new institutional actor in the *lex sportiva*. While its interventions remain relatively rare, compared to the number of CAS awards issued yearly, and costly (at least in terms of time), the ECtHR is nonetheless becoming a site of judicial contestation against the SGBs' transnational governance. Like the CJEU, its intervention is mostly *ex-post* and of a transnational constitutional nature.

European courts and administrations, be they national or supra-national, are often perceived as exercising external control over the *lex sportiva*. Yet, it might be more accurate to describe these institutions as engaging in a form of *dédoublement fonctionnel* or role splitting,[38] as they contribute to both national/European legal orders and the transnational regime of the *lex sportiva*. With regard to the latter, they discharge crucial functions of transnational constitutional review aimed at checking the legislative, executive and judicial governance exercised by the SGBs outside any democratic control. In doing so, they have a disproportionate influence, compared to other courts around the world, on the transnational governance of sports. This specific power of European judicial and administrative institutions can be traced back to the European anchoring of the Olympic Movement and the transnational strength of the collective organisation of European states. In short, this is a judicial embodiment of the Brussels

[35] *Mutu and Pechstein v Switzerland* (n 11).

[36] ibid.

[37] See Boisgontier, 'Is the *Lex Sportiva* on Track for Intersex Person's Rights? The World Athletics' Regulations Concerning Female Athletes with Differences of Sex Development in the Light of the ECHR' in chapter 11 of this volume.

[38] The concept was introduced in G Scelle, *Précis de droit des gens: Principes et systématique*, Vol. I (1932). See also A Cassese, 'Remarks on Scelle's Theory of "Role Splitting" (Dédoublement fonctionnel) in International Law' (1990) 1 *European Journal of International Law* 210.

effect and its cousins, the Luxembourg and Strasbourg effect. Not only is the *lex sportiva* a child of European laws, it can also be best resisted or changed through European legal institutions.

IV. GOING BEYOND: ENGAGING CRITICALLY WITH A EUROCENTRIC *LEX SPORTIVA*

This volume traces the European roots of the *lex sportiva* and centres the role of a variety of European laws (and legal professionals) in the transnational governance of international sports. It does not, however, include extensive and explicit critical reflections on the implications of this Eurocentrism. Yet, the central role played in particular by European institutions in regulating international sporting competitions and competitors worldwide will necessarily raise questions of legitimacy and imperialism.

In the concluding chapter of this volume, *Krüger* expands our horizons through a new materialist reading of the other contributions that promotes a novel understanding of *lex sportiva*. He demonstrates that new materialist theories can help us rethink transnational sports law and provides the basis for an immanent critique of *lex sportiva*. By approaching *lex sportiva* as not exclusively produced by humans, Krüger demonstrates how it, rather than fixed and distinct, can be viewed as always becoming, relational, entangled and connected to everything else material. When we do so, a number of previously under-considered questions are raised, as well as a novel framework for approaching these questions. One important but difficult question raised is that of responsibility in and for transnational sports law: 'in an era where the world is both increasingly mobile and humans are entangled with and (particularly the rich minority) co-producing the world we inhabit', the issue of responsibility in sports law needs to be seriously (re)considered, the author teaches us.[39]

An important contribution of our project consists of showing that the way we experience global sporting events, such as the Olympic Games or the FIFA World Cup, the way we decide who can compete in international competitions, or the way we regulate the private lives of athletes through anti-doping regulations, are largely conditioned by legal processes which are playing out in a European context. Our experience of international sports, and its definition through transnational regulations, is largely conditioned by national and supranational legal processes anchored in Europe. In sum, the global level playing field of international sports is primarily shaped by Europeans and their laws.

While representatives from other continents have a formal say inside the political bodies of the SGBs, their political powers are constrained by the legal framework in which they have to operate. The languages of Swiss law, EU law

[39] See Krüger, 'Lex Sportiva and New Materialism: Towards Investigations into Sports Law's Dark Materials?' in chapter 12 of this volume.

and the ECHR are the key legal discourses through which the governance of sports can be mediated. It is then unsurprising that the arbitrators that are appointed at the CAS rarely originate from outside Europe, and are generally extensively trained in Swiss or any other European law.[40] This eurocentrism is also visible in the institutional spaces open for legal challenges against the SGBs, which are extremely rarely being dragged before national or supranational courts outside Europe, and if they are there is generally little or no prospect for success.[41] Not only is the *lex sportiva* embedded in European laws, it is channelling challenges against SGBs to European judicial or administrative institutions forcing non-European citizens to turn to them in order to challenge decisions that profoundly affect them.

At the heart of this book lies a paradox: the *lex sportiva* is supposed to embody the global law of international sports and yet, as this volume has shown, it is profoundly European in its origins and institutional anchorage. Such a situation can easily be interpreted as a neo-colonial governance arrangement. Surely, there is room for various types of local resistance against the global rules and decisions of the *lex sportiva*, as there was room for legal pluralism during the colonial era. For example, compliance with the World Anti-Doping Code is in practice highly dependent on local institutional factors and interpreters.[42] In other words, many rules of the *lex sportiva* will be translated differently when they touch the ground in different legal contexts. Yet, there are rules and decisions, such as the World Athletics' (WA) Transgender and DSD Regulations challenged by Caster Semenya, that will not allow for much contextual interpretation or implementation.[43] In this regard, Caster Semenya, who was officially declared a woman at birth by the South African authorities, has seen her (sports) gender being called into question by the WA, an organisation based in Monaco, and has been forced to challenge the WA's fateful decision before the Swiss-based CAS[44] and SFT[45] and the Strasbourg-based ECtHR,[46] all courts with which she has no familiarity and which are entirely disconnected from her own social and cultural context. It might be that international sporting competitions can be governed only from some place, currently Europe, but then it is crucial to ensure that European legal institutions, in governing the world of sport, are fully aware of their transnational

[40] Lindholm (n 5).

[41] See, eg, the powerlessness of a Canadian court in attempting to overturn an IOC decision which it considered discriminatory, see Supreme Court of British Columbia, *Sagen v. Vancouver Organizing Committee for the 2010 Olympic and Paralympic Winter Games*, 2009 BCSC 942, 10 July 2009.

[42] A Duval, 'The Russian Doping Scandal at the Court of Arbitration for Sport: Lessons for the World Anti-Doping System' (2017) 16 *The International Sports Law Journal* 177.

[43] See Boisgontier, in this volume.

[44] *Mokgadi Caster Semenya & Athletics South Africa v International Association of Athletics Federations* (CAS 2018/O/5794 & 5798).

[45] *Caster Semenya v International Association of Athletics Federation (IAAF) & Athletics South Africa (ASA)* [2020] Swiss Federal Tribunal 4A_248/2019.

[46] *Semenya v Switzerland* (n 34).

responsibility. In such circumstances, there should, for example, be no room for a margin of appreciation of Switzerland in ECtHR cases involving the *lex sportiva*. Indeed, when the SFT reviews CAS awards, it is not ruling for Swiss society, but for the world. This neo-colonial dimension of the *lex sportiva* will need to be explored further in the future and institutional adjustments will need to be implemented to counter-balance Europe's dominance in shaping it. Hopefully, this volume will have contributed to highlighting the importance of this task.

Part I

The European Roots of *Lex Sportiva*

2

Embedded Lex Sportiva: *The Swiss Roots of Transnational Sports Law and Governance*

ANTOINE DUVAL*

LEX SPORTIVA IS often presented as an autonomous and anational legal order governing international sports, and in particular the Olympic Movement.[1] In fact, private organisations, such as the Fédération Internationale de Football Association (FIFA) or the International Olympic Committee (IOC), play a central role in the transnational governance of sports as they produce and enforce most of the rules that define the practice of international sports. Moreover, transnational sporting disputes are generally settled through a privatised justice system culminating at the Court of Arbitration for Sport (CAS), an arbitral tribunal seated in Lausanne. In short, *lex sportiva* offers a credible case study for the rise of transnational legality without a state.[2] Accordingly, its interactions with national or international laws are often presented as conflicts between strictly separated legal orders.[3] This chapter will attempt to nuance and in part challenge this image of the *lex sportiva* by highlighting instead its profound embeddedness in, and to a large extent its dependence on, Swiss law. In the spirit of this edited volume, the chapter will thus emphasise the local legal roots of the *lex sportiva*, which are traced back to the shores of the lac Léman and the steep hills of the city of Lausanne, the so-called 'Silicon Valley of Sports',[4] where many of the fundamental decisions conditioning the normative

* Antoine Duval is a Senior Researcher at TMC Asser Instituut.

[1] See F Latty, *Lex Sportiva : Recherche sur le droit transnational* (Martinus Nijhoff Publishers, 2007) and my own work on *lex sportive*, see A Duval, '*Lex Sportiva*: A Playground for Transnational Law' (2013) 19 *European Law Journal* 822 and A Duval, 'Transnational Sports Law: The Living Lex Sportiva' in P Zumbansen (ed), *The Oxford Handbook of Transnational Law* (Oxford University Press, 2021).

[2] It was already one of the examples referred to in G Teubner, '"Global Bukowina": Legal Pluralism in the World Society' in G Teubner (ed), *Global Law Without a State* (Dartmouth Publishing, 1997) 4.

[3] See Latty (n 1).

[4] R Ruiz, 'Swiss City is "the Silicon Valley of Sports"' *The New York Times* (23 April 2016), www.nytimes.com/2016/04/23/sports/olympics/switzerland-global-sports-capital-seeks-new-recruits.html.

substance and the institutional structure of the *lex sportiva* were and are being taken. While *lex sportiva* is primarily composed of private regulations, processes and institutions, this chapter argues that its existence is rendered possible by the constitutive framework of Swiss private law and its current shape is largely dependent on the interpretive decisions rendered by Swiss courts. Thus, the chapter ambitions to outline the legal determinants that made Switzerland the incontestable 'epicenter of global sport administration'.[5]

The chapter is inspired by the work of Wai, who studied the role of private (international) law in enabling the 'transnational liftoff'[6] of international businesses. Analogically, the argument will be that Swiss private law plays a fundamental role in facilitating the 'transnational liftoff' of the *lex sportiva*. Thus, it will support, in the context of the *lex sportiva*, Wai's contention that transnational private ordering occurs in the shadow of state law.[7] Sassen's work is another reference point insofar as she conceptualises the global 'as at least partly consisting of the denationalizing of specific forms of state authority which results from the location of particular components of global processes in national institutional orders'.[8] She emphasised in particular the fact that 'the state is one of the strategic institutional domains where critical work for developing globalization takes place'.[9] Consequently, she denoted the 'ironic outcome'[10] behind the dynamic of globalisation, and I would argue, behind the deployment of *lex sportiva's* transnational authority, which leads the state to contribute 'to strengthen the forces that can challenge or destabilize what have historically been constructed as state powers'.[11] Accordingly, this chapter advances that the *lex sportiva* is best understood as a transnational legal assemblage, which is at least partly embedded in the Swiss context and dependent on Swiss legal institutions to operate transnationally. The chapter is thus a challenge to the idea that *lex sportiva* could embody what de Sousa Santos referred to as an 'originally global condition' and emphasises instead its nature as 'globalized localism'.[12] Consequently, it rejects the presentation

[5] J-L Chappelet, 'Switzerland's Century-Long Rise as the Hub of Global Sport Administration' (2021) 28 *The International Journal of the History of Sport* 569, 569.

[6] R Wai, 'Transnational Liftoff and Juridical Touchdown: The Regulatory Function of Private International Law in an Era of Globalization' (2002) 40 *Columbia Journal of Transnational Law* 209.

[7] R Wai, 'Private v Private: Transnational Private Law and Contestation in Global Economic Governance' in H Muir Watt and DP Fernandez Arroyo (eds), *Private International Law and Global Governance* (Oxford University Press, 2014) 36.

[8] See S Sassen, *Territory, Authority, Rights: From Medieval to Global Assemblage* (Princeton University Press, 2006) and S Sassen, 'The State and Globalization: Denationalized Participation' (2004) 25 *Michigan Journal of International Law* 1141.

[9] S Sassen, 'Neither Global nor National: Novel Assemblages of Territory, Authority and Rights' (2008) 1 *Ethics & Global Politics* 61, 70.

[10] S Sassen, 'Globalization or Denationalization?' (2003) 10 *Review of International Political Economy* 1, 8 ('Furthermore, this work of states has an ironic outcome insofar as it has the effect of destabi- lizing some aspects of state power.').

[11] Sassen, 'The State and Globalization' (n 8) 1157.

[12] See B de Sousa Santos, 'Globalizations' (2006) 23 *Theory, Culture & Society* 393, 396.

of national law and *lex sportiva* 'as countervailing, separate normative orders, rather than interpenetrating orders'[13] and heeds the call to analyse 'the modes, processes, and institutions that enable a fruitful cooperation between state and non-state groups'.[14]

In order to do so, the chapter will engage with the existing Swiss legal scholarship looking at the intersection between Swiss law and the private regulation of sports, as well as with a number of decisions issued by the Swiss courts. The first section of this chapter will centre on showing how Swiss association law plays a constitutive role in conferring legal personality to international sports governing bodies (SGBs) and determining (or rather not determining) their structures and modes of operation. In the debates around *lex sportiva*, Swiss association law is often invisible, yet it provides the necessary foundations for the transnational projection of the private regulatory powers of the SGBs. The second part will focus on tracing the crucial role played by Swiss private international law and its interpretation by the Swiss Federal Tribunal (SFT) in the rise of the CAS as the supreme court of world sports. The chapter will show how the SFT gave the kiss of life to the CAS and protected it from external interferences, thus strengthening its institutional position in the *lex sportiva*. In fine, the chapter will come to the conclusion that Switzerland played (and still plays) an essential role in the emergence of the *lex sportiva* and that it has a disproportionate influence on the way in which sports is experienced and governed transnationally.[15] As discussed in the conclusion, this raises complex questions in terms of the transnational legitimacy and accountability of the Swiss institutions.

I. SWITZERLAND'S FRANKENSTEIN: HOW SWISS LAW GIVES THE KISS OF LIFE TO INTERNATIONAL SGBS AND SETS THEM FREE

Currently, most of the international federations (IFs) that are members of the Olympic Movement have their seat in Switzerland (mainly in or around Lausanne). This is not a coincidence. Besides the role of individual executives and the 'gravitational pull'[16] of the IOC, authors have long recognised the importance of Switzerland's 'unexacting legislation for associations'[17] in attracting international SGBs to Lausanne and its surroundings.[18] Yet, few are those who

[13] R Wai, 'The Interlegality of Transnational Private Law' (2008) 71 *Law and Contemporary Problems* 107, 112.

[14] R Michaels, 'The Mirage Of Non-State Governance' (2010) 1 *Utah Law Review* 31, 42.

[15] Coming to the same conclusion from a different disciplinary standpoint, see Chappelet (n 5) and J-L Chappelet, *La place olympique suisse, émergence et devenir* (Biere, Cabedita, 2019).

[16] Chappelet (n 5) 583.

[17] ibid.

[18] See M Mrkonjic, 'The Swiss Regulatory Framework and International Sports organisations' in J Alm (ed), *Action for Good Governance in International Sports Organisations* (Play the Game, Danish Institute for Sports Studies, 2013); LW Valloni and EP Neuenschwander, 'The Role of Switzerland

have identified the constitutive function of Swiss association law and studied its influence on the transnational operation and structure of the *lex sportiva*. In this section, I will first show how Swiss association law gives the kiss of life to SGBs, before highlighting its hands-off approach to the institutionalisation of the SGBs through private processes and regulations.

A. The Foundational Role of Swiss Private Law in Constituting the SGBs

Household names, such as FIFA, IOC, CAS and World Anti-Doping Agency (WADA), are all organisations that are incorporated under Swiss law as either Swiss associations (IOC, FIFA) or foundations (WADA, International Council of Arbitration for Sport (ICAS)). Inside the Olympic Movement, this is true as well of many of the IFs. While these organisations often act as if they are international organisations, from a formal standpoint they remain Swiss associations, taking the same corporate form as any local Swiss chess or football club. This formal congruence between local associations of Swiss citizens or residents and international SGBs epitomises the specificity of Swiss association law, as a cursory glimpse at the size and the scope of activities of FIFA or the IOC will quickly show that they are not of the same kind as local chess clubs. FIFA and IOC constitute colossal organisations, disposing of important revenue streams and administrative capacities in both material and human terms, and which are projecting their authority transnationally. In fact, as has been shown in recent years, they are often capable of imposing their will upon nation states.[19] This raises the question whether incorporating them in the same way, and therefore with similar constraints, as local associations affecting only a small number of local members is a sensible approach to structuring organisations of this size and with this transnational influence. Nevertheless, it is this incorporation as Swiss associations that provides SGBs with two essential resources to deploy transnational authority: legal personality and a constitutional legitimacy grounded in private autonomy and the freedom of association.

Legal personality enables SGBs to contract with a multitude of actors (members, sponsors, employees, other associations, etc). These contracts, in turn, enable them to raise funds, organise competitions and enforce their regulations. The entire

as Host: Moves to Hold Sports Organisations More Accountable, and Wider Implications' in Transparency International (ed), *Global Corruption of Sport* (Routledge, 2016) 321 ('It is no coincidence that these important bodies organising worldwide sports have all chosen the legal form of a Swiss association, granting maximum flexibility and autonomy to the organisation'); E Bayle, 'La gouvernance du sport international: Entre autonomie sportive et ingerence externe' in J-L Chappelet (ed), L'autonomie des organisations sportives (University of Lausanne, 2019) 20 ('Le mouvement sportif international, dirigé par le CIO, dispose d'une autonomie d'organisation lié à sa structure associative privée lui offrant une grande liberté notamment en raison d'un droit suisse associatif très libéral.').

[19] For concrete examples, see HE Meier and B Garcia, 'Protecting Private Transnational Authority against Public Intervention: FIFA's Power Over National Governments' (2015) 93 *Public Administration* 890.

edifice of the *lex sportiva* depends on this right of the SGBs to contract. Ultimately, it is Switzerland through its association law that confers to most international SGBs of the Olympic Movement their legal personality and therefore empowers them with the legal capacity to roam the world.[20] In doing so, it also provides them with a foundational myth that legitimises their power by grounding it in the freedom of association. Unlike international organisations which derive their legitimacy from the consent of sovereign states, the transnational authority of SGBs is philosophically grounded in the free will of its members (and their members' members). Put differently, they are constituted as an expression of the private autonomy of individuals.[21] In practice, not entirely unlike the limits and paradoxes linked to state consent as foundational myth for international treaties and organisations,[22] sportspeople have little choice but to adhere to the SGBs (and accept their foundational contracts) if they want to participate in organised sports.[23] However, formally the myth endures, and it is by recognising that SGBs constitute lawful Swiss associations despite their monopoly positions and their massive commercial interests,[24] that Swiss institutions provide them not only with the kiss of legal life but as well with the foundational fiction necessary to ground the legitimacy of their transnational authority.

International SGBs are born locally in Switzerland, but their lives are mostly lived transnationally. This is not a situation that is exclusive to SGBs, it is also true of many transnational corporations (TNCs).[25] However, the fundamental difference between SGBs and TNCs is that the former are born to govern a particular sporting activity or event in the interest of all sportspeople, while the latter have as their primary objective to enrich their shareholders. Crucially, international SGBs are public-oriented organisations meant to exercise transnational governance in the pursuit of the development of their competitions and/or sports.

[20] The same has been observed for corporations, see K Pistor, *The Code of Capital: How the Law Creates Wealth and Inequality* (Princeton University Press, 2019) 55 ('Not all features of the corporation, however, can be created by contract. Legal personality, which gives the entity the right to own assets, contract, sue, and be sued in its own name, can be obtained only by a state act.').

[21] The same consensual myth is central to the free operation of transnational corporations, see F Johns, 'The Invisibility of the Transnational Corporation: An Analysis of International Law and Legal Theory' (1994) 19 *Melbourne University Law Review* 893, 912.

[22] See W Werner, 'State Consent as Foundational Myth' in C Brölmann and Y Radi (eds), *Research Handbook on the Theory and Practice of International Lawmaking* (Edward Elgar Publishing, 2016) and N Krisch, 'The Decay of Consent: International Law in an Age of Global Public Goods' (2014) 108 *American Journal of International Law* 1.

[23] The lack of alternatives for members of sports associations has been analysed in detail by Margareta Baddeley in her book: *L'association sportive face au droit: les limites de son autonomie* (Helbing und Lichtenhahn, 1994) 78–87. This drives a search for post-consensual foundations, see, eg, in the context of the legitimacy of the CAS, A Duval, '*Not in My Name!* Claudia Pechstein and the Post-Consensual Foundations of the Court of Arbitration for Sport' in H Ruiz Fabri, A Nunes Chaib, I Venzke, A von Bogdandy (eds), *International Judicial Legitimacy* (Nomos Verlag, 2020).

[24] This is not a given as associations must have a non-economic goal. In the case of the international SGBs, it is being argued that their economic goals, which are undoubtedly prominent in their operations, are subordinated to their non-economic objectives linked to the organisation and promotion of their sport and competitions. See the discussion on this issue in Baddeley (n 23) 42–47.

[25] See Pistor (n 20) 52.

Accordingly, when they are amassing funds, it is not to redistribute them to their shareholders, but (at least in theory) to re-invest them in developing their administrative capacities to spread the reach of their sport (or sports in the case of the IOC). In other words, their core objective is not (or should not be) to enrich their employees and their members, but to trigger the participation of more players or clubs and to attract more public attention and participation to their events. They are built by design to rule sports transnationally and thanks to Swiss private law their transnational authority does not need to be grounded in the joint will of sovereign states but can rely on the exercise of private autonomy by associations and/or individuals. It is by certifying this fictitious fundament that Swiss law plays a decisive role in allowing the emergence of the central administrative and political organisations of the *lex sportiva*: the SGBs. Once brought to life, the SGBs escape in *Frankensteinian* style the control of their creator, Switzerland. They do so, ironically, with its benediction and encouragement.

B. Empowering SGBs Through Non-intervention: The *Laissez-Faire* Approach of Swiss Association Law

Freedom of association is recognised around the globe and enshrined in various national constitutions and international conventions. In practice, most countries allow for the constitution of associations, why then is there such a concentration of SGBs in Switzerland? The reason for this concentration cannot be traced back only to the proverbial Swiss ski resorts, neutrality or efficiency, rather, it is largely linked to the 'extraordinary autonomy'[26] afforded to the SGBs under Swiss association law. The rules applying to Swiss associations are enshrined in Articles 60 to 79 of the Swiss Civil Code (SCC) and were drafted at the beginning of the twentieth century with primarily small associations of Swiss citizens in mind.[27] Consequently, they impose 'minimal' constraints for the constitution of an association and its organisation.[28] This liberal model tailored to small associations bringing together Swiss citizens is being turbocharged by international SGBs which often have only one single Swiss member (the respective Swiss federation). It enables SGBs to set up, in almost complete autonomy, complex governance systems, dividing competences between multiple internal bodies and to rule their sports and competitions via internal regulations, which are enforced by internal institutions through the imposition of disciplinary sanctions, such as temporary bans from the activities of the

[26] M Baddeley, 'The Extraordinary Autonomy of Sports Bodies under Swiss Law: Lessons to be Drawn' (2020) 20 *The International Sports Law Journal* 3.

[27] Baddeley (n 23) 25 ('Dans l'esprit du législateur de 1908, l'association devait, en règle générale, servir de forme corporative à de *petites réunions* de personnes désireuses d'acquérir la personnalité juridique afin de poursuivre en commun des *buts idéaux:* politiques, religieux, scientifiques, artistiques, de récréation, etc (article 60 I CC *ab initia*).').

[28] ibid.

associations or fines.[29] Furthermore, Swiss association law also allows SGBs to exercise lucrative commercial activities, which for some of them (the Union of European Football Associations (UEFA), FIFA and the IOC in particular) bring in considerable revenue, reinvested in strengthening the regulatory capacity and reach of the SGB in question. Henceforth, the entire transnational governance system of the *lex sportiva* is conditioned on the liberalism of Swiss association law which lets the SGBs set their own rules, impose their own sanctions and police the compliance of their members (and their members' members). Combined with their monopoly control over international sporting competitions, the wide autonomy granted by Swiss law to international SGBs is a *conditio sine qua non* for their deployment of power and authority transnationally. Indeed, this autonomy secures both their freedom in defining their rules and their power in applying them, thus making submission to their rule-making and institutionalised processes a practical condition of access to international sporting competitions.

Moreover, the Swiss courts, which are generally competent under Article 75 SCC to resolve disputes related to associations, decided early on to exercise very limited oversight on the activities of SGBs.[30] In particular, they applied for a long time a doctrine that exempted the sporting regulations and decisions of SGBs from any judicial review.[31] Under this interpretation of Swiss association law, SGBs 'enjoyed unlimited freedom in issuing and applying a considerable portion of their rules for many years'.[32] Even when the Swiss courts started to exercise a slightly stricter control over the SGBs in the 1970s and 1980s, their rulings were described by Baddeley as 'only reminders of the overall limits to be respected by any association, and leaving therefore still considerable room for self-regulation'.[33] In any event, this relatively more active stance of the Swiss courts was swiftly stymied by the rise of the CAS in the 1990s, which was, as we will see in the next section, actively supported by the SFT.

This generous *laissez-faire* approach to the governance of associations was for a long time also reflected in Swiss criminal law.[34] Until recently, the passive corruption of sports administrators running the international SGBs remained unsanctioned under Swiss criminal law. Accordingly, the many instances of corruption involving executives of SGBs were not considered a crime and,

[29] See Baddeley (n 26) and Baddeley (n 23) 101–44.

[30] See the comprehensive survey of the approach of Swiss courts to reviewing decisions of SGBs in Baddeley (n 23) 344–80.

[31] ibid 352–67 and Baddeley (n 26) 6.

[32] Baddeley (n 26) 7.

[33] ibid 9.

[34] P Verschuuren, 'La corruption institutionnelle au sein du sport international: phénomène nouveau, problèmes anciens?' (2016) 101 *Revue internationale et stratégique* 141, 145 ('En outre, le fait que les organisations sportives soient hébergées en Suisse n'a pas, jusque-là, aidé à l'encadrement de leurs activités. Les dirigeants sportifs étaient en effet immunisés de toute instruction judiciaire pour des faits de blanchiment d'argent jusqu'à décembre 2014, et pour des faits de corruption jusqu'à juin 2015.').

therefore, executives who had accepted gifts of a financial or non-financial nature in return for favourable decisions (be they related to the allocation of the organisation of a competition or the attribution of commercial rights) escaped any consequences as Swiss prosecutors remained on the side lines. This state of affairs has changed after the recent FIFA-Gate, in which American federal prosecutors requested the Swiss police authorities to arrest FIFA executive committee members and to extradite them. The shame caused by the arrests and Switzerland's past passivity in the face of blatant instances of corruption triggered a reform of Swiss criminal law, which now outlaws passive corruption involving private actors.[35] Nevertheless, it remains to be seen whether the Swiss prosecutors will actively use these newfound investigative powers in order to more stringently supervise the governance of international SGBs.

In sum, the international SGBs as Swiss associations (or foundations) are dependent for their right to exist as legal persons on the recognition by the Swiss institutions (both administrative and judicial) of their foundation in 'the right to the collective exercise of individual autonomy'.[36] This endorsement is neither automatic nor natural, but the result of a fundamental political and legal choice of the Swiss state, which authorises SGBs to enter the world as legal beings and to exercise transnational authority and governance. In principle, Switzerland could at any time withdraw its recognition as it has the 'ultimate authority to allocate (and withdraw) constitutional functions'.[37] The Swiss contribution to the SGBs' existence does not stop at their birth, the *laissez-faire* approach of Switzerland's extremely liberal association law allows SGBs to autonomously devise their institutional structures and regulations while imposing them transnationally through a contractual cascade. In practice, to borrow from Sassen, Switzerland acts as the 'ultimate guarantor' and a 'major legitimator' of the claims of the *lex sportiva*.[38] Accordingly, a description of the *lex sportiva* that puts only the emphasis on its non-state nature would be understating 'the role of state law in framing and constituting non-state ordering, ie the embeddedness of private ordering in a network of other rules and laws'.[39] Paradoxically, therefore, the transnational reach of the *lex sportiva* is premised on the local embeddedness of its central institutions in Swiss private law. Furthermore, the rise of the CAS as the sole competent judicial institution where members of international SGBs can exercise their right

[35] On these reforms see Valloni and Neuenschwander (n 18) and Verschuuren (n 34) 147.

[36] KD Wolf, 'The Non-Existence of Private Self-Regulation in the Transnational Sphere and its Implications for the Responsibility to Procure Legitimacy: The Case of the *Lex Sportiva*' (2014) 3 *Global Constitutionalism* 275, 287.

[37] ibid 282.

[38] Sassen, 'The State and Globalization' (n 8) 1156 ('The background condition here is that the state remains as the ultimate guarantor of the "rights" of global capital, i.e., the protection of contracts and property rights, and, more generally, a major legitimator of claims.').

[39] Wai (n 7) 41; Wai (n 13) 114 ('Even as between contractual parties […] state law and process remains present in constituting the private ordering between contractual parties.').

to an independent review of decisions and regulations of the associations, as provided under Article 75 of the SCC, constitutes the ultimate step in the self-disempowerment of Swiss institutions in relation to the SGBs transnational governance activities.

II. HOW THE SWISS FEDERAL TRIBUNAL TURNED THE CAS INTO THE WORLD COURT OF SPORT

The CAS is often portrayed as the maker of *lex sportiva* and as the central institution of transnational sports law and governance.[40] In particular, it is the main judicial authority to hear appeals against the final decisions of most international SGBs. While CAS's statutes came into force in 1984, its activities started to pick up only at the turn of the century and reached a yearly total of 996 cases filed in 2021.[41] The CAS regularly makes the headlines of global newspapers and is the dispute resolution body that decides an overwhelming majority of the high-profile disputes related to international sports.

In this second part of my chapter, I will show that the transnational judicial authority of the CAS is premised on the active support of the SFT, which gave it the kiss of (legal) life, endorsed the central planks of its institutional structure and regularly secures the almost unchallengeable authority of its awards. In order to do so, the SFT made two essential determinations. First, it concluded that CAS arbitration clauses imposed by the SGBs onto their members were valid. Second, it decided that the CAS was sufficiently independent from the SGBs to constitute an arbitral tribunal. Finally, since taking the decision to back the CAS on these two fundamental issues, the SFT has continuously shored up the authority of its awards by adopting a hands-off approach to reviewing them.

A. The SFT's Embrace of Forced CAS Arbitration

The legitimacy of private arbitration is fundamentally undersigned by the free consent of the parties. This consensual fundament is central to the idea of arbitration, as 'a private initiative' and its ideal of 'freedom reconciled with law'.[42] However, as has been regularly highlighted by many authors over the years, CAS arbitration (in particular the so-called appeal arbitration) is in practice

[40] L Casini, 'The Making of a *Lex Sportiva* by the Court of Arbitration for Sport' (2011) 12 *German Law Journal* 1317. See as well J Lindholm, *The Court of Arbitration for Sport and Its Jurisprudence: An Empirical Inquiry into Lex Sportiva* (Springer, T.M.C. Asser Press, 2019).

[41] See the CAS statistics available at www.tas-cas.org/fileadmin/user_upload/CAS_statistics_2022.pdf.

[42] J Paulsson, *The Idea of Arbitration* (Oxford, Oxford University Press, 2013) 1.

a take it or leave it offer to the members of SGBs.[43] If they wish to participate in international sporting competitions, athletes and clubs (as well as other sports stakeholders) have to sign up to statutes or to entry forms which include a specific arbitration clause conferring exclusive jurisdiction to the CAS. In other words (those of the SFT itself), they have to choose between playing in their garden or signing up to arbitration.[44] Recently, the forced nature of CAS arbitration grounded in the athletes' lack of alternative options to practice their sport professionally has been recognised by the European Court of Human Rights (ECtHR) in its Mutu and Pechstein ruling.[45] In principle, this situation poses a fundamental challenge to the legitimacy of the CAS, which must therefore draw on post-consensual foundations to justify its existence.[46]

Prior to the ECtHR's ruling, the SFT played an essential role in buttressing the legitimacy of the CAS by embracing the validity of CAS arbitration clauses. In particular, it endorsed CAS arbitration clauses by reference, binding athletes and clubs to CAS arbitration through, for example, the general reference in the regulations of their national federation to the regulations of the IF which imposes a CAS arbitration.[47] In recent years, it has even started to consider that CAS arbitration clauses are *branchentypisch*,[48] standard practice in the sport sector and, therefore, presumed valid. This stand has been maintained despite the SFT's seemingly contradictory finding that a renunciation to the right to appeal a CAS award was invalid due to the lack of free will of an athlete.[49] The

[43] See A Rigozzi and F Robert-Tissot, '"Consent" in Sports Arbitration: Its Multiple Aspects' in E Geisinger and E Trabaldo de Mestral (eds), *Sports Arbitration as a Coach for Other Players* (Juris Publishing, 2015) 60 ('In other words, it is clear that sports arbitration is fundamentally non-consensual in nature, since athletes have no other choice but to agree to whatever is contained in the statutes or regulations of their sports governing bodies.'). See the many references in Duval (n 23).

[44] SFT 133 III 235, at 243–44 ('Mis dans l'alternative de se soumettre à une juridiction arbitrale ou de pratiquer son sport "dans son jardin" (FRANÇOIS KNOEPFLER/PHILIPPE SCHWEIZER, Arbitrage international, p. 137 in fine), en regardant les compétitions "à la télévision" (RIGOZZI, op. cit., n. 1509 et le premier auteur cité), l'athlète qui souhaite affronter de véritables concurrents ou qui doit le faire parce que c'est là son unique source de revenus (prix en argent ou en nature, recettes publicitaires, etc.) sera contraint, dans les faits, d'opter, *nolens volens*, pour le premier terme de cette alternative.').

[45] *Mutu and Pechstein v Switzerland* (2018) App nos 40575/10 & 67474/10 (ECtHR, 2 October 2018) paras 109–23.

[46] See Duval (n 23).

[47] SFT 4P.230/2000, para 2a (Dieser Nachweis erfordert nicht, dass die Schiedsklausel in den von den Parteien ausgetauschten Vertragsdokumenten selbst enthalten ist. Vielmehr genügt zum Nachweis der Schiedsklausel durch Text, dass in solchen Dokumenten darauf verwiesen wird. Der Verweis braucht die Schiedsklausel nicht ausdrücklich zu nennen, sondern kann auch als Globalverweis ein Dokument einbeziehen, welches eine solche Klausel enthält); SFT 4A_460/2008, para 6.2; SFT 4A_548/2009, para 4.1.

[48] SFT 4A_428/2011, para 3.2.3 ; SFT 4A_314/2017, para 2.3.1.

[49] SFT 133 III 235, at 245 ('Qu'il y ait un certain illogisme, en théorie, à traiter de manière différente la convention d'arbitrage et la renonciation conventionnelle au recours, sous les rapports de la forme et du consentement, est sans doute vrai (dans ce sens, cf. FRANÇOIS KNOEPFLER, in François Knoepfler/Philippe Schweizer, Jurisprudence suisse en matière d'arbitrage international, in RSDIE 2006 p. 105 ss, 159). Toutefois, en dépit des apparences, ce traitement différencié obéit à une

SFT has justified its 'benevolence'[50] in this regard by using a 'there is no alternative' style of argument, in other words: 'there is no professional sport without consent to sports arbitration' (*'il n'y a pratiquement pas de sport d'élite sans consentement à l'arbitrage du sport'*).[51]

In sum, the SFT is interpreting the consensual basis underpinning the validity of arbitration loosely in order to accommodate the CAS and its operation. Without the readiness of the SFT to adopt what has been called 'a clear "pro-CAS arbitration" case law',[52] CAS awards would have lacked any authority. Accordingly, fundamental interpretive choices of the SFT, or its 'flexibility'[53] as it is referred to in its jurisprudence, gave the kiss of life to the CAS and constitutes the main legal fundament upon which its central institutional role in the *lex sportiva* is dependent. Hence, while the CAS has been invented by the IOC and is very much displaying transnational judicial authority,[54] its legal existence cannot be detached from a discretionary decision of the SFT to assimilate CAS arbitration to international arbitration in spite of it being 'far from the traditional idea of arbitration being the consensual alternative dispute adjudication process that we read about in every textbook on arbitration'.[55]

B. The SFT's Leniency on the Independence of the CAS

This liberal approach to the consensual fundament of CAS arbitration could (some would say should) have led the SFT to adopt a stricter assessment of the structural independence of the CAS from the SGBs. Indeed, if private parties can be coerced into a CAS arbitration, then it makes sense to ensure that they can rely on the same guarantees of independence that would be afforded to

logique qui consiste, d'une part, à favoriser la liquidation rapide des litiges, notamment en matière de sport, par des tribunaux arbitraux spécialisés présentant des garanties suffisantes d'indépendance et d'impartialité (au sujet du TAS, cf. **ATF 129 III 445** consid. 3.3.3.3), tout en veillant, d'autre part, à ce que les parties, et singulièrement les sportifs professionnels, ne renoncent pas à la légère à leur droit d'attaquer les sentences de la dernière instance arbitrale devant l'autorité judiciaire suprême de l'Etat du siège du tribunal arbitral.').

[50] SFT 133 III 235, at 245 ('Exprimée d'une autre façon, cette logique veut que le maintien d'une possibilité de recours constitue un contrepoids à la "bienveillance" avec laquelle il convient d'examiner le caractère consensuel du recours à l'arbitrage en matière sportive (RIGOZZI, op. cit., n. 1352).'). See since then the regular reaffirmation of this '*bienveillance*' in SFT 4A_548/2009, para 4.1; SFT 4A_246/2011, para 2.2.2; SFT 4A_428/2011, para 3.2.3; SFT 4A_314/2017, para 2.2.1.

[51] SFT 4A_428/2011, para 3.2.3.

[52] A Rigozzi, 'Challenging Awards of the Court of Arbitration for Sport' (2010) 1 *Journal of International Dispute Settlement* 217, 244.

[53] SFT 133 III 235, at 244 ('Le libéralisme qui caractérise la jurisprudence relative à la forme de la convention d'arbitrage en matière d'arbitrage international se manifeste également dans la souplesse avec laquelle cette jurisprudence traite le problème de la clause arbitrale par référence [...].').

[54] The evolution in the function of international arbitration towards judicialisation has been noted by other authors in other contexts, see A Stone Sweet and F Grisel, *Evolution of International Arbitration: Judicialization, Governance, Legitimacy* (Oxford University Press, 2017).

[55] Rigozzi and Robert-Tissot (n 43) 59.

them before a national judge.[56] In practice, since its 'cornerstone'[57] *Gundel* decision related to CAS arbitration, the SFT has always considered the CAS to be sufficiently independent to be recognised as a legitimate arbitral tribunal issuing binding awards. Nonetheless, in *Gundel* it did point out certain issues with regard to the independence of the CAS from the IOC and hinted at the need for some institutional changes.[58] The decision was followed by a set of institutional reforms at the CAS, referred to as the Paris Agreement, which are still largely in place nowadays.[59] These changes were endorsed by the SFT in its *Lazutina* decision from 2003, which famously recognised the CAS as sufficiently independent from the IOC for its awards to be considered equivalent to decisions of national courts.[60] In particular, it endorsed the use of a closed list of CAS arbitrators and the role of the ICAS in the selection of these arbitrators.[61] The SFT concluded its visibly 'political'[62] assessment by stressing that the CAS has become 'one of the main pillars of organized sports'.[63] Since its *Lazutina* decision, the SFT was asked in numerous instances to revisit the independence of the CAS, but has systematically endorsed the current institutional set-up and unwaveringly concluded that it constitutes an independent arbitral tribunal under Swiss law.[64]

However, this conclusion of the SFT is far from universally shared and has been strongly criticised in the literature.[65] In a similar vein, two judges of the

[56] For a similar view, see A Rigozzi, 'L'importance du droit suisse de l'arbitrage dans la résolution des litiges sportifs internationaux' (2013) 132 *Revue de droit suisse* 301, 305 (Le caractère obligatoire de l'arbitrage sportif requiert qu'il ne puisse exister aucun doute dans l'esprit des athlètes quant à l'indépendance structurelle du TAS (vis-à-vis des fédérations sportives qui leur imposent l'arbitrage).) and Rigozzi and Robert-Tissot (n 43) 71 ('We would like to stress however that the compulsory nature of sports arbitration requires athletes to have no doubts as to the independence and impartiality of the CAS arbitrators *vis-à-vis* the particular sports governing body which compelled the athlete to arbitrate').

[57] A Rigozzi, *L'arbitrage international en matière de sport* (Helbing & Lichtenhahn, 2005) 273 (… l'arrêt Gundel a été défini à juste titre comme la pierre angulaire sur laquelle repose le système d'arbitrage du TAS.).

[58] SFT 119 II 271, at 280.

[59] On these institutional changes, see the page on the 'History of the CAS' on the CAS website, available at www.tas-cas.org/en/general-information/history-of-the-cas.html.

[60] SFT 129 III 445, at 463 ('Le TAS est suffisamment indépendant du CIO, comme de toutes les autres parties qui font appel à ses services, pour que les décisions qu'il rend dans les causes intéressant cet organisme puissent être considérées comme de véritables sentences, assimilables aux jugements d'un tribunal étatique.').

[61] SFT 129 III 445, at 456–458.

[62] Rigozzi (n 57) 287 ('Que faut-il retenir de l'arrêt Latuzina ? Tout d'abord le caractère « politique » de cet arrêt qui transparaît non seulement du soin avec lequel le Tribunal fédéral a analysé le système d'arbitrage du TAS, mais aussi de la surabondance d'arguments d'opportunité.').

[63] SFT 129 III 445, 463.

[64] See recently: SFT 4A_260/2017, para 3.4 and 4A_520/2021, para 5.5.

[65] See Rigozzi (n 57) 292–293; D H. Yi, 'Turning Medals into Metal: Evaluating the Court of Arbitration of Sport as an International Tribunal' (2006) 6 *Asper Review of International Business and Trade Law* 289; R Downie, 'Improving the Performance of Sport's Ultimate Umpire: Reforming the Governance of the Court of Arbitration for Sport' (2011) 12 *Melbourne Journal of International Law* 315; Rigozzi (n 56) at 305–306; A Duval and B Van Rompuy, 'Protecting Athletes' Right to a Fair Trial Through EU Competition Law: The *Pechstein* Case' in C Paulussen, T Takacs, V Lazić, B Van

ECtHR published a strongly argued dissent under the *Mutu and Pechstein* decision on the lack of independence of the CAS from the SGBs.[66] The ECtHR itself, however, did conclude that the CAS fulfilled the independence requirements of Article 6§1 European Convention of Human Rights (ECHR).[67] This steady endorsement of the current structure of the CAS by the SFT, embodies what Whytock called the 'governance support function'[68] of national courts in the context of international commercial arbitration. It confers a seal of approval allowing the CAS to legitimately operate in its current institutional form and allows its awards to travel the world with the authority necessary to secure their almost unchallengeable finality.[69] Accordingly, if the CAS looks like it does nowadays, it is mainly because of the unwillingness of the SFT to require that its structure be set up differently. In sum, the SFT bears a direct responsibility for the institutional contours of the CAS. While the internal structure and organisation of the CAS is also dependent on decisions taken by its governing body, the ICAS, in practice it is equally (or more decisively) determined by the (non-) interventions of the SFT. Hence, the Swiss Supreme Court has not only a decisive influence on the existence of the CAS, it shapes its structure and processes. Ironically, the institutional embodiment of global sporting justice is highly dependent on the decisions taken by a court seated 500 metres away from the historical seat of the CAS and hardly representative of the wide range of people ultimately affected by the decisions of the CAS. In fact, the decisive influence of the SFT on the successful operation of the CAS does not stop there; it is also strengthening the legitimacy and finality of CAS awards by allowing challenges against them while at the same time rendering them hopeless.

C. Illusory Review: The Swiss Federal Tribunal Hands-Off Approach to Challenges against CAS Awards

Arbitral awards are valuable in the sporting context, as well as in commercial disputes, because they are relatively easy to enforce and difficult to challenge. This is especially true of CAS awards because they rarely require an exequatur by a national court to be enforced against the losing party. Indeed, SGBs dispose of the private power necessary to force most concerned parties into complying with CAS awards, as they can simply restrict access to their competitions (or the competitions of their members) to recalcitrant individuals or clubs. This means

Rompuy (eds), *Fundamental Rights in International and European Law* (Springer, T.M.C. Asser Press, 2016).

[66] See the joint partly disssenting, partly concurring Opinion of judges Keller and Serghides under *Mutu and Pechstein v Switzerland* (n 45).

[67] ibid paras 150–59.

[68] CA Whytock, 'Litigation, Arbitration, and the Transnational Shadow of the Law' (2008) 18 *Duke Journal of Comparative and International Law* 449.

[69] Rigozzi (n 56) 304 ('Cette reconnaissance par le Tribunal fédéral a permis au TAS de devenir une institution mondialement reconnue pour la résolution des litiges en matière sportive.').

that unlike commercial awards, CAS awards very rarely necessitate the intervention of state courts to be implemented. Consequently, beyond the relatively straightforward opportunity to challenge a CAS award before the SFT on the basis of the grounds listed in Article 190 Private International Law Act (PILA), there are very few realistic options available to overturn or block the application of such an award. This central position of the SFT in reviewing CAS awards explains the 'spectacular rise'[70] in the absolute number of challenges lodged before the Swiss court against CAS awards. Ultimately, the finality or fragility of CAS awards is mainly a function of the review exercised by the SFT.

In general, the SFT is known for being extremely reluctant to overturn international arbitral awards. Experienced observers note that 'only in particularly grievous cases will the Swiss courts disturb an international arbitration award'.[71] As documented by Dasser and Wojtowicz, between 1989 and 2019 only 7.56 per cent of challenges lodged with the court against international awards were successful. In 2022, the success rate of challenges against CAS awards reached a low point of 0 per cent (out of 33 SFT decisions). Despite the increasing absolute number of appeals against CAS awards, the SFT limits strictly the scope and intensity of its review. In general, the SFT refuses to act as an appellate court when reviewing international awards and to reconsider the facts of the case.[72] This reluctance is also reflected in its extremely narrow interpretation of the notion of public policy, be it in its procedural or substantial form.[73] For example, the SFT does not consider a mistaken interpretation of the law or even a *contra legem* application of a rule by an arbitrator as running afoul of Swiss public policy, neither does the arbitrariness of a decision constitute a violation of public policy in the sense of Article 190(2)e PILA.[74] Accordingly, the SFT acknowledges that the quashing of an award on the basis of public policy is 'extremely rare'.[75] In fact, it has only once struck down an international award (a CAS award) on the basis of substantial public policy in its famous *Matuzalem* decision.[76] In recent years, in light of a growing tendency of parties to invoke the ECHR, the SFT has also started to regularly stress that the incompatibility of a CAS award with the ECHR is not as such a valid basis for a successful challenge of a CAS award.[77] Finally, even in the extremely rare cases in which the SFT allows a challenge to stand and decides to set aside a CAS award, the case is

[70] F Dasser and P Wojtowicz, 'Swiss International Arbitral Awards Before the Federal Supreme Court: Statistical Data 1989–2019' (2021) 39 *ASA Bulletin* 7, 11.

[71] P Landolt, 'Judicial Control of Arbitral Awards in Switzerland' in LA Di Matteo, M Infantino and NM-P Potin (eds), *The Cambridge Handbook of Judicial Control of Arbitral Awards* (Cambridge University Press, 2020) 336, 351.

[72] See recently, SFT 4A_434/2022, para 4.2.

[73] Rigozzi (n 56) 320.

[74] SFT 4A_406/2021, para 7.1.

[75] SFT 4A_246/2022, para 6.1 and 4A_248/2019, para 2.

[76] SFT 138 III 322.

[77] For recent examples of this stable jurisprudence, see SFT 4A_406/2021, para 7.2; SFT 4A_564/2021, para 4.1; SFT 4A_248/2019, para 3.2.

usually sent back to the CAS for a new decision to be issued. In such situations, athletes who are challenging the SGBs have to assume again the costs of CAS proceedings with limited prospect of success.[78]

In sum, as stressed by the SFT, it 'should not be assimilated to an appeal court overseeing the CAS, which would freely assess the merits of its international awards'.[79] In general, as noted by Swiss observers, the court 'does not like to second-guess Swiss arbitral tribunals'[80] and adopts a true 'hands-off approach'[81] when dealing with CAS awards. This is not specific to CAS arbitration or Switzerland, as Whytock has shown national courts play a crucial role in emancipating arbitration from judicial monitoring throughout the world.[82] Yet, in the context of CAS arbitration, this extreme 'permissiveness'[83] is more problematic. As pointed out by Rigozzi,

> one can also think that some sort of control by the Supreme Court would constitute a minimum quality guarantee of the arbitrators' work on the merits and that the athletes should be allowed such a guarantee given that they were compelled to accept arbitration.[84]

Moreover, in light of the extreme difficulties faced by athletes (and other parties) to challenge CAS awards in other national courts around the world, the SFT is in practice the only court which can provide a systematic and robust supervision of the decisions of the CAS.[85] Yet, the Swiss Court has renounced any active role in reviewing CAS awards, as it offers only a questionable 'security net'[86] limited at best to the most egregious cases. This decision of the SFT to remain on the side lines insofar as CAS awards are concerned has a 'radiating effect'[87]

[78] In the *Sun Yang* case, for eg, the first CAS award (CAS 2019/A/6148 *World Anti-Doping Agency v Mr Sun Yang & Fédération Internationale de Natation* (FINA), 28 February 2020) was annulled by a decision of the SFT (SFT 147 III 65) due to the partiality of one of the arbitrators involved. Yet, the case was sent back to the CAS, which issued a second award (CAS 2019/A/6148 *World Anti-Doping Agency v Mr Sun Yang & Fédération Internationale de Natation* (FINA), 22 June 2021), which was then unsuccessfully challenged by Sun Yang before the SFT (SFT 4A_406/2021).

[79] SFT 4A_406/2021, para 8 and SFT 4A_248/2019, para 2.

[80] Dasser and Wojtowicz (n 70) 40.

[81] Rigozzi (n 52) 219.

[82] Whytock (n 68) 469.

[83] A Rigozzi, 'L'importance du droit suisse de l'arbitrage dans la résolution des litiges sportifs internationaux', (2013) *Zeitschrift fur Schweizerisches Recht* 301–25, 320.

[84] Rigozzi (n 52) 254. For a similar view, see M Baddeley, 'La décision Cañas: nouvelles règles du jeu pour l'arbitrage international du sport' (2007) *Causa Sport* 155.

[85] Claudia Pechstein, who engaged in a never-ending crusade against the CAS over an award confirming a doping ban issued by the International Skating Union, has experienced this difficulty first hand, as her long-fought battle to overturn the decision contributed directly to her personal bankruptcy. See Die Welt, Pleite zwingt Pechstein zu dramatischem Hilferuf (1 July 2015), www.welt.de/sport/article143390802/Pleite-zwingt-Pechstein-zu-dramatischem-Hilferuf.html.

[86] Rigozzi (n 52) 264 ('The question is thus whether the Supreme Court's case law constitutes such a security net in CAS cases and contributes to ensure the quality of CAS awards. As a matter of fact, it is clear that while the number of actions filed is increasing exponentially, the number of awards set aside remains very limited.').

[87] On the 'radiating effect' of court judgments, see M Galanter, 'The Radiating Effects of Courts' in KO Boyum and L Mater (eds), *Empirical Theories about Courts* (Longman, 1983) 117.

worldwide, as it hardens the finality of these awards and implies that athletes and other stakeholders are likely to have their final (and often only) chance in a (relatively independent) court in Lausanne, not at the SFT, but a few hundred metres up the hill at the Château de Béthusy (and now at the Palais de Beaulieu), home to the CAS.[88]

Ultimately, the existence, shape and power of the CAS are all dependent on fundamental legal determinations made by the SFT. This is not to say that Swiss law and institutions are fully in control, they always remain at risk of being blackmailed with a threat of collective exit by the international SGBs and the CAS.[89] Nevertheless, this is a relationship of interdependency and the SFT has consciously provided the legal capital, in Sassen's words the 'new legalities',[90] necessary for the CAS to emerge and solidify its position as the supreme court of world sport.[91] Henceforth, the *lex sportiva*, not unlike the new *lex mercatoria*,[92] must be understood as a hybrid, combining both state and non-state elements in a transnational functional regime. International sports arbitration exists not outside the state, without its support, but instead because the Swiss state is consciously putting its legal weight behind it.[93] In this regard, the 'enduring success' of the CAS, like the general appeal of Switzerland for international arbitration, can indeed be traced back to 'the efficient, speedy, no-nonsensical, and arbitration-friendly resolution of challenges of awards'.[94] However, as pointed

[88] Rigozzi (n 52) 265 ('the CAS is becoming the only instance where they [the athletes] can assert their rights').

[89] Although unsuccessful in this specific instance, as the Swiss authorities refused to confer to the IOC the status of an international organisation, such an attempt at exit blackmail is presented in Q Tonnerre, 'Un chemin semé d'embûches: les relations entre la Confédération suisse et le CIO des années 1970 à nos jours' in E Bayle, A Bonomi, J-L Chappelet, S Caneppele (eds), *La régulation du sport mondial – Global Sport Regulation* (niversité de Lausanne, 2021) 212, 222 ('Le CIO en profite pour faire savoir à ses interlocuteurs que des villes concurrentes cherchent toujours à attirer le siège de l'organisation et qu'une amélioration de son statut juridique pourrait résoudre en partie cette question, lui permettant d'obtenir une reconnaissance plus importante de la part de l'ONU.').

[90] Sassen, 'The State and Globalization' (n 8) 1155 ('It is becoming clear that the role of the state in the process of deregulation involves the production of new types of regulations, legislative items, court decisions, in brief, the production of a whole series of new legalities') and Sassen (n 10) (Governments of countries articulated with the global economic system have had to pass multiple legislative measures, regulations, executive orders, and court decisions, enabling foreign firms to operate in their territories, their own firms to operate abroad, and markets generally to become global).

[91] Wai refers to a 'dialectical relationship' between transnational private dispute-resolution and state law, see Wai (n 6) 267.

[92] R Michaels, 'The True Lex Mercatoria : Law Beyond the State' (2007) 14 *Indiana Journal of Global Legal* 447, 466 ('Within this debate, a lex mercatoria that combines both state and non-state elements can only be explained as a hybrid.'). Similarly, Whytock (n 68) 471 ('Second, it follows that transnational arbitration is probably better characterized as a "mixed" rather than a purely private form of governance.').

[93] More generally on international arbitration being premised on the active support of national law and courts, see Wai (n 6) and Whytock (n 68) and CA Whytock, 'Private-Public Interaction in Global Governance: The Case of Transnational Commercial Arbitration' (2010) 12 *Business and Politics* 1.

[94] Dasser and Wojtowicz (n 70) 41.

out by *Wai* already 20 years ago, there 'are significant risks to parties when there is inadequate judicial oversight for problems such as limited information and unequal bargaining power in many contexts where arbitration, forum-selection and choice of law clauses are "agreed" to'.[95] Translated to the context of this chapter, if the main reason for the CAS being located in Switzerland is because it can operate without real checks in spite of its non-consensual set-up, then there is probably little cause to celebrate this 'success'. In addition to allowing the CAS to exercise transnational authority with few strings attached, we will see in the final part of this chapter that the SFT's endorsement has also become a bill of health acting as a powerful shield in proceedings brought against CAS awards outside Switzerland.

III. WHAT HAPPENS IN LAUSANNE STAYS IN LAUSANNE: THE SWISS FEDERAL TRIBUNAL'S ENDORSEMENT OF CAS AS A POTENT EXTERNAL SHIELD

The role of the SFT is not only crucial for the existence of the CAS and in strengthening its authority inside the transnational governance structure of international sports, it is also essential in shielding the CAS (and its awards) from challenges outside Switzerland. This external legitimation function of the SFT has in the past been instrumental in convincing other national and European courts and competition authorities to embrace the legitimacy of the CAS and the legality of its awards, as will be documented in this section with references to German courts, the ECtHR and the European Commission.

A. The Role of the SFT's Jurisprudence in the *Pechstein* Judgment of the BGH

Claudia Pechstein is a German speed skater, who has been attempting to challenge a CAS award, which confirmed a doping sanction issued against her by the International Skating Union, since 2009.[96] Unsurprisingly, the CAS award was endorsed by the SFT and, therefore, she was excluded from the Vancouver 2010 Winter Olympics.[97] Nevertheless, Claudia Pechstein lodged an application against Switzerland before the ECtHR, which will be discussed in the next section, and started proceedings before local German courts claiming damages

[95] Wai (n 6) 271. For similar considerations on the limits of arbitration, see Wai (n 7) 51 ('The generalized broad support for dispute resolution clauses may reduce then the traditional oversight role for private law courts to examine issues of information, voluntariness, and bargaining power of the parties to an arbitration agreement or a contract containing such a clause.') and Pistor (n 20) 226.

[96] CAS 2009/A/1912 &1913, *Claudia Pechstein et al v International Skating Union*, 25 November 2009.

[97] SFT 4A_612/2009.

from the ISU, while contesting the validity of the CAS award (and CAS arbitration clause). In the context of the latter proceedings, the Regional Court of Munich (OLG Muenchen) questioned the validity of CAS arbitration clauses, as well as the independence of the CAS.[98] Yet, the ISU appealed the decision to the highest German Civil Court (*Bundesgerichtshof* or BGH) in Karlsruhe, which overruled the decision of the OLG in July 2016.[99] In 2022, the German Constitutional Court annulled this decision and referred the case back to OLG Muenchen.[100] For our purposes, the focus will be on the reasoning relied on by the BGH to endorse the validity of the CAS arbitration clause and, in particular, on the role played by the SFT's support for the CAS.

First, with regard to the validity of the consent of Claudia Pechstein, the BGH is of the view that German courts must apply Swiss law 'in the same way as the courts of the foreign country in question interpret and apply it'.[101] The BGH simply noted that the

> case law of the Swiss Federal Tribunal on the question of 'involuntary signing' of arbitration agreements in favour of the CAS which are imposed on professional athletes by the sports federations shows that although a professional athlete will only sign the arbitration agreement under duress because he knows that he will not be able to exercise his profession otherwise, the arbitration agreement will still be valid'.[102]

Accordingly, unlike the OLG, it decided to defer to the SFT in matters related to the interpretation of Pechstein's consent to CAS arbitration. Consequently, the BGH narrowed considerably the possibility to challenge the validity of CAS arbitration clauses which are endorsed by the SFT. Through the operation of private international law rules determining the applicable law in a particular matter, the SFT's determination on this question becomes decisive even outside Switzerland, and extremely difficult to overturn.

Second, the BGH when assessing whether the CAS constituted a 'true' arbitral tribunal, largely relied on the conclusions reached by the SFT in this regard. From the outset, it considered, referring to the *Danilova and Lazutina* decision of the SFT, that the CAS is 'independent of the sports federations and Olympic Committees that support it'.[103] Furthermore, when assessing the impact of the closed list of arbitrators on the independence of the CAS, the BGH refers decisively to academic commentaries reporting on the key Lazutina decision of the SFT.[104] Third, and finally, the judges stressed the fact that Claudia Pechstein

[98] OLG München, *Az. U 1110/14 Kart, Claudia Pechstein v/ International Skating Union (ISU)*, 15 January 2015.

[99] BGH, KZR 6/15, *Claudia Pechstein v/ International Skating Union (ISU)*, 7 June 2016.

[100] BverfG, 1 BvR 2103/16, 3 June 2022.

[101] BGH, KZR 6/15, II.3. c)ee)(2) (hereinafter I refer to the translation of the ruling available on the CAS website, www.tas-cas.org/fileadmin/user_upload/Pechstein___ISU_translation_ENG_final.pdf).

[102] ibid.

[103] ibid II.1)b).

[104] ibid II.1)c)bb), referring to F Öschütz, 'Anmerkung zur Entscheidung des schweizerischen Bundesgerichts im Fall Danilova und Latsutina' (2004) *SchiedsVZ* 211, 212.

had 'also the option […] of having the arbitral awards of the CAS reviewed by the federal courts of Switzerland to a certain extent',[105] and invoked the New York Convention on the Recognition and Enforcement of Arbitral Awards to justify the fact that it would not engage in any further review of the award. In other words, there 'is no further reaching right for a decision particularly by a German state court'.[106]

These holdings incarnate the trust put by the German court in the SFT's assessments of the validity of the arbitration clause, despite its acknowledged forced nature, and of the independence and impartiality of the CAS. Accordingly, the SFT's certification of the CAS constitutes a very strong presumption of legality playing in favour of CAS awards in the eyes of the BGH. Under the guise of private international law principles, which were devised specifically to apply to situations in which parties freely renounce their right to go to national courts, the conclusions reached by the SFT were deferred to. In this way, the SFT's non-interventionist approach to the CAS is spreading almost seamlessly beyond the borders of Switzerland. This ensures, at least in Germany, but other cases of challenges against CAS awards would likely be dealt with similarly in most countries around the world, that CAS awards become a hard legal currency whose authority and finality are extremely difficult to challenge in national courts throughout the globe.

B. The Role of the SFT's Jurisprudence in the ECtHR's Review of CAS Awards: The *Mutu and Pechstein* and *Platini* Cases

In recent years, CAS awards have also increasingly been the subject of applications lodged against Switzerland before the ECtHR.[107] While these cases do not directly challenge CAS awards, they at least aim to challenge the human rights compatibility of the lenient review of CAS awards exercised by the SFT. The main decision in this regard is the *Pechstein and Mutu* judgment rendered in 2018. It concerns the compatibility of the CAS with Article 6§1 ECHR. In particular, Pechstein and Mutu argued that, for the former, the CAS as an institution and, for the latter, the CAS arbitrators involved in the proceedings lacked the independence and impartiality required under Article 6§1 ECHR. Pechstein also challenged the compatibility of the confidential nature of her hearing before the CAS with the same provision.

In the ruling, the Strasbourg judges recognised that CAS arbitration was in general forced arbitration and, therefore, needed to fully comply with

[105] ibid II.3.c)bb)(3).

[106] ibid.

[107] For recent decisions, see *Mutu and Pechstein v Switzerland* (n 45), *Bakker v Switzerland* (2019) App no 7198/07 (ECtHR, 3 September 2019), *Platini v Switzerland* (2020) App no 526/18 (ECtHR, 11 February 2020). One application remains officially pending at the ECtHR, it concerns the South-African runner Caster Semenya, see *Semenya v Switzerland* App no 10934/21.

Article 6§1 ECHR.[108] However, the Court also came to the conclusion that the CAS was to be regarded as an independent and impartial arbitral tribunal. In doing so, it emphasised the fact that the SFT had recognised that CAS awards amount to 'proper judgments comparable with those of a national court'.[109] Furthermore, the ECtHR considered, against the dissenting opinion of judges Keller and Serghides, that

> there are insufficient grounds for it to reject the settled case-law of the Federal Court to the effect that the system of the list of arbitrators meets the constitutional requirements of independence and impartiality applicable to arbitral tribunals, and that the CAS, when operating as an appellate body external to international federations, is similar to a judicial authority independent of the parties.[110]

The emphasis put in this paragraph on the SFT's 'settled case-law' seems to indicate that the ECtHR displays some deference to the determinations reached by the SFT and, therefore, puts a higher burden on the claimants aiming to challenge them.

In the more recent *Platini* case, the ECtHR rejected the application submitted by the former FIFA official and endorsed the findings of the SFT.[111] In particular, it stressed the fact that Platini had had the opportunity to appeal the CAS award to the SFT, which supported the legality of the award with a 'plausible and convincing' reasoning.[112] Moreover, the Strasbourg judges insisted that Platini had 'sufficient institutional and procedural safeguards, including a private (CAS) and state (SFT) jurisdiction before which he could raise his claims, and which conducted a real balancing of the relevant interests and responded to the applicants claims with duly motivated decisions'.[113] Finally, the ECtHR also stressed the 'considerable margin of appreciation'[114] enjoyed by Switzerland in the context of this case. In practice, as emphasised by the dissenting judges in the *Mutu and Pechstein* ruling, there are serious concerns regarding the independence of the CAS. Furthermore, as evidenced statistically and recognised in the (Swiss) literature, the SFT's review of CAS awards is extremely limited in scope and can hardly count as a strong safeguard for parties challenging CAS awards. Ironically, the SFT even bluntly refuses to review the compatibility of CAS awards with the ECHR. Nevertheless, the ECtHR's position on this issue is illustrative of the considerable symbolic power conferred to the CAS by the SFT's endorsement and of its fundamental role in shielding the CAS and its awards from external challenges.

[108] A Duval, 'Time to Go Public? The Need for Transparency at the Court of Arbitration for Sport' in A Duval and A Rigozzi (eds), *Yearbook of International Sports Arbitration* (T.M.C. Asser Press, Springer, 2019).

[109] *Mutu and Pechstein v Switzerland* (n 45) para 156.

[110] ibid 157.

[111] *Platini v Switzerland* (n 107) para 68.

[112] ibid para 69.

[113] ibid para 70.

[114] ibid.

The SFT's lenient endorsement of the CAS is thus held against applicants before the ECtHR and justifies the rejection of their claims. Not unlike before the BGH, the endorsement by the SFT is not seriously called into question and operates as a strong presumption in favour of the CAS and its decisions. The reference to the margin of appreciation of Switzerland in the *Platini* decision is further evidence of the importance of the SFT's endorsement in shielding the CAS from any critical review by the ECtHR. Yet, this reference is all but unproblematic in a context in which the CAS does not primarily affect Swiss citizens, but constitutes a transnational judicial body which defines the rights and obligations of a large group of people across the globe.[115] In this context, is it reasonable to invoke the margin of appreciation of a state when the exercise of this margin of appreciation has consequences primarily for a transnational constituency? There is no doubt that Swiss interests might be at play, in particular economic and reputational interests, but it is also evident that the interests of many individuals who are not Swiss citizens, and who therefore have no political say in Swiss institutions, are being primarily affected.

C. The Role of the SFT's Jurisprudence in the European Union's Approach to the CAS

Finally, the SFT's endorsement of the CAS also played a limited role in the way in which EU institutions were treating the CAS in the early 2000s. This is reflected, for example, in decisions of the European Commission (EC) in competition law cases. In its *Meca-Medina* decision, the EC referenced the *Lazutina* decision of the SFT and, in particular, the paragraph in which the Swiss judges recognised that the CAS could be considered a proper arbitral tribunal in instances in which the IOC is a party.[116] This reference supported the rejection, without further discussions, of the claim that the CAS lacked impartiality. In *Cañas*, the EC rejected a complaint and stressed that the claimant, an Argentinean tennis player, had not exercised his right to appeal to the SFT.[117] This subsequently led the EC to insist that it does not constitute an appeal body in individual doping cases, thus implying that the SFT was the right body to turn to for such a challenge against a CAS decision. Both decisions illustrate how the SFT's jurisprudence has been used by the EC as a shield against claims that the CAS

[115] For a similar argument, see M Krech, '"Sport Sex" before the European Court of Human Rights' (*Volkerrechtsblog*, 22 March 2021), https://voelkerrechtsblog.org/sport-sex-before-the-european-court-of-human-rights/.

[116] EC's rejection decision in *Meca Medina and Majcen v IOC* (Case COMP/38158), 1 August 2008, para 66.

[117] EC's rejection decision in *Certain joueur de tennis professionnel v Agence mondiale antidopage, ATP Tour Inc et Fondation Conseil international de l'arbitrage en matière de sport* (Case COMP/39471), 12 October 2009, para 49 ('Le plaignant aurait pu exercer un deuxième recours auprès du Tribunal fédéral suisse après la deuxième sentence du TAS du 23 mai 2007, mais il a choisi de ne pas le faire et de saisir la Commission européenne.').

lacks independence or impartiality, and how its power of review is presented as a considerable procedural safeguard for claimants. It is true, however, that since then the EC has been more sceptical in its assessment of the CAS as an avenue for review in competition law complaints.[118]

In conclusion, the SFT not only allows the CAS to take off the ground and become an active global court, it also confers to it the necessary legitimacy to resist external challenges from other courts. Consequently, it secures the transnational authority of its awards and their efficacy in determining the outcome of fundamental sporting disputes affecting sporting citizens throughout the world. In short, without this resounding Swiss endorsement, there would not be an effective and authoritative transnational *lex sportiva* to speak of. Hence, analogically to global capitalism in Pistor's work,[119] international sports is sustained mostly by a single domestic legal system, in this case Swiss law, thanks to the recognition of the legitimacy of its legal coding by other states and international institutions.

IV. CONCLUSION

This chapter has aimed to show primarily that the *lex sportiva*, the transnational legal regime which rules international sports and in particular the Olympic movement, is not anational and radically autonomous from the state,[120] but instead profoundly embedded in Swiss law and dependent for its transnational 'liftoff'[121] on the active support of Swiss institutions. In this regard, the *lex sportiva* embodies well what *Wai* calls the 'interlegality of transnational private law'.[122] The chapter also showcases a fundamental paradox of globalisation highlighted in Sassen's work, the fact that 'some of the components of the nation-state and the state apparatus are themselves part of the new centrifugality'.[123] In fact, the existence of the *lex sportiva* is made possible by its embeddedness in the Swiss context, which is key to securing the legitimacy and effectiveness of its transnational authority. Accordingly, *lex sportiva* should be seen as a glocal assemblage of legal components from

[118] EC's decision in *International Skating Union's Eligibility rules* (Case AT.40208), 8 December 2017, paras 268–286. Even though the General Court annulled the EC's decision on this point, see Case T-93/18 *International Skating Union v European Commission* [2020] ECLI:EU:T:2020:610, paras 131–164.

[119] Pistor (n 20) 132.

[120] In this regard, the chapter comes to the same conclusion as Wolf (n 36).

[121] Wai (n 6).

[122] Wai (n 13).

[123] Sassen (n 9) 74. See as well, S Sassen, 'Embedding the Global in the National: Implications for the Role of the State' (1999) 7 *Macalester International* 31, 40 ('Some of what we code as national because it takes place in national territory has become the global. And some of what we code as global is contingent on the national state as an administrative capacity and as a source of legitimacy.').

different horizons in which Swiss law (and Swiss lawyers[124]) play a central role.[125] It illustrates the fact that 'globalization is always the successful globalization of a particular localism'.[126] The so-called liberalism of Swiss private law, its *laissez-faire* approach to associations and international arbitration, is a fundamental pre-condition to the transnational power and authority of the institutions, regulations and decisions of the *lex sportiva*. The reluctance of these same Swiss institutions to intervene in the affairs of the SGBs or the CAS amounts to a positive endorsement of their current institutional processes and substantive regulations or decisions. Switzerland's stand is not neutral, and unlike what Swiss institutions often try to project, it has profound distributive and political consequences for those involved in international sports across the globe. Formulated differently, below the veneer of neutrality and respect for private autonomy, the 'depoliticizing flatness'[127] referred to by *Wai*, lies the empowerment of certain individuals or interests over others.[128] *Lex Sportiva*, then, must be understood as essentially co-constructed by Swiss legal institutions. The fact that this seemingly benign form of Swiss transnational legal imperialism expresses itself negatively, by a refusal to intervene, does not make it less intrusive for those at the receiving end of transnational sports law and governance.[129] Instead, as we have documented, the non-intervention of Swiss institutions acts as a crucial endorsement to the SGBs and as a necessary condition for their deployment of almost unchallengeable transnational private authority.

Once the fundamental nature and the considerable implications of the Swiss contribution to the *lex sportiva* become clear, it raises a number of difficult questions, such as: Is Swiss law and are Swiss institutions well placed to defend the interests of non-Swiss citizens subjected to the *lex sportiva*? Can sportspeople really entrust Swiss institutions with the responsibility of protecting their fundamental rights within the *lex sportiva*? Have Swiss institutions

[124] Documenting the intricate, at times almost incestuous, relationships between Swiss lawyers inside the Swiss Government and their Swiss counterparts at SGBs, see Tonnerre (n 89) 217 and 224. In general, an extensive sociological analysis of the transnational social field of lawyers behind the *lex sportiva* would be an important research project to pursue.

[125] On the glocal nature of *lex sportiva*, see A Duval, 'The Russian Doping Scandal at the Court of Arbitration for Sport: Lessons for the World Anti-Doping System' (2017) 16 *International Sports Law Journal* 177. On how the CAS weaves together legal fragments to produce the *lex sportiva*, see A Duval, 'Seamstress of Transnational Law: How the Court of Arbitration for Sport Weaves the Lex Sportiva' in N Krisch (ed), *Entangled Legalities beyond the State* (Cambridge University Press, 2021) 260.

[126] de Sousa Santos (n 12) 396.

[127] Wai (n 7) 36 ('A kind of depoliticizing flatness, and a connected lack of legitimacy, seems associated with the reality of complex transnational pluralism in economic law.').

[128] For a similar argument in the context of the regulation of capital and transnational economic activities, see Pistor (n 20).

[129] Identifying the same concerns with regard to the lenient supervision by national courts of commercial arbitration, see Whytock (n 68) 472 ('Third, from a governance-oriented normative perspective, it is precisely this "odd relationship between the public and private" – this combination of minimal judicial monitoring and strong judicial support – that raises concerns'.).

done a good job in doing so until now? Should other courts that have to deal with challenges against the *lex sportiva* show deference to the assessments of the SFT? Should the ECtHR recognise a margin of appreciation to Switzerland in matters related to the *lex sportiva*? All these questions are not hypothetical, they are at the core of many debates currently being waged before a number of jurisdictions on the legality of CAS awards and the scope of control that other European or national courts should exercise over them.[130]

This chapter is not the right place to answer them, but they will need to be thoroughly tackled in the near future. Ultimately, the tight entanglement between the private rules and decisions of the SGBs and Swiss law ought to be meticulously and critically deconstructed in order to better understand the inner workings of the *lex sportiva* and determine the extent of the responsibility (and potentially of the complicity) of Switzerland in the current state of transnational sports governance and regulation. Indeed, while the Swiss *laissez-faire* approach to the SGBs' rule over international sports might have clear economic benefits for Switzerland,[131] its potential negative consequences for athletes, fans, and others affected by the *lex sportiva* should not be overlooked. Instead, it is essential to be mindful of the fact that '[w]hen private actors assume public functions this does not unburden the state/world of states of their ultimate responsibility to mitigate the problems of legitimation associated with transnational private norm-setting and norm-enforcement'.[132]

[130] Many of them are discussed in the other chapters included in this volume.

[131] Chappelet makes reference to around 3000 well-paid jobs linked to the presence of international SGBs, see Chappelet (n 5) 569. For a more comprehensive quantitative analysis of the significant economic impact of international SGBs in Switzerland, see C Stricker and G-B Derchi, *The Economic Impact of International Sports Organisations in Switzerland: 2014–2019* (International Academy for Sports Science and Technology, 2021), https://aists.org/wp-content/uploads/2022/01/AISTS-Ecoimpact-21-Full-Report-FINAL-EN.pdf.

[132] Wolf (n 36) 301.

3

Putting the Lex into Lex Sportiva: *The Principle of Legality in Sports*

JOHAN LINDHOLM*

I. KEEPING SPORTS ON THE STRAIGHT AND NARROW

When international sports federations and other sports governing bodies (SGBs) act, do they do so with the authority of law and are they subject to the requirements of the principle of legality? Under traditional legal thinking, the answers to both those questions would seem to be no. Sports rules are in several respects similar to state-based law, for example, in that they contain general norms established by actors internally designated as norm makers and in a particular prescribed order and may be functionally similar to administrative law norms.[1] Formally, however, they are a collection of private horizontal agreements based on private law and consent, and while this collection is admittedly vast, complex and sophisticated unlike state-based law, it has not sprung forth from the exercise of public power.[2] Since the principle of legality serves as a check on the exercise of public power, it follows, seemingly naturally, that the principle should not apply to sports rules.

It is therefore puzzling that the Court of Arbitration for Sport (CAS) has in fact recognised the principle of legality as one of the general principles included in *lex sportiva*.[3] The term *lex sportiva* is used by different authors to mean slightly different things,[4] but it is here used to refer to the set of rules and principles that govern sports transnationally or globally and that

* Professor of Law, Umeå University. Email: johan.lindholm@umu.se.

[1] See, eg, CAS 98/200, *AEK Athens and SK Slavia Prague v UEFA*, para 58.

[2] See, eg, MJ Beloff et al, *Sports Law*, 2nd edn (Hart Publishing, 2012) 35–36, 45–46.

[3] I am not the first to make this observation, see, eg, F Latty, *La Lex Sportiva : Recherche Sur Le Droit Transnational* (Martinus Nijhoff Publishers, 2007) 319–20; K Vieweg and P Staschik, 'The Lex Sportiva: The Phenomenon and Its Meaning in the International Sporting Arena' in K Vieweg (ed), *Lex Sportiva* (Duncker & Humblot, 2015) 26. I have also previously written on the topic in J Lindholm, *The Court of Arbitration for Sport and Its Jurisprudence: An Empirical Inquiry into Lex Sportiva* (TMC Asser Press, 2019) 194–99.

[4] See, eg, A Duval, 'Lex Sportiva: A Playground for Transnational Law' (2013) 19 *European Law Journal* 21, 827–28; Lindholm (n 3) 7–14; Latty (n 3) 31–39; Vieweg and Staschik (n 3).

is developed through public, private, judicial and legislative/formal norm-making processes.[5] The CAS is the foremost authoritative interpreter of *lex sportiva* and a main contributor by weaving together private-made norms with various national and international state-based norms into an entangled, transnational legal order.[6]

Besides describing this jurisprudence, this chapter also, and perhaps more interestingly, seeks to explain it. As noted above, the CAS's case law on legality raises a thought-provoking legal puzzle: why does a principle that serves to check public power apply to what is formally a web of private-law agreements between private entities? It also presents a strategic puzzle: why would the CAS, being a central power-wielding institution in sports,[7] introduce a principle that serves to check how sports institutions exercise their powers? This investigation into legality in sports law aims to address these questions. It is thus primarily descriptive and explanatory in nature, placing less emphasis on the normative implications.[8]

The chapter proceeds as follows. Section II provides the reader with a brief introduction to the principle of legality as it applies to this specific context. Section III explores how the CAS recognises, understands and enforces the principle of legality. As demonstrated below, the CAS's jurisprudence contains a plurality of aspects of the principle of legality that range from the relatively narrow principle of non-retroactivity for (quasi-) criminal offences to a 'thicker', normative understanding that overlaps significantly with Fuller's criteria for moral law. Section IV builds on and seeks to explain those observations. Drawing on various theories on international arbitration and transnational law, three complementary explanations for the CAS's jurisprudence are presented. The chapter rounds off with some concluding reflections and questions for further research in section V.

As this chapter hopefully demonstrates, the principle of legality is an excellent case study that can contribute to our understanding of the nature of *lex sportiva* in this transnational order, how the CAS goes about shaping it, as well as the influence that national and regional European law plays in this process.

[5] *cf* A Duval, 'What *Lex Sportiva* Tells You About Transnational Law' in P Zumbansen (ed), *The Many Lives of Transnational Law: Critical Engagements with Jessup's Bold Proposal* (Cambridge University Press, 2020). As seen in section IV.C, the character of *lex sportiva* is also closely connected to sports' claim for autonomy vis-à-vis state-based legal orders.

[6] A Duval, 'Seamstress of Transnational Law: How the Court of Arbitration for Sport Weaves the Lex Sportiva' in N Krisch (ed), *Entangled Legalities beyond the State* (Cambridge University Press, 2022). see also B Hess, 'The Development of Lex Sportiva by the Court of Arbitration for Sport' in K Vieweg (ed), *Lex Sportiva* (Duncker & Humblot, 2015); Latty (n 3) 257–59.

[7] L Casini, 'The Making of a Lex Sportiva by the Court of Arbitration for Sport' (2011) 12 *German Law Journal* 1317, 1318–19; A Duval, 'Not in My Name! Claudia Pechstein and the Post-Consensual Foundations of the Court of Arbitration for Sport' (2017) 2, https://ssrn.com/abstract=2920555.

[8] Specifically, there is no ambition here to determine normatively whether transnational sports law complies (sufficiently) with the principle of legality or identify 'normative shortcomings'. *cf* N Walker, 'The Idea of Constitutional Pluralism' (2002) 65 *MLR* 317, 322–23.

II. VARIETIES OF LEGALITY: AN OVERVIEW

The principle of legality, and the concept of legality more broadly, can be understood in a variety of ways and no universally agreed upon definition of the principle of legality exists.[9] Whereas some of these understandings are relatively narrow and straightforward, others are broad and vague. There are also noticeable differences between legal traditions in how the term is used.[10] Finally, the principle of legality is so deeply connected to a number of core legal concepts and jurisprudential questions that it is nearly impossible to draw its boundaries.

There is, however, broad agreement that the function of the principle is to guard against the arbitrary exercise of power on the part of those who govern for the benefit of those who are governed.[11] Through its function, the principle of legality is consequently closely connected with the rule of law. While the principle of legality can be distinguished from the rule of law, the two are deeply intertwined and legality can be understood as a subset of the rule of law, its formal element. As demonstrated herein, the principle of legality is not (only) a general legal value but a practical legal tool that can be and is invoked by individuals to protect their rights and interests in real-world situations. Thus, while the principle of legality is both complex and fuzzy, its importance cannot be denied.

Legality can be understood as a 'way of framing and understanding the relation between the ruler and the ruled, the administrator and the administrated, the governor and the governed'.[12] Traditionally, the principle of legality covers individuals' relationship with the state and acts as a limitation on the latter's exercise of public power over the former.[13] As it has become understood in the continental European legal tradition,[14] the principle was born out of the

[9] LFM Besselink, F Pennings and S Prechal, 'Legality in Multiple Legal Orders' in L FM Besselink, F Pennings and S Prechal (eds), *The Eclipse of the Legality Principle in the European Union* (Kluwer Law International BV, 2011); A Somek, 'Is Legality a Principle of EU Law?' in S Vogenauer and S Weatherill (eds), *General Principles of Law: European and Comparative Perspectives* (Hart Publishing, 2017) 53–54.

[10] Besselink, Pennings and Prechal (n 9).

[11] See, eg, AV Dicey, *The Law of the Constitution* (edited by JWF Allison) (Oxford University Press, 2013) 97.

[12] B Kingsbury, 'The Concept of "Law" in Global Administrative Law' (2009) 20 *European Journal of International Law* 23, 39.

[13] Besselink, Pennings and Prechal (n 9) 2.

[14] See also Dicey (n 11) 95–119 on the constitutional development in England. Dicey's influence has contributed to the diverging terminology. FA von Hayek, *The Road to Serfdom* (Routledge, 2006) 76. For example, it is sometimes used to mean a collection of common law principles of interpretation. See, eg, B Chen, 'The Principle of Legality: Issues on Rationale and Application' (2015) 41 *Monash University Law Review* 329; R French, 'The Principle of Legality and Legislative Intention' (2019) 40 *Statute Law Review* 40. This can be thought of as an operationalisation of the principle of legality. See, eg, *US v Fisher*, 6 U.S. 358, 390 (1805) ('Where rights are infringed, where fundamental principles are overthrown, where the general system of laws is departed from, the legislative intention must be expressed with irresistible clearness to induce a court of justice to suppose a design to effect such objects.').

French Revolution in response to a perceived need to protect the people's rights and freedoms against the state's arbitrary exercise of power.[15] The solution was as simple as it was brilliant: only through law can the state limit people's rights and freedoms.[16] This places the exercise of public power under the regulation of law and requires 'that whatever government does, it should do through laws'.[17] It follows from the basis-in-law requirement that the exercise of executive power becomes subject to the control of parliament, a legislative body over which the people ideally exercise significant influence. As it 'enables rule-makers to control rule-administrators',[18] the principle of legality is connected to popular sovereignty and democracy in orders where the legislative power is exercised by a democratically elected body.[19]

The requirement imposes rule *by* law, a 'thin' version of the rule *of* law.[20] While rule by law is a necessary element of the principle of legality, as well as of the formal rule of law,[21] it is insufficient insofar that it does not ensure that subjects' behaviour can be guided by the law.[22] In a well-functioning democracy, the legislation requirement may ensure popular influence, but it does not protect individual subjects against the arbitrary exercise of power. To ensure this, law must not only exist but also exhibit certain qualities, such as generality, certainty and clarity.[23] By requiring law to have such characteristics, the principle of legality contributes to and serves as the basis for a 'thicker' understanding of (formal) rule of law.[24] Scholars have proposed such qualities,[25] but the arguably most well-known and influential is Lon Fuller's criteria of formal

[15] Besselink, Pennings and Prechal (n 9) 3–10. See also Somek (n 9) fn 7; A Andrijauskaitė, 'The Principle of Legality and Administrative Punishment under the ECHR: A Fused Protection' (2021) 13 *Review of European Administrative Law* 33, 35. *cf* NB Reynolds, 'Grounding the Rule of Law' (1989) 2 *Ratio Juris* 1, 5 ('The rule of law is a solution to a problem, and as the classical tradition has always recognized, the problem is tyranny …').

[16] Déclaration des droits de l'homme et du citoyen de 1789, Art 4 ('La liberté consiste à pouvoir faire tout ce qui ne nuit pas à autrui : ainsi, l'exercice des droits naturels de chaque homme n'a de bornes que celles qui assurent aux autres membres de la société la jouissance de ces mêmes droits. Ces bornes ne peuvent être déterminées que par la loi.').

[17] Reynolds (n 15) 3.

[18] Kingsbury (n 12) 32.

[19] A de Vries and L Francot-Timmermans, 'As Good as It Gets: On Risk, Legality and the Precautionary Principle' in Besselink, Pennings and Prechal (eds), *The Eclipse* (n 9) 12. In this manner, formal legality provides law with its legitimacy in democratic societies. BZ Tamanaha, *On the Rule of Law: History, Politics, Theory* (Cambridge University Press, 2004) 99. Inherent in this construction is also the organisational separation of legislative and executive bodies and that legislative bodies do not themselves apply their laws to individual cases. Andrijauskaitė (n 15) 38.

[20] Tamanaha (n 19) 92.

[21] ibid 91–93.

[22] Hayek (n 14) 75–76; J Raz, 'The Rule of Law and Its Virtue' in J Raz, *The Authority of Law: Essays on Law and Morality* (Oxford University Press, 2002) 214.

[23] Tamanaha (n 19) 96–97.

[24] ibid 91. These are commonly also seen as necessary to ensure freedom and liberty. see BZ Tamanaha, 'A Concise Guide to the Rule of Law' in Gianluigi Palombella and Neil Walker (eds), *Relocating the Rule of Law* (Hart Publishing, 2009) 7.

[25] See, eg, Raz (n 22) 214–18 (proposing eight principles).

legality or, as he varyingly refers to them, 'principles of legality'.[26] We will return to Fuller and his criteria in section III.D.

The origin of the principle of legality explains its focus on public power and, more specifically, state-based conception of public power that maps closely to a Westphalian understanding of law, law-making and legal orders.[27] It also helps explain why the principle of legality, under a traditional understanding, applies to limit governments' (and other public entities') exercise of power,[28] but not to horizontal dealings between private entities whose rights and obligations vis-à-vis one another rest on consent, not force or public power.

Finally, legality can refer to the property or characteristics of norms that are legal. In this sense, the principle of legality is used to make the distinction between law and non-law. Through that use, the principle of legality is connected to and depends on the core jurisprudential question of what constitutes or deserves to be seen as law, law's authority, law's legitimacy and subjects' duty to obey the law.[29] In this manner, the principle of legality serves to guard against the arbitrary exercise of public power, but also to attribute and legitimise public power.[30]

III. SLAM-DUNKING THE PRINCIPLE: THE CAS ON LEGALITY

A. Introduction

In this section, I present the internal sports perspective on the principle of legality as a general principle of transnational sports law by considering the jurisprudence of the CAS. Established as a Swiss arbitration institution, the CAS is one of several actors that contribute to the development of *lex sportiva*. The CAS occupies a particularly important role when it comes to the establishment and application of general principles, such as the principle of legality: through its case law the CAS is the foremost arbiter of the principles that are included in *lex sportiva*, and its decisions on such matters de facto function as precedent.[31]

It can easily be observed that the principle of legality is one of the unwritten general principles contained in *lex sportiva* according to the CAS's case law. The CAS frequently and explicitly recognises and applies the principle of legality to SGBs' regulations and decisions, including in many recent awards.[32] This is not

[26] LL Fuller, *The Morality of Law*, 2nd edn (Yale University Press, 1964) 197.

[27] Besselink, Pennings and Prechal (n 19) 4; de Vries and Francot-Timmermans (n 19) 12.

[28] See, eg, Tamanaha (n 24) 4–6.

[29] See, eg, J Raz, *Between Authority and Interpretation: On the Theory of Law and Practical Reason* (Oxford University Press, 2009); S Shapiro, *Legality* (Harvard University Press, 2011).

[30] Besselink, Pennings and Prechal (n 9) 5–6.

[31] Lindholm (n 3) 85–114.

[32] For a few recent examples, see CAS OG 00/004, *COC and Kibunde v AIBA*, para 11; CAS 2018/A/6069, *Cardoso v UCI*, para 281; CAS 2019/A/6226, *WADA v Spanish Anti-Doping Agency*

limited to awards concerning certain areas or issues, decided by a small group of arbitrators, or during a limited time period. It can therefore, in my view, not be disputed *that lex sportiva* includes the principle of legality.

It is less clear *what* this means and the presentation of CAS jurisprudence below reveals that the CAS presents and approaches the principle of legality in various ways, ranging from the very narrow to the equally broad. This is not surprising since the principle of legality can be understood in a variety of ways. However, how the principle is understood affects its scope and demands, and therefore also its relevance.

B. Criminal Legality in Quasi-Penal Disciplinary Matters

SGBs have the power to regulate what actions are acceptable and unacceptable in sports; the power to decide what sanctions shall follow if an actor fails to respect the rules and the power to enforce their own rules. In addition, SGBs extensively engage in sanctioning clubs, athletes, officials and other sports actors for such commonly occurring actions as doping, other forms of cheating, match-fixing, corruption and disallowed player transactions. Sanctioned actors have a strong interest in challenging such decisions and a significant portion of the CAS's case load consequently consists of appeals of SGBs' sanctioning decisions. In numerous such cases, appellants have sought to invoke general principles of criminal law, such as the principle of *nulla poena sine culpa*, the presumption of innocence and the principle of *lex mitior*,[33] prompting the CAS to consider whether such principles form part of *lex sportiva*. This question turns on a conundrum similar to the one associated with the application of the principle of legality to sports. A seemingly important distinction between criminal and sports sanctions is that the latter, unlike the former which are based on the exercise of public power, are based on private and supposedly consensual agreements.

The CAS has nevertheless recognised that certain criminal law principles form part of the general principles included in *lex sportiva*. For example, in *S v FEI*, a case concerning the disqualification and suspension of an equestrian for doping, the CAS held that

> taking into account the seriousness of the measures which may be pronounced against him and which are, moreover, akin to penalties, there is no doubt that, in application of a general principle of law, the person responsible has the right to clear himself through counter-evidence.[34]

and Salas Zorrozua, para 143; CAS 2019/A/6500, *Islamic Republic of Iran Judo Federation v International Judo Federation*, paras 115–116; CAS 2020/A/7019 and 7035, *Olympiacos v HFF and PAOK* and *Xanthi FC and PAOK v HFF*, paras 111.

[33] See, eg, CAS 94/128, *ICU and CONI*; CAS 2006/A/1035, *Xavier v UEFA*; CAS 2011/A/2433, *Diakite v FIFA*.

[34] CAS 91/56, *S v FEI*, para 4.

This decision forms part of a broader jurisprudence on the application of criminal law principles as part of *lex sportiva*,[35] including on many principles that are of great importance in that particular area of sports.[36]

The application of criminal law principles in sports is based on a functional comparison between states' power to impose criminal penalties and SGBs' power to impose sporting sanctions. Although disciplinary rules, actions and sanctions in sports are formally of a private nature, they are in many regards similar to their criminal law counterparts and have therefore been aptly characterised by the CAS as 'quasi-penal'.[37] Broadly speaking, the argument goes that to the extent that regulations and decisions in sports carry consequences for individuals that are comparable in nature and severity to other negative actions that presuppose public power, the most obvious comparison being between sports sanctions and criminal penalties, comparable principles should apply.[38]

While *lex sportiva* includes many criminal law principles, the one of greatest relevance in this context is of course the principle of criminal legality. This includes foremost the general principle of *nullum crimen, nulla poena sine lege* (*scripta*) that has been seen as the basis for criminal law and incorporates the core ideas of legality. The general principle contains more specific, corollary principles strongly connected to legality. This includes the requirement of specificity (or prohibition of ambiguity), the principle of narrow interpretation, prohibition of analogous use, which in CAS jurisprudence is largely operationalised through what it refers to as the 'predictability test',[39] as well as the principle of non-retroactivity.[40]

[35] See, eg, CAS 2009/A/1931, *Iourieva and Akhatova v UBI*, para 24 (*lex mitior*). The Swiss Federal Tribunal has expressly declined to answer whether Swiss law requires disciplinary actions in sports to comply with criminal principles as a matter of public policy. *Iourieva and Akhatova v International Biathlon Union (IBU)* [2010] Swiss Federal Tribunal 4A_620/2009, para 4.2 ('Les recourantes font grief au TAS d'avoir méconnu les principes de la lex mitior et de la non-rétroactivité des normes qui constituent, à leurs yeux, des principes juridiques fondamentaux relevant de l'ordre public matériel. Il n'est pas nécessaire de trancher ici la question de savoir si les deux principes invoqués par les recourantes ressortissent l'un et l'autre à l'ordre public ...'). However, compare *Kop v International Association of Athletics Federations (IAAF) and Turkish Athletic Federation (TAF)* [2010] Swiss Federal Tribunal 4A_624/2009, para 3.2.2, where the Court's engagement in substance suggests that the principles form part of public policy.

[36] However, it has also importantly refused to include the presumption of innocence which if included would conflict with the use of strict liability in doping.

[37] See, eg, CAS 98/222, *Bernhard v ITU*, para 26; CAS 2000/A/289, *UCI v Chiatti and FFC*, para 7.

[38] *cf* CAS 2006/A/1164, *Scassa and MV Agusta Motor Spa v FIM*, para 15 ('where sports associations are involved this requirement of clarity and predictability is crucial due to the complexity of the technical regulations often involved and the serious sanctions that can result from offences thereto.').

[39] As far as I have been able to determine, this term originated in CAS 2001/A/330, *Reinhold v FISA*, para 17.

[40] S Glaser, 'Nullum Crimen Sine Lege' (1942) 24 *Journal of Comparative Legislation and International Law* 29; A Mokhtar, 'Nullum Crimen, Nulla Poena Sine Lege: Aspects and Prospects' (2005) 26 *Statute Law Review* 41.

The CAS has in a number of decisions applied the principle of criminal legality to SGBs measures. An illustrative example is the CAS's decision in *Rebagliati*. After initially winning an Olympic Gold medal, a snowboarder tested positive for marijuana and for this reason the International Olympic Committee (IOC) decided to rescind his medal. The applicant challenged the legal basis for the IOC's decision. Although the IOC Medical Code identified marijuana as a drug 'subject to certain restrictions', the Code also stated that marijuana only constituted a prohibited substance if there was an 'agreement with the International Sports Federations', and in the case at hand no such agreement had been reached with the relevant international federation.[41] Without hesitation, the CAS overturned the IOC's decision on the basis of the principle of criminal legality:

> We have been told that the decision to sanction R. was reached after difficult deliberations at the level of the IOC Executive Board as well as at that of its Medical Commission. Our own decision is not difficult. Although we have taken pains to explain our reasoning in some detail, and although we understand that the ethical aspects of the question have given pause as to appropriate sanctioning policies – and may result in further reflection in this regard – the existing applicable texts leave us no alternative whatsoever. It is clear that the sanctions against R. lack requisite legal foundation.[42]

Another example is *Liebherr Ochsenhausen*. The case concerned a German table tennis club, Liebherr Ochsenhausen, which had competed in the Men's European Champions League and been eliminated in a competition against a Belgian club, Charleroi, in the quarter finals. After the final, one of the Charleroi players competed for another club in the Chinese Super League. As this was contrary to the applicable rules, Liebherr Ochsenhausen sought to have the outcome of their matches against Charleroi invalidated. The responsible federation, the European Table Tennis Union (ETTU), sanctioned Charleroi but refused the request of invalidation, inter alia on the grounds that it was not clear from the rules that retroactive disqualification was a possible sanction. Liebherr Ochsenhausen appealed this decision to the CAS which upheld the ETTU's decisions. In its award, the CAS panel concluded that it was 'in line with the principle of legality and predictability of sanctions which requires a clear connection between the incriminated behaviour and the sanction and calls for a narrow interpretation of the respective provision'.[43]

The expression 'in line with' used by the CAS in *Liebherr Ochsenhausen* could be read as the principle of legality having a relatively weak, incidental and supplemental role in the determination of the case in question. However, the CAS has subsequently interpreted and relied on *Liebherr Ochsenhausen* as the principle of criminal legality constituting a binding and mandatory principle

[41] CAS OG 98/002, *Rebagliati v IOC*, paras 13–14, 22.
[42] ibid para 27.
[43] CAS 2007/A/1363, *TTF Liebherr Ochsenhausen v ETTU*, para 16.

in *lex sportiva*.[44] In CAS jurisprudence, *Liebherr Ochsenhausen* is invoked as an authority for the rule that *lex sportiva* requires both 'that sports regulations proscribe the misconduct with which the subject is charged, i.e. nulla poena sine lege (principle of legality), and that the rule be clear and precise, i.e. nulla poena sine lege clara (principle of predictability)'.[45] In addition, it imposes a requirement of narrow interpretation and in its entirety promotes a high standard of legality in terms of clarity and foreseeability.

Thus, to summarise, CAS jurisprudence leaves little uncertainty or disagreement that the principle of criminal legality is a general principle of *lex sportiva* that applies to sanctioning measures and, consequently, acts as a restriction of SGBs' sanctioning power.[46]

C. Legality Beyond the Quasi-Penal

The case law regarding the applicability of the principle of criminal legality to 'quasi-penal' cases can be described as the hard core of the CAS's legality jurisprudence. However, the latter is not limited to the former, and the scope and content of the principle of legality in *lex sportiva*, as understood through CAS case law, extends considerably beyond the 'quasi-penal' and the principle of criminal liability.

In many situations it is difficult to draw a clear distinction between, on the one hand, the exercise of sanctioning power and quasi-criminal sanctioning actions and, on the other, the exercise of regulatory power. Sanctions are based on – and according to the principle of legality must be based on – previous regulation. While many sanctions challenged before the CAS concern the enforcement of anti-doping regulations and other quasi-criminal substantive rules, it would be a mistake to assume that this is always the case, and the CAS has held that 'the different elements of the rules of a federation shall be clear and precise, in the event they are legally binding for the athletes …'[47] Thus, all legally binding rules – not only those that are sanctioning or quasi-penal – must be clear and precise or, differently stated, comply with the principle of legality.[48]

[44] See, eg, CAS 2010/A/2284, *Arzhanova v CMAS*, para 34 ('The principle of legality and predictability of sanctions requires a clear connection between the behaviour in question and the sanction and calls for a narrow interpretation of the respective provision (CAS 2007/A/1363).').

[45] CAS 2017/A/5086, *Chung v FIFA*, para 149, citing inter alia *Liebherr Ochsenhausen*.

[46] See, eg, *UCI v Chiatti and FFC* (n 37) para 7; CAS 2008/A/1545, *Anderson et al v IOC*, paras 30–35; CAS 2014/A/3665–3667, *Suárez et al v FIFA*, paras 71–74; CAS 2017/A/5056 and 5069, *Ittihad FC v Troisi and FIFA*, paras 126–128.

[47] See, eg, CAS 2007/A/1437, *Diethart v FIS* (unpublished decision, quoted in CAS 2013/A/3316, *WADA v Bataa and IPF*, para 50); CAS 2014/A/3832 and 3833, *Vanakorn v FIS*, para 85.

[48] The wording used is interesting and somewhat confusing. The CAS plainly held that *if* sports rules are legally binding, *then* they must be clear and precise. From this it does not necessarily conversely follow that *if* rules are clear and precise, *then* they are legally binding. However, as discussed in section II, legal philosophers have convincingly argued that no duty can exist to follow rules that are

An illustrative example is *Racing Club Asociación Civil v FIFA*. The case concerned a football club that had been involved in a so-called 'bridge transfer', meaning the transfer of a player due to non-sporting interests. Such transfers were banned under the FIFA Regulations on the Status and Transfer of Players (RSTP) and rules governing the FIFA Transfer Matching System (TMS), which served the purpose of ensuring that FIFA had accurate information about player transfers. Although those regulations govern commercial dealings between clubs buying and selling players, they were enforced through sanctions and such sanctions had been imposed on the applicant football club. The club challenged the decision on the grounds that the rules were not clear and foreseeable. The CAS agreed:

> The Panel … adheres to the view that FIFA is responsible for preparing a set of rules which, in a clear and transparent manner, regulate these matters and the consequences derived from committing such unlawful practices. The Panel considers that the parties involved, not least the players, in conformity with the principle of legality, shall be provided with specific guidelines in order to know how to act when international transfers of players take place.[49]

The CAS's decision in *Racing Club Asociación Civil v FIFA* illustrates how regulatory power, in order to be effective, is frequently dependent on sanctioning power and how the application of the principle of criminal legality is accordingly often difficult to distinguish from the application of the principle of legality more generally.

However, the principle of legality also applies to situations that do not involve any sanctions (non-quasi-penal situations). There are clear examples of the CAS applying the principle of legality as a limitation on SGBs' exercise of power in cases that neither involve the imposition of sanctions nor are otherwise of a 'quasi-penal' nature. One such example can be found in *Kibunde*, a case that concerned a boxer's eligibility to compete in the Olympic Games. The boxer had initially qualified for the Games but was subsequently struck from participation after he failed to appear for a mandatory weigh-in and medical examination. The case concerned eligibility and the CAS explicitly classified the regulations in question as the 'rules of the game', but it nevertheless found that the principle of legality applied as an unwritten general principle.[50]

Similarly, *Grasshopper v Alianza Lima* concerned a dispute between two football clubs regarding one club's right to economic compensation for the training of a player employed by the other club. The case turned on the application of different sports regulations governing such matters. Despite the purely

insufficiently clear and precise. It would seem to follow from this that unclear and imprecise rules are in fact not legally binding.

[49] CAS 2014/A/3536, *Racing Club Asociación Civil v FIFA*, para 9.18.

[50] *COC and Kibunde v AIBA* (n 32), para 11. The panel did not, however, find a breach in that particular case.

commercial nature of the dispute, the CAS held that the principle of legality applied.[51] In *Grasshopper v Alianza Lima*, and other similar cases,[52] the principle of legality specifically concerned respect for the hierarchy of norms.

A final example is *PFC Rostov v RFU* which concerned the refusal of the RFU (the Russian Football Federation) to grant one of its clubs a licence to participate in the UEFA Europa League, even though the club had qualified by winning the Russian Cup. According to the RFU, the club had failed to comply with the financial criteria, including by not paying solidarity contributions on transferred players. The club, on the other hand, pointed out that the Federation had never filed a written request for such payments. Even though the dispute concerned club licensing and financial matters, the CAS found that the principle of legality is 'applicable to regulations that govern procedures that may have very important consequences on a party' and on this basis imposed a duty on the RFU to file a written request for the solidarity contributions.[53]

D. *Quigley* and Fullerian Legality

Finally, and arguably most importantly, the requirements that follow from the principle of legality, as included in *lex sportiva*, extend beyond the narrower subprinciples of the principle of criminal legality. The most extensive expression of the principle of legality in CAS jurisprudence is also the oldest.

Quigley,[54] arguably one of the CAS's most important decisions,[55] concerned an American skeet shooter, George Quigley, who fell ill while competing for his national team at a World Cup event held in Cairo. His coach called for the hotel doctor who diagnosed Quigley with bronchitis. The doctor prescribed a cough syrup that, unknowingly to Quigley and contrary to the doctor's assurances, contained a substance that was prohibited under the doping regulation of the governing international federation. The case eventually ended up before the CAS that was charged with determining what consequences Quigley should face. The parties agreed that the objective condition laid out in the doping regulation, the use of a prohibited substance, was met. They disagreed, however, on whether the rules additionally contained a subjective condition for sanctioning according to which the athlete must have intentionally consumed the substance for the purpose of enhancing his or her performance. The regulations were somewhat unclear and contradictory on this point.

[51] CAS 2008/A/1705, *Grasshopper v Alianza Lima*, para 25.

[52] See, eg, CAS 2013/A/3090, *BFU v FIFA*, para 60, where the CAS invoked *Grasshopper v Alianza Lima* as a source for the rule that the principle of legality limits the power of international federations to sanction national federations.

[53] CAS 2014/A/3621, *JSC PFC Rostov v RFU*, paras 115–117, para 116 quoted.

[54] CAS 94/129, *USA Shooting and Quigley v Union Internationale de Tir* (UIT).

[55] Lindholm (n 3) 126–28, 194–95.

The CAS had previously established that SGBs' regulations, decisions and actions are subject to certain general principles of law,[56] but in *Quigley*, the CAS held for the first time that the principle of legality is one of those principles:

> The fight against doping is arduous, and it may require strict rules. But the rule-makers and the rule-appliers must begin by being strict with themselves. Regulations that may affect the careers of dedicated athletes must be predictable. They must emanate from duly authorised bodies. They must be adopted in constitutionally proper ways. They should not be the product of an obscure process of accretion. Athletes and officials should not be confronted with a thicket of mutually qualifying or even contradictory rules that can be understood only on the basis of the de facto practice over the course of many years of a small group of insiders.[57]

The quoted paragraph has subsequently been cited with approval and applied by the CAS in such a great number of cases that 'the classic dictum'[58] arguably constitutes one of the CAS's most firmly established precedents.[59] The CAS has even applied its holding to itself, refusing to define or apply requirements retroactively.[60]

The *Quigley* panel did not invoke the principle of legality by name. However, the requirements expressed by the CAS in the quoted section map out almost to perfection Fuller's understanding of legality as a characteristic of moral law. Fuller defines the principles of legality as norms that are general (not ad hoc), public (not secret), prospective (not retroactive), comprehendible, consistent in form (not contradictory or conflicting) and reasonably consistent in implementation and application. The thinking that underpins these requirements is straightforward: subjects of norms should actually be able to orient their behaviour in accordance with the norms and failing this they cannot be legitimately expected to comply. In other words, legal norms must be capable of having the guiding effect inherent to law and Fuller's criteria for legality thereby also become criteria for determining whether norms deserve to be recognised as law.[61]

The CAS's decision in *Quigley* contains multiple elements of Fuller's principles of legality, including publicity, clarity, coherence, possibility of compliance and constancy over time. Not only do the *Quigley* criteria substantively match Fuller's, I believe that Fuller would also whole-heartedly agree with the CAS's

[56] See, eg, *S v FEI* (n 34) para 4 (procedural rights).

[57] *USA Shooting and Quigley v UIT* (n 54) para 34.

[58] CAS 2017/A/5114, *Juliano et al v FEI*, para 62.

[59] See, eg, CAS 96/149, *Cullwick v FINA*, paras 21–22; CAS 95/150, *Volkers v FINA*, paras 14–15; *Reinhold v FISA* (n 39) para 17; CAS 2004/A/725, *USOC v IOC and IAAF*, para 19; CAS 2006/A/1164, *Scassa and MV Agusta Spa v FIM*, paras 15–16; CAS 2007/A/1377, *Rinaldi v FINA*, paras 40–41; *Anderson et al v IOC* (n 46) paras 77–78; CAS 2009/A/1768, *Hansen v FEI*, para 17; CAS 2011/A/2612, *Hui v IWF*, para 103; CAS 2013/A/3435, *Stepien v Polish Rugby Union*, para 88; *JSC PFC Rostov v RFU* (n 53) para 115.

[60] *Rebagliati v IOC* (n 41) para 26.

[61] Fuller (n 26) 33–94.

reasons for imposing them. Expanding on *Quigley*, the CAS explained in *USOC v IOC and IAAF*:

> The rationale for requiring clarity of rules extends beyond enabling athletes in given cases to determine their conduct in such cases by reference to understandable rules. As argued by the Appellants at the hearing, clarity and predictability are required so that the entire sport community are informed of the normative system in which they live, work and compete, which requires at the very least that they be able to understand the meaning of rules and the circumstances in which those rules apply.[62]

Thus, it is in my opinion clear that the CAS in *Quigley* adopted a 'Fuller' understanding of the principle of legality that in a qualitative sense extends beyond the core requirements of the principle of *nulla poena sine lege* or the existence of a legal basis per se and instead incorporates a legality ideal based on the internal morality of law.

While *Quigley* stands for an ideal, its effects are not limited to stating ideals. The holding in *Quigley* has in subsequent CAS jurisprudence been accepted and applied as a concrete test. This is, for example, illustrated by *Rinaldi* where the CAS extensively and diligently considered whether FINA's representation rules met the *Quigley* criteria, ultimately concluding that the rules were 'straightforward and clear', predictable and understandable to the average reader and that the applicant therefore did not fall 'foul of unpredictable requirements'.[63]

To summarise, it follows from CAS jurisprudence that: (i) the general principles included in *lex sportiva* include the principle of legality; (ii) the principle applies to all legally-binding rules, including but not limited to 'quasi-penal' situations; and (iii) the demands on rules that come with the principle include not only a 'thin' understanding of legality, such as the requirements of a formal legal basis for actions and non-retroactivity, but also a 'thick' understanding that demands that the governed are actually able to understand, predict and direct their actions based on the rules. While the CAS in some cases focuses on the narrow aspects of the principle, such as the requirement of non-retroactivity for disciplinary sanctions, this can be explained by the fact that this was all that the case called for and there are, as far as I have been able to determine, no examples of the CAS denying that *lex sportiva* includes the broadest definition of the principle of legality.

[62] *USOC v IOC and IAAF* (n 59) para 20. see also ibid para 12 ('To take a rule that plainly concerns individual ineligibility and the annulment of individual results, and then to stretch and complement and construe it in order that it may be said to govern the results achieved by teams, is the sort of legal abracadabra that lawyers and partisans in the fight against doping in sport can love, but in which athletes should not be required to engage in order to understand the meaning of the rules to which they are subject.').

[63] *Rinaldi v FINA* (n 59) paras 15–47.

IV. WHY LEGALITY IS A HOME RUN FOR SPORTS LAW

A. Introduction

It was demonstrated above that the principle of legality according to the CAS constitutes one of the general principles included in *lex sportiva* and that the principle is applicable to and invokable against SGBs. Why is this? Is the functional similarity between SGBs and state entities in terms of governing power or the similarity between the effects of their actions enough to warrant the principle of legality's applicability to SGBs and their actions?[64] The SGBs and their sub-bodies have and exercise an exceptional amount of power and the examined case law demonstrates why it is appropriate, even necessary, to check that power.[65]

That the principle of legality ought to be included in *lex sportiva* is not, however, a satisfactory explanation for why this is also the case, at least not by itself. As discussed in the introduction to this chapter, this puzzling finding runs counter to the traditional view that the principle of legality applies to public entities exercising public power and that private entities, under which we traditionally sort SGBs, fall outside the principle's scope *ratione personae*. Moreover, you would assume that the masters of *lex sportiva*, which includes the CAS,[66] would seek to avoid limiting their power to regulate and govern sports and that they would therefore be strategically disinclined to adopt the principle of legality since limiting power is the principle's *raison d'être*.[67] The SGBs have largely freely selected the CAS as its dispute-resolving institution and they could relatively easily revoke their consent if they were altogether unhappy with the limitations imposed on them by the CAS.[68] In this section of the chapter, I seek to explain why the CAS has come to its thus somewhat puzzling and counterintuitive position.

Why-questions are notoriously difficult to answer, and the one studied here is no exception to the rule. The explanations for why legality applies explicitly

[64] *cf AEK Athens and SK Slavia Prague v UEFA* (n 1) para 58 ('there is an evident analogy between sports-governing bodies and governmental bodies with respect to their role and functions as regulatory, administrative and sanctioning entities, and that similar principles *should* govern their actions'[emphasis added]). See also Latty (n 3) 320–21.

[65] See also the *Mutu and Pechstein v Switzerland* [2018] ECtHR 40575/10, 67474/10, partly dissenting, partly concurring Opinion of Judges Keller and Serghides, para 18 ('Where a body has as much power as the CAS and is able and prepared to determine the civil rights and obligations of its members (in the present case, the athletes), with the authority to give enforceable decisions, the Court must first ensure that such a body is a tribunal "established by law", within the meaning of Article 6 of the Convention, before determining whether or not it is impartial.').

[66] See above section I.

[67] See, eg, *Mutu and Pechstein v Switzerland* (n 65) partly dissenting, partly concurring Opinion of Judges Keller and Serghides.

[68] In most non-doping appeals cases, the CAS's jurisdiction rests on arbitration clauses that SGBs have inserted into their charters or rules. Before SGBs started inserting such clauses, the CAS saw very few cases. Lindholm (n 3) 61–66.

offered by the CAS in its awards is a natural point of departure for such an enquiry. However, it is important to keep in mind that the award texts do not necessarily offer a complete account of those reasons, nor do they provide a single and consistent account as individual arbitrators can be expected to differ in their thinking on these matters. It is therefore submitted that no single explanation for why the CAS has adopted the principle of legality into *lex sportiva* can be formulated.

At the same time, this does not mean that we cannot say anything relevant on the causes of this development. By drawing on different theories on transnational law and international arbitration, it is possible to formulate different, plausible and non-exclusive explanations for why the CAS has recognised the principle of legality. While they should be seen as coexisting,[69] each of these explanations have distinct benefits and may be appealing to different audiences as they rest on distinct theoretical foundations. It follows that CAS arbitrators probably adhere to different theories on transnational law and international arbitration which in turn contributes to shaping their different perspectives on what the principle of legality is and how it applies in the sports context. However, when combined, they can explain the CAS's jurisprudence on legality.

B. 'The State(s) Made Us Do It': A Traditionalist Explanation

A first account departs from the proposition that arbitration panels seek to ensure the validity, recognition and enforcement of their awards and that they for this depend on national legal orders. While SGBs and other actors in sports contribute a great deal of normative content, this account acknowledges in a traditionalist and realist manner that global sports law is connected to and dependent on state-based legal orders. On the basis of these ideas, the principle of legality is part of the requirements made by state-based law for the validity, recognition and enforcement of sport decisions and CAS awards.

Drawing on the theoretical framework formulated by Emmanuel Gaillard, this traditionalist account can be built on two representations of international arbitration. The first of these is the *mono-local representation* under which 'the sole source of the arbitrator's power is the legal order of the seat of the arbitration'[70] and 'the award's legal force stems exclusively from the law of the State where the arbitration took place',[71] making the arbitral tribunal one of many courts that make up a national legal order. This view builds on a positivist

[69] *cf* E Gaillard, 'The Arbitral Order: Evolution and Recognition' in Thomas Schultz and Federico Ortino (eds), *The Oxford Handbook of International Arbitration* (Oxford University Press, 2020) 559.

[70] E Gaillard, 'The Representations of International Arbitration' (2010) 1 *Journal of International Dispute Settlement* 271, 277–79, 277 quoted.

[71] E Gaillard, *Legal Theory of International Arbitration* (Martinus Nijhoff Publishers, 2010) 15.

thinking, where the *lex arbitrii* serves as the *Grundnorm*, and promotes order and simplicity by anchoring international arbitration in a single state,[72] and 'the legal order of the seat is the one having the most complete and effective control over the arbitration'.[73] An obvious example of such state control, and an observation in favour of a mono-local perspective, is when the national courts of the arbitration seat review and invalidate arbitration awards.

For the CAS, and by extension for global sports (law), a direct and immediate concern is that its awards can survive review by the Swiss Federal Tribunal (SFT), applying the requirements that Swiss law imposes by merit of being the *lex arbitrii*.[74] Although recognition and enforcement by national legal orders is important for the effective realisation of arbitration awards, a direct review of their legality is even more so. Additionally, many SGBs are established in Switzerland and Swiss law frequently applies substantively to sports-related disputes in general and in proceedings before the CAS in particular, either by default or by merit of a choice-of-law clause.[75] Swiss law thus exercises significant influence on the outcome of individual disputes, regardless of Switzerland's geographical connection with the parties and the factual circumstances, but also more generally over the CAS's jurisprudence and *lex sportiva*.[76]

Swiss law plays an important role in the CAS's incorporation of the principle of legality as a general principle of *lex sportiva*. The CAS has on numerous occasions held that by merit of Swiss law, legal principles apply to and limit the powers of SGBs to the extent that they are 'an expression of a fundamental value system that penetrates all areas of law'.[77] As Baddeley explains, Swiss law requires SGBs to respect general legal principles when exercising their powers, and especially their sanctioning power, and this includes the principle of legality.[78] This limitation on SGBs' powers follows from the Swiss Civil Code,[79] which also provides that the obligation can be enforced before Swiss courts.[80] This also means that there is an obligation to respect general legal principles when Swiss law applies.

[72] ibid 21–24.

[73] ibid 22.

[74] M Baddeley, 'The Extraordinary Autonomy of Sports Bodies under Swiss Law: Lessons to Be Drawn' (2020) 20 *The International Sports Law Journal* 3, 9. See, eg, *Reinhold v FISA* (n 39) paras 15–16.

[75] CAS Code (2021), Articles R45 and R58.

[76] See also Duval, 'Embedded *Lex Sportiva*: The Swiss Roots of Transnational Sports Law and Governance' in chapter two of this volume.

[77] CAS 2008/A/1583 and 1584, *Benfica v UEFA and FC Porto and Vitória Sport Clube de Guimarães v UEFA and FC Porto*, para 42.

[78] M Baddeley, *L'association sportive face au droit: Les limites de son autonomi* (Helbing & Lichtenhahn, 1994) 108. See also, eg, CAS 2007/O/1381, *RFEC and Valverde v UCI*, paras 54–61. In some cases, the CAS finds support for the requirements of predictability using a hybrid or mixed approach that includes private law principles such as the principle of good faith. See, eg, *Scassa and MV Agusta Motor Spa v FIM* (n 38) paras 9–17; *Rinaldi v FINA* (n 59) para 18.

[79] Article 63 of the Swiss Civil Code.

[80] Article 75 of the Swiss Civil Code.

However, the impact of Swiss law is not limited to such situations and the CAS appears to attach particular importance to the Swiss conception of legality and the legality requirements of Swiss law, including the application of the requirements of Swiss law and the Swiss Civil Code in cases where it does not apply. For example, in *Hui*, the CAS noted that:

> [a]ccording to Swiss association law a federation may base a disciplinary measure against a (direct or indirect) member only on provisions that provide a clear and unambiguous authority to do so [... but that t]his principle is also part of general considerations of sports law that have been taken into account by CAS Panels in the past irrespective of the (subsidiarily) applicable law to the merits ...[81]

The CAS is not always explicit or intentional about this. An example of how a Swiss conception of legality seemingly unintentionally sneaked its way in can be found in *Omeragik*. The case concerned a dispute between a Macedonian federation and a Macedonian sports official where Macedonian law was the substantive law applicable to the case. Nevertheless, the CAS explicitly applied the principle of legality to SGBs,[82] based on previous CAS jurisprudence, in which Swiss law was the applicable substantive law, as precedent.[83]

A second, slightly modified representation of international arbitration, which Gaillard refers to as *multilocal*, maintains arbitration's and arbitration awards' dependence on state-based legal orders but emphasises the *international* character of international arbitration. It specifically attaches importance to arbitral awards being recognised as valid not only by the legal order of the arbitral seat, but by a plurality of legal orders. The multilocal representation takes seriously the Westphalian model of law and international relations under which each state is equally sovereign to decide whether to recognise or enforce an arbitration award, regardless of each other's positions, including the position of the seat of arbitration.[84] Under this representation, arbitrators focus on ensuring the validity, recognition and enforcement of the award in as many jurisdictions as possible, particularly those that have a connection with the dispute but ideally globally.[85] In order to achieve this, arbitrators will seek to comply with the mandatory rules of multiple jurisdictions, more broadly than what may follow from a narrow understanding of the applicable procedural and substantive law or from the mono-local representation.[86]

The multilocal representation is an intuitive fit for international sports arbitration: sport is a global activity and decisions and arbitral awards in sports, such as a doping suspension, need to be enforced globally in order

[81] *Hui v IWF* (n 59) para 103.

[82] CAS 2011/A/2670, *Omeragik v FFM*, paras 5.1 and 8.13–8.14. see also *JSC PFC Rostov v RFU* (n 53) (applying Russian law and invoking *Quigley*).

[83] It is impossible to say whether this was intentional or unintentional on the part of the CAS.

[84] Gaillard (n 71) 28–29.

[85] Inherent to this model is the possibility of asymmetrical validity.

[86] Gaillard (n 71) 28–31. See also Gaillard (n 70) 280–81.

to be effective, especially at the highest level of competition. The multilocal representation helps to explain why CAS jurisprudence and *lex sportiva* contains conceptions of the principle of legality that go beyond what Swiss law requires. If arbitrators seek to maximise multi-jurisdictional recognition and enforcement, they should adopt a broad, generous or 'thick' understanding of legality that meets the requirements of as many legal orders as possible. A multilocal representation of international arbitration is, in other words, conducive to choosing the broadest variant of legality, regardless of whether the law governing the arbitration or the dispute so requires.

The CAS is sometimes open and explicit about these concerns. For example, in *Salas Zorrozua* a Spanish athlete challenged being suspended for doping on the basis of an Athlete Biological Passport (ABP). The Spanish Administrative Court of Sport set aside the decision for being too vague and uncertain and therefore being in violation of the principle of legality enshrined in the Spanish Constitution.[87] On appeal, the CAS upheld the suspension on the grounds that '[i]t is well-established under the CAS jurisprudence' that *lex sportiva* includes a broad principle of legality – implicitly that met or exceeded the requirements of the Spanish Constitution – and that the applicable rules were 'sufficiently clear, precise and unambiguous' to comply with that principle.[88]

It is arguably particularly appropriate to apply a multilocal perspective on international arbitration when it comes to constitutional issues. Over the last few decades, there has been a growing awareness of what is commonly referred to as constitutional pluralism, that is 'the phenomenon of a plurality of constitutional sources which creates a context of potential constitutional conflicts between different constitutional orders to be solved in a non-hierarchical manner'.[89] The principle of legality is one such constitutional issue for which there may be multiple, conflicting sources that cannot be ordered hierarchically. A simple but illustrative example of the ensuing complexity can be found in the European Court of Human Rights' (ECtHR) decision in *Platini* in which the Court suggested that Switzerland may have a positive obligation under Article 7 of the European Convention on Human Rights to ensure that FIFA respects the criminal principle of legality.[90]

While the sports sector's global character speaks in favour of the validity and importance of multilocal representation, the ability of sports institutions

[87] *WADA v Spanish Anti-Doping Agency* (n 32) para 24.

[88] ibid para 143. See also, eg, CAS 2000/A/289, *UCI v Chiotti and FFC* (in relation to French law).

[89] M Poiares Maduro, 'Interpreting European Law – Judicial Adjudication in a Context of Constitutional Pluralism' (2007) 1 *European Journal of Legal Studies* 137, 137. The work of Neil Walker has been particularly influential on the European discussion, eg Walker (n 8); N Walker, 'Constitutional Pluralism Revisited' (2016) 22 *European Law Journal* 333.

[90] *Platini v Switzerland* [2020] ECtHR 526/18, paras 43–49. Instead of dismissing the claim on the grounds that Art 7 ECHR does not apply to sporting sanctions, the ECtHR declined to apply the provision to the specific sanctioning of Platini because it concerned disciplinary actions against a limited group of individuals possessing a special status (*cf Volkov v Ukraine* [2013] ECtHR 21722/11), suggesting that measures that apply more broadly would be covered by the provision (*cf Matyjek v Poland* [2007] ECtHR 38184/03).

to enforce their own decisions could be levied as an argument in the opposite direction. At the core of the multilocal representation lies a need for, or at least a utility of, states and state agents assisting in the enforcement of arbitral awards. Since SGBs can effectively enforce awards themselves, ultimately by merit of their capacity to deny actors access to sporting competitions, state recognition and enforcement is relatively unimportant in sports compared to other sectors. However, this does not mean that the CAS can safely ignore the views of non-Swiss state legal orders. An illustrative example of this is the case of *Pechstein* where the CAS's award[91] was upheld by the SFT[92] but subsequently challenged in German courts, in a case for damages,[93] as well as before the ECtHR.[94]

C. 'Because We are the Law': A Transnationalist Explanation

What the accounts discussed thus far have in common is that they are based on a perception of rules, decisions and awards in sports being dependent on – and to some extent defined in relation to – national legal orders. They depart from an understanding of arbitrators as actors who administer justice on behalf of sovereign states and who give them their legitimacy and force, and, more modestly and realistically, on which they in practice rely. The third representation of international arbitration rejects its dependence on the legal order of any individual state (monolocal representation) or a plurality of states (multilocal representation). This representation conceives the arbitral legal order as an autonomous legal order unto itself, a legal order whose legitimacy comes from the international community that it serves. This representation, which challenges the Westphalian understanding of law, can be referred to as *the transnational representation*.[95]

The transnational representation is a natural fit for understanding the CAS and *lex sportiva*, as well as how the two relate to each other. Transnational legal theory holds that one of the primary goals of a transnational order is to retain and enhance its autonomy from state-based law,[96] and the establishment of a transnational legal order for sports, *lex sportiva*, supports sports' ambitions of disentanglement and independence from state-based governance.[97] As explained

[91] CAS 2009/A/1912 and 1913, *Pechstein v ISU and DESG v ISU*.

[92] *Pechstein v International Skating Union (ISU) and Deutsche Eisschnelllauf Gemeinschaft eV (DESG)* [2010] Swiss Federal Tribunal 4A_612/2009.

[93] LG München I 37. Zivilkammer, 26 February 2014, 37 O 28331/12; OLG München, 15 January 2015, U. 1110/14 Kart; Bundesgerichtshof, 7 June 2016, KZR 6/15.

[94] *Mutu and Pechstein v Switzerland* (n 65).

[95] Gaillard (n 71) 35–37; Gaillard (n 70) 277–78; Gaillard (n 69) 557–58.

[96] *cf* R Michaels, 'The True Lex Mercatoria: Law Beyond the State' (2007) 14 *Indiana Journal of Global Legal Studies* 447; A Stone Sweet, 'The New *Lex Mercatoria* and Transnational Governance' (2006) 13 *Journal of European Public Policy* 627; Lindholm (n 3) 7–8.

[97] See, eg, K Foster, 'Global Sports Law Revisited' (2019) 17 *Entertainment and Sports Law Journal* 2 ('Global sports law has developed an ideology that it is an autonomous transnational legal

by Beloff, 'one of [lex sportiva's] key objectives is to immunise sport from the reach of the law, to create in other words a field of autonomy within which even appellate sports tribunals should not trespass'.[98]

The principle of legality is an integral element of the quest of the world of sport to establish *lex sportiva* as an autonomous transnational legal order, and thereby also allowing the autonomous power of sports governing bodies to govern. As explained in section II, while the principle of legality is a concrete principle that courts apply to decide specific cases, it is also the property of being legal. Differently phrased, the principle of legality not only applies *to* law; it also identifies what *is* law. It follows from this that any order that claims to be a legal order must comply with the principle of legality.[99]

And being law matters, for example, to those who are invested in *lex sportiva* being recognised as a transnational *legal* order. To label something as law has an impact on power relations between actors because of the authority and respect that law demands and the heightened position that law enjoys in relation to other normative systems. To recognise something as law acknowledges that the actor that created the norm is a 'lawmaker' and legitimises the actor's power.[100] As Schultz explains, 'the presence of law reduces the legitimacy of the intervention in a given social context of other legal orders'.[101] However, it also follows that 'if legality accounts for what makes some organized human activity into law then a legal system that fails to exhibit elementary features of legality it is not really law'.[102] No legality, no law; it is as simple as that.

This makes for something of a paradox. In order to protect and increase the power to govern by credibly claiming the character of being the law – ie legality as a characteristic – it is beneficial or even necessary to impose exceptional restrictions on those powers, limitations that are normally reserved for public actors and extend beyond what we normally expect of private actors – ie legality as a check. This phenomenon has been expressed by Kingsbury who argues that 'in choosing to claim to be law …, a particular global governance entity or regime embraces or is assessed by reference to the attributes, constraints and normative commitments that are immanent in public law'.[103] Transnational (private) legal orders, such as the *lex sportiva*, may claim autonomy and states may even grant them autonomy, but that does not mean that they deserve autonomy. To deserve the privilege that comes with being recognised as a law-maker

order. This supposed autonomy has allowed international sporting bodies to claim an effective immunity from review by national courts and enabled them to maintain a degree of self-governance and non-accountability that is arguably unrivalled among international organisations.').

[98] MJ Beloff, 'Is There a Lex Sportiva?' [2005] *International Sports Law Review* 49, 53.

[99] *cf* Somek (n 9) 53 (on whether EU law is a legal order).

[100] T Schultz, *Transnational Legality: Stateless Law and International Arbitration* (Oxford University Press, 2014) 12–14.

[101] T Schultz, 'The Concept of Law in Transnational Arbitral Legal Orders and Some of Its Consequences' (2011) 2 *Journal of International Dispute Settlement* 59, 85.

[102] Somek (n 9) 53.

[103] Kingsbury (n 12) 30.

and to deserve one's norms to be recognised as the law, private entities must 'meet the regulative standards of the rule of law',[104] or, as Kingsbury puts it, 'be examined from the standpoint of their legal basis and other qualities associated with law'.[105]

Viewed from this perspective, the CAS's jurisprudence on the principle of legality may be the product of a strategic bargain: in order to be recognised and treated as a proper legal order, *lex sportiva* benefits from subjecting itself to the heightened requirements that apply to legal regimes and systems of laws. In other words, to be recognised as a true transnational legal order, *lex sportiva* needs to include 'the elementary features of law' included in the principle of legality,[106] such as being reasonably predictable.[107] This would also suggest that if the surrounding community acknowledges and accepts that the principle of legality applies to sport rules, it also to some extent acknowledges and accepts that sport rules *is* law or significantly 'law-like'.

To the extent that it is allowed to apply general principles of law, transnational arbitration is well-suited to incorporate the principle of legality,[108] but this does not mean that we should expect a clear understanding of legality in *lex sportiva*. The lack of a single, shared and clear understanding of the principle of legality is perhaps particularly likely in a transnational context. Transnational arbitrators will draw on the understanding of various legal orders, borrowing and adapting as needed.[109] In hard cases and on questions on which legal orders disagree, arbitrators 'endeavor to identify rules that are generally endorsed at a given time by the international community and determine that they should prevail over those reflecting a State's isolated position …'[110] This is true for the CAS.[111] As CAS arbitrators are trained in different legal orders and legal orders differ in how they conceive and apply the principle,[112] some divergence can be expected.[113] The principle of legality in *lex sportiva* is in this regard an illustrative example of constitutional pluralism.

104 Schultz (n 101) (passim, 82 quoted).

105 Kingsbury (n 12) 24.

106 *cf* Schultz (n 101). Schultz uses the criteria included in the principle of legality to evaluate whether transnational arbitral legal orders, such as the *lex sportiva*, ought to be recognised as law. I do not conduct such a normative evaluation but rather rely on this observation to answer the research questions. Even so, I want to make clear that I do not mean to suggest that invoking or even complying with the principle of legality is sufficient for a private legal order constituting law. See Kingsbury (n 12) 32–33.

107 Schultz (n 100) 17–18.

108 See, eg *Rebagliati v IOC* (n 41); *COC and Kibunde v AIBA* (n 32). This also includes many awards where the CAS does not make it clear what is the legal basis for including the principle, most importantly *Quigley* and cases that invoke it directly as the authority, see, eg, *JSC PFC Rostov v RFU* (n 53) paras 115–17.

109 Gaillard (n 69) 557. See also Latty (n 3) 320–21.

110 Gaillard (n 71) 37.

111 See Lindholm (n 3) 10.

112 See above section I.

113 For a similar argument, see Duval (n 6) 286.

There is some clear evidence of this line of thinking in the CAS's jurisprudence.[114] In the section in *Quigley* quoted in section III.D, the CAS made the normative claim that rule-making and rule-applying entities in sports ought to live up to the moral qualities that follow from a Fullerian understanding of the principle of legality. Nothing in the award indicates that this is an obligation imposed on sports by state-based legal orders. On the contrary, when read together with the rest of the award, it becomes clear that the CAS's normative stance rests on what it considers appropriate. In connection with the above-quoted statement, the CAS argues that '[a]ny *legal regime* should seek to enable its subjects to assess the consequences of their actions' (emphasis added).[115] It also explains elsewhere in the award that '[t]his is a matter of legitimate expectations, and it is crucial to any decent *system of laws*' (emphasis added).[116]

It seems to follow from *Quigley* that the recognition of the principle of legality as a general principle follows from *lex sportiva's* character as a 'legal regime' and 'system of laws'. To be clear, it seems that it is *because lex sportiva* constitutes a transnational legal order *that* the principle of legality is or ought to be one of the general principles included in this order. In other words, the obligations of law apply to the rules laid down by SGBs because they are law in the CAS's opinion. Much like the elements of the principle of legality identified in *Quigley* bearing a strong similarity to those formulated by Fuller, the CAS's reasons for the inclusion of the principle of legality in *lex sportiva* have a distinct Fullerian tone. The role (and justification) of law is that it directs the subjects' behaviour and provides order to society and in order for law to fulfil this function, it must be possible for the subjects to be able to understand the rules and decide to act in accordance with the rules, or not.[117]

This line of reasoning is even more clearly expressed by the CAS in its decision in *USOC v IOC and International Association of Athletics Federations (IAAF)*. The case is, as the CAS pointed out, 'a most peculiar case, arising in most unusual circumstances'.[118] The story begins in 1999, when Jerome Young, an American track-and-field athlete, tested positive for doping while competing in the United States. Young was initially found guilty of and suspended for doping, but this decision was overturned by the national federation's appeals board. Young subsequently participated in the 2000 Olympic Games in Sydney as one of six athletes on the US team that went on to win the gold medal in the Men's 4 x 400 metre relay. After the Games, the doping violation

[114] As a general point, the CAS has held that the principle of legality may apply to sports regulations regardless of whether any state-based legal orders so require by merit of the CAS's own jurisprudence. See, eg, CAS 2013/A/3324 and 3369, *GNK Dinamo v UEFA*, para 9.11.

[115] *USA Shooting and Quigley v UIT* (n 54) para 30.

[116] ibid para 33.

[117] R Stacey, 'Popular Sovereignty and Revolutionary Constitution-Making' in D Dyzenhaus and M Thorburn (eds), *Philosophical Foundations of Constitutional Law* (Oxford University Press. 2016) 171.

[118] *USOC v IOC and IAAF* (n 59) 1.

was reconsidered, and the CAS held in its award in *Young* that the athlete had indeed committed a doping offence and therefore should not have been allowed to participate in the Olympic Games.[119]

Following *Young*, the IAAF annulled the result of the entire US relay team. This decision was appealed and the main issue in the case that followed, *USOC v IOC and IAAF*, was whether the measure complied with the principle of legality. Specifically, the case turned on whether the IAAF's rule governing the consequences of a doping offence, which consistently referred to a specific athlete,[120] could serve as the basis for the annulment of the entire team's result. Reaching such a conclusion would require interpreting the rule purposely, extensively and contrary to its plain meaning in a manner that would quite clearly conflict with the principle of legality.[121] Invoking *Quigley*, the CAS explained why the principle of legality bars such an interpretation:

> The rationale for requiring clarity of rules extends beyond enabling athletes in given cases to determine their conduct in such cases by reference to understandable rules. As argued by the Appellants at the hearing, clarity and predictability are required so that the entire sport community are informed of the normative system in which they live, work and compete, which requires at the very least that they be able to understand the meaning of rules and the circumstances in which those rules apply.[122]

USOC v IOC and IAAF stands for a systemic approach to legality that places comprehensibility, clarity and predictability at the centre of a legitimate normative system capable of governing human behaviour. The similarities between the CAS's reasoning in *USOC v IOC and IAAF* and Fuller's on the principles of the internal morality of law are striking.[123]

D. 'In the Name of the Law': A Legitimacy Explanation

The cases in which the CAS is asked to apply the principle of legality have something in common. In section III we learned that cases involving the principle of legality can involve any sport, type of stakeholder and type of measure. However,

[119] CAS 2004/A/628, *IAAF v USATF and Young*.

[120] IAAF Rule 59.4, reproduced in *USOC v IOC and IAAF* (n 59) para 4 ('If *an* athlete is found to have committed a doping offence and this is confirmed after a hearing or *the* athlete waives *his* right to a hearing, *he* shall be declared ineligible. In addition, where testing was conducted in a competition, *the* athlete shall be disqualified from that competition and *the* result amended accordingly. *His* ineligibility shall begin from the date of suspension. Performances achieved from the date on which the sample was provided shall be annulled' [emphasis added]).

[121] *USOC v IOC and IAAF* (n 59) para 12 ('To take a rule that plainly concerns individual ineligibility and the annulment of individual results, and then to stretch and complement and construe it in order that it may be said to govern the results achieved by teams, is the sort of legal abracadabra that lawyers and partisans in the fight against doping in sport can love, but in which athletes should not be required to engage in order to understand the meaning of the rules to which they are subject.').

[122] ibid para 20.

[123] Whether the CAS panel actually drew on or was inspired by Fuller's work is unknown and unknowable to anyone not on the panel.

these cases all involve what can be described as judicial review, meaning that the CAS had to test whether the SGB's measures should be set aside.[124] How to resolve such disputes without losing legitimacy is a challenge for the CAS.

When deciding cases, dispute resolution institutions, public as well as private, face a potential legitimacy cost that, if mismanaged, could escalate to a legitimacy crisis.[125] The role of the dispute resolver is to hold the litigants to their obligations on a reciprocal basis. On the one hand, the institution's legitimacy for the litigants rests on it being seen as fair and impartial. On the other, when adjudicating individual disputes, the institution needs to declare winners and, more sensitively, losers. In so doing, the institution is keen to convince the losing party that even though it ultimately agreed with the opposing party, it is impartial and not on either side.

This is something that dispute resolution institutions must bear in mind regardless of whether their jurisdiction rests on consent or force. An institution that depends on party consent for jurisdiction (*consensual dispute resolution*) is obviously dependent on the parties' views of the legitimacy of the institution and its decisions in order to conduct business. If the losing party has freedom in the choice of engaging the institution again, it is important that it perceives the decision as legitimate.[126] Institutions that have the power to force parties to submit to its jurisdiction (*compulsory dispute resolution*), which includes many state-based public courts, must nevertheless ensure its legitimacy in the eyes of the public. To such institutions, the risk of a legitimacy hit is particularly strong when an institution adjudicates a dispute where one of the parties can be perceived as belonging to the same system as the institutions, such as when a state-based court resolves a public law dispute, and finds in favour of that party.[127] To resolve this legitimacy conundrum, dispute resolution institutions seek to use 'rule-based justifications' that enable the institutions to justify adverse outcomes based on it being mandated by law.[128]

While adjudication before the CAS in some cases can be characterised as consensual, in many cases the institution's relationship to the parties is asymmetrical. Although the CAS's jurisdiction, like that of other arbitration tribunals, technically rests on consent, it is in many situations and to many classes of litigants (eg, clubs and athletes) de facto compulsory.[129] When those litigants are

[124] If those cases concerned state actors instead of SGBs, this would clearly be the term we used.

[125] Here I draw broadly on the theoretical framework of Shapiro and Stone Sweet. See, eg, M Shapiro, *Courts: A Comparative and Political Analysis* (The University of Chicago Press, 1986) ch 1; A Stone Sweet, 'Judicialization and the Construction of Governance' (1999) 32 *Comparative Political Studies* 147; A Stone Sweet and F Grisel, *The Evolution of International Arbitration: Judicialization, Governance, Legitimacy* (Oxford University Press, 2017) 11–20.

[126] For traditional arbitration panels, formed to decide individual disputes, this largely becomes a legitimacy issue for the individual arbitrator. As arbitration is institutionalised, it increasingly becomes a question of institutional legitimacy.

[127] This is one of the reasons why perceived (and real) judicial independence is important.

[128] Stone Sweet and Grisel (n 125) 17–18. This is one possible explanation for judicial law-making.

[129] *Mutu and Pechstein v Switzerland* (n 65) paras 113–15.

involved in a dispute with an SGB on the opposing side, which is the situation in virtually every case that involves the application of the principle of legality, those actors may reasonably have some pre-litigation concerns over the CAS's impartiality considering the SGBs' influence over the institution.[130] The SGBs, by comparison, have, as discussed above, largely freely consented to the CAS's jurisdiction and thereby also its power to review their rules, but the SGBs could relatively easily revoke this consent.[131]

In such a context it makes good sense for the CAS to invoke and apply the principle of legality as a norm. Whether or not the non-SGB party ultimately wins or loses, by explicitly engaging with the principle of legality, the CAS signals its independence from the SGBs and that it serves as an effective check against them arbitrarily exercising their power. When the CAS strikes down SGB rules, invoking the principle of legality to do so, it enables the CAS to play the law-made-us-do-it card while at the same time signalling respect for the SGBs as law-makers by holding them to the law-maker standard.

V. CONCLUSIONS

This study has demonstrated that the principle of legality applies to a significant extent to SGBs when they exercise their power to govern sports. *Lex sportiva* includes a thin understanding of the principle of legality, such as narrowly construed quasi-criminal principles of non-retroactivity and *nullum crimen, nulla poena sine lege scripta*. However, the principle clearly extends far beyond that, both with regard to scope, which includes non-sanctioning cases, and substantive content, which includes the criteria of moral law. While the CAS may in some cases choose to apply a thin conception, for example, justified by the demands of Swiss law, it is willing to go further when circumstances so demand and its jurisprudence provides the basis for doing so.

We have also learned that there is no clear, single authority or reason for why the principle of legality forms part of *lex sportiva*. Instead of clear boundaries and hierarchies between (autonomous and sovereign) private, national and international legal orders, we find a context dominated by polycentric dynamics. National and international state-based legal orders intermingle with the internal processes of sport, which depart from and introduce different logics, to produce the observed results. In this respect, the principle of legality in sport demonstrates a general point about transnational legal governance: the application of the principle of legality in *lex sportiva* is an illustrative example of how neither public actors nor private actors can govern autonomously in

[130] See, eg, ibid, the partly dissenting, partly concurring Opinion of Judges Keller and Serghides.
[131] See section IV.A.

transnational spaces.[132] The case studied here is thus a manifestation of both transnational legality[133] and entangled legalities.[134]

The CAS's own legality case law is a good illustration of how the institution 'borrows magpie-like' from various legal orders,[135] but also of the particularly strong influence of Swiss law on *lex sportiva*, including in cases where Swiss law does not apply. The 'freer' relationship to rules in national legal orders associated with the transnational model can be seen in the CAS's legality jurisprudence. For example, in some cases the CAS does not apply the principle of legality directly to SGBs, but interprets sports rules and regulations in the light of the principle of legality and other general legal principles.[136] For example, in *Anderson*, the CAS held that the Olympic Charter 'is to be properly read in accordance with the "principle of legality" …'.[137] To use EU law language, you could say that the principle of legality in such instances applies indirectly and has an effect on sports rules and that the principle in this manner has a tangible impact on rights, obligations and outcomes in concrete cases.

It is clear that the relationship between SGBs and other sports actors is also not a traditional, horizontal and contractual relationship.[138] Even though SGBs lack the monopoly on violence associated with and seen as a defining characteristic of a state,[139] they are in fact able to effectively enforce their regulations themselves and without significant assistance from state-based legal orders. The foundation of the SGBs' power is their de facto monopoly power to decide who is allowed to participate in various areas of sports. For example, as the SFT pointed out in *Cañas*, athletes that are interested in exercising their sports anywhere besides their own backyards have no option but to submit to the governance and regulations of established SGBs.[140] This thinking is echoed in

[132] *cf* P Zumbansen, 'Piercing the Legal Veil: Commercial Arbitration and Transnational Law' (2002) 8 *European Law Journal* 400.

[133] *cf* Schultz (n 100).

[134] *cf* N Krisch, 'Framing Entangled Legalities beyond the State' in N Krisch (ed), *Entangled Legalities beyond the State* (Cambridge University Press, 2022).

[135] Beloff (n 98) 52.

[136] See, eg, CAS 92/80, *B v FIBA*, para 10 ('[Le tribunal arbitral] interprétera les dispositions de ce droit fédératif à la lumière des principes généraux du droit.').

[137] *Anderson et al v IOC* (n 46) para 30.

[138] See, eg, the SFT's decision of 27 May 2003 in case 4P.267–270/2002, *Lazutina and Danilova v IOC*, para 3.3.3.2, reported in 129 ATF 445 ('Etablies sur un axe vertical, les relations entre les athlètes et les organisations qui s'occupent des diverses disciplines sportives se distinguent en cela des relations horizontales que nouent les parties à un rapport contractuel.').

[139] M Weber, 'Politics as a Vocation' in HH Gerth and C Wright Mills (trs), *Essays in Sociology* (Oxford University Press, 1946) 78 ('a state is a human community that [successfully] claims the monopoly of the legitimate use of physical force within a given territory.').

[140] The SFT's decision of 22 March 2007 in 4P.172/2006, *Cañas v APT Tour*, reported in ATF 133 III 235, para 4.3.2.2 ('Ainsi l'athlète qui souhaite participer à une compétition organisée sous le contrôle d'une fédération sportive dont la réglementation prévoit le recours à l'arbitrage n'aura-t-il d'autre choix que d'accepter la clause arbitrale, notamment en adhérant aux statuts de la fédération sportive en question dans lesquels ladite clause a été insérée, à plus forte raison s'il s'agit d'un sportif professionnel. Il sera confronté au dilemme suivant: consentir à l'arbitrage ou pratiquer son sport en dilettante …').

the case law of the Court of Justice of the European Union (CJEU).[141] When viewed from this perspective, it appears that the 'monopoly on participation' can, and perhaps should, act as an alternative to the 'monopoly on violence' as a nexus to the principle of legality.

These findings raise some questions for further enquiry. First, what other 'public law' principles besides the principle of legality form part of the general principles of *lex sportiva* and apply to SGBs? Considering the traditional view that the principle of legality only applies to public entities, this constitutes an important finding and calls for a reconsideration of the public-private divide. As Duval points out, 'the formalist divide between public and private organizations at the transnational level conceals the material power and regulatory authority of many corporations and associations …'[142] Considering its exceptionally fundamental position in any legal order, it is natural that the principle of legality might be one of the first principles to traverse that divide, but having accepted that private expressions of power can justify breaching the public-private divide, we should consider which other principles apply by the same logic. For example, are basic human rights also associated with a thick understanding of the rule of law or good governance general principles in *lex sportiva*?

Second, does the principle of legality form part of other private transnational legal orders beyond *lex sportiva* and apply to private entities in sectors other than sports? As discussed above, SGBs owe their powerful positions to the structural aspects of sport that are more or less specific to each sector of sport. Private governance is not, however, unique for the field of sports and there are many sectors governed by powerful private entities. In this regard, the puzzle analysed herein is general.

[141] It fits very well with the focus of the Court and EU internal market law on market access and market access gatekeepers. The CJEU's extension of the scope of Union citizenship rights to SGBs in *Topfit and Biffi* shows that the same is true outside the economic sphere: because an SGB 'exercises a certain power over individuals', specifically over its ability to integrate into society, the exercise of that power is subject to the principle of proportionality and consequently effectively, as discussed above, the principle of legality. Case C-22/18, *TopFit eV and Daniele Biffi v Deutscher Leichtathletikverband eV*, para 39.

[142] A Duval, 'Taking Feminism beyond the State: FIFA as a Transnational Battleground for Feminist Legal Critique' [2022] *International Journal of Constitutional Law* 1, 21–22.

4

*Europeanisation of the Olympic Host (City) Contracts**

YULIYA CHERNYKH[1]

I. INTRODUCTION

AT THE ENTRANCE to the exhibitions at the Olympic Museum in Lausanne, one finds the words of Pierre de Coubertin. Written in large white letters on a dark wall, the phrase brings the universal aspiration of the Olympic Games to the forefront. The message appears to be clear: the Olympic Games are '*not French, Latin or European, but universal*'.

However, what this universal aspiration means is open to various interpretations. In a narrow sense, it may be viewed as emphasising geography. Since their revival, the Olympic Games have indeed taken place in various places around the world, outside Europe – in Asia, Australia, North and South America. And while Africa as a continent has not (yet) been chosen and the repetitiveness in the selection of some countries may also be open to criticism, the territorial reach, at least as far as the covered continents are concerned, is largely universal. In a more profound and broader sense, the universal aspiration of the Olympic Games may be associated with the common Olympic values that include excellence, respect and friendship as permeating principles. These principles and other values communicated through Olympism are not French, Latin or European, but universal.

Whether the legal framework behind the Olympic Games is equally universal is not an easy question to answer. From one perspective, the Olympic Games are primarily organised on the basis of the Olympic regulations that express transnational rules not belonging to a single jurisdiction – *lex olympica*. In this sense, the legal framework is indeed universal. From another, the contractual arrangements behind the Olympic Games are predominantly tied to one single

*I would like to thank Anna-Maria Strittmatter for her comments on the initial draft of this chapter.

[1] Inland Norway University of Applied Sciences.

European jurisdiction: Switzerland, and through it to the European legal tradition. In this sense, the legal framework does have a European 'nationality'.

By combining archival work with doctrinal and comparative legal analysis, this chapter accordingly investigates how and why Host City Contracts (HCCs),[2] as the principal contractual legal framework enabling the Olympic Games, are Europeanised. The chapter starts by describing a theoretical lens/perspective for assessing the Europeanisation of the HCCs. It then provides details on the data used for this research consisting of the HCCs, minutes of the International Olympic Committee (IOC) sessions, contemporaneous reports and correspondence, memoirs, and other historical and contemporary material. Thereafter the chapter turns to the HCCs in their historical development evidencing the persistent choice of Swiss law as applicable law and Switzerland as the place of dispute resolution. Finally, the chapter explores the scope that the choice of law and dispute resolution brings for defining centres of gravity for the HCCs vis-à-vis Swiss law and with it the European legal tradition, as well as implications of such a Europeanisation of Olympic sports law.

II. THE CONCEPT OF 'EUROPEANISATION'

As a name for the process and the result of something becoming European, the concept of 'Europeanisation' may convey various meanings in different contexts. In the context of contract law, that is of relevance for this chapter, Europeanisation may capture the growing awareness of the core common features in European contract law (*inward-looking Europeanisation*). Such an understanding has previously inspired efforts to harmonise European contract law and resulted in the Principles of European Contract Law (PECL)[3] and the Draft Common Frame of Reference (DCFR).[4] Despite the overall failure to create a common European Civil Code, the products of harmonisation remain authoritative.[5] Europeanisation may also refer to the EU legal order's narrower

[2] With Brisbane 2032, the IOC has started to refer to the HCCs as Olympic Host Contracts (OHCs). The change reflects the possibility to conduct the Olympic Games in larger geographical units than cities (regions, states or countries can become hosts for the Olympic Games). Apart from terminological precision, the change in itself does not entail anything substantial. Therefore, all contracts for hosting the Olympic Games will be *collectively* referred to in this chapter as HCCs; *individually*, when a contract in relation to Brisbane 2032 is named, this chapter will use the proper reference – OHC, the 2032 Brisbane OHC.

[3] The Principles of European Contract Law are a result of an academic initiative of the Commission on European Contract Law set up by Ole Lando. The Principles of European Contract Law are available at www.trans-lex.org/400200/_/pecl/.

[4] The Draft Common Frame of Reference is a result of broader academic efforts, partly funded by the EU, on the identification of common harmonised rules of private law. The Draft Common Frame of Reference is available at www.law.kuleuven.be/personal/mstorme/2009_02_DCFR_OutlineEdition.pdf.

[5] N Jansen and R Zimmermann, *Commentaries on European Contract Laws* (Oxford University Press, 2018) 2–18.

and more distinct role for contract law in Europe (*EUnisation*). While still largely fragmented, the significance of the EU legal order in this field is undoubtedly growing.[6] Apart from the successful unification of regulation on the protection of consumers,[7] EU rules spread further to regulate the supply of digital content and services.[8] Overall, the EU legal order has a penetrating effect on other fields of national law regulation that are in one way or another connected with contractual relationships, such as data protection,[9] competition rules,[10] state aid regulation,[11] etc. Finally, Europeanisation may also identify the external – mostly historical and occasional colonial – influence of the European contractual legal tradition for non-European countries (*outward-looking Europeanisation*). For example, recent comparative studies show the impact to a varying degree of the European contract law tradition on contract law in Hong Kong, India, Japan, Korea, Malaysia, Thailand, Singapore and other countries.[12]

In one way or another Swiss contract law is part of all described dimensions of Europeanisation. To begin with, the key source of Swiss contract law – the Swiss Code of Obligations of 1911 – is itself a product of the European private law tradition. The document is premised on a careful comparative analysis of the, at the time, fragmented cantonal contract law regulations and strongly inspired by the nineteenth century codifications of civil law in Germany, France and Austria.[13] Its concise pragmatic style and clarity of language served as a model for contemporary efforts to codify European private law (*inward-looking*

[6] J Basedow, *EU Private Law: Anatomy of a Growing Legal Order* (Intersentia, 2021) V–VI, 59–163.

[7] Directive 2011/83/EU of the European Parliament and of the Council of 25 October 2011 on consumer rights, amending Council Directive 93/13/EEC and Directive 1999/44/EC of the European Parliament and of the Council and repealing Council Directive 85/577/EEC and Directive 97/7/EC of the European Parliament and of the Council [2011] OJ L304/64.

[8] Directive (EU) 2019/770 of the European Parliament and of the Council of 20 May 2019 on certain aspects concerning contracts for the supply of digital content and digital services [2019] OJ L136/1.

[9] Regulation (EU) 2016/679 of the European Parliament and of the Council of 27 April 2016 on the protection of natural persons with regard to the processing of personal data and on the free movement of such data, and repealing Directive 95/46/EC (General Data Protection Regulation) [2016] OJ L119/1. The HCCs expressly incorporate General Data Protection Regulation in their recent editions.

[10] Articles 101–106 of the Treaty on the Functioning of the European Union (TFEU). See also E Szyszczak, 'Application of EU Competition Rules to Sport' in J Anderson, R Parrish and B García (eds), *Research Handbook on EU Sports Law and Policy* (Edward Elgar, 2018) 261–84.

[11] Article 107 of TFEU. See also A Cattaneo, 'State Aid and Sport' in Anderson, Parrish and García, ibid 197–227.

[12] M Chen-Wishart and S Vogenauer (eds), *Contents of Contracts and Unfair Terms* (Oxford University Press, 2020) 62–65, 93, 111–13, 161–63, 207–208, 242–43, 339, 413, 479–80.

[13] SM Maksimović and D Despotović, 'The Origin of the Civil Law Codification in Europe' (2022) 39 (1) *Pravo, teorija i praksa* 45, 52–54; K Mathis and PA Burri, 'Nudging in Swiss Contract Law? An Analysis of Non-Mandatory Default Rules from a Legal, Economic and Behavioural Perspective' in K Mathis and A Tor (eds), *Nudging – Possibilities, Limitations and Applications in European Law and Economics* (Springer International Publishing, 2016) 211.

Europeanisation).[14] Further, the impact of Swiss contract law on other non-European contract law traditions is also well documented, and includes, for instance, complete reception of the Swiss Code of Obligations by Turkey in 1926[15] and varying role in shaping contract law in Asia[16] (*outward-looking Europeanisation*). Finally, because of the series of bilateral agreements with the EU, Swiss contract law (and Swiss law in general) is not entirely isolated from the role that EU law continuously and increasingly plays in the field of private law and some other fields (*EUnisation*).[17]

Drawing on the European *belonginess* of Swiss contract law described above, this chapter reveals the Europeanisation of the HCCs by introducing a simple and rather *instrumental* notion of Europeanisation. 'European' here primarily implies *substantive* and *procedural* bonds that tie these contracts to Europe. The application of a substantive law of a European country as part of the European contract law tradition instead of any other non-European national law is such a substantive bond. The localisation of dispute resolution and enabling the ultimate (even if limited in the case of arbitration) judicial control to Europe instead of any other place is such a procedural bond. In other words, the connection between the HCCs and Swiss law are perceived to be signs of the Europeanisation of the HCCs.

The adopted approach is premised on a theoretical perspective that critically assesses the possibility of a complete disengagement of contracts from applicable national law, either because of a broad party autonomy and detailed/exhaustive contractual regulation or because of the influence of international arbitration, or both.[18] However detailed, autonomous and self-sufficient a contract might appear, its governing law determines all critical aspects of regulation, such as formation, interpretation, performance, termination and validity. The adopted approach does not negate broad party autonomy that many national contract laws worldwide provide to parties, but rather recognises a nuanced perspective of existing limits to party autonomy and control that applicable law has on the content of contractual terms and throughout the entire contract's lifespan.[19] Furthermore, this work also endorses well-established views about the capacity of the mandatory rules of the forum statutes to override chosen law, if it

[14] O Lando, 'Salient Features of the Principles of European Contract Law: A Comparison with the UCC' (2001) 13 *Pace International Law Review* 339, 342–43; A Morin, 'Efficiency and Swiss Contract Law' in K Mathis (ed), *Law and Economics in Europe: Foundations and Applications* (Springer, 2014) 212.

[15] Morin, ibid.

[16] ibid; E Bucher, *Introduction to Swiss Law* (Kluwer 2004) 103.

[17] A Epiney, 'How Does European Union Law Influence Swiss Law and Policies?' in S Nahrath and F Varone (eds), *Rediscovering Public Law and Public Administration in Comparative Policy Analysis: A Tribute to Peter Knoepfel* (Presses polytechniques et universitaires romandes, 2009) 179–96.

[18] G Cordero-Moss, *International Commercial Contracts: Applicable Sources and Enforceability* (Cambridge University Press, 2014) 308–309.

[19] On the scope and limits of party autonomy, see A Mills, *Party Autonomy in Private International Law* (Cambridge University Press, 2018).

is foreign to the forum (not the case for the HCCs), and the role of the seat of arbitration for the ultimate control over arbitral awards.[20]

The described notion of Europeanisation shapes the chapter in a simple and comprehensive way. The applicable law of a European country, such as of Switzerland, and dispute resolution also being localised in Europe, such as in state courts and/or arbitration in Switzerland, become the focal point of discussion. The chapter accordingly proceeds to empirically verify and critically assess these substantive and procedural aspects of Europeanisation and question their impact on the Europeanisation of transnational sports regulations, or *lex sportiva*.

III. DATA

This chapter relies on unique data as not all the HCCs are publicly available. Only the most recent HCCs and occasionally a few others can be easily accessed through open online resources belonging to the Olympic Studies Centre/the IOC and to a lesser extent various platforms and official websites maintained by authorities in the respective jurisdictions.[21] The majority of the material analysed in this chapter could only be accessed in the archives of the Olympic Studies Centre in Lausanne.[22] However, even the archives, at the time of their

[20] Ml Wilderspin, 'Overriding Mandatory Provisions' in J Basedow, G Rühl, F Ferrari, and P de Miguel Asensio (eds), *Encyclopedia of Private International Law* (Edward Elgar, 2017) 1331–36; Cordero-Moss (n 18) 308–309;.

[21] The HCCs for Tokyo 2020, Beijing 2022, Paris 2024, Milano-Cortina 2026, Los Angeles 2028 and Brisbane 2032 were published because of the revised 2020 Olympic Agenda that expressed an undertaking that the HCCs were to be made public. The remaining HCCs in relation to the Olympic Games in Vancouver, London and Rio do not fall under the duty of transparency and have become available through various official and non-official sources. The following HCCs were thus accessed: Vancouver 2010 (available at www.gamesmonitor.org.uk/archive/node/1166.html), London 2012 (available at www.gamesmonitor.org.uk/files/Host%20City%20Contract.pdf), Rio 2016 (available at www.rio.rj.gov.br/documents/8822216/10480306/Contrato_Cidada_Anfitria_Olimpiadas_2016_assinado.pdf), Tokyo 2020 (available at www.2020games.metro.tokyo.lg.jp/eng/taikaijyunbi/taikai/hcc/index.html), Beijing 2022 (available at https://stillmed.olympic.org/Documents/Host_city_elections/Host-City-Contract-XXIV-Olympic-Winter-Games-in-2022--Beijing-Execution-no-signature.pdf), Paris 2024 (available at https://stillmed.olympic.org/media/Document%20Library/OlympicOrg/Documents/Host-City-Elections/XXXIII-Olympiad-2024/Host-City-Contract-2024-Principles.pdf), Milano-Cortina 2026 (available at www.milanocortina2026.org/media/ljcdhpcf/host-city-contract-2026-principles.pdf), Los Angeles 2028 (available at https://stillmed.olympic.org/media/Document%20Library/OlympicOrg/Documents/Host-City-Elections/XXXIV-Olympiad-2028/Host-City-Contract-2028-Principles.pdf) and Brisbane 2032 (available at https://stillmed.olympics.com/media/Documents/Olympic-Games/Brisbane-2032/Host-Contract/Host-City-Contract-2032-Principles.pdf).

[22] The IOC's historical archive is maintained by the Olympic Studies Centre in Lausanne at its address Villa du Centenaire, Quai d'Ouchy 1, 1006 Lausanne, Switzerland. The archive was accessed during my visits to the Olympic Studies Centre in Lausanne that took place on 17–18 February 2022 and 15–16 September 2022. I would like to thank the staff of the Olympic Studies Centre for facilitation and help with archival documents.

consulting, were not able to provide full access because of an embargo on the general files classified by the IOC as 'for internal use' that has been in place for the last 20 years.[23] The available archive documents cover Olympic Games held from 2000 back to 1964. This chapter accordingly relies upon 21 HCCs (including one OHC)[24] out of 27 known HCCs, whereas six HCCs remain confidential.[25]

The figure below summarises the available material as well as the remaining gap in the knowledge:

Figure 4.1 Host City Contracts

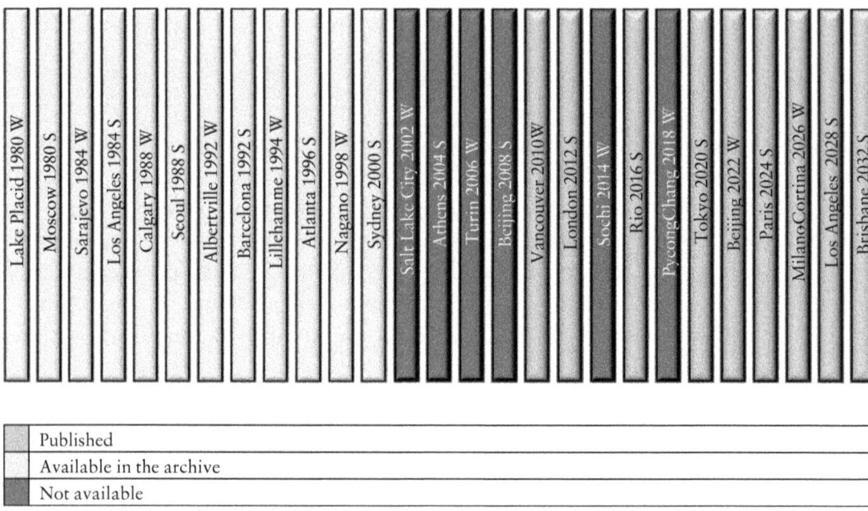

IV. THE HCCS AND THEIR HISTORICAL DEVELOPMENT

Before assessing the significance of substantive and procedural bonds with European legal culture, it is worth taking a closer look at the contemporary features of the HCCs and their historical development. What are these contracts all about? How detailed are they? Have they experienced stability or change in terms of applicable law and dispute resolution provisions across time?

[23] The IOC Access Archive Rules are available at https://library.olympics.com/default/historical-archives.aspx?_lg=en-GB.

[24] Among these documents, the very first HCCs for the Olympic Games in 1964 in Tokyo and Innsbruck were not signed, thus leaving 12 signed HCCs for the Olympic Games from 1980 to 2000 (Lake Placid 1980, Moscow 1980, Sarajevo 1984, Los Angeles 1984, Calgary 1988, Seoul 1988, Albertville 1992, Barcelona 1992, Lillehammer 1994, Atlanta 1996, Nagano 1998 and Sydney 2000).

[25] The HCCs in relation to Salt Lake City 2002, Athens 2004, Turin 2006, Beijing 2008, Sochi 2014, and PyeongChang 2018 remained inaccessible and were not considered.

A. Contemporary Shape

While being contracts on *event organisation*, the HCCs bear unique features. Their uniqueness is directly tied to the magnitude of the event and specificity of the governance of the Olympic movement. With regard to the event's magnitude, it is difficult to find any other contemporary event that would compare with the Olympic Games, as regards size, recognition or cost. Indeed, the Olympic Games are commonly recognised as '*the largest, the highest-profile, and the most expensive megaevent that exists*'.[26] To enable these extraordinary sport events to take place, the HCCs are accordingly concluded well in advance of the Olympic Games and as a result of the bidding procedure. With regard to the role of governance of the Olympic movement, the entire organisation of the event is vested in the hands of one single organisation – the IOC. This organisation as the 'owner' of the Olympic Games manages the bidding procedure and defines the critical terms of cooperation with the local organising committee (OCOG). While the IOC ensures that it is free from any financial liability,[27] it retains a unilateral right to amend its operational requirements and terminate the respective HCC.[28] All necessary work on the actual organisation of the games is done by the OCOG, usually consisting of the representatives of the National Olympic Committees (NOCs) of the respective host states and host cities/venue. Accordingly, the core parties involved in delivering the Olympic Games are the IOC, the elected host city and a host NOC. In addition, and once created, the organising committee for the OCOG also becomes a party to the HCC. This is a rather peculiar arrangement where a non-existent organisation at the time of the conclusion of a contract subsequently joins it as a party. National authorities do not usually appear as a formal party to these contractual arrangements but are actively involved in securing the successful delivery of the Olympic Games through necessary guarantees and other commitments that raises some democratic concerns.[29] Finally, the Olympic Charter – the codified fundamental principles of Olympism – is incorporated into the HCCs and thus directly applicable and legally enforceable between the contractual parties.

In view of the above features, it is no wonder that the contemporary edition of the HCCs represents a rather complex and detailed matrix of contractual

[26] B Flyvbjerg, A Budzier and D Lunn, 'Regression to the Tail: Why the Olympics Blow Up' (2021) 53(2) *EPA: Economy and Space* 234.

[27] See, for instance, para 4 of the Joint and several liabilities of the Host Cities, the Host NOC and the OCOG in the 2026 Milano-Cortina HCC that contains the typical wording for the joint and several liability of the Host City, the Host NOC and the OCOG: 'The Host City, the Host NOC and the OCOG shall be jointly and severally liable for all their obligations, guarantees, representations and other commitments under the HCC, whether entered into individually or collectively' 2026 Milano-Cortina HCC (n 21) para 4.1.

[28] See, for instance, 2026 Milano-Cortina HCC (n 21) para 30.

[29] A Duval, 'From Global City to Olympic City: The Transnational Legal Journey of London' in H P Aust and JE Nijman (eds), *Research Handbook on International Law and Cities* (Edward Elgar, 2021) 293–304.

provisions on dozens of pages. These provisions are aimed at ensuring the core exchange between the parties under the HCCs. The IOC provides expertise and contributes to *benefits and rights* connected with marketing, ticketing, licensing and broadcasting. In turn, the host city, the respective host NOC and the OCOG are supposed to carry out all the actual work on the delivery of the Games and bear the joint and several liability for all their commitments. Overall, the IOC essentially entrusts the elected host city/venue, the respective host NOC and the OCOG '*with planning, organising, financing, and staging of the Games*'.[30]

As presently structured, the HCCs consist of the Olympic Host Principles and the Olympic Host Contract Operational Requirements together with the Games Delivery Plan and the Candidature Commitments. The Olympic Host Principles provide an essential legal framework for commercial, organisational, reporting and financial obligations and consists of seven parts: General Responsibilities of the Parties; Contribution of the IOC to the Success of the Games; Core Requirements; Coordination with the IOC; Key Deliverables and Operational Areas; Paralympic Games; and Miscellaneous. These Olympic Host Principles are the core of the agreement, whereby the parties agree on all critical undertakings along with responsibilities, principles of interpretation, Swiss law as governing law, and the Court of Arbitration for Sport (the CAS) as the primary dispute resolution mechanism. The Olympic Operational Requirements set the OCOG's specific obligations in each of the delivery areas; the Games Delivery Plan specifies the main milestones and timelines in the performance of the operational requirements under the HCC and the Candidature Commitments specify those commitments which the candidate city presents during the course of the bidding. In recognising Swiss law as the governing law, the HCCs also attempt to make clear that the obligations of the Parties shall be defined first by the terms of the contract, second by the Olympic Charter, and only third by the principles of interpretation of Swiss law.

The wording of the HCCs' provision on applicable law and dispute resolution is illustrated in the latest edition of the 2032 Brisbane OHC, as follows:

> 52. Governing law and arbitration
>
> 52.1. This contract is exclusively governed by the substantive, internal laws of Switzerland, to the exclusion of the rules regarding conflicts of laws.
>
> 52.2. Any dispute concerning the validity, interpretation or performance of the OHC shall be determined conclusively by arbitration, to the exclusion of the state courts of Switzerland, of the Host Country or of any other country; it shall be decided by the Court of Arbitration for Sport and resolved definitely in accordance with the Code of Sports-Related Arbitration of such Court. The arbitration shall take place in Lausanne, Switzerland. If, for any reason, the Court of Arbitration for Sport denies its competence, the dispute shall then be determined conclusively by the state courts in Lausanne, Switzerland.

[30] See, for instance, 2032 Brisbane OHC (n 21) para 2.

> 52.3. The Hosts, the Host NOC and the OCOG hereby expressly waive the application of any legal provision under which they may claim immunity against any lawsuit, arbitration or other legal action which is either:
>
> a. initiated by the IOC or any other IOC Indemnitee;
> b. initiated by a third party against the IOC or any other IOC Indemnitee; or
> c. initiated in relation to the commitments undertaken by the Host Country Authorities (or any authority of a country other than the Host Country pursuant to §5.3).
>
> Such waiver shall apply not only to the jurisdiction but also to the recognition and enforcement of any judgment, decision or arbitral award.[31]

In response to the growing criticism,[32] the latest editions of HCCs also started to include innovative commitments relating to sustainability and human rights protection. HCCs commit the IOC, the host city and the host NOC to ensuring that the Games are at the forefront in the field of sustainability and are organised in a manner that complies with the Olympic Charter, the IOC Code of Ethics and the United Nations Guiding Principles on Business and Human Rights.[33] Recognition of these values reflect an important trend in operationalising the increasing role of sustainability and human rights in international transactions.

Overall, the HCCs do not belong to a specific type of contract expressly regulated in civil law tradition. From a general perspective, the HCCs represent *mid- or long-term* contractual arrangements as the IOC and all relevant parties conclude contracts well in advance to secure necessary infrastructure delivery and proper organisational arrangements. These contracts involve *high-value* undertakings that with each year increase progressively with the profits from broadcasting and various marketing revenues.[34] Finally, one may question some of the *asymmetry* regarding the parties' rights and obligations, particularly as regards the exclusive right of the IOC to terminate an HCC[35] and cash the guarantee from the General Retention Fund as liquidated damages.[36]

B. Historical Evolution

However, the HCCs have not always been about mega-sized events and huge financial undertakings. They were not always as detailed and elaborate as they

[31] ibid.

[32] Human Rights Watch, 'Olympics: Host City Contract Requires Human Rights' (28 February 2017), www.hrw.org/news/2017/02/28/olympics-host-city-contract-requires-human-rights#.

[33] UN Guiding Principles on Business and Human Rights, www.ohchr.org/sites/default/files/documents/publications/guidingprinciplesbusinesshr_en.pdf.

[34] By way of example, the latest HCC for Brisbane estimates that the IOC contributions and granted benefits and rights to the OCOG to be one billion, eight hundred million United States dollars, 2032 Brisbane OHC (n 21) para 7.1(a).

[35] ibid para 39.

[36] ibid para 37.

are now. The earlier editions of the HCCs could be drafted on a single page and be rather simple, resembling more a framework agreement than a detailed operational document. Over time and as the IOC's revenues from media rights increased significantly,[37] the contractual arrangement became more sophisticated. The precision and detail in contractual arrangements grew in tandem with the growth of the Olympic Games and the institutionalisation of the IOC.

A historical insight into the development of the HCCs shows that the first modern Olympic Games were held without any formal contract at all, whereas the detail and complexity of the concluded contracts have grown steadily. The first time the idea of having a formal contract between the IOC and the organising committee emerged dates back to August 1960. At that time, the IOC informed the Austrian delegation that the IOC would renounce its television rights in favour of the organising committee if an indemnity of USD 20,000 was paid. The Austrian delegation had perceived the sum to be too high in view of earlier discussions. The question of the indemnity was postponed to another IOC session in Athens and later on the same amount upon which the IOC had insisted was agreed. Reacting to the situation at the IOC session in Rome, Comte de Beaumont, an IOC member, proposed 'that in future, a contract drawn in good and due form be signed between the contracting parties, namely the I.O.C. and the Organizers of the Games'.[38] Comte de Beaumont also reiterated this idea at the following IOC session in Athens where he stressed the importance of defining in a contract 'the chief demands and responsibilities which are incumbent to the cities which have been attributed the Games by the I.O.C.'[39] However persuasive the idea of having a specific contract for the organisation of the Olympic Games was, the drafts of contractual agreements in relation to the Olympic Games in Tokyo and Innsbruck dated 1964 remained unsigned and no contract was concluded until 1974.

One may well ask oneself what the reasons for the absence of contracts between the IOC and organising committees before 1974 were. They were numerous. Most importantly, the Olympic Games were only just starting to attain their status as mega sporting events, which they now undoubtedly enjoy. Their organisation did not require the same level of coordination and allocation of responsibility as do contemporary Olympic Games. Disagreements or misunderstandings between the IOC and the local organising committees, even if they existed, did not have serious ramifications at the time, before high revenues

[37] International Olympic Committee, *The International Olympic Committee – One Hundred Years: The Idea – The Presidents – The Achievements, Volume III produced under supervision of Raymond Gafner* (International Olympic Committee, 1996) 167–79. See also, L Delpy Neirotti, 'Olympic Broadcast Rights' in D Chatziefstathiou, B García and B Séguin (eds), *Routledge Handbook of the Olympic and Paralympic Games* (Routledge, 2020) 109–19.

[38] Minutes of the 57th session of the International Olympic Committee in Rome, 22–24 August 1960 (archive).

[39] Annex 3 to the 58th session of the International Olympic Committee in Athens 19–21 June 1961 (archive).

could be made from broadcasting. Finally, the IOC itself did not become a legal entity until the early 1980s.[40]

The formalisation of the legal status of the IOC appeared in fact as a crucial moment for the emergence of the HCCs. Numerous factors prompted the necessity to register the IOC as a legal entity: such as an exponential growth in revenue, a corresponding growth in the number of formal employees at the secretariat, risks of individual responsibility for the IOC members that had to be minimised, and the need for a legal entity in order to protect the emblems of the Olympic Games. All these factors were named at the IOC session in Vienna in 1974 where a Swiss lawyer and the head of the 'juridical committee', Marc Hodler,[41] presented a report about the legal status of the IOC. He prepared the report in cooperation with René Bondoux from France, John Emerys Lloyd from England, Luc Silance from Belgium, and Dr František Kroutil from Czechoslovakia. Consisting of European lawyers, the group unanimously recommended that legal status be given to the IOC, and Switzerland was chosen as the place of registration.[42] Non-European jurisdictions were not discussed for this purpose at all. The working group considered either France, being the birthplace of the IOC, or Switzerland, where its headquarters were located at the time. And while the decision to register in Switzerland took place already in 1974, some time passed before the actual registration, negotiated with officials in Switzerland, was finalised.[43]

With the internal decision on the formalisation of the legal status of the IOC in Switzerland came the very first two HCCs that were signed jointly on 23 October 1974 in relation to the Olympic Games at Lake Placid and Moscow. These were one-page contracts titled 'Contract between the International Olympic Committee and the National Olympic Committee of the Elected City' concluded in Vienna and signed by the President of the IOC, the President of the relevant NOC and the members of the bidding committees. Interestingly, the cities were not formal signatories of the HCCs. Of the six brief provisions in the two HCCs, none concerned governing law or dispute resolution. Clause 1 provided that the selected city shall confirm the replies given to the *questionnaire*[44] and was responsible for the organisation of the Games 'to the satisfaction of the IOC'.[45] Clause 2 described who signed the contract and in what capacity. Clause 3 specified that the prior agreement of the IOC was

[40] International Olympic Committee (n 37) 66–68.

[41] Marc Hodler was also the Swiss IOC member and President of the International Skiing Federation, and honorary IOC Treasurer.

[42] The 75th session of the International Olympic Committee in Vienna, 21st–24th October 1974 (archive).

[43] International Olympic Committee (n 37) 66–68.

[44] The questionnaires were used to ensure all the terms that were used to map all the necessary practical aspects in the organisation of the Olympic Games, an analogue of pre-election commitments in modern HCCs.

[45] 'Contract between the International Olympic Committee and the National Olympic Committee of the Elected City' 23 October 1974 (archive).

necessary for the conclusion of all 'important'[46] contracts and 'those concerning the IOC and its rights'.[47] Clause 4 made it clear that the IOC was supposed to enter into direct contracts with broadcasters in relation to the broadcasting rights. Clause 5 specified that the IOC rules and regulations were applicable in all relevant contracts relating to the organisation of the Olympic Games. Article 6 covered the indemnity of 250,000 Swiss francs that was supposed to be paid to the IOC as an advance of the income derived from the Games for Lake Placid and twice as much for Moscow. Vienna was expressly identified as the place of contract conclusion.

The first HCC that was more elaborate and included provisions on governing law and dispute resolution was the HCC for the winter Olympic Games in Sarajevo. Concluded on 18 May 1978, it was three pages long, stipulated the law of Switzerland as the applicable law and mentioned the court of first instance of Geneva as having exclusive jurisdiction over any dispute arising out of the HCC. Importantly, the HCC already provided that the city waived the application of any federal or state law or any other legal provision under which the city could claim immunity against a lawsuit.

In line with the twin contracts for the winter and summer Olympic Games in Lake Placid and Moscow, one would expect the same terms to have been agreed for the summer Olympic Games in Los Angeles as for the winter Olympic Games in Sarajevo. That indeed was the intention of the IOC. However, contracting on the same conditions proved to be more complex. Los Angeles was the only candidate for the summer Olympic Games[48] and did not readily accept the IOC's terms. The core disagreement turned around the financial guarantee that the IOC required under Rule 4 of the Olympic Charter.[49] For the IOC, making Los Angeles accept its terms was important, particularly because all previously concluded contracts in relation to the Olympic Games in Lake Placid, Moscow and Sarajevo featured unconditional acceptance of the IOC terms. However, the tension became so serious that the IOC considered holding the Olympic Games elsewhere.[50] Following the somewhat confrontational discussion in 1978,

[46] ibid.

[47] ibid.

[48] International Olympic Committee (n 37) 82. According to Gafner, numerous factors led to the shortage of candidates in that period, including the economic crisis, scale of the Olympic Games, deficits in Munich and Innsbruck, uncontrolled construction costs of the Montreal Games, political problems and risks of boycotts, other political tensions, and '*the personal diplomacy of Lord Killanin, by which he* stayed clear of soliciting any candidatures' – ibid.

[49] Rule 4 of the 1978 Olympic Charter provided that: 'Application to hold the Games shall be made by the official authority of the city concerned with the approval of the National Olympic Committee (NOC) which must guarantee that the Games shall be organised to the satisfaction of an in accordance with the requirements of the IOC. The NOC and the city chosen shall be jointly and severally responsible for all commitments entered into and shall assume complete financial responsibility for the organisation of the Games.' On the process of negotiating concessions, see RB Perelman (ed), *Official Report of the Games of the XXIIIrd Olympiad Los Angeles, 1984*, Volume I. Organisation and Planning (Los Angeles Olympic Organizing Committee, 1985) 9–12.

[50] The 80th session of the International Olympic Committee in Athens, 17–20 May 1978 (archive).

the IOC nevertheless decided to give a second chance to Los Angeles by awarding the Olympiad provisionally on the condition that the HCC incorporating the Olympic rules be concluded before 1 August 1978.[51] The records show that the HCC was indeed concluded on terms that were satisfactory to the IOC – yet with considerable delay and inevitable concessions from both sides.[52] Similar to the contract with Sarajevo, Swiss law was selected as the law applicable to the HCC.[53] The dispute resolution clause, however, was different and instead of Swiss state courts as agreed in the HCC for Sarajevo, it provided for arbitration under the rules of the International Chamber of Commerce.[54]

For the subsequent two contracts for Calgary and Seoul, the negotiating power was fully returned to the IOC as several cities competed to become the venue for the Olympic Games. Calgary along with two other cities (Cortina d'Ampezzo and Falun) competed for the XV (winter) Games. While Seoul and one more city (Nagoya) competed for the XVI (summer) Games. For both contracts a reference to the Swiss state courts appeared again along with the unchanged provision on Swiss law being applicable. Concluded on 30 September 1980, the HCC for the Olympic Games in Calgary already comprised four pages and provided that it was 'subject to the law of Switzerland' and that 'the court of first instance of Geneva, canton of Switzerland' had exclusive jurisdiction in the case of dispute and the parties' failure to settle amicably. Similarly, the HCC in relation to the Olympic Games in Seoul contained the same provisions on the applicable law and dispute resolution. Overall, according to the IOC's own assessment, both contracts appeared more advanced than the preceding contracts,[55] as they, for example, introduced cities as immediate parties to HCCs.

The first reference to the CAS with its seat in Lausanne appeared in 1986 in the HCC concluded for the Olympic Games in Albertville. This contract had already grown to be 16 pages long and it contained provisions on Swiss law as the applicable law. The reason why the CAS appeared only in the seventh HCC

[51] ibid.

[52] Lord Killanin, the IOC President at the time, described the concessions in his memoires with the following words: 'Over the next ten months it was agreed that there should be two contracts, one between the IOC and the organising committee, which would take on the responsibility normally vested in a city, and one between the organising committee and the USOC. It took much negotiating to achieve a position in which each party found the outcome satisfactory. The biggest stumbling block in terms of delay was brought about by the need for the USOC, rightly, to be indemnified against the possible financial failure of the organising committee.' Lord Killanin, *My Olympic Years* (William Morrow and Company, Inc, 1983) 98–99.

[53] The contract is contained in the Amendments to the Minutes of the 81st session of the International Olympic Committee in Montevideo, 5–7 April 1979 (archive).

[54] The contract did not contain a reference to the seat (or the place of arbitration). According to Article 12 of the ICC arbitration rules applicable at the time, the place of arbitration was supposed to be fixed by the Court, unless agreed upon by the parties, www.international-arbitration-attorney.com/wp-content/uploads/1975-ICC-Rules-of-Arbitration-English.pdf.

[55] A letter dated 23 March 1982 written by the legal counsel for the IOC as a response to a letter dated 17 March 1982 from IOC director Monique Berlioux, 'Contrats avec les villes olympiques reponse' (archive).

is rather straightforward: the CAS was in its infancy in the early 1980s. The very first proposal for the creation of the CAS emerged in 1982 when Kéba M'Baye at the invitation of Juan Antonio Samaranch, IOC President at the time, presented the idea 'to establish a body that would settle any disputes within the sports world that were outside the competence either of the Executive Board in relation to the organisation of the Olympic Games, or the International Federations on technical matters' at the 85th IOC session in Rome in 1982. Already at the following IOC session in New Delhi in March 1983, the statute of the new institution was presented and not long thereafter the CAS became the preferred dispute resolution body to be included in the HCCs. Rather than being created specifically for the HCCs, the CAS was, however, mostly discussed as an urgent need for the sports community as a whole, essentially reflecting the role that the IOC was increasingly assuming concerning global sport. Since 1986, the CAS, as the dispute resolution body, became omnipresent in all the HCCs analysed in this chapter that followed: the 1992 Barcelona HCC, the 1994 Lillehammer HCC, the 1996 Atlanta HCC, the 1998 Nagano HCC, the 2000 Sydney HCC, the 2010 Vancouver HCC, the 2012 London HCC, the 2016 Rio de Janeiro HCC, The 2020 Tokyo HCC, the 2022 Beijing HCC, the 2024 Paris HCC, the 2026 Milano-Cortina HCC, the 2028 Los Angeles HCC up to the most recent one addressed at the beginning of this section – the 2032 Brisbane OHC.

V. SUBSTANTIVE BONDS: SWISS LAW AS THE APPLICABLE LAW

That Swiss law is chosen for sport-related contracts is not very surprising. As the second choice for international commercial contracts worldwide,[56] Swiss law is traditionally the first choice for sport disputes.[57] The precise reasons for this choice can be debated from many angles ranging from convenience and coincidence and the overall somewhat *ritual* significance of Switzerland for the Olympic movement to the impression of neutrality of Swiss law,[58] or its capacity

[56] Swiss law is the second most often chosen law according to the empirical research of Gilles Cuniberti conducted on 4,400 international contracts that appeared in arbitration proceedings administered by the International Chamber of Commerce (ICC) – G Cuniberti, 'The International Market for Contracts: The Most Attractive Contract Laws' (2014) 4 *Northwestern Journal of International Law and Business* 455, 459. Cuniberti's other empirical study of Asian arbitration institutes show, however, that Swiss law was not that popular for the cases submitted to Asian arbitration institutes for adjudication – G Cuniberti, 'The Laws of Asian International Business Transactions' (2016) 25 (1) *Washington International Law Journal* 35, 38.

[57] The default position under Rule 45 of the Code of Sports-related Arbitration, is that Swiss law applies in the absence of the parties' choice (in force as from 1 July 2020, but also present in earlier versions). The very first draft of the CAS Statute prepared in 1983 already provided that 'Failing any specific clause in the agreement the CAS applies Swiss Law.' – The minutes of the 86th session of the IOC in New Delhi, 26–28 March 1983. See also IS Blackshaw, *International Sports Law: An Introductory Guide* (TMC Asser Press, 2017) 130, 132.

[58] On the ambiguity of the neutrality of substantive law see Cuniberti with further references: Cuniberti, 'The International Market for Contracts' (n 56) 455, 484–86.

to endorse a broad party autonomy for contractual relations[59] as well as to ensure the autonomy of associations,[60] etc. The consulted archives are silent as to why Swiss law was chosen for the HCCs. There is no internal memo or correspondence on this subject. What the archives do reveal though is that the choice of Swiss law has remained unchanged for the HCCs since the first time that choice was expressly made in 1978 and that this coincided approximately in time with the choice of Switzerland as the place for the IOC registration as a legal entity.

Even if Swiss law does not have specific background regulations for contracts on event organisation, its implications are difficult to overstate. First and foremost, Swiss law defines the scope of party autonomy to agree on contractual terms.[61] However broad party autonomy under Swiss law is, it is not limitless. Swiss law controls the content of contractual provisions in what relates to illegality or compliance with mandatory provisions of the Swiss Code of Obligations, and even, on rare and limited occasions, fairness between the parties.[62] Second, Swiss law governs all critical aspects of the lifespan of a contract such as contract formation, performance, termination, liability, validity, and interpretation, and thus contractual provisions cannot be assessed in total isolation from this regulation.[63] For contract interpretation, for instance, Swiss law expects the real and common intent of the parties to be considered. In addition, and unlike some countries, it enables a broad range of evidentiary material to be taken into account in establishing this intent.[64] Third, the application of Swiss law to the HCCs is not frozen in time as Swiss law as a whole applies to the HCCs, including all relevant jurisprudential clarifications and developments at the EU level when and if they are made part of Swiss law.

[59] Bucher (n 16) 105; R Pahud de Mortanges, *Swiss Legal History* (Peter Lang GmbH, Internationaler Verlag der Wissenschaften, 2020) 280–81.

[60] M Baddeley, 'The Extraordinary Autonomy of Sports Bodies under Swiss Law: Lessons to Be Drawn' (2020) 20(3) *The International Sports Law Journal* 3, 4–5.

[61] G Cordero-Moss, 'Limitations on Party Autonomy in International Commercial Arbitration' (2014) 372 *Recueil des Cours de l'Académie de Droit International* 133, 215–319.

[62] S Marchand, *Clauses contractuelles. Du bon usage de la liberté contractuelle* (Helbing Lichtenhahm, 2008) 3–49.

[63] Article 116 of the Swiss Private International Law provides that 'contracts are governed by the law chosen by the parties'.

[64] None of the evidence is excluded for this exercise. Indeed, according to Article 18 of the Code of Obligations: 'In order to decide on the form and clauses of a contract, it is necessary to seek the real and common intention of the parties, instead of relying on the incorrect expressions and terms which the parties used in error or with the aim of disguising the real nature of the contract'. Further, an interpreter is expected to consider clarifications of the Federal Supreme Court on contract interpretation as follows: 'A judge will first seek to establish the real and common intention of the parties, adopting an empirical approach, without stopping at the inaccurate expressions or denominations they may have used. If he or she is unable to do so, he or she will seek, by applying the principle of trust, the meaning that the parties could and should have given, pursuant to the rules of good faith, to their reciprocal manifestations of intent, taking into account all the circumstances.' (Decision of the Federal Supreme Court 4A_124/2014 of 7 July 2014, para 3.4.1.) See also, A Cemil Yildirim, *Interpretation of Contracts in Comparative and Uniform Law* (Kluwer Law International, 2019) 69–81.

The described omnipresent role of Swiss law does not stop at supplying specific rules or principles for the interpretation of the HCCs or regulating general issues of contract formation, performance, liability, termination and validity, although all the above effectively define the identity of a contract or its DNA. As governing law, it may become critical in assessing any asymmetry in regard to the rights and obligations that one may observe in relation to the HCCs and understanding the *concepts* that the HCCs rely upon. While possibly bearing generic appeal, some of the concepts used in the HCCs have their roots in and shall be understood as part of the Swiss contract law tradition. By way of example, *a duty to negotiate in good faith* in the case of unforeseen or undue hardship[65] or because of a change in the management process[66] shall be understood in light of the interpretation under Swiss contract law of the concept of good faith.[67] Indeed, comparative research shows that the interpretation of the precise content and implications of *good faith* in contractual relationships is not identical across jurisdictions.[68] The role of good faith as a meta-norm under Swiss law may bring surprises for those coming from legal traditions where good faith does not enjoy a similar importance. Another example relates to the concept of *liquidated damages* which the IOC can withdraw from the General Retention Fund in the case of contract termination. Swiss law will determine enforcement conditions for liquidated damages, including the standards of assessment of their reasonableness and proportionality, and the scope of the power of an adjudicator to cut their amount. Under Article 163 of the Code of Obligations,[69] an adjudicator applying Swiss law may reduce the amount of damages awarded if they consider them excessive. Depending on the circumstances of the particular dispute, the amounts accumulated in the General Retention Fund, currently five per cent of all amounts paid to the OCOG,[70] might be considered excessive and thus the contractual provision will not be fully enforced because of the controlling role of the governing law. In the same vein, the *extent of an agreed waiver*[71] and the effect of a *non-waiver clause*,[72] if tested in arbitration, shall be understood in light of what Swiss contract law provides for regarding the possibility and terms of effective waivers and non-waivers, including the omnipresent principle of good faith.

[65] For instance, 2026 Milano-Cortina HCC (n 21) para 30.5 'Change management process'; 2032 Brisbane OHC (n 21) para 31.

[66] For instance, 2026 Milano-Cortina HCC (n 21) para 42 'Unforeseen or undue hardship', 2032 Brisbane OHC (n 21) para 43.

[67] Morin (n 14) 216–18.

[68] R Zimmermann and S Whittaker (eds), *Good Faith in European Contract Law* (Cambridge University Press, 2000).

[69] Marchand (n 62) 217–18.

[70] For instance, 2026 Milano-Cortina HCC (n 21) para 8.2(c) and the 2032 Brisbane OHC (n 21) para 8.2 (c).

[71] For instance, 2026 Milano-Cortina HCC (n 21) paras 37.3, 37.5 'Indemnification and waiver of claims'; 2032 Brisbane OHC (n 21) para 38.

[72] For instance, 2026 Milano-Cortina HCC (n 21) para 44 'Non-waiver'; 2032 Brisbane OHC (n 21) para 45.

Even contractual techniques that the HCCs use appear to be influenced by Swiss law. By way of example, the preamble to the 2032 Brisbane OHC provides that 'the Parties agree that the foregoing Preamble shall form an integral part of the OHC – Principles'. This is a technique recommended to Swiss lawyers to ensure that in preambles, undertakings are operationalised, or in the words of Sylvain Marchand 'contractualised'.[73] As highlighted by Marcel Fontaine and Filip de Ly in their book, approaches to the role of contractual preambles vary across jurisdictions,[74] and thus the HCCs' approach to this issue is yet another sign of the preeminent role that Swiss law plays in their drafting.

However, let us not be misled by the express choice of the Olympic rules and regulations in the HCCs, as well as the overall hierarchy of legal sources prioritising the Olympic rules and regulations over Swiss law. Indeed, there was a time in which Olympic rules and regulations exclusively governed the organisation of the Olympic Games in the absence of any written contractual arrangements between the parties (ie prior to 1974). In the very first HCC editions, the IOC's regulations determining the conditions under which the Olympic Games were organised were integrated into the contracts. Already the very first HCCs for Lake Placid 1980 and Moscow 1980 incorporated by reference the Olympic rules and regulations.[75] However, these regulations did not provide an autonomous framework for *contractual regulation* and cannot – in their past or present form – autonomously solve contract-related questions that may arise in the course of the organisation of the Olympic Games. Beyond the determination of the core roles of the parties involved in the organisation of the Olympic Games, these regulations are completely silent on contract-related questions. They do not clarify the entire scope or nature of the liability of the parties, they say nothing about the legal regime of contract termination, they do not explain principles of contract interpretation, etc. Furthermore and for the same reason, the hierarchy[76] that the contemporary HCCs set for applicable sources/rules and

[73] Marchand (n 62) 98.

[74] M Fontaine and F de Ly, *Drafting International Contracts* (Brill | Nijhoff, 2006) 59–102.

[75] The 1980 Lake Placid HCC and the 1980 Moscow HCC provided that: 'In every contract in any way concerning the organising of the games the city or the Organising Committee to be formed shall mention the IOC rules and regulations and make them compulsory applicable'.

[76] The HCCs analysed here demonstrate a certain evolution of the provision on the precedence of the Contract. For instance, the 2010 Vancouver HCC, the 2012 London HCC and the 2016 Rio HCC provide the following wording: 'Should there be any conflict between the provisions of this Contract and the Olympic Charter, the provisions of this Contract shall take precedence.' The 2020 Tokyo HCC provides as follows: 'In case of conflicts or discrepancies in relation to the interpretation or implementation of this Contract, such conflicts or discrepancies shall be determined by applying, in the following order of preference: the present Contract, the Olympic Charter and applicable laws.' The 2022 Beijing HCC provides: 'In case of conflicts or discrepancies in relation to the interpretation or implementation of this Contract, such conflicts or discrepancies shall be determined by applying, in the following order of preference: first the terms defined herein; second the Host City Contract Detailed Obligations referred to in Sections 6 and 69 above; third the Olympic Charter and applicable laws.' The 2024 Paris HCC, the 2026 Milano-Cortino HCC and the 2028 Los Angeles HCC provide: 'The obligations of the Parties under the HCC shall be defined, first, by the

regulations is somewhat misleading. What is defined as the subsidiary option is effectively the primary one. Swiss law does not play a residual role, but effectively defines the scope of party autonomy, principles of contract interpretation, period of limitation, as well as informing and controlling various other contractual provisions.

VI. PROCEDURAL BONDS: SWITZERLAND AS THE PLACE OF DISPUTE RESOLUTION

Similarly to the situation surrounding substantive Swiss law, the parties to the HCCs did not specifically discuss Switzerland as a place of dispute resolution. The first two HCCs for the Olympic Games in Lake Placid and Moscow in 1980 did not contain any dispute resolution provision.[77] The first provision covering dispute resolution introduced by the IOC appeared in the 1984 Sarajevo HCC; it provided for an exclusive competence of a state court in Geneva and has not raised any concerns.[78] Despite the general complexities surrounding the conclusion of the 1984 Los Angeles HCC and a change from a state court to arbitration, the seat for ICC arbitration in Switzerland did not trigger any particular disagreement either. In the same vein, the creation of the CAS and its subsequent inclusion in all HCCs that followed the 1988 Seoul HCC did not provoke any debate. Starting (presumably) with the 2010 Vancouver HCC,[79] the IOC also began reinforcing the choice of Switzerland as a place of dispute resolution by including additional provisions that subjected all non-arbitrable issues arising out of the HCCs to the direct jurisdiction of a state court in Lausanne.

terms of the HCC, second, by the terms of the Olympic Charter and, third, by application of the principles of interpretation of Swiss law.' The 2032 Brisbane OHC essentially contains the same wording as the 2024 Paris HCC, the 2026 Milano-Cortino HCC and the 2028 Los Angeles HCC, albeit with some variation: 'The Olympic Host Contract (or OHC), as referred to herein, consists of the following documents and commitments, which are all binding upon the Parties and which, in case of any conflict or discrepancy, will apply in the following order of precedence: a. The OHC – Principles (including all appendices which form an integral part thereof); b. The OHC – Operational Requirements; c. The Games Delivery Plan; and d. The Pre-election Commitments.' Of relevance regarding the expressed criticism are mostly the 2020 Tokyo HCC and the 2022 Beijing HCC and to a somewhat lesser extent (because of the emphasis of interpretation) the 2024 Paris HCC, the 2026 Milano-Cortino HCC, the 2028 Los Angeles HCC and the 2032 Brisbane OHC. These HCCs allocate to the governing law, at least as far as the explicit formulations are concerned, the residual character.

[77] Both HCCs were concluded with the respective NOCs and not cities as such.

[78] In 1978, when considering biddings from Sarajevo and the two other competing cities Sapporo and Gothenburg, the IOC President enquired if the delegates agreed to the draft HCC between their cities and the IOC, to which all delegates replied in the affirmative – Minutes of the 80th Session of the International Olympic Committee, Athens 17–20 May 1978.

[79] The first HCC that exhibits this change is the 2010 Vancouver HCC (it might be the case that one of the four unavailable HCCs – the 2022 Salt Lake City HCC, the 2004 Athens HCC, the 2006 Turin HCC and the 2008 Bejing HCC – already contained this choice.

Again, the step has not brought any controversy. Finally, provisions on a waiver of immunity by which the NOC, the OCOG, and respective cities waived any legal provision under which they could claim immunity in a legal procedure or arbitration have not raised any particular disagreement or concern.[80]

Various factors explain why Switzerland appeared in the HCCs as a place of dispute resolution and was not strongly opposed or challenged. Convenience for the IOC and the asymmetry in negotiation powers are the most plausible reasons. As discussed, Switzerland was the home of the IOC, and a Swiss lawyer led its legal department. Even if somewhat complicated at the time,[81] Swiss procedural regulations were still the closest and most understandable choice in comparison with unknown options elsewhere. The 'procedural gravity' for the HCCs was centred in two cantons in the physical vicinity of the IOC office – the canton of Geneva (for the 1984 Sarajevo HCC, the 1988 Calgary HCC and the 1988 Seoul HCC) and the canton of Vaud for arbitration and limited state jurisdiction (for all subsequent HCCs). When the IOC took the initiative to create an arbitration institute, Switzerland, unsurprisingly, was again chosen as a seat. The IOC took the promotion of the CAS seriously.[82] Luckily, Swiss statutory arbitration provisions are more comprehensive and supportive for international users than purely national proceedings in state courts.[83] The appeal of neutrality that created favourable conditions for other parties to accept Switzerland as the place of dispute resolution even without a precise understanding of what neutrality may or may not bring for dispute resolution should not be discarded. Above all, the scarcity of actual disputes arising out the HCCs prior to and after the creation of the CAS[84] limits the practical relevance of a broader debate on the choice of the seat of the forum, at least for now, although a debate can certainly take place in the abstract.

While the precise implications of this choice vary somewhat depending on whether Swiss *courts* or Swiss *arbitration* were chosen primarily, Switzerland has in any event retained ultimate control over any decision rendered. There

[80] Views on the enforceability of waiver clauses may differ, but the point here is that the choice of Switzerland as a place of dispute resolution remained uncontroversial and was reinforced by various other contractual provisions that attempted to preclude any adverse effect of any existent regulation that could undermine this choice.

[81] Pahud de Mortanges (n 59) 280–81.

[82] See the report of the Executive President of the CAS presented at the IOS session in Berlin – Minutes of the 90th session of the IOC in Berlin, from 1st to 6th June 1985. See also the report of the Executive President of the CAS with the similar content presented at the IOC session in Istanbul – Minutes of the 92nd session of the IOC in Istanbul, 9th to 12th May 1987.

[83] Just a couple of years after the CAS was created, Switzerland passed the Swiss Private International Law Act that included progressive liberal regulation of international arbitration and enabled Switzerland to become one of the most popular arbitration venues today.

[84] The only known dispute concerning the Olympic Games appears to be the one arising out of the 2012 London HCC. The dispute was settled without provoking discussions about the suitability of the choice of dispute resolution. This observation is without prejudice to a strong strand of literature criticising procedural fairness and human rights protection for athletes in the CAS.

are essentially three different models of the control exercised by Switzerland integrated in the HCCs: (1) the full and complete control by Swiss courts as to the entire dispute on merits; (2) a limited control by Swiss courts over arbitration without any express choice of dispute resolution for non-arbitrable issues; and (3) a limited control by Swiss courts over arbitration combined with express choice for full and complete control on merits as to non-arbitrable parts of a dispute. All three have been practised over different periods of time. The first model of full and complete control by Swiss courts over the entire dispute was chosen for three HCCs (the 1984 Sarajevo HCC, the 1988 Calgary HCC, and the 1988 Seoul HCC) and is history now. The second model was practised in the period after the 1988 Seoul HCC until (presumably) the 2010 Vancouver HCC. The third model was (presumably) introduced as of the 2010 Vancouver HCC and is still in practice.

To put it differently, the practical implications of these models could be as follows. When the HCCs provided for a state court as a forum, Swiss state courts were empowered to finally resolve on merits any potential dispute arising out of the HCCs. The entire judicial system could be put in operation with all instances and all possible intensity of review being invoked. When the HCCs provided for arbitration only, Swiss courts still retained some control. That control was primarily limited to the grounds for setting arbitral awards aside and could be practised regardless of the choice of arbitration being the ICC Court of Arbitration or the CAS insofar as Switzerland was chosen as the seat. And while Switzerland has a longstanding arbitration-friendly reputation, setting awards aside is not entirely unknown to it.[85] The jurisdiction for non-arbitrable parts of disputes had to be determined based on applicable conflict-of-laws rules. Finally, when the HCCs provided (and continue to provide) for a combination of arbitration (the CAS) and express residual jurisdiction of Swiss courts over non-arbitrable matters, Swiss courts enjoyed (and continue to enjoy) a limited control over arbitration in setting aside procedures and a full control over non-arbitrable issues.[86] Arguably, Swiss courts also enjoy

[85] The grounds for setting awards aside are defined in Article 190(2) of the Private International Law Act, according to which an award can be set aside on four occasions as follows: '(a) if the sole arbitrator was not properly appointed or if the arbitral tribunal was not properly constituted; (b) if the arbitral tribunal wrongly accepted or declined jurisdiction; (c) if the arbitral tribunal's decision went beyond the claims submitted to it, or it failed to decide on one of the prayers for relief; (d) if the principle of equal treatment of the parties or the right of the parties to be heard was violated; (e) if the award is incompatible with public policy'. See also, M Arroyo, 'Commentary on Chapter 12 PILS, Article 190 [Finality, challenge: principle]' in M Arroyo (ed), *Arbitration in Switzerland: The Practitioner's Guide*, 2nd edn (Kluwer Law International, 2018) 266–350; D Mavromati, 'The Role of the Swiss Federal Tribunal and Its Impact on the Court of Arbitration for Sport (CAS)', https://papers.ssrn.com/sol3/papers.cfm?abstract_id=2845237.

[86] Because Swiss law defines arbitrability broadly, it is difficult to identify specific examples of non-arbitrable disputes in the context of the HCCs. It is potentially possible to think of some aspects of disputes intervening with public policy and lying exclusively within the competences of Swiss

full control over those parts of disputes that are not covered by an arbitration agreement. Curiously enough, the scope of an arbitration agreement in the most recent HCCs, including the 2032 Brisbane OHC and the 2026 Milano-Cortina HCC, is not expressed broadly as 'all disputes arising from or in connection with the contract', but narrowly covering validity, interpretation and performance, but not formation and termination. Arguably, you may submit that any potential dispute about formation and termination will not fall within the jurisdiction of the CAS and thus will end up in a Swiss court.[87] To sum up, in one way or another, Swiss courts exercise control over potential disputes arising out of the HCCs.

Since the procedural regulations cannot be frozen in time, Switzerland retains control over the precise shape of the procedural rules and can amend or change the regime whenever it so desires. To illustrate this control, you may recall that when a state court in the canton of Geneva was first chosen for the 1984 Sarajevo HCC and two other HCCs, Swiss procedural rules were not harmonised or unified at the federal level. Each canton had its own peculiarities and it was not entirely clear to what extent the jurisprudence of the Federal Supreme Court might affect the application of procedural rules at the cantonal level.[88] Arbitration was rapidly evolving and Swiss courts were gaining an arbitration-friendly reputation already in the 1970s.[89] Yet, there were many limitations, and the judiciary system of two levels exercised control (cantonal and federal) over arbitral awards. The progressive changes in 1988, just a few years after the creation of the CAS, further liberalised the arbitration regime by restricting grounds for setting awards aside.[90] The unification of procedural laws in state courts only took place in 2011,[91] whereas more recently, in 2021, arbitration procedural regulations have undergone further changes, enabling, for instance, parties to seek evidentiary support directly from Swiss state courts.[92] Regardless of the cursory description and actual content of these procedural changes, the point is simple – the general procedural framework depends on the state policy and is not immune from future changes.

state courts, such as the registration of intellectual property rights or bribery. See also, M Orelli, 'Commentary on Chapter 12 PILS, Article 177 [Arbitrability]' in M Arroyo (ed), *Arbitration in Switzerland: The Practitioner's Guide*, 2nd edn (Kluwer Law International, 2018) 62–63.

[87] See with further references C Müller and O Riske, 'Chapter 2, Part II: Commentary on Chapter 12 PILS, Article 178 [Arbitration agreement]' in Arroyo (n 86).

[88] Pahud de Mortanges (n 59) 292–94.

[89] ME Schneider and P Michele Patocchi, 'The New Swiss Law on International Arbitration' 1–3, www.lalive.law/wp-content/uploads/2019/10/mes_new_swiss_law_1989.pdf.

[90] ibid 10–12.

[91] Pahud de Mortanges (n 59) 293–94; A Wallerman Ghavanini, 'Harmonization of Civil Procedure: Can the European Union Learn from Swiss Experiences?' (2016) 24 (5) *European Review of Private Law* 855, 860–69.

[92] G von Segesser and AM Petti, 'The Changing Legal Landscape of Arbitration in Switzerland' in Global Arbitration Review, *The European Arbitration Review 2022* (Law Business Research Ltd, 2021) 151–71.

VII. CONCLUSION

Despite setting a legal framework for organising global sporting events, the HCCs' legal gravity has been and still is located in Switzerland, Europe. Swiss law is the governing law and the starting point for defining the contractual legal framework. Effectively, it is the governing law that defines the scope of party autonomy to agree on the terms contained in the HCCs, complements where a contract may be silent and provides a combination of guiding and mandatory rules and principles. One may theorise to what extent Swiss contract law may be characterised as being truly international or European. The fact remains that while popular for international transactions worldwide and being omnipresent for sport-related contracts, Swiss contract law remains the product of one single *European* jurisdiction – Switzerland; furthermore, it is not carved in stone and might be subject to change.

Similarly, regarding the procedural dimension, the predominant choice of arbitration instead of state courts – the CAS – does not make dispute resolution provisions entirely neutral. The CAS is a *localised* arbitration court with its seat in Switzerland that makes Swiss courts competent to exercise their, albeit limited, control over awards. Furthermore, the contemporary HCCs expressly state that if the CAS declines jurisdiction, ordinary Swiss courts become competent. Accordingly, Swiss courts may retain jurisdiction if the CAS panel declines its jurisdiction to hear disputes say on the *formation* and *termination* of an HCC. In the past, Swiss courts had complete jurisdiction over all disputes stemming from the HCCs.

Apart from the direct substantive and procedural *Swiss bonds* that determine the entire system of coordinates for the HCCs identified in this chapter, these contracts are filled with concepts that are generally well-known in European contract law and may have a particular meaning under Swiss law. This chapter has touched upon the concepts of good faith and liquidated damages as an illustration. If one considers the HCCs as part of a transnational Olympic regulation, then one would identify these concepts in the texts as *transplants* from the European private law tradition.

And while it is not possible to measure Europeanisation in a precise manner, one may attempt to assess its scope by contrasting it with alternatives. An alternative to European contract law would be the applicability of contract law of non-European countries or (questionably) the disconnection of HCCs to the extent possible from any national law. Here, one may theoretically think about HCCs being subject to the applicable law of the place where the Olympic Games are being held. One may also consider an attempt at maximum possible disengagement from national law through the creation of a special uniform convention addressing major sport events similar to the Convention on the International Sales of Goods or application of *ex aequo et bono*.[93] An alternative to European

[93] *Ex aequo et bono* (from Latin 'according to the right and good') is frequently considered as an opportunity for the parties in arbitration to disengage their dispute (fully or partially) from applicable national law.

legal concepts would be the integration of legal concepts that are firmly rooted in other legal traditions. An alternative to ultimate European judicial control would be the seat of arbitration being located in some other country with the role of non-European state courts for the exercise of permissible control over arbitration. One may also potentially think of delocalised arbitration courts that would not be subject to judicial control in any particular jurisdiction, similar to the International Court for the Settlement of Investment Disputes with their own autonomous system of appeal, or initial jurisdiction of non-European state courts. None of these alternatives have yet found their way into the HCCs.

All these direct or indirect points of influence of the European legal tradition raise a final important observation. While the resulting symbiosis of *Swiss contract law* and *sports regulation* has not been conclusively tested before any adjudicatory body, their continuous *reproduction* for each Olympic Games raises a question concerning their *stability* and *appeal*. Suppose that one characterises the HCCs and other relevant regulations that stem from them as evidence of *lex sportiva*, no complexity should arise in recognising the distinct role of the European legal tradition behind their normative matrix. In other words, European anchors in the HCCs make it possible to suggest that the emerged and emerging *lex olympica* insofar as contractual arrangements are concerned does not represent a *self-referential normative framework* but is premised on the European legal tradition or is Europeanised.

5

The Influence of European Legal Culture on the Evolution of Lex Olympica *and Olympic Law*

MARK JAMES AND GUY OSBORN*

I. INTRODUCTION

THIS CHAPTER EXPLORES the impact of European laws and legal thinking on the evolution of both *lex Olympica*, a distinct but powerful influencer of *lex sportiva*, and Olympic Law, the legislative product of the indirect law-making capability of the International Olympic Committee (IOC). It does this through an analysis of the IOC and its legal norm-creating powers, focussing specifically upon the IOC's requirement that an Olympic host criminalises the phenomenon of ambush marketing. It illustrates that Europe's impact is substantive, procedural and cultural, and further examines the effect of, and critiques the extent of, the IOC's leverage in creating legal and regulatory frameworks in host cities.

The Olympic Movement, the IOC, and indeed the Olympic Games in general, are being subjected to unprecedented levels of social, political and legal scrutiny and criticism. Of particular interest to lawyers is the interrogation of the normative framework developed by the IOC that enables it to create Olympic Law from its own internal legal norms, the *lex Olympica*. This novel approach to law creation is grounded in highly Eurocentric notions of contract law, intellectual property law, and comparative legal theory. In particular, the interlocking series of contracts that underpins *lex sportiva* is replicated in the key relationships between the IOC, the International Sports Federations (ISFs), the National Olympic Committees (NOCs), the World Anti-Doping Agency (WADA), the

* Mark James is Professor of Sports Law at Manchester Metropolitan University. Guy Osborn is Professor of Laws at the University of Westminster. The authors would like to express their thanks to the editors and contributors to the Workshop in Umeå who provided valuable input and academic camaraderie throughout the drafting process. We are also grateful to Chris Ellins of Westminster Law School for his thoughts and input on an early draft of this chapter.

Court of Arbitration for Sport (CAS), the hosts of the Olympic Games, and the athletes, creating an Olympic-specific *lex sportiva*: the *lex Olympica*. Alongside this internal legal framework, the use of 'forced transplants' has underpinned the creation of national laws in host cities since the Sydney 2000 Games, developing a separate body of Olympic Law.[1]

This chapter will focus on how Euro- and Anglo-centric notions of contract law and intellectual property law, in the context of the protection of a mega sports event's commercial rights strategies, underpins the decision-making process that determines which disputes need litigating and why. The indirect law-making capability of the IOC will be analysed through the evolution of the anti-ambush marketing legislation required of host jurisdictions. This analysis will focus in particular on the step change in the regulation of ambush marketing that was introduced by the United Kingdom Parliament for London 2012, and the ways that this Anglo-European extension of traditional notions of intellectual property law has influenced legislative interventions at subsequent editions of the Olympic Games, through the lens of forced transplants. Before doing so, however, it is important to explore some of the origins of sports governance and the broader influence and impact of European legal cultures on the regulatory frameworks of sport, its internal laws, and their relationship with more traditional forms of law, before exploring the concept of *lex Olympica*.

Broadly speaking, the evolution of many of the world's most popular sports can trace both their regulatory origins, and the formation of their governing bodies, to Europe. Whilst the precise pre-history of association football is somewhat uncertain,[2] the sport's first Laws were formalised in London in 1863, with the (English) Football Association formed later in the same year.[3] As Vamplew notes, rules emerge because of competition,[4] at which point a degree of standardisation is required. These formalised regulatory frameworks usually preceded, or were coterminous with, the formation of governing bodies. As with football, both the Broughton Rules and the Queensbury Rules, which provide the basis for modern professional boxing, predate the formation of the first official governing body of the sport, the Amateur Boxing Association.[5] What is particularly striking is that this process of standardisation and formalisation of

[1] M James and G Osborn, 'The Olympics, Transnational Law and Legal Transplants: The International Olympic Committee, Ambush Marketing and Ticket Touting' (2016) 36(1) *Legal Studies* 93.

[2] There is a voluminous literature on this topic. See, eg, G Curry (ed), *The Early Development of Football. Contemporary Debates* (Routledge, 2019); P Swain, 'The Origins of Football Debate: Football and Cultural Continuity, 1857–1859 (2015) 32(5) *The International Journal of the History of Sport* 631.

[3] Note that in a very self-regarding sense, even today, it is not the *English* FA but merely 'The FA.'

[4] W Vamplew, 'Playing with the Rules: Influences on the Development of Regulation in Sport' (2007) 24(7) *The International Journal of the History of Sport* 843.

[5] See further S Greenfield and G Osborn, 'A Gauntlet for the Glove: The Challenge to English Boxing Contracts' (1995) 5 *Marquette Sports Law Journal* 153. The British Boxing Board of Control was formed in Cardiff in 1929.

laws and governance structures in many modern sports emerged from Europe in the late nineteenth and early twentieth centuries. The influence of the United Kingdom is especially strong, with a number of key governing bodies emerging in London in particular.

The formalisation of sports' rules and/or laws was quickly followed by the creation of national, continental and world governing bodies as the self-appointed guardians of individual sports, related groups of sports, and multi-sport events such as the Olympic Games. Europe's influence in global sporting terms is highly significant. The IOC was founded on 23 June 1894. Its European credentials are marked by its foundational meetings taking place in Paris and its domination by European members. The original IOC comprised 16 members from 13 different nations, and although avowedly international in its outlook, the only representation from outside of Europe in its early membership was from the USA, Australia and Argentina.[6] Similarly, the Fédération Internationale de Football Association (FIFA) was founded in the headquarters of the Union Française de Sports Athlétiques in Paris on 21 May 1904.[7] The founding member associations were all European: Belgium, Denmark, France, Germany, The Netherlands, Spain, Sweden and Switzerland.

These links to Europe have been reinforced by the decision of many ISFs to locate their headquarters in European states, and in particular in Switzerland.[8] Of the 34 members of the Association of Summer Olympic International Federations, 23 are based in Switzerland, with a further eight headquartered elsewhere in Europe;[9] all members of the Association of International Olympic Winter Sports Federations are based in Europe, with four of the seven headquartered in Switzerland.

Europe's influence on the legal and regulatory structures applied to world sport can be seen as being substantive, procedural and cultural. With so many of the world's major ISFs, including the IOC, established, located in, and operating from European jurisdictions, the influence of Europe and its legal cultures is writ large upon the evolution of both *lex sportiva* and *lex Olympica*. This is compounded by several European legal systems having significant influence far beyond their original geographical boundaries; many legal systems, with the notable exception of those in Russia and China, are heavily influenced by the English common law or the civil codes of France and Germany. Within these contexts, a European-influenced model of contractual relationships provides the vehicle, or space, in which the IOC is able to regulate the Olympic Movement and operate as a commercially independent entity. As discussed below in terms

[6] J Krieger and S Wassong, 'The Composition of the IOC' in D Chatziefstathiou, B Garcia and B Seguin (eds), *Routledge Handbook of the Olympic and Paralympic Games* (Routledge, 2021) 204.

[7] IOC history archived at olympics.com/ioc/history.

[8] See J-L Chappelet, 'Switzerland's Century-Long Rise as the Hub of Global Sports Administration' (2021) 38(6) *The International Journal of the History of Sport* 569.

[9] See the list provided by the Association of Summer Olympic International Federations at www.asoif.com/members.

of ambush marketing, European influence on the evolution of intellectual property laws generally is significant, as are the ways that the law has developed to provide a legal means of prohibiting unwanted commercial associations with major sporting events.

The influence of European legal cultures and thinking on the regulation of international sport is marked, particularly insofar as the Olympic Movement and Olympic Charter embrace, or are influenced by, many aspects of European legal traditions including administrative law, criminal law, employment law, and human rights law. In this chapter, we will focus on the impact of European notions of contractual interpretation, intellectual property law, and the use of legal alternative dispute resolution mechanisms. Before returning to the influence of European legal culture more explicitly later, it is important to examine the relationship between *lex sportiva*/sports law and *lex Olympica*/Olympic Law.

II. THE RELATIONSHIP BETWEEN *LEX SPORTIVA*/SPORTS LAW AND *LEX OLYMPICA*/OLYMPIC LAW

For many years, there was a vague acceptance that the actions of organisations associated with the running of sport were, if not above the law, then certainly outwith its normal jurisdiction. However, the expectations of effective and operational good governance, and the requirements of the rules of natural justice, or due process, in ISFs' decision-making processes have ensured that sport is, ultimately, subject to the law. As ISFs have adjusted their behaviours to take account of developments in national, EU and international law, a clear split between '*lex sportiva*' and 'sports law' has evolved. In contradistinction to more traditional forms of law, *lex sportiva* encapsulates the internal rules and regulations of sport, including the various governing statutes and charters, key contracts, and the decisions of the IOC, the ISFs, the WADA and the CAS.[10] On the other hand, sports law incorporates the bodies of national and EU legislation, the jurisprudence of national, EU and international courts, and the international treaties that apply to sport.[11] Whereas sports law is applied to, or imposed on, sport by the appropriate legal jurisdiction governing the dispute in question, the authority and applicability of *lex sportiva* is grounded in a series of interlocking contracts that require adherence to the internal legal norms and regulatory frameworks of specific sports bodies,[12] and is increasingly transnational in its outlook and application.[13]

[10] For a more detailed discussion of the scope and definition of *lex sportiva*, see, eg, A Duval, '*Lex Sportiva*: A Playground for Transnational Law' (2013) 6 *European Law Journal* 822.

[11] See generally M James, *Sports Law*, 3rd edn (Palgrave, 2017) and A Cattaneo and R Parrish, *Sports Law in the European Union* (Kluwer Law International, 2020).

[12] K Foster, '*Lex Sportiva*: Transnational Law in Action' (2012) 3-4 *The International Sports Law Journal* 20.

[13] A Duval, 'Transnational Sports Law: The Living Lex Sportiva' in P Zumbandsen (ed), *The Oxford Handbook of Transnational Law* (Oxford University Press, 2021).

The regulatory frameworks of different sports usually operate alongside each other, as there is a general acceptance that sport should be granted a degree of legal and political autonomy over its own governance. The autonomy of sports organisations from political interference is a requirement of the Olympic Charter,[14] however, their autonomy from legal oversight is only ever conditional.[15] The law retains ultimate regulatory oversight of sport and, unless specific exemptions are granted to it, sport must operate in accordance with the law, and in many cases that law is European in origin.

Despite the growth of interest in the subject, agreement on the definitions of both *lex sportiva* and sports law remain elusive. Foster considers that *lex sportiva* is often defined too narrowly, focussing on either the internal rules of sport, the decisions of the CAS, or a combination of the two. Instead, he prefers the term 'global sports law', which fuses both of these meanings with general principles of law, including global administrative law. This leaves his extended understanding of *lex sportiva*, or global sports law as:

> [An] autonomous transnational legal order established by international sporting federations and those subject to their sporting jurisdiction[s] and which emerges from the statutes and regulations of federations as interpreted by institutions of alternative dispute resolution created by those federations. It is a private regulatory order, which is legitimised by contract and consent, operating transnationally to transcend national variation. The key element of this definition is the notion of autonomy. The ideology embodied within the concept of global sports law is that it is a law without a state and so outside the governance of national laws, that it is immune from state regulation and a legal order in its own right, and that it is legitimated by its subjects. This claim of immunity and autonomy makes global sports law of interest to a wide range of legal theorists, but it also exemplifies a political struggle … between self-regulation and public accountability.[16]

Duval provides a more detailed account of *lex sportiva* that goes beyond the simple contractual framework to embrace a plurality of legal sources that includes: the written constitutions of the ISFs, including in particular the Olympic Charter; and the interpretation of these documents by both the relevant judicial committees of specific sports and the CAS.[17] This results in a more all-encompassing, living definition of *lex sportiva* that captures the many interactions between sport and a wider understanding of what constitutes 'law' in all of its forms. More importantly, perhaps, Duval states explicitly that rather than being a genuinely self-regulating, fully autonomous transnational legal construct, *lex sportiva* operates in reality in intimate connection with the legal

[14] Fundamental Principle 5. Further, Rule 2(5) requires the IOC to promote its political neutrality and to preserve the autonomy of sport, and 27(2.1(6)) requires similar autonomy of NOCs.

[15] S Weatherill, 'Is there such a thing as EU Sports Law' in R Siekmann and J Soek (eds), *Lex Sportiva: What is Sports Law?* (TMC Asser Press, 2012) 305.

[16] K Foster, 'Global Sports Law Revisited' (2019) 17(1) *Entertainment and Sports Law Journal* 4, at www.entsportslawjournal.com/article/id/851/#B11.

[17] Duval (n 13).

and political contexts in which it is grounded. It is this more nuanced understanding of *lex sportiva* that is used here.

The dual legal-regulatory approach of sport through *lex sportiva* and sports law is replicated in the Olympic legal framework by *lex Olympica* and Olympic Law. The importance of *lex Olympica* in particular is that the norms created by the IOC are often incorporated into the *lex sportiva* of ISFs, or at the very least, seen as the legal benchmarks and standards that are aspired to as ideals. Focussing specifically on the Olympic Charter, Duval analyses its importance within a transnational contractual framework, observing that, 'All the members of the [Olympic Movement] commit to abiding by the Olympic Charter, which stands supreme as an overarching constitution of the *lex sportiva*.'[18] He goes on to state that the Olympic Charter exerts a centripetal force over the ISFs, as well as having an emerging constitutional function in respect of the CAS.[19] In that way, the Olympic legal framework is both integral to and a key influencer of *lex sportiva*, both of which are heavily influenced by European legal cultures as a result of the presence of so many ISFs, including the IOC, in European jurisdictions.

III. THE OLYMPIC LEGAL FRAMEWORK

The law-making capability of the IOC remains an underexplored aspect of transnational sports legal scholarship.[20] As the IOC is neither a nation state, nor a transnational body created by nation states through treaty provisions governed by international law, it has no formal legal sovereignty justifying a direct law-making capability. Despite this lack of a formal jurisdiction, if we remain agnostic to the origins of an entity's law-making powers,[21] then the IOC as a transnational organisation is a creator of legal norms, of *lex Olympica*, which provides it with wide-ranging legal powers derived from, and implemented in accordance with, a series of interlocking contracts with the constituents of the Olympic Movement. This *lex Olympica* has much in common with transnational sports law, with *lex sportiva*, in terms of structure and enforceability, whereas Olympic Law is the manifestation of the legal norms underpinned by *lex Olympica* into regional, national, international and transnational laws. The two interrelated sources of law form the basis of the Olympic legal framework, both of which are distinctly European in origin and culture.

[18] ibid 494.

[19] See further, Duval (n 10) and A Duval, 'The Olympic Charter: A Transnational Constitution Without a State?' (2018) 45 *Journal of Law and Society* 245.

[20] Notable exceptions include: A Mestre, *The Law of the Olympic Games* (TMC Asser Press, 2009); F Latty, *La lex sportiva: recherche sur le droit transnational* (Martinus Nijhoff, 2007) and Le Comité International Olympique et le Droit International (Montchrestien, 2001); and M James and G Osborn, *Olympics Laws. Culture, Values, Tensions* (Routledge, 2024).

[21] Duval (n 10) 836.

Founded in France in 1894 and headquartered in Lausanne, Switzerland, since 1915 following its relocation from Paris, the IOC's relationships with its key stakeholders, the ISFs, NOCs, host city organising committees of the Olympic Games (OCOGs), and the athletes are governed by a complex, interlocking contractual framework. At the apex of this framework sits the Olympic Charter.[22] First published in 1908, the Olympic Charter is the founding and governing document, of which each member of the Olympic Movement must be a signatory. The introduction to the Olympic Charter states that it fulfils three purposes:

1. As a basic instrument of a constitutional nature, it defines the Fundamental Principles and essential values of Olympism.
2. To serve as the statutes for the International Olympic Committee.
3. To define the main reciprocal rights and obligations of the three main constituents of the Olympic Movement: the IOC, the ISFs, and the NOCs, as well as the Organising Committees for the Olympic Games, all of which are required to comply with the Olympic Charter.[23]

The Olympic Charter operates as the key document in the contractual framework that defines the rights and responsibilities of all stakeholders in the Olympic Movement. The Olympic Movement, the IOC, and issues relating to the hosting of the Olympic Games are currently being subjected to unprecedented levels of social, political and legal scrutiny and critical appraisal.[24] As with *lex sportiva* and sports law, there is a bifurcation of regulatory mechanisms applicable to the Olympic Movement: *lex Olympica* is the internal legal framework governed by contract and can be seen as an Olympic-specific form of *lex sportiva*; whereas Olympic Law is the corpus of laws that the IOC requires to be enacted for its benefit, and the benefit of its sponsors, as part of the Olympic Host Contract.

Of particular interest is the interrogation of the normative framework created by the IOC that enables it to create Olympic Law in host countries through the enactment of its own internal legal norms, the *lex Olympica*. This novel approach to law creation through the use of 'forced transplants' has underpinned the creation of national laws in host cities since the Sydney 2000 Games and is grounded in Eurocentric notions of contract law, the protection

[22] IOC Olympic Charter (2021), available at stillmed.olympics.com/media/Document%20 Library/OlympicOrg/General/EN-Olympic-Charter.pdf?_ga=2.73625490.1287301814.1636013909-728463178.1636013909. This is the edition as of 8 August 2021. Previous iterations are available via olympics.com/ioc/olympic-charter.

[23] ibid. It should be noted that although athletes are not considered to be one of the main constituents of the Olympic Movement, they are subject to the requirements of the Olympic Charter, along with additional rights and responsibilities via the Athletes' Declaration: olympics.com/ athlete365/who-we-are/athletes-declaration/#:~:text=The%20Athletes'%20Rights%20and%20 Responsibilities,strong%20athlete%20representative%20Steering%20Committee.

[24] See in particular, J Boykoff, *NOlympians* (Fernwood Publishing, 2020) and B Flyvbjerg, A Budzier and D Lunn, 'Regression to the Tail: Why the Olympics Blow' (2021) 53(2) *Environment and Planning A* 233.

of intellectual property and commercial rights, and comparative legal theory.[25] The interlocking series of contracts that underpins *lex sportiva* is replicated in the governance framework for the key relationships between the IOC, the hosts of the Olympic Games, the NOCs, the ISFs and the athletes. Beyond the broader European influence upon sport outlined above, the issue of Europeanisation is in fact more prevalent and important than perhaps has been acknowledged historically. The importance of this Europeanism is developed further below by highlighting Eurocentric approaches in cases such as *Pechstein and Mutu*,[26] and our case study on ambush marketing, stressing the continuing European influence upon Olympism, *lex Olympica* and Olympic Law.

The importance of analysing the Olympic legal framework is its extent and breadth, and the impact that this can have on the operations of ISFs and NOCs worldwide.[27] This in turn facilitates a range of unique possibilities driven by the importance, and enduring legacy, of *lex Olympica* and Olympic Law. Essentially, as part of the procedure to win and host an edition of the Games, the IOC requires the creation of Olympics-specific municipal, and/or national, laws by host nations. These laws are primarily for the benefit of the IOC and its key stakeholders; the OCOGs and members of the official sponsorship programmes.[28] This indirect legislative capability is different in both form and scope from *lex sportiva* and sports law in that the IOC uses its leverage to insist on contractual relationships that force the creation of law into existence where otherwise it would have no such capacity.[29] Although many ISFs request this level of protection for their own events, the vast majority are denied; only the IOC requires contractual guarantees that such legislative protections will be in place as a pre-condition of being awarded the Games, which can result in a breach of contract and the withdrawal of the invitation to host if they are not provided.

This 'Olympic Law' is the wide-ranging body of laws that is created by national, regional and/or city legislatures. It includes the regulations that are put in place to allow specific traffic lanes between key transport interchanges and Olympic venues, no fly zones over venues, advertising and trading regulations, tax provisions for visiting competing athletes and administrators, amongst many other legislative provisions.[30] These are created to ensure the smooth

[25] See further, James and Osborn (n 1) and M James and G Osborn, 'Pliant Bodies: Generic Event Laws and the Normalisation of the Exceptional' (2017–2018) 12(1) *Australian and New Zealand Sports Law Journal* 77.

[26] *Mutu and Pechstein v Switzerland* (2018) App nos 40575/10 & 67474/10 (ECtHR, 2 October 2018).

[27] Latty (n 20) 251–52 describes the Olympic Charter as, 'constitution mondiale du sport'.

[28] See further, James and Osborn (n 1).

[29] K Foster, 'Is there a Global Sports Law?' (2003) 2 *Entertainment Law* 1 and more generally on the various interpretations of *lex sportiva*, R Siekmann and J Soel (eds), *Lex Sportiva: What is Sports Law?* (TMC Asser Press, 2012).

[30] The authors outline many of these within the context of London 2012 in M James and G Osborn, 'London 2012 and the Impact of the UK's Olympic and Paralympic Legislation: Protecting Commerce or Preserving Culture?' (2011) 74(3) *MLR* 410. As detailed there, further legislative

running of each edition of the Olympics from an operational perspective, and the protection of associated commercial rights and revenue streams from unauthorised association with the Games. In both cases, the legislation is enacted at the express requirement of the IOC. A refusal, or failure to provide the required legislative infrastructure can, at least in theory, lead to the removal of the right to host the Olympics by the IOC.[31]

A. Defining, Developing and Deconstructing *Lex Olympica*

Latty states that *lex Olympica* is the *lex sportiva* originating from the IOC and that the Olympic Charter is at the core of *lex Olympica*.[32] The Olympic Charter is the foundational document of *lex Olympica* and stands at the apex of the contractual framework that governs the relationships within the Olympic Movement. Rule 15 Olympic Charter states that the IOC is an international non-governmental, not-for-profit organisation, of unlimited duration, in the form of an association with the status of a legal person. Its corporate mission, as defined in Rule 2 Olympic Charter, is to promote the Fundamental Principles of Olympism (FPOOs) throughout the world and to provide leadership for the Olympic Movement. Key amongst its roles is to ensure the celebration of the Olympic Games in a manner that is consistent with the Charter's requirements in general and the FPOOs in particular.

Membership of the Olympic Movement requires each sporting body to be a signatory of, and act in compliance with, the Olympic Charter. For ISFs, this is essential as without compliance with the Charter, their sports cannot be considered for inclusion in the Olympic Games. For example, International Rugby League has long hoped to gain acceptance as a full member of the Global Association of International Sports Federations so that it can become a signatory of the Olympic Charter and have Rugby League Nines considered for inclusion in the programme for Brisbane 2032.[33] Once an NOC is a signatory,

requirements include: a prohibition on the unauthorised resale of tickets, and the regulation of street trading, London Olympic Games and Paralympic Games Act 2006, ss 19–21 and London Olympic Games and Paralympic Games (Advertising and Trading) (England) Regulations 2011/2898; income tax exemptions for Olympic accredited personnel, London Olympic Games and Paralympic Games Tax Regulations 2010/2913. Under Reg 5, the list of people who were not ordinarily resident in the UK and thereby capable of claiming tax exempt status under the Regulations included: competitors; media workers; representatives of governing bodies and the IOC; service technicians; team officials; technical officials; and the provision of dedicated traffic lanes, Olympic Route Network Designation Order 2009/1573.

[31] Olympic Charter (n 22) Rule 59(1.6) and s 38(2)(b) Olympic Host Contract – Principles: Games of the XXXIII Olympiad in 2024, available at stillmed.olympic.org/media/Document%20Library/OlympicOrg/Documents/Host-City-Elections/XXXIII-Olympiad-2024/Host-City-Contract-2024-Principles.pdf.

[32] Latty (n 20) 173.

[33] See further M Rowbottom, 'Rugby League Unveils Olympic Ambitions after Brisbane Awarded 2032 Games' (*Inside the Games*, 23 July 2021), www.insidethegames.biz/articles/1110609/troy-grant-irl-brisbane-2032-olympics.

failure to comply with the requirements of the Charter can result in suspension, or expulsion, from the Olympic Movement and the inability to send a delegation to the Olympics.

There continues to be significant disagreement about the definition and scope of *lex Olympica*, which is to some extent a replication of the debate about the meaning of *lex sportiva*. On one side is the claim that *lex Olympica* is central to an understanding of the operation of global sports law itself, whilst on the other is an assumption that it is an autonomous and distinct body of private law.[34] Acknowledging both sides of the argument and utilising a more conciliatory approach, it is possible to provide a more specific definition of *lex Olympica* that encompasses both the operation of Olympic-specific sporting-legal norms and their evolution from a transnational legal space.

Where transnational law embraces all legal rules, independently of their origin, that exceed the framework of a single national legal order, transnational sports law includes in particular the private rules of the ISFs and the IOC.[35] Emerging from this framework, *lex Olympica* can be seen as a specific driver of transnational sports law that provides the normative framework for the Olympic Movement through a series of interlocking contracts in a similar way to how *lex sportiva* operates to regulate the behaviour of the ISFs. Defined in this way, *lex Olympica* is operationalised by the Olympic Charter and the other documents flowing from it,[36] including in particular the Olympic Host Contract, the athlete participation agreement, the Athletes' Declaration, and the IOC's relationships with WADA and the CAS. Thus, the Olympic Charter is the prime contract underpinning all key relationships within the Olympic Movement, from which all other contractual arrangements flow, and is the foundational source of *lex Olympica*.

The interpretation of the Olympic Charter is governed by Swiss law, as applied in the first instance by the IOC Executive Board, on appeal by the CAS (Rules 59–61 Olympic Charter), and ultimately by the Swiss Federal Tribunal. Similarly, the Olympic Host Contract states that:

> The obligations of the Parties under the Olympic Host Contract shall be defined, first, by the terms of the Olympic Host Contract, second, by the terms of the Olympic Charter (…) and, third, by application of the principles of interpretation of Swiss law.[37]

Further, as the ultimate interpretative body for disputes relating to the Charter,[38] the CAS has reserved for itself the general ability to rely upon a range of 'universal legal principles' to assist its panels in forming their opinions. As Faut explains, the fundamental legal and moral principles acknowledged by Swiss

[34] R Siekmann, 'What is Sports Law? Lex Sportiva and Lex Ludica: A Reassessment of Content and Terminology' (2011) *International Sports Law Journal* 3.

[35] F Latty, 'Transnational Sports Law' (2011) 1-2 *International Sports Law Journal* 34, 35.

[36] Mestre (n 20).

[37] Olympic Host Contract (n 31) cl I-1.2.

[38] Olympic Charter (n 22) Rule 61.

law, and therefore expected as a minimum to be used by the CAS in all sports arbitrations are:

> The scope of principles falling under this definition is broad and contains, inter alia, the rule of *pacta sunt servanda* [agreements must be kept], the prohibition of abuse of rights, the prohibition of discrimination, the prohibition of corruption, spoliation and bribery, the need to act in good faith, the prohibition of expropriation without compensation or the protection of incapables.[39]

Alongside the rules requiring a fair hearing, or natural justice, or due process, it is clear that the CAS is reliant on interpretative norms of statutory interpretation, fairness, and contract derived from Eurocentric understandings of what these mean and how they should be applied. So, Europe's influence is *procedural* as well as substantive and cultural. This in turn demonstrates that the interpretation and enforcement of the requirements of the Olympic Charter, and therefore *lex Olympica*, is heavily influenced by European legal traditions of contractual interpretation and dispute resolution. The IOC's location in Switzerland and the governing law of all of its key relationships being Swiss law, any challenges to the creation, substance and interpretation of *lex Olympica* are dominated by European legal thinking.

This Eurocentric approach was confirmed in the *Pechstein* decision,[40] which requires that the CAS must abide by the procedural requirement to provide a fair trial in accordance with Article 6.1 European Convention on Human Rights (ECHR).[41] The importance of this case is that it created the potential to impose ECHR requirements that go beyond the procedural and into the substantive. It demonstrates that the CAS, as the body identified as the sole arbiter of disputes relating to the Olympic Charter, is bound by the ECHR and in future could be expected to interpret the Charter in accordance with the pan-European norms that it protects. This need for ISFs, and by extension the IOC, to adhere to fundamental human rights was reinforced in the *Semenya* decision,[42] where the ECtHR held that the ability to appeal from the CAS to the Swiss Federal Tribunal creates the necessary nexus between the case and the State of Switzerland, bringing its decisions within the jurisdiction of the ECtHR. Thus, *lex Olympica* is grounded in the European legal tradition of the sanctity of contractual relationships, interpretative norms, and human rights. The importance of the Olympic

[39] F Faut, 'The Prohibition of Political Statements by Athletes and its Consistency with Article 10 of the European Convention on Human Rights: Speech is Silver, Silence is Gold? (2014) 14 *International Sports Law Journal* 253, 256.

[40] See D Goertz, 'Recap of the Pechstein Saga: A Hot Potato in the Hands of the Sports Arbitration Community' (*Kluwer Arbitration Blog*, 1 February 2020), arbitrationblog.kluwerarbitration.com/2020/02/01/recap-of-the-pechstein-saga-a-hot-potato-in-the-hands-of-the-sports-arbitration-community/.

[41] See European Court of Human Rights, *Guide on Article 6 of the European Convention on Human Rights, Right to a Fair Trial (Civil Limb)* (updated to 31 August 20222), www.echr.coe.int/documents/guide_art_6_eng.pdf.

[42] *Semenya v Switzerland* (2023) App no 10934/21 (ECtHR 11 July 2023). See further J Cooper, 'Protecting Human Rights in Sport: Is the Court of Arbitration for Sport Up to the Task? A Review of the Decision in Semenya v IAAF' (2023) 2 *International Sports Law Journal* 151.

Charter and *lex Olympica* cannot be understated. As all of the major world governing bodies are signatories of the Charter, *lex Olympica* has a much wider impact than on the IOC alone, and is a major influencer of the ongoing evolution of *lex sportiva*, which in turn cements the importance of European legal culture on both *lex Olympica* and *lex sportiva*.

B. The IOC's Indirect Power to Create Olympic Law

Where *lex Olympica* is the internal legal norms governing the IOC's relationships with the wider Olympic Movement, Olympic Law is the manifestation of the associated requirements of *lex Olympica* transplanted into the applicable legal regimes of host cities, regions and countries. This is most evident when the host is required to enact specific legislation for the benefit of the IOC, the OCOGs, and their commercial partners. This process of 'forced law creation' occurs when the law enacted by a previous host is transplanted from that jurisdiction into the law of a successor host. This unique process provides the IOC with an indirect law-making power by enabling it to have its legal norms enacted by dedicated legislation in the host jurisdiction of each edition of the Olympic Games. It is this forced transplantation into the domestic legal system of the host jurisdiction that causes Olympic Law to fall outside of the usual definitions of both sports law and transnational law, and, it is argued, should be considered to be a new category of each.

Olympic Law can therefore be defined as the body of national laws that is forced into existence by a privately constituted transnational organisation, the IOC, which by using its leverage over the host's legal and political institutions, seeks to bring to life its transnational legal norms, the *lex Olympica*, to protect and enhance its commercial and economic interests, and its revenue streams. The IOC is not discharging its duties in cooperation with the host jurisdictions,[43] but is instead compelling them to act on its behalf. The compulsion to enact this Games-specific legislation is made under the threat of the removal of the invitation to host the Olympics.[44] Whereas in traditional contractual terms, the relationship between the IOC, OCOG, host city and NOC is ostensibly consensual, the reality is a 'take it or leave it' position, with an ever-present threat of the invitation to host the Games being withdrawn for non-compliance, and an implicit threat of legal action being taken against the host for breach of contract where requirements are not met or the Games do not go ahead as planned.[45]

[43] S Hobe, 'Global Challenges to Statehood' (1997) 5 *Indiana Journal of Global Legal Studies* 191, 196.

[44] Olympic Charter (n 22) Rule 36(2).

[45] B Kaplan, 'Why Did the Olympics Go Forward? An Examination of the Host City Contract' (*Brooklyn Sports and Entertainment Law Blog*, 28 July 2021), https://sports-entertainment.brooklaw.edu/sports/why-did-the-olympics-go-forward-an-examination-of-the-host-city-contract/.

The Olympic Host Contract requires the host jurisdiction to guarantee that there are either laws in place already, or that new laws will be enacted, which will provide the required protections and perceived operational necessities associated with hosting the Games. For example, the IOC requires legislative protection for its commercial properties and those of the OCOG from ambush marketing,[46] including in particular the Olympic symbol, emblem, mascots and 'CITY + YEAR' designation (for example, Tokyo 2020).[47] Legislative protection is also required for Rule 50(1) Olympic Charter, which requires that Olympic venues and competition routes, including the surrounding areas and routes to and from key transport interchanges, are 'clean'. Here, 'clean' means that the venues themselves are free from any sponsorship or advertising, and that the surrounding areas are free from all non-official advertising and unlicensed trading. When the need for such legislation was queried in the UK Parliament, the Government's response was simply the truism that the laws had been enacted because the IOC required it as a term of the Host City Contract.[48]

The process by which this forced law creation occurs is through a form of legal diffusion.[49] When normative and legal orders co-exist in the same context of time and space, as is the case with the IOC and the host jurisdiction of an edition of the Olympics, sustained interaction is inevitable. Diffusion of the law takes place when one normative or legal order, system, or tradition influences another in a significant way.[50] Olympic Law is created when the normative framework devised by the IOC requires changes in the domestic law of the host nation. This legal diffusion takes place by means of a legal transplant,[51] by which the norms of the originator jurisdiction, the IOC, are transplanted, either in whole or in part, into that of the new host.

The creation of Olympic Law has two unique elements. First, the diffusion does not involve the wholesale, or partial, transplantation of one country's law to a second jurisdiction.[52] Here, the original normative framework is created at the transnational level by a private, transnational non-state organisation, the IOC, before it becomes state-based law for the first time in the jurisdictions in which the host city is located. Before each subsequent process of diffusion and

[46] London Olympic Games and Paralympic Games Act 2006, s 33 and sch 4.

[47] Olympic Host Contract (n 31) cl 41.

[48] Lord Davies of Oldham, HL Deb, Vol 677, col 249 (11 January 2006). See also the general House of Commons debate at HC Deb, Vol 444, cols 208–213 (21 March 2006), where the scope of, but not the need for, these provisions is discussed. The need for the Olympic-specific legislation is attributed solely to the demands of the IOC as defined in the Host City Contract.

[49] Diffusion is used here as the overarching general term, of which there are many more nuanced variations. For a review of this field of study see in particular, W Twining, 'Diffusion of Law: A Global Perspective' (2004) 49 *Journal of Legal Pluralism* 1 and its sequel, 'Social Science and Diffusion of Law' (2005) 32 *Journal of Law and Society* 203.

[50] Twining (n 49) 'Diffusion of Law' 14.

[51] Contrast the approaches of O Kahn-Freund, 'On Uses and Misuses of Comparative Law' (1974) 37 *MLR* 1 and A Watson, 'Legal Transplants and Law Reform' (1976) 92 *LQR* 79.

[52] Twining (n 49) 'Social Science' 207.

transplantation, the legislation returns to the IOC to be internalised into its own normative framework. The Olympic Law requirements are then updated by the IOC following debriefings provided by the outgoing OCOG, creating new *lex Olympica*, which is then diffused into the Olympic Host Contract before being transplanted into the host jurisdiction of the next edition of the Olympics. Thus, the diffusive effect of this process is a transnationalised phenomenon.

Figure 5.1 The Transnationalised Process of the Creation of Olympic Law from the *Lex Olympica*

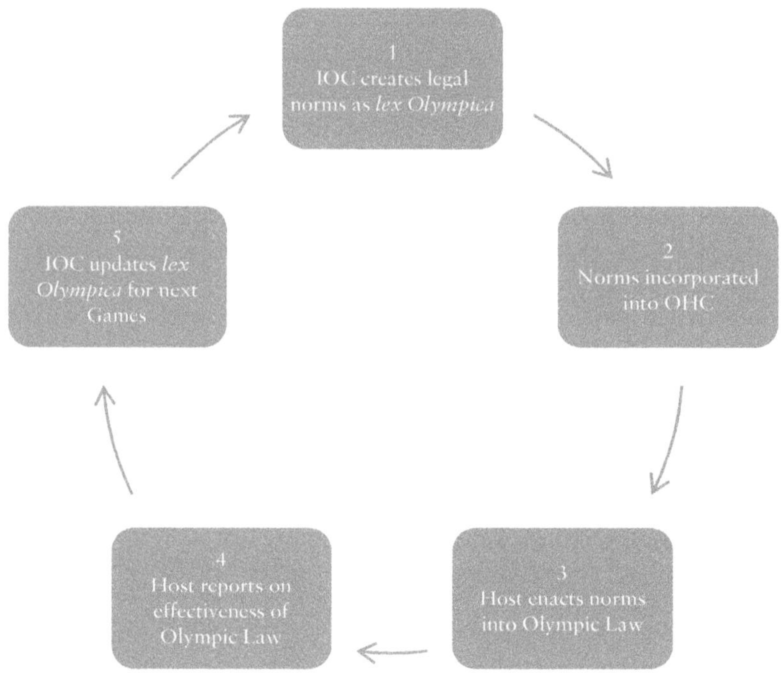

Secondly, the host of the transplanted law is forced to enact legislation for the benefit of the IOC and its affiliates, rather than choosing to do so, under threat of having the right to host the Olympics rescinded. This process of forced diffusion and transplantation of the requirements of *lex Olympica* provides the IOC, albeit indirectly or vicariously, with the formal law-making capability that it otherwise lacks and, 'detaches legally the Olympic city from its host country by creating an ephemeral local legal regime, reminiscent of a special economic zone'.[53]

[53] A Duval, 'From Global City to Olympic City: The Transnational Legal Journey of London 2012' in H Aust and J Nijman (eds), *Research Handbook on International Law and Cities* (Edward Elgar, 2021).

IV. THE CONTINUING EUROPEAN INFLUENCE: THE CASE OF AMBUSH MARKETING

In its most recent incarnation, the mission of the IOC includes a specific requirement to oppose any political or commercial abuse of sport and athletes.[54] This opposition to commercial 'abuse' has manifested itself in two distinct ways. First, growing out of the IOC's original requirement that all participants in the Olympics must be amateur, the previous iterations of Rule 40 have attempted to restrict athletes' ability to exploit commercially their participation in the Games.[55] Since the relaxation of the rules governing amateurism in the 1986 version of the Olympic Charter, the restrictions now found in Rule 40 Olympic Charter have morphed into a means of protecting one of IOC's key revenue streams: The Olympic Partnership (TOP) programme. Although there has been some relaxation in the strictures of Rule 40's application following the Deutscher Olympischer Sportbund case,[56] Rule 40 continues to operate, in effect, to restrict athletes from promoting themselves freely in ways that the IOC sees as being in competition with the official sponsorship programmes. In other words, the athletes are prohibited from operating commercially on threat of disqualification and withdrawal of Olympic accreditation, where they are considered to be ambushing the official sponsors of specific editions of the Games and/or diluting the value of the TOP programme.

Secondly, the IOC has shown an increasing determination to protect the TOP sponsors, and the edition-specific sponsors of each Olympic Games, from ambush marketing more generally. Where Rule 50(1) Olympic Charter requires all Olympic venues to be advertising free, specific legislation to guarantee not only clean venues, but a regulated space around those Olympic sites, was introduced at Sydney 2000.[57] The perceived success of the legislation at Sydney 2000, and later editions of the Games, saw more innovative marketing techniques developed by ambushers. This in turn resulted in a step change in the protections offered by the UK Government for London 2012 and the creation of a new intellectual property right, a super-intellectual property right:[58] the association right. This highly unusual level of protection for an event has been developed incrementally by the IOC and implemented unquestioningly by subsequent hosts.

[54] Olympic Charter (n 22) r 2.11.

[55] See further, A Geurin and E McNary, 'Athletes as Ambush Marketers? An Examination of Rule 40 and Athletes' Social Media Use during the 2016 Rio Olympic Games' (2021) 21 *European Sport Management Quarterly* 116 and James and Osborn (n 20).

[56] Bundeskartellamt Commitment Decision (Case B226/17) held that Rule 40 operated as an abuse of a dominant position by the Deutscher Olympischer Sportbund and the IOC. See further, J de Werra, 'Athletes & Social Media: What Constitutes Ambush Marketing in the Digital Age? The Case of Rule 40 of the Olympic Charter' in T Trigo et al, *Vers les sommets du droit: "Liber amicorum" pour Henry Peter* (Schulthess éditions romandes, 2019) 3.

[57] James and Osborn (n 25).

[58] M James and G Osborn, 'Guilty by Association: Olympic Law and the IP Effect' (2013) 2 *Intellectual Property Quarterly* 97.

This approach to protecting Olympic revenue streams by means of an association right will be analysed to demonstrate how European and Anglocentric contract law and theories of intellectual property protectionism have shaped the development of both *lex Olympica* and Olympic Law.

Modern intellectual property law is based on theories originating in Europe, and developed further by theorists in the United States of America, in particular, and diffused at the transnational level through the World Intellectual Property Organisation (WIPO).[59] Although intellectual property rights are national, or territorial, in nature, they are informed by global trends and developments. This has enabled protected properties to be moved and traded internationally, and protected transnationally. During the nineteenth century, a number of mainly European countries entered two multinational conventions: the Paris Convention and the Berne Convention.[60] The primary effect of these two Conventions was to offer the same protections across largely European signatory nations. This had the effect of harmonising at an early stage the approaches of the signatories to the protection of intellectual endeavours, whilst leaving individual states to enact their own specific legislative provisions. A variety of international treaties have followed.[61] The theoretical and philosophical underpinnings of these intellectual property laws and approaches are very much of European origin, evolving from and developing the work of theorists such as John Locke and Jeremy Bentham.[62] The role of Europe is further embedded, when its influence is seen in a broader sense, because of the harmonising effects of the international treaties promoted by WIPO, which is itself based in Switzerland.

Following the perceived success of the extended 'clean' areas around Olympic venues at Sydney 2000,[63] the IOC began to require as a matter of course that legislative protection against ambush marketing was provided by the host nation. This resulted in the step change in the scope of the protections offered by the UK Government at London 2012. Whereas previous legislative restrictions had focused on preventing non-official sponsors from advertising around Olympic venues, the London Olympic and Paralympic Games Act 2006 created a novel form of intellectual property, the London Olympic Association Right, which extended traditional notions of intellectual property law. Thus, an Olympic-specific solution was created from Anglo-European traditions on how to protect the goodwill inherent in a sporting mega event that could be incorporated into the *lex Olympica* and transplanted into the national law of host nations.

[59] See generally here works such as L Bently and B Sherman, 6th edn, *Intellectual Property Law* (Oxford University Press, 2022).

[60] The Paris Convention for the Protection of Industrial Property 1883 and the Berne Convention for the Protection of Literary and Artistic works 1886.

[61] See Bently and Sherman (n 59) ch 1, which covers the impacts of WIPO, the General Agreement on Tariffs and Trade (GATT) system, and the Agreement on Trade-Related Aspects of Intellectual Property Rights (TRIPS).

[62] See, eg, E Hettinger, 'Justifying Intellectual Property' (1989) 18(1) *Philosophy and Public Affairs* 31.

[63] James and Osborn (n 25).

A. Ambush Marketing – What is it and why is it Problematic?

As the IOC became increasingly aware of the value of its commercial and intellectual property rights, it began to protect them more proactively. The Olympic Partnership sponsorship programme began in 1985, restricting dramatically who could use the Olympic Symbols and associated iconography identified in Rules 7–14 Olympic Charter. Alongside this was the IOC's increasing concern that the value of its commercial and intellectual property rights could be undermined by ambush marketing.

Whereas Rule 50(1) and its predecessors require advertising-free, clean stadiums, little attention had been paid to what might be happening outside of, and along the main transport routes to, Olympic venues. After Atlanta 1996, the IOC took a much more sophisticated approach to protecting its revenue streams, particularly those driven by sponsorship fees, throughout Olympic host cities. As is the case with all ambush marketing, although such practices may be problematic from an economic, sociological and ethical perspective, there is nothing inherently wrong in law with running a rival advertising campaign in public or media spaces, provided that the ambusher does not use any protected intellectual property and is not claiming an official association with the event. In intellectual property law terms, providing that the ambush is not confusing people to think that they are an official sponsor, nor passing off that they are formally associated with the event, then the event organiser has no legal recourse against the ambusher. This lacuna in the protection afforded by intellectual property law would require specific legislation to be implemented to prevent, and ultimately criminalise, ambush marketing.

Initially, the focus of the legislation required by the IOC was to ensure that the Olympic venues and their immediate environs were clean, which had been one of the key problems at Atlanta. In other words, there was a particular need to protect the Games from intrusive ambush marketing, where ambushers access areas where advertising is prohibited or highly regulated, as not even the TOP sponsors are allowed to advertise within an Olympic venue.[64] The legislation required to protect Sydney 2000 prevented unauthorised advertising in designated areas in and around Olympic venues, providing a protected environment of up to 1500m around each.[65] The perceived success of this approach has seen these protections developed incrementally at each edition of the Games since. However, as ambushers became increasingly sophisticated, it became clear that a more robust response was required to protect the official sponsors.

[64] The only branding seen at Olympic events is that on the clothing and equipment used by athletes and officials and, where needed, on the official timing devices. See further Olympic Charter (n 22) r 50 and its byelaws.

[65] Sydney 2000 Games (Indicia and Images) Protection Act 1996 (Cth), State Environmental Planning Policy No 38 – Olympic Games and Related Projects (NSW) cl 11C, and Olympic Arrangements Act 2000 (NSW).

Ambush marketing is seen by many event and competition organisers as a direct challenge to the value of the commercial rights owned by sports bodies by undermining official exclusivity arrangements with official sponsors. These exclusive arrangements create scarcity that ensures (at least a perception of) a high commercial value to the official sponsor, which in turn enables the rights owner to demand high fees to associate with an event. Any dilution of that exclusivity by multiple brands claiming, or appearing to claim, to be associated with the event can lead to a significant diminution of the value of the official right to be associated with an event and its iconic logos and branding.[66]

Essentially, the key to an ambushing marketing strategy is that it offers brands an alternative, and cheaper, way of capitalising on the increased public attention on a specific event, team, athlete or brand. Traditionally it was seen as a detrimental or predatory activity, and often described as parasitical, but the forms and types of ambush have evolved over time. The problem faced by rights owners and event organisers is that unless the ambusher actually uses copyrighted or trademarked materials, or claims to be an official sponsor when they are not, there is in general no legal recourse for a well-thought out marketing campaign that undermines that of the official sponsors. What is striking over recent Olympic cycles is that technological and other societal changes have facilitated multiple new methods for potential infractions of this amorphous right to associate with an event. Discussing the thematic space traditionally reserved for Olympic sponsors, McKelvey, Grady and Moorman note:

> [as] the Olympic marketing and sponsorship landscape has shifted, the exponential growth of 'social media has helped create the perfect storm to fuel ambush marketing at an amplified level' and further enable non-official sponsors to activate marketing campaigns in the Olympic thematic space.[67]

Ambush marketing is a highly contentious term, with little agreement on either its definition or its commercial, legal, ethical, and moral acceptability. Coined as a term in the 1980s,[68] its original conception was fairly narrow and focussed on activity conducted by 'non-sponsors' that impacted on 'official sponsors'. Nufer noted that there were three basic objectives to ambush marketing: *economic* (increased profit and greater brand awareness); *psychological* (generating greater attention on and awareness of a brand); and *competition* (weakening of official sponsors' relationships with the event).[69]

[66] Global Language Monitor, 'Official Ambush Marketing Rankings for the Tokyo 2020 Olympics', https://languagemonitor.com/olympic-games/5584/.

[67] S McKelvey, J Grady and A Moorman, 'Ambush Marketing and Rule 40 for Tokyo 2020: A Shifting Landscape for Olympic Athletes and their Sponsors' (2021) 31 Journal *of Legal Aspects of Sport* 95.

[68] P Johnson, 'Defining the Indefinable: Legislating for "Ambush Marketing"' (2020) 15(5) *Journal of Intellectual Property Law and Practice* 313.

[69] G Nufer, 'Ambush Marketing in Sports: An Attack on Sponsorship or Innovative Marketing?' (2016) 6(4) *Sports, Business and Management: An international Journal* 476, and see generally Geurin and McNary (n 55) 116.

The need to examine the implications of ambush marketing in terms of the power afforded to a private body, the IOC, over elected governments was suggested by Ellis, Scassa and Seguin in their 2011 review, as was the need for further research on this topic.[70] We addressed their concerns in our article for *Legal Studies*,[71] which examined the phenomenon of ambush marketing through the lens of legal transplant, making an initial attempt at a legal definition of the concept. Ambush marketing is, however, a broad and amorphous concept; Zhou noted that a formal definition of ambush marketing is problematic because there is little consensus as to its precise meaning and ambit.[72] Chadwick and Burton initially described ambush marketing as:

> [a] form of associative marketing which is designed by an organisation to capitalize on the awareness, attention, goodwill and other benefits generated by having an association with an event or property, without the organisation having any official or direct connection to that event or property.[73]

They noted that ambush marketing had become an increasingly attractive strategy for non-sponsors as marketers recognised the possibilities, and cost savings, that it afforded. Concomitantly, its increased use and sophistication became a more direct challenge for event organisers and their official sponsors to combat. Chadwick and Burton's original typology identifies three general tropes of ambush marketing, with sub-categories of how each operated in practice: direct ambush activities (including predatory ambushing, coat tail ambushing and property infringement); associative ambush activities (including sponsor self-ambushing, associative ambushing, distractive ambushing, values ambushing, insurgent ambushing and parallel property ambushing); and incidental ambush marketing (unintentional ambushing and saturation ambushing).

They refined their typology further in 2018, when three strategic approaches to ambush marketing were defined: incursion; obtrusion; and association.[74] Incursive ambushing is the deliberate activity of a non-sponsor that is designed to threaten, undermine, or distract attention from an event and/or official sponsors of the event. Obtrusive ambushing is the prominent or undesirably visible (according to the rights holder) marketing activities of non-sponsors that distract from an official event sponsorship. Associative ambushing is the attempt by a brand that has no official or legal right of association with an event to imply or create an allusion that it has an official connection with that event.

[70] See D Ellis, T Scassa and B Seguin, 'Framing Ambush Marketing as a Legal Issue: An Olympic Perspective' (2011) 14 *Sport Management Review* 297.

[71] James and Osborn (n 1).

[72] W Zhou, 'Responses of Chinese Laws to Ambush Marketing' (2018) 9(2) *Asian Journal of Law and Economics* 2017–0015.

[73] S Chadwick and N Burton, 'The Evolving Sophistication of Ambush Marketing: A Typology of Strategies' 53(6) *Thunderbird International Business Review* 709, 714.

[74] N Burton and S Chadwick, 'Ambush Marketing is Dead, Long Live Ambush Marketing' (2018) 58(3) *Journal of Advertising Research* 282, 289 et seq.

From a legal and regulatory perspective, the key distinction is between intrusive ambushing (incursive or obtrusive), where the ambusher is impinging on the spaces reserved for the event and/or its official sponsors, and associative ambush marketing, where the ambusher is suggesting a formal link with the event. Whichever aspect of ambush marketing is in focus, the key is that rights holders, or event organisers, see the rights linked to their events being eroded or diminished by the ambush and want these protected.

In terms of how ambush marketing has been combatted, Burton and Bradish present an important distinction between reactive and proactive measures.[75] Reactive measures include naming and shaming, a somewhat ineffective tactic, and emphasising enforcing events' intellectual property rights and associated legal remedies. As they put it:

> Ultimately, the reactive tactics employed by rights holders have offered little protection from ambush marketers. Given the short timeframes during which most sporting events take place, and the often quick, timely campaigns utilised by ambushers to maximise their association with an event, lengthy legal proceedings and *ex post facto* public relations campaigns provide little protection for sponsors.[76]

Accordingly, more proactive measures have been sought by the mega sporting events that have sufficient leverage to demand additional protections from ambush marketing. These have included creating specified spatial and temporal event zones that are regulated by event specific, anti-ambush marketing legislation. The key problem associated with such proactive measures is the need to provide a formal and legally robust definition of ambush marketing. For example, section 12(4) UEFA European Championship (Scotland) Act 2020 defines ambush marketing as, '[an] act or a series of acts intended specifically to advertise within an event zone at a prohibited time – (a) a good or service, or (b) a person who provides a good or service'. Similar definitions can be found in the UK legislation developed for the Glasgow 2014 and Birmingham 2022 editions of the Commonwealth Games,[77] all of which have evolved from the London 2012 legislation examined below.

Additional proactive approaches can be found in event tickets' terms and conditions. For example, the Ticket Terms and Conditions for entry to any event at the Birmingham 2022 Commonwealth Games adopted the following definition:

> 'Ambush Marketing' means any activity by which a person purports to take advantage of the benefits, goodwill or footfall associated with and generated by the Games, including without limitation the unauthorised use of a Ticket as a prize or gift or in a lottery, raffle, sweepstake, fundraiser or competition or for any other promotional,

[75] N Burton and C Bradish, 'Commercial Rights Management in Post-Legislative Olympic Sponsorship' (2019) 9(2) *Sport, Business and Management: An International Journal* 201.

[76] ibid 204.

[77] Glasgow Commonwealth Games Act 2008 (Games Association Right) Order 2009/1969 and Birmingham Commonwealth Games Act 2020 ss 3–9.

> advertising or commercial purpose and/or any other activity by a person not authorised by Birmingham 2022 which: (a) associates the person with the Games; or (b) exploits the publicity or goodwill of the Games; or (c) has the effect (in the reasonable opinion of Birmingham 2022) of conferring the status of a Commercial Partner on a person who is not a Commercial Partner or otherwise diminishing the status of any Commercial Partner.[78]

Thus, a variety of approaches have been adopted in an attempt to mitigate the effects of ambush marketing on official sponsors and, ultimately, on the value of these association rights. In terms of legislative responses, as Johnson notes, whilst it may be the case that laws are required, this extension of law should not be undertaken blindly.[79] Not only is ambush marketing difficult to define in a way that is clear and understandable to non-sponsors and event attendees, it also runs the risk of being interpreted by its enforcers in a disproportionately restrictive manner.

By London 2012 it had become much more difficult to ambush an event by intrusion, requiring increasingly subtle and nuanced advertising campaigns if an association with the Games was going to be attempted. Sections 19-31E and schedules 3 and 4 of the London Olympic Games and Paralympic Games Act 2006 (LOGPGA 2006) were enacted in an attempt to prohibit all unauthorised associations with London 2012 by means of ambush marketing and street trading. Where American Express' infamous 1994 campaign that claimed that, 'You don't need a visa to go to Norway …' is the paradigm associative ambush pre-London, as the law came in, the ground rules were set for what could, and what could not, be lawful ambush marketing.

B. London Olympic Games and Paralympic Games Act 2006: A Step Change against Ambush Marketing

Much of the Olympic iconography is protected in the UK by the Olympic Symbol etc (Protection) Act 1995 (OSPA 1995). Section 1 OSPA 1995 creates the Olympic Association Right (OAR). In its original form, the OAR conferred on the British Olympic Association (BOA) the exclusive right to use the Olympic symbol, the Olympic motto or any of the following protected words: Olympiad, Olympian, Olympic and their plurals.[80] Infringement of the OAR, as defined in section 3 OSPA 1995, occurred where an ambusher either (a) used a representation of the Olympic symbol, the Olympic motto or a protected word, or (b) used a representation of something so similar to the Olympic symbol or the Olympic motto *as to be likely to create in the public mind an association with it*.[81] It is

[78] See 'Notices and Policies' at www.birmingham2022.com/terms-and-conditions/ticketing/.
[79] Johnson (n 68).
[80] OSPA 1995, ss 3 and 18(2)(a).
[81] ibid s 3(1).

this concept of association, rather than use of a protected symbol, or the creation of confusion in the minds on the public, that creates the novel extension of intellectual property law.

Under section 6 OSPA 1995, infringement of the OAR is actionable by the BOA, which can seek relief by way of damages, injunctions, accounts or any other remedy that is available in respect of the infringement of a property right. Where the OAR is infringed with a view to making a gain to the infringer or another, and/or a loss to another in commercial circumstances, then a criminal offence can be committed under section 8 OSPA 1995.

The LOGPGA 2006 made three specific changes to the framework of protections available for the symbols and words most closely associated with the Olympic Movement in general and London 2012 in particular. First, for the period of its existence, the London Organising Committee of the Olympic Games (LOCOG) was granted proprietor status in respect of the OAR. Secondly, the scope of the OAR was increased significantly by extending it to cover 'a representation of something so similar to the Olympic symbol or the Olympic motto as to be likely to create in the public mind an association with the Olympic Games or the Olympic movement'.[82] Thirdly, there was the creation of a London 2012-specific association right: the London Olympic Association Right (LOAR).[83]

The LOAR, for which the LOCOG was granted the exclusive power to grant authorisations, was created by section 33 LOPGA 2006 and defined in schedule 4 of the Act. Going much further than the OAR, infringement of the LOAR is defined in schedule 4, paragraph 2 as when, in the course of a trade or business, *any representation of any kind* is made in a manner that is likely to suggest to the public that there is an association between the business and London 2012. When determining whether an association with London 2012 was being made, account could be taken of the use of the following specific words or phrases: Group A – games, Two Thousand and Twelve, 2012, and twenty twelve; Group B – gold, silver, bronze, London, medals, sponsor, and summer. If a word or phrase in Group A was used in combination with either another word or phrase in Group A, or with a word in Group B, then this would be indicative of an attempt at making an unlawful association with London 2012.[84] The same civil actions and remedies were available for infringement of the LOAR as are for the OAR.

The creation of these association rights is highly contentious. Writing before the Games, Harris et al analysed this development with some trepidation, particularly its extraordinarily wide-ranging scope, and that it appeared

[82] ibid s 3(1)(b).

[83] For more detail on this, see V Horsey, R Montagnon and J Smith, 'The London Olympics 2012 – Restrictions, Restrictions, Restrictions' (2012) 7(10) *Journal of Intellectual Property Law and Practice* 715.

[84] LOPGA 2006, sch 4, para 3.

to monopolise anything that attempted to make any connection with London 2012:

> The protection of a blanket 'association' right strikes fear into brand owners and lawyers alike. This is because, in the absence of definable boundaries, there is no way of saying what will, or will not, fall within the legislation. That is, until we see how the wording of the 2006 Act will be interpreted by the courts. Certainly, it seems likely that High Court judges may see fit to fetter the broad protection currently offered by the legislation.[85]

The creation of the LOAR, and the amendments to the OAR, evidence a further development of traditional protections offered by intellectual property law. Instead of simply prohibiting the use of the specific symbols, words and phrases most obviously connected to the Olympics, the LOAR and amended OAR extend significantly the situations in which an ambusher can be held to have made an unlawful association with the Games. By extending the protections offered by traditional concepts of copyright and trademark to merely creating a perception of association with London 2012, the Olympic Games and/or the Olympic Movement, the LOAR and OAR can be seen as a new category of intellectual property, or super-IP.[86] There is no need to prove intent to infringe, or to create confusion in the minds of the public. Instead, the LOAR is infringed on the suggestion of an unlawful association, and the OAR where it is 'likely' to create in the public mind a commercial, structural or contractual 'association' with the Games.

Chavanat and Desbordes provide a useful review of the ambushes that occurred at London 2012,[87] noting that the restrictions were the most rigorous and far reaching in Olympic history, at least up to that point. The instances of ambushing that they identify demonstrate a very high degree of sophistication, providing examples of each of incursive, obtrusive and associative ambushing that was able to subvert the spirit, if not the letter of the law. Although no legal actions for infringement of either the OAR or LOAR were pursued, a heavy-handed cease and desist approach was taken in respect of anyone perceived to be making any kind of an association with the Games without the appropriate consent.[88]

The UK's approach to preventing ambush marketing at London 2012 was considered a success, with subsequent editions of the Games building on it as part of their own anti-ambushing strategies that underpin the legal guarantees

[85] P Harris, S Schmitz and R O'Hare, 'Ambush Marketing and London 2012: A Golden Opportunity for Advertising, or Not?' (2009) 20(3) *Entertainment Law Review* 74, 75–76. See also James and Osborn (n 30).

[86] James and Osborn (n 58).

[87] N Chavanat and M Desbordes, 'Towards the Regulation and Restriction of Ambush Marketing? The First Truly Social and Digital Mega Sports Event: Olympic Games, London 2012' (2014) 15(3) *International Journal of Sports Marketing and Sponsorship* 2.

[88] BBC News, 'Sausages Exploit Olympic Logo' (31 August 2007), news.bbc.co.uk/1/hi/england/dorset/6972224.stm.

provided for in the OHC. To date, no challenges to any of the anti-ambush marketing provisions have been recorded. The IOC does not want to risk the legislation being struck out for being too vague, or an infringement of commercial free speech.[89] The ambushers do not want to establish that the restrictions are lawful and are instead prepared to continue to push the boundaries of the definitions provided in the legislation, with the result that the UK's novel approach to anti-ambush marketing legislation has influenced significantly the development of subsequent versions of both *lex Olympica* and Olympic Law.

V. CONCLUSION

This chapter has explored the influence of European legal culture upon a specific aspect of *lex Olympica* and Olympic Law, and further illustrated that the European influence is not only substantive, but procedural and cultural. Both *lex Olympica* and Olympic Law are clearly influenced by Anglo-European legal thinking and creative legislative developments, in this case intellectual property law, contract law, and alternative dispute mechanisms, and the ways that they have been used to develop a framework of protection for the IOC's revenue streams.[90] The creation and operationalisation of the association right is an extension of Anglo-European notions of intellectual property law that has resulted in the creation of a new form of intellectual property right that extends much more widely than traditional copyright and trademark law, and goes beyond the protections offered by the action in passing off.

Further, we have illustrated that the leverage that the IOC is able to utilise can force the creation of legal and regulatory provisions that operate to the benefit of itself, local organising committees and their sponsors. We have previously argued that this leverage is often unchecked and that the cyclical process of Olympic Law creation is in need of rethinking or recalibration. Further to this this we would add that the IOC has missed an opportunity by its insistence on a rigid and all-encompassing approach to regulating the exploitation of its commercial rights. If the IOC was instead to take a more nuanced and relational approach, then a genuinely novel, transnational framework could be developed that is more inclusive of non-European approaches. More broadly, it ensures that both *lex Olympica* and Olympic Law continue to be defined and influenced by euro legal principles, theories and laws at the expense of developing a genuinely novel, transnational approach.

[89] K de Beer, 'Let the Games Begin – Ambush Marketing and Freedom of Speech' (2012) 6 *Human Rights and International Legal Discourse* 284.

[90] For the operation of the law at recent Games see: A Epstein, 'The Ambush at Rio' (2017) 16 *John Marshall Review of Intellectual Property Law* 350 and D Fields and A Muller, 'Running Rings around Ambush Marketing: How the Tokyo Games Propose to Prevent Misuse of the Olympic and Paralympic Brands' (2020) 31(7) *Entertainment Law Review* 237.

Lex Olympica continues to operate as a major influencer of *lex sportiva*. Where the Olympic Movement leads, other ISFs and event organisers seek to follow. This in turn creates an event legacy that remains unacknowledged by scholars of mega sporting events.[91] The legal legacy can be seen in three specific manifestations. First, through the mechanism of Olympic-specific forced transplants. Secondly, through the recycling and updating of Olympic-specific legislation in former hosts, as has occurred in particular in the UK in respect of the Commonwealth Games. Thirdly, by similar protections being demanded by, though usually denied to, other ISFs. The distinction between the responses of governments to the IOC and to other ISFs demanding similar protections is one of leverage; the IOC is (currently) able to exert its leverage over governments wanting to host the Games by insisting on these legislative changes being a term of the Olympic Host Contract, whereas other ISFs rarely have the same level of leverage and must either accept the refusal or move the event elsewhere. With the next two editions of the Olympics located in Europe, in Paris in 2024 and Milan-Cortina in 2026, the power and influence of European and Anglo-European legal cultures on the ongoing evolution of *lex Olympica* and *lex sportiva* will continue to shape the sporting-legal system for the foreseeable future.

[91] J Grix (ed), *Leveraging Mega-Event Legacies* (Routledge, 2018).

6

Who Regulates the Regulators? How European Union Regulation and Regulatory Institutions May Shape the Regulation of the Football Industry Globally

CHRISTOPHER A FLANAGAN

I. REGULATORY AUTONOMY

'And what on earth has this all got to do with European competition law?'

– Gianni Infantino (2006)[1]

A. Introduction

It has been said that 'association football is generally accepted as the world's most popular spectator sport'.[2] In common with most sports, its rule-making structures have generally been defined by the pursuit of autonomy; that is to say that football's governing bodies, in common with most sports governing bodies (SGBs), have defended their right to conceptualise, design, and execute their own rules and regulatory frameworks. This has carried with it a degree of friction where conflicts have arisen between prevailing background laws and the policy objectives of those SGBs. Football, as a sport of cultural and financial significance, has been central to that friction; with an epicentre forming in Europe, wherein SGBs have 'lobbied hard' for the recognition of the specificity of sport

[1] G Infantino, 'Meca-Medina: A Step Backwards for the European Sports Model and the Specificity of Sport?' (UEFA.com).
[2] T Jewell, 'Major League Soccer in The USA' in J Goddard and P Sloane (eds), *Handbook on the Economics of Professional Football* (Edward Elgar Publishing, 2014) 351.

in instruments of European Union (EU) law.[3] Overtly, this appears to signify a relationship of discomfort between SGBs and those rule-making bodies able to exert a degree of control over the limits of SGBs' regulatory autonomy. However, recent developments show that the relationship between SGBs and EU law is not exclusively antipathetic; a key SGB having subsumed into its regulatory ecosystem aspects of secondary EU legislation (specifically regulations and directives). Football's apex regulator, the *Fédération Internationale de Football Association* (FIFA), has made moves towards harmonisation with external regulatory measures in respect of data protection, and perhaps more strikingly, in the inception of a new clearing house for international player transfers, has moved towards the ambit of secondary EU law. This not only shows the influence of EU law; it brings FIFA's activities within the oversight and direct regulatory competence of regulatory bodies outside the sports ecosystem. This chapter will take as case studies both FIFA's approach to data protection and its approach to establishing an international player transfer clearing house. Both of these measures are influenced by, and in many respects defined by, EU law. Beyond the hegemonic influence on FIFA's own regulatory approach, this chapter will consider how the movement of the organisation of professional football towards external regulators in the cases of data protection and the centralised clearing and settlement of player transfers may influence football's historically (mostly) autonomous systems, and what that says of the influence of EU law on sport globally.[4]

By examining sources of regulatory influence on sport, and in particular the influence of EU law on the regulation of football, this chapter will explore the question: Who regulates the regulators? Each of FIFA's data protection and clearing regimes reveals a fact pattern that might be considered surprising in view of the traditionally held ideal of an SGB fiercely defending itself against the 'interference' of EU law: an observable 'Brussels Effect'[5] made manifest in global football, under which FIFA adopts and imposes EU legal regulatory systems, directly and indirectly, into jurisdictions outside the direct ambit of EU regulatory competence. Not only does FIFA's introduction of rules based systems of data privacy, and centrally controlled player transfer financial distributions, demonstrate how EU law has come to influence the internal rules of sport, it also highlights (and in the case of the FIFA clearing house, directly introduces) an EU-level regulatory oversight and influence on football and its governing bodies.

B. Regulators

Before exploring influences on the regulation of football, it is helpful to give a framework to the concept of 'regulation'. Morgan and Yeung describe regulation

[3] A Duval (2013) 'Lex Sportiva: A Playground for Transnational Law' (2013) 19 *European Law Journal* 6, 822–42.

[4] For discussion, see section I.C.

[5] Being the 'EU's unilateral ability to regulate the global marketplace', A Bradford, *The Brussels Effect: How the European Union Rules the World* (Oxford University Press, 2020) Preface.

as 'notoriously difficult to define with clarity and precision',[6] but draw on Hood et al's explanation of regulation as involving a capacity for: (i) standard setting; (ii) information gathering; and (iii) behaviour modification.[7] Similarly, Baldwin et al[8] and Black[9] define regulation as 'the intentional use of authority to affect behaviour' by reference to information gathering and behaviour modification tools.

As regulation has matured, both as praxis and as a field of academic discourse, so have the activities within its purview. As Baldwin et al explain, 'regulation has become a much wider concern than an interest in governing by rule'.[10] Notwithstanding this wider view of regulation,[11] the systems within and supervising professional football have tended to sit within the traditional paradigm of a regulator, imposing traditional archetypes of regulation, by 'command and control'.[12]

Assessing FIFA's regulation of the international transfer market in football players against Hood et al's three-point explanation of regulation, we can see that FIFA has the capacity to set standards, specifically by reference to its Regulations on the Status and Transfer of Players (RSTP) and the guidance notes thereto issued by FIFA;[13] it has information gathering powers under the system of regulatory oversight and enforcement it has created, and more specifically pursuant to the implementation of its 'Transfer Matching System' (TMS);[14] and modifying the behaviour of the subjects of its regulatory measures both through the regulations (including the RSTP and the FIFA Clearing House Regulations) and through enforcement and disciplinary measures in instances of breach as well as through its Disciplinary Committee and the private system of dispute resolution it facilitates through its Football Tribunal system.[15]

[6] B Morgan and K Yeung, *An Introduction To Law And Regulation – Texts And Materials* (Cambridge University Press, 2012).

[7] See C Hood, H Rothstein and R Baldwin, *The Government of Risk: Understanding Risk Regulation Regimes*, 2nd edn (Oxford University Press, 2004).

[8] R Baldwin, M Cave and M Lodge, *The Oxford Handbook of Regulation* (Oxford University Press, 2010).

[9] J Black, 'Decentring Regulation: Understanding the Role of Regulation and Self-Regulation in a 'Post-Regulatory World' (2001) 54 *Current Legal Problems* 1, 103–46.

[10] Baldwin, Cave and Lodge (n 8) 6.

[11] Consider, for example, the popular rejection of the putative 'European Super League', see 'How Europe Has Reacted To Super League' (*BBC Sport*, 19 April 2021), www.bbc.co.uk/sport/football/56801498.

[12] 'Command and control' systems having been 'the traditional starting point of both regulators and regulatory scholars', Baldwin, Cave and Lodge (n 8) 8.

[13] Namely, the FIFA, *Commentary on the Regulations on the Status and Transfer of Players*, Edition 2021 (2021), https://digitalhub.fifa.com/m/346c4da8d810fbea/original/Commentary-on-the-FIFA-Regulations-on-the-Status-and-Transfer-of-Players-Edition-2021.pdf.

[14] For information on the FIFA Transfer Matching System and its role in the regulation of the international transfer market, see K Morris and B Lysaght, 'How FIFA TMS Investigations Increase Transparency and Accountability in International Football Transfers (*LawInSport*, 13 June 2016), www.lawinsport.com/topics/item/how-fifa-tms-investigations-increase-transparency-and-accountability-in-international-football-transfers.

[15] Instituted pursuant to Article 54 of the FIFA Statutes. For an overview of the FIFA Dispute Resolution Chamber, see F de Weger, *The Jurisprudence of the FIFA Dispute Resolution Chamber* (TMC Asser Press, 2016).

From this we can conclude that FIFA, and indeed most SGBs, do perform a regulatory function. One aspect of that regulatory function that separates sport from other regulated industries is that SGBs do not generally derive their power from national laws or international treaties, whereas other command-and-control supervisory regulators of the independent administrative kind more commonly derive power from state-based laws within a public law framework.[16] It has been stated that '[n]either FIFA nor UEFA have immanent regulatory power', and '"well established" that sports governing bodies derive their regulatory power as a function of a complex contractual or quasi-contractual nexus to which other participants in football submit'.[17] This is in contrast to the typically conceived regulator, either in the case of industry specific regulation (such as the regulators of financial services or the environment) or cross-industry regulators of specific risks (such as the regulators of competition or data protection), whose creation and powers are typically rooted in national (or as the case may be, international treaty-based) laws.[18]

Occasionally, activities will come within the purview of more than one competent regulator. For example, a data leak at a financial institution may attract regulatory scrutiny from a financial services regulator as well as a data protection regulator,[19] or spheres of competence may be shared and enforcement co-ordinated between regulatory bodies.[20]

[16] As noted above, the sources of power and constitutional composition of regulatory authorities are complex. For a survey of various independent administrative authorities, see R Caranta, M Andenas and D Fairgrieve, *Independent Administrative Authorities* (British Institute of International and Comparative Law, 2005); for an analysis of sources of power in regulatory systems, see T Prosser, *The Regulatory Enterprise Government, Regulation, and Legitimacy* (Oxford University Press, 2010).

[17] CA Flanagan, The Corridor of Uncertainty: Part Two, Why Attempts to Regulate the Financial Aspects of Football are Met with Legal Challenges (2018) *International Sports Law Journal* 18, 29–38.

[18] Take, for eg, the European Banking Authority, established pursuant to the 2007-2008 financial crisis under Regulation (EU) No 1093/2010 of the European Parliament and of the Council of 24 November 2010 establishing a European Supervisory Authority (European Banking Authority), amending Decision No 716/2009/EC and repealing Commission Decision 2009/78/EC [2010] OJ L331/ 12–47, and whose tasks and powers are defined by Article 8 of that Regulation. In contrast to the prevailing orthodoxy, English football appears set to introduce a statutory regulator, which should prove a fertile case study in optimal structures in sport.

"Government to Introduce Football Regulator' (*BBC Sport*, 25 April 2022), www.bbc.co.uk/sport/football/61211255?at_campaign=64&at_custom3=%40BBCNews&at_custom1=%5Bpost+type%5D&at_medium=custom7&at_custom4=EA54868C-C44B-11EC-AF0D-6EEF4744363C&at_custom2=twitter.

[19] See, eg, the fine of Tesco Bank by the UK Financial Conduct Authority following a cyber-attack on the bank: Financial Conduct Authority, 'FCA Fines Tesco Bank £16.4m for Failures in 2016 Cyber Attack' (*FCA*, 1 October 2018), www.fca.org.uk/news/press-releases/fca-fines-tesco-bank-failures-2016-cyber-attack.

[20] For eg, in the UK the Financial Conduct Authority and the Competition and Markets Authority hold concurrent powers in respect of competition law pursuant (in the case of the Financial Conduct Authority specifically) to sections 234I to 234O of the Financial Services and Markets Act 2000. The framework for co-operation between the two regulators is set out in a memorandum of understanding, available at www.fca.org.uk/publication/mou/fca-cma-concurrent-competition-powers-mou.pdf.

Sport differs somewhat. SGBs' lack of intrinsic, statute-based power, alloyed to the commercial role most SGBs take,[21] mean that they are, as a matter of fact, subject to some degree of supervisory regulation. In general, regulation is conceptualised as a corollary to specific risk.[22] There is a well-established and manifest risk in the case of the activities of SGBs that the regulatory regime they institute may infract domestic or international law. The most prominent friction in that regard has arisen in the context of regulatory initiatives in sport raising questions of compliance with the four freedoms of the internal market, and with EU competition law. The European Commission, as the executive branch of the EU and thus *de jure* regulator of compliance with EU law, should accordingly have regulatory authority over SGBs insofar as their activities affect the EU's internal market.[23] Given the economic centrality of Europe to football (both within and outside the EU), there can be little doubt that the regulatory authority of FIFA, UEFA, and the myriad other football SGBs in Europe, intersect with the European Commission's.

This, however, has not always been agreed by football's governing bodies.

C. Is Football Self-Regulating?

Football, like most sports, has historically been a self-regulated affair, and defended its freedom from external interference or supervision. Geeraert et al describe how '[t]he highest governing bodies of sport … regulated their sports or events autonomously through self-governing networks with their own rules and regulations', whereby SGBs are 'very reluctant to give up their cherished autonomous status and point to the "specificity" of their sector to justify this'.[24] The ideation of regulatory autonomy free from external interference is predicated on the sanctity of the 'specificity of sport', the idea that 'the peculiar characteristics of sport in comparison to other sectors of the economy … mean it should be, to a greater or lesser extent, subject to its own sui generis treatment in law'.[25]

[21] As Andrews and Harrington state, 'FIFA and the other governing bodies have completely undermined the legitimacy of their political and commercial roles, and have not done enough to fulfil the regulatory roles they should be playing'. M Andrews and P Harrington, 'Off Pitch: Football's Financial Integrity Weaknesses, and How to Strengthen Them' (CID Working Paper No 311, January 2016) 68–103.

[22] See Hood et al (n 7) 4.

[23] This is an authority it has exercised: see Commission Decision C(2017) 8230 (final), adopted on 8 December 2017 relating to proceedings under Article 101 TFEU and Article 53 of the EEA Agreement (Case AT/40208 – International Skating Union's eligibility rules). For an analysis of that case, see E Szyszczak, 'Competition and Sport: No Longer So Special?' (2018) 9 *Journal of European Competition Law & Practice* 3, 188–96; A Cattaneo, 'International Skating Union v Commission: Pre-Authorisation Rules and Competition Law' (2021) 12 *Journal of European Competition Law and Practice* 4, 318–20.

[24] A Geeraert, J Scheerder, H Bruyninckx, 'The Governance Network of European Football: Introducing New Governance Approaches to Steer Football at the EU Level' (2012) 5 *International Journal Sport Policy* 1–20.

[25] Flanagan (n 17).

This idea, when considering the regulation of football – or indeed any sport – as primarily about designing and enforcing rules which affect play on the field, has a certain logic. The design of rules affecting the organisation of sport on the field of play can be considered, at least superficially, best performed by the relevant SGB. It is easy, too, to see how the sports industry could convince itself that the specificity of sport carried weight for matters beyond the pitch: It is truly an idiosyncratic industry in which one participant relies on the survival of its direct competitors for its own success.[26]

Indeed, the soft competence of the EU in the field of sport is expressly framed in those terms, Article 165(1) on the Treaty of the Functioning of the European Union (TFEU) says '[t]he Union shall contribute to the promotion of European sporting issues, while taking account of the specific nature of sport, its structures based on voluntary activity and its social and educational function'.

The European Commission's White Paper on Sport notes[27] that 'sporting organisations and Member States have a primary responsibility in the conduct of sporting affairs, with a central role for sports federations'.[28] However, this is not framed in terms of an absolute discretion for SGBs. Rather, 'sporting organisations have to exercise their task to organise and promote their particular sports "with due regard to national and Community legislation"'.[29]

After all, sport and SGBs are not merely concerned with regulating what happens during games, as an abstract activity without impact beyond the match. Sporting regulatory frameworks frequently go beyond setting out how a game is to be played; and even if they did not, the rules determining who can play and under what conditions have broader implications. Sport represents a major economic sector; players being the labour in that sector. This is particularly true of football. Aggregate revenues in the European football market alone are reported to have been euro28.9 billion for the 2018/2019 season.[30] Thus,

> regardless of the unique nature of sport, it cannot be divorced from its reality as a significant economic sector … Rules made by FIFA and UEFA affect the economic capabilities of undertakings such as clubs; their employees such as players; and an entire supporting economy such as agents, sponsors, and broadcasters.[31]

[26] '[All] clubs rely on their competitors completing the season for the sake of their own commercial endeavours and for the validity of the league season. Football clubs – and sports teams generally – have a mutual economic dependence'. CA Flanagan, 'Paid in Full: A Critical Look at the Law and Economics of the Football Creditors Rule' (2016) *Entertainment and Sports Law Journal* 14, 3.

[27] And in doing so cites the European Council's Declaration on the specific characteristics of sport and its social function in Europe, of which account should be taken in implementing common policies (The Nice Declaration, 2000).

[28] European Commission, *White Paper on Sport* COM(2007) 391 final. Available at https://eur-lex.europa.eu/legal-content/EN/TXT/?uri=CELEX%3A52007DC0391.

[29] ibid.

[30] Deloitte, 'Annual Review Of Football Finance 2021' (*Deloitte*, July 2021), www2.deloitte.com/content/dam/Deloitte/uk/Documents/sports-business-group/deloitte-uk-annual-review-of-football-finance-2021.pdf.

[31] Flanagan (n 17).

D. The Boundaries of Self-Regulation

Consequently, the requirement to pay 'due regard to national and Community legislation' has fettered the regulatory autonomy of SGBs. Cases relating to sport emerged at the European Court of Justice (ECJ) as early as the 1970s (*Walrave and Koch*[32] or *Donà*[33]), but as Chappelet states:

> it was the ECJ's judgment of 1995 concerning the Belgian footballer Bosman that really unleashed a series of complaints by sportsmen and women against their organisations, whose decisions and/or rules were thus challenged in the European courts, resulting in restrictions on their autonomy to determine sporting regulations.[34]

The case of *Bosman*[35] was, and remains, a landmark case for sports law and for shaping the rule-making powers of SGBs; reinforcing the finding in *Walrave and Koch* that sport, notwithstanding its specificity, is subject to the *acquis communautaire* where relevant law is engaged by sporting activities. *Bosman* established core principles for SGBs' rule-making and, as Duval and van Rompuy state, '[t]his general analytical framework for applying EU law to sport has not changed since'.[36]

That general analytical framework takes the principles established in EU law – principally in the case of *Gebhard*[37] – for the assessment of circumstances in which fundamental freedoms of the EU are restricted. It is established that those restrictions may be permissible where they are: (i) non-discriminatory; (ii) justified by an objective of imperative requirements in the general interest; (iii) suitable for attaining that objective; and (iv) a proportionate means of doing so.[38] So, even in the case of non-discriminatory restrictions of the fundamental freedoms of the EU, an SGB must demonstrate that the relevant rule is necessary, suitable, and proportionate.

Whereas the primary focus in *Bosman* was a restriction on the freedom of movement, the more persistent challenge to SGBs' rules has come under the auspices of EU competition law challenges. However, the framework described above applies similarly to competition law challenges to SGBs' rules.

[32] Case 36-74 B.N.O. *Walrave and L.J.N. Koch v Association Union cycliste internationale, Koninklijke Nederlandsche Wielren Unie and Federación Española Ciclismo* (1974) ECR 1423.

[33] Case C 13-76 *Gaetano Donà v Mario Mantero* (1976) ECR 1333.

[34] JL Chappelet, 'Autonomy of Sport in Europe' (*Council of Europe*, 2010), https://rm.coe.int/autonomy-of-sport-in-europe/168073499f.

[35] Case C-415/93 *Union Royale Belge des Sociétés de Football Association ASBL v Jean-Marc Bosman* (1995) ECR I-4921.

[36] A Duval and B van Rompuy, 'Introduction' in A Duval, B van Rompuy (eds), *The Legacy of Bosman* (ASSER International Sports Law Series. TMC Asser Press, 2016) 2.

[37] Case C-55/94 *Reinhard Gebhard v Consiglio dell'Ordine degli Avvocati e Procuratori di Milano ECR* (1995) I-4165.

[38] ibid (see para 6 of the 'Operative Part' of the judgment).

Sport-focussed EU competition law cases[39] followed with their roots in the (again, non-sport related) decision in *Wouters*,[40] in which the principle sometimes referred to as 'regulatory ancillarity'[41] was established, which enables 'a balancing of restrictions of competition against the reasonableness of regulatory rules'.[42] As with restrictions to fundamental freedoms, that balancing act is performed by reference to necessity, suitability, and proportionality.

It is also now clear that the framework for assessing the legality of SGBs' rules pervades the spectrum of those SGBs' regulatory authority and rule-making powers, having transmogrified to apply even in respect of 'what might be classified as "purely" sporting rules'[43] such as sanctions for doping offences.[44] In any event, given the sophistication of the commercial exploitation of modern sport, and football in particular, the distribution between the 'purely' sporting and the economic is increasingly indistinct.[45]

What can be demonstrated by the erosion of the specificity of sport by the jurisprudence of the ECJ is the fuzzy boundary of the SGBs' rule-making powers. In that sense, EU law, as interpreted by the ECJ, has shaped sport not by laying down positive obligations that an SGB must follow; but by setting the outer limits for SGBs' own regulatory authority.

Weatherill conceptualises this as giving SGBs 'conditional autonomy':[46] SGBs are at liberty to construct their own regulatory systems *provided that* they do so in compliance with the prevailing systems of law to which they are subject (specifically the EU fundamental freedoms and competition law).

A function of this conditional autonomy is that SGBs have what Weatherill describes as a margin of appreciation within which they can create and enforce rules, even where those roles entail some prima facie impingement on a provision of EU law.[47] This is in many respects a necessary concession in order to enable the existence of SGBs as regulators. The creation of rules in sporting ecosystems – particularly complex ones such as those in professional football – will, near axiomatically in many circumstances, have a restricting or

[39] Case C-519/04 P *David Meca-Medina and Igor Majcen v Commission of the European Communities* (2006) ECR I-6991. For analysis see C Zardini Filho, 'European Union Competition Law in Sports: Cases and Relevant Aspects of Articles 101 and 102 of the Treaty on the Functioning of the European Union, their Importance and Influence on Sport Managers and Institutions' (2017) *PODIUM Sport, Leisure and Tourism Review* 6, 392–408.

[40] Case C-309/99 *J.C.J. Wouters et al. v Algemene Raad van de Nederlandse Orde van Advocaten* (2002) ECR I-1577.

[41] A phrase coined by Whish and Bailey, see R Whish and D Bailey, *Competition Law*, 8th edn (Oxford University Press, 2015).

[42] Per Whish and Bailey, ibid.

[43] Flanagan (n 17).

[44] See *Meca-Medina and Majcen v Commission* (n 39).

[45] For further exploration, see B van Rompuy, 'The Role of EU Competition Law in Tackling Abuse of Regulatory Power by Sports Associations' (2015) 22(2) *Maastricht Journal of European and Comparative Law* 174–204.

[46] S Weatherill, 'The Influence of EU Law on Sports Governance' in S Weatherill, *European Sports Law: Collected Papers* (Asser Press, 2013); S Weatherill, *Principles and Practice in EU Sports Law* (Oxford University Press, 2017).

[47] Weatherill, *Principles and Practice*, ibid 167.

distorting impact on competition (in comparison to a countervailing circumstance in which sports were, somehow, unregulated) or fundamental freedoms. If SGBs did not have a margin of appreciation in which to operate, they could not regulate sport in a meaningful way.

Weatherill describes this margin of appreciation as follows: 'A measure within the lex sportiva must be manifestly inappropriate having regard to its objective before the choice will be regarded as invalid'.[48] It is also depicted as being buttressed and legitimised by social dialogue.[49] However, conversely, this margin of appreciation can be construed as undermining the regulatory authority of SGBs as the rules they propagate are amenable to challenge, if not always amenable to ultimately being struck down. This has been described in the context of the financial regulation of football as creating a 'corridor of uncertainty' within which new financial regulation is created; the requirement for proportionality being 'a nebulous measure to assess ex ante, so rule making is performed in the dark'.[50]

There is a continuing friction that exists in SGBs' ability to regulate within this structure. In the specific case of football, though, the manifestation of that friction has generally accrued between football's regulatory bodies and the participants in (or adjacent to) its ecosystem through systems of internal and external dispute resolution. It has less commonly been a friction that has arisen between regulators. That is to say that the regulatory oversight exercised by the European Commission in respect of the regulatory activities of football's governing bodies has in recent years been relatively inert. The real drivers of scrutiny have been the subjects of football's regulatory initiatives.

There can be little doubt that EU law has played a significant part in defining the boundaries of SGBs' regulatory powers and that it has, in thematic terms, shaped the content of FIFA's regulations. Whilst a regulatory friction remains in football's system of conditional autonomy, underpinned by the acts of questionable compatibility with EU law by participants in the football ecosystem, the central legal boundaries – of legitimacy and proportionality –have some equilibrium. The particular assessment may vary from case to case, but the underlying legal test is stable.

II. 'IF THE MOUNTAIN WON'T COME': NEW REGULATORY PARADIGMS

A. Beyond Competition: The Legitimacy Sanctuary of EU Law

Where the intersection of EU competition law and sport may be somewhat settled in approach (if not in application to a particular set of facts), the economic

[48] ibid.
[49] ibid.
[50] Flanagan (n 17).

and technological development of football moves the game into new territories. Concurrently and inevitably, EU law continues to develop, with the regulatory initiatives of the EU colliding with the football industry in interesting new ways.

Whereas football once spent considerable energy evading the reaches of EU law, what is now seen, in a more mature economic and regulatory ecosystem, is a move towards EU law, particularly and unfamiliarly, to secondary EU law; and indeed towards external, supervisory regulatory systems in doing so.

It may not be superficially apparent how EU data protection and financial services law may come to affect the *lex sportiva*, but as football becomes increasingly data rich, and as the monetary value and regulatory control over the flow of money in the international player transfer system increase, those legal and regulatory systems become increasingly important to football.

The invocation of EU secondary legislation and regulatory systems that do not specifically pertain to sport says something of FIFA's moves towards being a multi-faceted, all-purpose regulator of the sporting and economic activities relating to football; it also says something of the power of EU law. Much ink has been spilled over that power: Bradford, in her seminal 2012 work, describes 'Europe's unilateral power to regulate global markets', a phenomenon she referred to as the 'Brussels Effect'.[51] Bradford builds on the work of Vogel,[52] whose notion of the 'California Effect' positions large multi-national (or multi-state) enterprises as central to the spread of regulatory standards, where those enterprises comply with the 'highest' regulatory standards imposed upon them, and apply those standards in all states in which they act whether or not there is a legal or regulatory burden to do so. This results in the transmission of standards, 'not just in terms of legislative change, but also in terms of what corporate board rooms around the world view as the "gold standard" to guide or otherwise shape their behaviour'.[53]

That EU law should affect the regulation of football is neither surprising (given 'EU regulations penetrate numerous aspects of people's everyday lives around the world'[54] and 'The Brussels Effect affects the food [people] eat, the air they breathe, and the products they produce and consume'[55]), nor is it novel;[56]

[51] A Bradford, 'The Brussels Effect' (2012) 1 *Northwestern University Law Review* 107, 1–68. Bradford built upon this work in A Bradford, 'Exporting Standards: The Externalization of the EU's Regulatory Power via Markets' (2015) 42 *International Review of Law and Economics* 158–73 and Bradford (n 5).

[52] D Vogel, 'Trading Up: Consumer and Environmental Regulation in a Global Economy' (Harvard University Press, 1995) ch 8.

[53] L Bygrave, 'The "Strasbourg Effect" on Data Protection in Light of the "Brussels Effect": Logic, Mechanics and Prospects (2021) 40 *Computer Law & Security Review*.

[54] Bradford (n 5) Introduction, xv.

[55] ibid.

[56] Consider, eg, the centrality of the *Bosman* case to the player transfer regulatory system. For analysis of the Brussels Effect and sport more generally, see J Kornbeck, 'Sport Regulation Between Brussels Effect and Brexit Dividend' in J Kornbeck (ed), *Sport and Brexit*, 1st edn (Routledge, 2021), ch 15.

nevertheless, FIFA's place in the Brussels Effect model as an exporter of EU regulation is an interesting one. On the one hand, FIFA is a large and influential multi-national enterprise like many others, performing commercial functions; FIFA, though, as an SGB, also performs its own regulatory functions. In that latter capacity, FIFA *qua* regulator, may not seem the archetype of 'markets forces' spreading EU law beyond its territorial boundaries, yet it is in that capacity that we see the Brussels Effects inferred by the regulatory regimes described in this chapter – in respect of EU data protection and financial services laws. However, it is perhaps misleading to conceptualise FIFA's regulatory power alone as being the vehicle on which EU law is carried. It is illusory to think of FIFA's regulatory functions as being wholly divisible from its commercial functions; there is no neat delineation, the two are intertwined. As Meier and García posit: 'FIFA's regulatory ambitions probably reflect football's massive commercialization, setting a strong incentive for the governing body to maintain concentrated control over international football and its revenues'.[57] Thus, whilst FIFA's promulgation of EU law is carried along regulatory lines, its basis for doing so is not absent a commercial dimension, and as a consequence, as Bradford says of the Brussels Effect generally, it 'emerges from market forces and ... self-interest to adopt relatively stringent EU standards globally'.[58]

B. Data Protection

The protection of personal data has been of concern at EU level for more than a quarter of a century.[59] In 1995, Directive 95/46/EC (the Data Protection Directive)[60] was enacted. The Data Protection Directive laid the foundations for much of the modern data protection regulatory framework that still remains in place, having established in law the legal concept of 'personal data', the conditions for processing such data, the rights of data subjects, and so on. The Data Protection Directive is described as having 'marked the creation of the world's largest area of free flow of personal data on the basis of commonly agreed safeguards'.[61]

[57] HE Meier and B García, 'Protecting Private Transnational Authority Against Public Intervention: FIFA's Power Over National Governments' (2015) *Public Administration* 93: 890–906.

[58] Bradford (n 5) 2.

[59] In fact, the data protection framework in the EU goes back further than the Data Protection Directive, to 'the Council of Europe's Convention of 28 January 1981 for the Protection of Individuals with regard to Automatic Processing of Personal Data (Convention 108), which was the first binding international legal instrument for data protection'. M Kuschewsky *Data Protection & Privacy*, 3rd edn (Sweet & Maxwell, 2016).

[60] Directive 95/46/EC of the European Parliament and of the Council of 24 October 1995 on the protection of individuals with regard to the processing of personal data and on the free movement of such data (the Data Protection Directive) [1995] OJ L281/31–50.

[61] V Reding, 'Forward' in M Kuschewsky, *Data Protection & Privacy*, 1st edn (Sweet & Maxwell, 2012) 7.

The criticality of data protection to EU citizens is enforced by Article 8 of the EU Charter of Fundamental Rights (given legal force by the Treaty of Lisbon), which states:

> 1. Everyone has the right to the protection of personal data concerning him or her.
> 2. Such data must be processed fairly for specified purposes and on the basis of the consent of the person concerned or some other legitimate basis laid down by law. Everyone has the right of access to data which has been collected concerning him or her, and the right to have it rectified.
> 3. Compliance with these rules shall be subject to control by an independent authority.

In order to reflect the development of data usage in society in the intervening years, in 2018, the Data Protection Directive was repealed and replaced by Regulation 2016/679, the General Data Protection Regulation (GDPR).[62] The GDPR is an evolution of the framework established by the Data Protection Directive, and 'upgrades data protection and the humanist values upon which our legal system is based so as to make them more effective in the digital world'.[63] It does so by building a 'stronger and more coherent data protection framework in the EU, backed by strong enforcement'.[64]

Unlike the Data Protection Directive, the GDPR is a regulation, and thus is directly applicable in Member States. In order to promote the harmonisation of approaches in the case of cross-border data processing, the GDPR also introduces a 'one-stop-shop' mechanism, which necessitates co-ordination between the competent data protection regulators of Member States.[65] It is a requirement under Article 51 of the GDPR for a Member State to have in place at least one independent public authority 'responsible for monitoring the application of this Regulation, in order to protect the fundamental rights and freedoms of natural persons in relation to processing and to facilitate the free flow of personal data within the Union'. Overseeing and ensuring co-ordination among the national regulators is the European Data Protection Board (EDPB).[66]

Supporting the legislative and regulatory framework is a European judicial system that has been unafraid to make far-reaching decisions where it considers there to have been instances of non-compliance. As Buttarelli posits: 'the courts, and in particular the Court of Justice of the European Union (CJEU), are

[62] Regulation (EU) 2016/679 of the European Parliament and of the Council of 27 April 2016 on the protection of natural persons with regard to the processing of personal data and on the free movement of such data, and repealing Directive 95/46/EC (General Data Protection Regulation) [2016] OJ L119/1–88.

[63] I Falque-Pierrotin, 'Foreword' in Kuschewsky (n 59).

[64] Kuschewsky (n 59) ch 1.1.

[65] Article 51(2) of the GDPR provides that '*Each supervisory authority shall contribute to the consistent application of this Regulation throughout the Union. For that purpose, the supervisory authorities shall cooperate with each other and the Commission*'. See also Arts 4(23), 55–56, 60–70, and Recitals 124 and 140 of the GDPR.

[66] Established pursuant to GDPR Art 68.

applying the rights and freedoms of individuals in the digital age with remarkable vigour and precision'.[67] The consequence of this framework is that '[d]ata protection is a highly developed and regulated area of law'.[68]

Personal data manifests itself in football in various ways, from the prosaic to the controversial; everything from a top goal scorers table to use in algorithms to derive betting odds relies on the processing of personal data. EU data protection law has been examined in the context of anti-doping,[69] genetic testing,[70] sporting regulatory investigations,[71] and player performance data analytics.[72] There can be little doubt that EU data protection law plays a significant part in the sporting ecosystem, and that its relevance will grow as the prevalence and use cases for personal data in sport increase as they have in wider society.

That position is true, however, for all data rich industries. The influence of EU data protection law on football specifically goes further. In 2019, FIFA adopted its own Data Protection Regulations (the 'FIFA DPRs').[73] Whilst personal data may seem incidental to FIFA's regulatory functions, it is in fact a core component – from the commercial exploitation of data, such as the use of player names and characteristics in FIFA licensed video games, to the organisation of tournaments (necessarily involving the processing of information relating to players and other data subjects), to, most pertinently for present purposes, a more complex intersection with FIFA's regulatory systems.

Of particular significance is the international player transfer system as governed by the RSTP. Article 5 of the RSTP states that 'Each association must have an electronic player registration system … Only electronically registered players identified with a FIFA ID are eligible to participate in organised football.' Thus, the processing of player personal data now commences at the start of each player's involvement in the organised game, whether professional or amateur.[74] This system is used to bring players within FIFA's global regulatory ambit, as 'By the act of registering, a player agrees to abide by the FIFA Statutes and

[67] G Buttarelli, 'Foreword' in Kuschewsky (n 59).

[68] CA Flanagan, 'Stats Entertainment: The Legal and Regulatory Issues Arising from the Data Analytics Movement in Association Football. Part Two: Data Privacy, the Broader Legal Context, and Conclusions of the Legal Aspects of Data Analytics in Football' (2022) *Entertainment and Sports Law Journal* 19(1).

[69] M Viret, 'How Data Protection Crystallises Key Legal Challenges in Anti-Doping' (*Asser International Sports Law Blog*, 7 May 2019), www.asser.nl/SportsLaw/Blog/post/how-data-protection-crystallises-key-legal-challenges-in-anti-doping-by-marjolaine-viret.

[70] S Patel and I Varley, 'Exploring the Regulation of Genetic Testing in Sport' (2019) 17 *Entertainment and Sports Law Journal* 5, 1–13.

[71] B Hessert, 'Cooperation and Reporting Obligations in Sports Investigations (2020) *International Sports Law Journal* 20, 145–156.

[72] Flanagan (n 68).

[73] FIFA, Data Protection Regulations, October 2019 edition, available at https://digitalhub.fifa.com/m/787f00d0380f4120/original/dr9labmtd63ctx6o3erk-pdf.pdf.

[74] Article 5 RSTP states that 'A player must be registered at an association to play for a club as either a professional or an amateur in accordance with the provisions of article 2'.

regulations, the confederations and the associations.'[75] This dependence on data processing is further entrenched by other regulatory functions of FIFA. FIFA's TMS, through which international transfers are processed,[76] is predicated on the sharing of personal data. The FIFA Clearing House, described in greater detail below, is reliant on an electronic player passport, another instance of personal data collection and processing.[77] FIFA's internal dispute resolution systems will typically involve processing data concerning the players involved – and so on.

So, any determination of compliance with the RSTP, and any determination on the rights and duties that arise under it (such as those relating to training compensation and solidarity payments), necessarily entail an amount of personal data collection and processing. Accordingly, personal data processing permeates FIFA's activities.

The FIFA DPRs are described as having 'considerable conceptual overlap with the GDPR',[78] although (unsurprisingly) comprising just 12 Articles, the FIFA DPRs are considerably less detailed than the GDPR (which comprises 99 Articles and 173 Recitals). There are, consequently, some variances in approach.

Both the GDPR and the FIFA DPRs relate to the processing of 'personal data'. In each case, 'personal data' is defined as information relating to an 'identified or identifiable natural person'.[79] Like the GDPR, the FIFA DPRs separate out 'special category' data from other forms of personal data,[80] although the treatment of special category data varies. Whereas the GDPR allows the processing of special category data on narrower grounds than the processing of other forms of personal data,[81] the FIFA DPRs apply a diluted standard, stating that special category data must 'be afforded special protection against unauthorised access',[82] that 'All persons Processing Special Categories of Personal Data must be expressly advised of the importance of treating these Special Categories of Personal Data as strictly confidential',[83] and that such data 'may only be transferred to Third Parties if there are legal reasons for doing so or with the express Consent of the Data Subject'.[84] The standards afforded to special category data under the FIFA DPRs are in likelihood standards that apply to the processing of all personal data under the GDPR (and indeed with the remainder of the FIFA DPRs).

[75] ibid.

[76] See Morris and Lysaght (n 14).

[77] See FIFA Circular 1654 (26 November 2018) and FIFA Circular 1679 (1 July 2019), Art 7 RSTP, and 'FIFA Clearing House' (FIFA.com), www.fifa.com/en/legal/football-regulatory/clearing-house.

[78] Flanagan (n 68).

[79] GDPR Art 5; FIFA DPRs Art 2.

[80] GDPR Art 9; FIFA DPRs Arts 2 and 4(2). Special category data relates to 'racial or ethnic origin, political opinions, religious or philosophical beliefs, or trade union membership … genetic data, biometric data for the purpose of uniquely identifying a natural person, data concerning health or data concerning a natural person's sex life or sexual orientation'.

[81] See GDPR Art 9.

[82] FIFA DPRs Art 2.

[83] FIFA DPRs Art 4(2).

[84] ibid.

Like the GDPR,[85] the FIFA DPRs establish principles of data protection. These principles are generally aligned, although as is noted by Bellamy, the FIFA DPRs impose two further principles:

1. that personal data is only to be accessible by people who need it for their activity ('the need-to-know principle');[86] and
2. that each FIFA entity shall ensure that all infrastructure used for processing personal data is adequately protected with 'state-of-the-art technical and organisational measures, taking into consideration the risks to data subjects'[87] ('the protection principle').[88]

Whilst the need-to-know principle and the protection principle do not have a direct counterpart in the GDPR as conditions of processing, they are, as a matter of practice, covered by other requirements of the GDPR.[89]

Again following the GDPR in a truncated format, the FIFA DPRs implement a suite of rights for data subjects, including a right to be informed about the collection and use of data, the right to rectification, the right to be forgotten, the right to restrict processing and so on – concepts lifted from the GDPR.

As mentioned, there are areas of divergence, one of the most notable of which is the lack of distinction between 'controllers' and 'processors' found in the GDPR. Article 4(7) of the GDRP defines a data controller as a 'body which, alone or jointly with others, determines the purposes and means of the processing of personal data', whereas Article 4(8) defines a processor as a 'body which processes personal data on behalf of the controller'. This distinction is important as '[r]isks, roles, and responsibilities under data protection law vary dependent on whether a party using personal data does so as a controller or a processor'.[90] There is, though, an attenuated echo of this structure in Article 6 of the FIFA DPRs, which states that '[t]he transmission of Personal Data to Third Parties shall be carried out in such a way that the Third Party processes the data in accordance with the sender's instructions', which is a structure required pursuant to Article 28(3) of the GDPR in any controller-processor relationship governed by the GDPR.

[85] The GDPR establishes data protection principles at Art 5, stating that personal data must be processed only where that processing can be performed: lawfully, fairly and transparently; for specified, explicit and legitimate purposes; minimising personal data use; accurately, with up-to-date data; for no longer than is necessary; and with integrity and confidentiality.

[86] FIFA DPRs Art 4(1).

[87] Ibid.

[88] J Bellamy, 'An Overview of FIFA's New Data Protection Regulations' (*LawInSport*. 2020), www.lawinsport.com/topics/item/an-overview-of-fifa-s-new-data-protection-regulations.

[89] Amongst other relevant provisions of the GDPR Art 25 requires data protection by design and by default, including a requirement for data controllers to 'implement appropriate technical and organisational measures for ensuring that, by default, only personal data which are necessary for each specific purpose of the processing are processed. That obligation applies to the amount of personal data collected, the extent of their processing, the period of their storage and their accessibility' (GDPR Art 25(2)).

[90] Flanagan (n 68).

One of the more controversial aspects of the GDPR in practice has been the way it controls the transfer of personal data to third countries,[91] which has resulted in high-profile decisions of the CJEU.[92] The FIFA DPRs allow '[c]ross-border (i.e. outside Switzerland) Disclosure of Personal Data (including the granting of remote access)' either 'where the legislation in the country in question guarantees an adequate level of data protection according to the list published by the [Swiss Federal Data Protection and Information Commissioner]'[93] or otherwise where:

a) [the FIFA DPRs] are complied with;
b) sufficient guarantees are agreed with the recipient in the form of a contract or in another legally enforceable form;
c) the Data Subjects grant their Consent on an exceptional basis;
d) the Processing of Personal Data is closely connected to the conclusion or performance of a contract and the data consists of the contractual partner's Personal Data;
e) it is required for the substantiation of claims before courts;
f) the Disclosure takes place within the same legal person or company, provided that the applicable internal data protection guidelines provide an appropriate level of protection.

This is a more permissive regime than its GDPR counterpart. Nevertheless, the influence of the GDPR – which at its core aims to ensure that personal data is only transferred outside the direct scope of the GDPR in circumstances whereby the data protection standards set by the GDPR can continue to be achieved – is seen.[94] This is reflective of a broader, and instructive, point: The GDPR has a very broad territorial scope. By virtue of its Article 3, the scope of the GDPR 'can effectively extend worldwide', as it applies to the processing of personal data 'in the context of the activities of an establishment of a controller or a processor in the Union, regardless of whether the processing takes place in the Union or not',[95] and where data is processed outside of the EU but in respect of either goods and services offered to EU citizens, or where the monitoring of the behaviour of EU citizens takes place.[96] This is likely to bring some of the data processing activities of FIFA itself within the scope of the GDPR given the importance of the European football market, notwithstanding FIFA's location in Switzerland, ie outside the EU.

[91] That is to say countries outside the European Economic Area.

[92] Notably C-362/14 *Maximillian Schrems v Data Protection Commissioner* (2015) and Case C-311/18 *Data Protection Commissioner v Facebook Ireland Limited and Maximillian Schrems*, colloquially known as 'Schrems I' and 'Schrems II'.

[93] FIFA DPRs Art 7(1).

[94] It has been suggested that the regulation of international data transfers has had an influence on the GDPR's position as a global standard bearer. See O Lynskey, *The Foundations of EU Data Protection Law* (Oxford University Press, 2015) 41–44.

[95] GDPR Art 3(1).

[96] ibid Art 3(2).

Whether or not FIFA is required to comply with the GDPR in respect of some of its data processing activities, it was not required to implement its own iteration and thus act as a global vector of the principles enshrined in the GDPR. The specific application of the FIFA DPRs is narrow, described as 'relating only to personal data processed by, or on behalf of, or with FIFA; where exchanged with FIFA or a FIFA Member Association; or where relying on infrastructure provided by FIFA'.[97] Such 'infrastructure provided by FIFA' would presumably include the FIFA TMS system on which the international player market is dependent. Whilst the scope of activities subject to the FIFA DPRs is narrow, the territorial scope is effectively worldwide.[98] The GDPR itself has as a starting point a wide territorial scope in its direct application, it has also been heralded as paradigmatic, 'an example par excellence',[99] of the Brussels Effect,[100] having a strong hegemonic influence on data privacy globally.[101] In terms of the global imposition of GDPR-like standards, there may not be a better example than that of the FIFA DPRs.

Whereas the GDPR institutes a system co-ordinating national regulators overseen by the EDPB, the FIFA DPRs interpose FIFA as a data protection regulator of sorts, with 'Data Security Incidents'[102] to be reported to FIFA.[103] Failure to comply with the FIFA DPRs could result in sanctions pursuant to Article 12(2), which state that '[a]ny infringement of these Regulations may incur sanctions under the Applicable Data Protection Laws, the FIFA Statutes or any other FIFA regulations'.[104] The FIFA DPRs do not specify the actions to be taken by FIFA in the event of a Data Security Incident of FIFA's responsibility, although such incident would in likelihood be subject to prevailing data protection law in Switzerland (the revised Swiss Federal Data Protection Act, passed on 25 September 2020, the 'Swiss DPA 2020') or potentially the GDPR where its extra-territorial effect applies.

[97] Flanagan (n 68). Note that the FIFA DPRs expressly do not apply to personal data processed '… to Member Associations and their members in relation to any Personal Data that they cumulatively process: using their own infrastructure; for their own purposes; and in their own right.' See Article 3, FIFA DPRs.

[98] Particularly so given FIFA has some 211 Member Associations, more than the number of countries recognised by the UN (as of the date of writing, 193). For a list of FIFA Member Associations, see www.fifa.com/about-fifa/associations.

[99] Bygrave (n 53).

[100] Furthermore, it has also been suggested that European data protection law displays a 'Strasbourg Effect', see Bygrave (n 53).

[101] See Bradford (n 5), S Gunst and F de Ville, 'The Brussels Effect: How the GDPR Conquered Silicon Valley' (2021) 26 *European Foreign Affairs Review* 3, 437–58.

[102] Defined as 'Any event of loss of confidentiality, integrity and availability with the potential of constituting a risk for FIFA, any other Entity or any Data Subject' (FIFA DPRs Art 2).

[103] This is in itself influenced by the GDPR, with GDPR Art 33 requiring personal data breaches to be notified by data controllers to the relevant supervisory authority ('without undue delay and, where feasible, not later than 72 hours after having become aware of it', GDPR Art 33(1)).

[104] It is somewhat unclear how FIFA would enforce sanctions under Applicable Data Protection Laws (as defined in the FIFA DPRs).

Whereas the impact of EU internal market and competition law has been to define the outer boundaries of the regulatory power of FIFA and other SGBs, the impact of the GDPR has been much more prescriptive, with FIFA having co-opted the form, and indeed some of the substance, of the EU data protection regime. Bellamy states that 'FIFA was not required to adopt the Regulations by Swiss legislation, a national data protection regulator or, of course, any organ of the European Union. They were passed and adopted by the consent of FIFA and its member associations'.[105]

There are various explanations as to why FIFA may have been influenced to create its own data protection regime in this way. First, the GDPR has had a powerful hegemonic influence on data protection standards globally.[106] In addition to its direct implementation into the 27 Member States, the GDPR has been at the vanguard of a global advancement in data protection laws, with new regimes implemented in jurisdictions including California,[107] China,[108] the United Arab Emirates,[109] and indeed Switzerland[110] influenced to a greater or lesser degree by the GDPR.

Just as *Bosman* drew out and built upon latent principles established in cases such as *Walrave and Koch*, the GDPR reinvigorated interest in and built upon the principles enshrined in the earlier Data Protection Directive. Compliance programmes across all industries, including football, generated questions about data flows and good data governance. Taking aside (although in doubt in part because of) the GDPR's wide territorial scope, it had the effect of promoting good data compliance principles globally.

The implementation of the FIFA DPRs can also be seen as a defensive move by FIFA. Where data protection laws apply, FIFA is not just the author of data protection regulations, but also the subject of applicable data protection law, and in order to help facilitate the transfer of personal data by FIFA across borders, as

[105] Bellamy (n 88).

[106] Per R Mahieu, et al, 'Measuring the Brussels Effect through Access Requests: Has the European General Data Protection Regulation Influenced the Data Protection Rights of Canadian Citizens? (2021) *Journal of Information Policy* 11, 301–49, 'It is undeniable that through various mechanisms, European data protection law has impacted the creation of data protection laws elsewhere'. See also Lynskey (n 94) 41–44.

[107] CAL. CIV. CODE § 1798.100 et seq. Taking an approach to data protection which includes 'Bearing a resemblance to GDPR's definition [of personal data]', per Linklaters, 'New California Law Marks A Progressive Movement For U.S. Data Protection' (*Linklaters.com*, 2018), www.linklaters.com/en/insights/blogs/digilinks/new-california-law-marks-a-progressive-movement-for-us-data-protection.

[108] Under which 'many articles are modelled on similar concepts under the GDPR' per Linklaters, 'China: The New Privacy Law Is Passed And The Wait Is Over' '(*Linklaters.com*, 2021), www.linklaters.com/en/insights/blogs/digilinks/2021/august/china-the-new-privacy-law-is-passed-and-the-wait-is-over.

[109] C Williams and L Tyson, 'UAE Law Regarding The Protection Of Personal Data' (*National Law Review*, 2021), www.natlawreview.com/article/uae-law-regarding-protection-personal-data.

[110] The provisions of which 'are similar to those of the GDPR' per Linklaters and Vischer, 'Data Protected Switzerland' (*Linklaters.com*, 2021), www.linklaters.com/en/insights/data-protected/data-protected---switzerland.

is necessary to aspects of its functions.[111] FIFA has a material interest in raising global data protection standards so that it is not unduly impinged in its activities by data protection regulators with the benefit of the force of law.[112] For example, where FIFA DPRs impose an obligation to report to FIFA '[a]ny event of loss of confidentiality, integrity and availability with the potential of constituting a risk for FIFA, any other Entity or any Data Subject', that in turn allows FIFA to assess and manage its own risk of being subject to enforcement measures and administrative fines, with each of the GDPR and the Swiss DPA 2020 requiring the reporting of data breaches to supervisory authorities.[113]

The FIFA DPRs also follow considerable pressure on FIFA to ensure that due regard is paid to human rights in football.[114] The protection of personal data is a critical aspect of the right to privacy, and consequently must be meaningfully engaged with by FIFA as a part of a broader human rights compliance framework.

There has also been a great deal of focus on data exploitation within football. At the forefront of this has been FIFPro, the global football players' union. In 2020, FIFPro published a policy paper, 'A Future Oriented Player Data Policy For the Digital Football Industry',[115] which set out its agenda for the (restrictions on the) exploitation of player's personal data, which included the application of 'collective standards for the collection, protection, and use of player data', which should be 'established on the basis of existing privacy laws such as the General Data Protection Regulation'. To the degree that the FIFA DPRs apply to the processing of players' personal data (such as when players' personal data is

[111] Consider, for example, the transfer of personal data involved in an international player transfer, with attendant upload and transmission of personal data concerning the relevant player via the FIFA TMS.

[112] Conduct of this nature is promoted by the GDPR, and the FIFA DPR regime is thematically similar to the concept of 'codes of conduct' enshrined in Art 40 of the GDPR. Under that system, 'specific features of the various processing sectors and the specific needs of micro, small and medium-sized enterprises' can be accommodated and guided by codes of conduct developed by associations or other bodies and approved by a supervisory data protection regulator. In the specific case of the FIFA DPRs, neither the regulations themselves nor the FIFA Circular 1697 adopting the FIFA DPRs mentions the code of conduct concept, nor do they appear to have been adopted by a supervisory body, but the conceptual overlap is nevertheless striking.

[113] Under the GDPR regime, pro-active management in this way may also result in clemency in the event of enforcement action. Article 83(2) of the GDPR together with Guidance published by the Article 29 Working Party (the predecessor to the EDPB) and endorsed by the EDPB makes clear that making clear and transparent notifications of breaches to supervisory authorities and co-operating with supervisory authorities thereafter is a relevant factor (inter alia) in mitigation of breach; as is 'any action taken by the controller or processor to mitigate the damage suffered by data subjects', which purpose the FIFA DPRs could also be held to serve. Article 29 Data Protection Working Party, 'Guidelines On The Application And Setting Of Administrative Fines For The Purposes Of The Regulation 2016/679 17/EN WP 253' (2017).

[114] For framing, see A Duval and D Heerdt, 'FIFA and Human Rights – a Research Agenda' (2020) 25 *Tilburg Law Review* 1.

[115] FIFPro, 'A Future Oriented Player Data Policy For the Digital Football Industry – The Collection, Protection, and Use of Player Data' (*FIFPro*, 2020), www.fifpro.org/media/31intkan/fifpro-policy-position_player-data_eng.pdf.

transferred by FIFA to a Member Association outside the EU), FIFPro's desired policy approach is, to an extent, met – the FIFA DPRs apply, and are heavily influenced by the GDPR, albeit in a slimline format.

As Bellamy concludes, 'the adoption of the [FIFA DPRs] will apply whenever FIFA, its member associations and their members undertake joint processing activities and will therefore significantly raise the bar for member associations and their members that are not subject to the GDPR'.[116]

Whereas the FIFA DPRs show the colonising effect of EU law on the *lex sportiva*, their direct impact to date is unquantified, but will likely be subtle; a gentle raising of data protection standards for a limited class of persons. The more tangible impact is of the GDPR itself, with the FIFA DPRs representing proof of concept in the de facto spread of EU data protection standards and concepts into jurisdictions where those standards and concepts may not (yet) apply de jure.[117]

C. The FIFA Clearing House

The implementation of the FIFA Clearing House is intended to ameliorate certain dysfunctional elements of the international player transfer market: '[t]he prevailing circumstances and worrying trends of today's transfer market indicate that [the objectives of the RSTP[118]] have not been yet fully achieved or are being undermined'.[119] As part of a suite of changes in FIFA's 'landmark reform package'[120] were proposals to create a 'FIFA Clearing House', intended principally to automate the distribution of monies to those parties in the football ecosystem who may become entitled to payment when a football player is traded.[121] A particular problem associated with the regulatory framework of the international player transfer market, and the proper enforcement of the RSTP, related to a market failure[122] in the appropriate distribution of training compensation and solidarity payments owing to clubs in accordance with the provisions

[116] Bellamy (n 88) 68.

[117] Noting that Bradford, 'The Brussels Effect' (n 51), in her analysis of the 'Brussels Effect', distinguishes between de facto and de jure manifestations, with the former presaging the latter.

[118] Namely 'the protection of contractual stability; encouragement of training; solidarity between the elite and grassroots; protection of minors; competitive balance; and ensuring the regularity of sporting competitions': FIFA, 'FIFA Takes the First Step for the Establishment and Operation of the FIFA Clearing House' (*Fifa.com*, 25 July 2019), www.fifa.com/about-fifa/who-we-are/news/fifa-takes-the-first-step-for-the-establishment-and-operation-of-the-fifa-cleari.

[119] ibid.

[120] T Gunawardena, 'Changing the Game: Dissecting the Landmark Reforms Endorsed by the FIFA Football Stakeholders Committee' (*LawInSport*, 2018), www.lawinsport.com/topics/item/changing-the-game-dissecting-the-landmark-reforms-endorsed-by-the-fifa-football-stakeholders-committee.

[121] 'FIFA expects that the adoption of the FIFA Clearing House system will effectively ensure the payment of the Solidarity Contribution and Training Compensation amounts to training clubs all around the world, with the potential to increase the amount of money distributed to training clubs by up to four times of what they currently receive.': FIFA (n 118) 85.

[122] Lenarduzzi reports that 'In 2018, it was reported that just USD$67.7m of the USD$351.5m due to be distributed in solidarity contributions, was actually paid. That is a mere 19.3% of what

of Articles 20 and 21, and Annexes 4, 5 and 6 of the RSTP, which facilitate the redistribution of money to clubs involved in the development of players.[123] Moreover, FIFA estimates that 'the gap between the solidarity contribution and training compensation rewards due to training clubs and the actual training rewards paid by engaging clubs to training clubs is growing every season'.[124]

The historically decentralised nature of financial flows within the global player transfer market also introduce other risks, such as those associated with financial crime. A 2009 Financial Action Task Force study, 'Money Laundering through the Football Sector',[125] specifically identifies the transfer market and ownership of players as a potential vector for financial crime, partly because of its opacity:

> The transfer market is vulnerable to various forms of misuse, such as tax evasion, insider fraud and also money laundering. Vulnerabilities are connected with lack of transparency in relation to the funding for certain transfer transactions and the opportunity for funds to be paid offshore with limited disclosure requirements regarding beneficial ownership of destination accounts.[126]

Consequently, it has been argued that '[g]iven the level of autonomy exercised over the industry by its regulatory bodies, it is incumbent on those organisations to put in place an appropriate framework to prevent or mitigate the risk of financial crime occurring'.[127]

However, by controlling and distributing monies to whom third parties have an entitlement, FIFA potentially brings itself within the ambit of a complex web of financial services laws and regulations. Given the centrality of various EU jurisdictions to football, and given the multiplicity of EU banking and financial services laws,[128] the creation of the FIFA Clearing House cannot be contemplated without considering the potential for FIFA's activities to fall within the regulatory perimeter of EU financial services law.

should have trickled down and perhaps just as alarming is that this percentage has been worsening.': R Lenarduzzi, 'Revisiting FIFA'S Training Compensation And Solidarity Mechanism – Part. 2: The African Reality – By Rhys Lenarduzzi' (*Asser International Sports Law Blog*, 2020), www.asser.nl/SportsLaw/Blog/post/revisiting-fifa-s-training-compensation-and-solidarity-mechanism-part-2-the-african-reality-by-rhys-lenarduzzi. Primary data is available in FIFA's Global Transfer Market Report (2019), https://digitalhub.fifa.com/m/248987d86f2b9955/original/x2wrqjstwjoailnncnod-pdf.pdf.

[123] For background on training compensation and solidarity payments, see A Smith, 'A Guide To Training Compensation And Solidarity Payments In Football' (*LawInSport*, 2015), www.lawinsport.com/topics/item/a-guide-to-training-compensation-and-solidarity-payments-in-football.

[124] FIFA, 'FIFA Clearing House' (*Fifa.com*, 2021), www.fifa.com/en/legal/football-regulatory/clearing-house.

[125] Financial Action Task Force, 'Money Laundering through the Football Sector' (2009), www.fatf-gafi.org/content/dam/fatf-gafi/reports/ML%20through%20the%20Football%20Sector.pdf.coredownload.pdf.

[126] ibid para 70.1.

[127] CA Flanagan, 'Teenage Kicks: How The Structural Adolescence Of The Football Sector Engenders A Risk Of Money Laundering, Corruption And Other Economic Crimes' in L Pasculli and N Ryder (eds), *Corruption in the Global Era*, 1st edn (Routledge, 2019).

[128] For a list, see 'EU Banking And Financial Services Law' (*European Commission*, 2021), https://ec.europa.eu/info/law/law-topic/eu-banking-and-financial-services-law_en.

This was clearly anticipated by FIFA. In its Request for Proposal (RFP) Establishment and Operation of the FIFA Clearing House,[129] it stated that 'bidders should estimate the effort to comply with the proposed jurisdiction's regulatory requirements', suggesting that

> [e]xamples of such regulation for central counterparties and financial institutions are:
>
> – The Financial Market Infrastructure Act (FMIA or FinfraG) and the Anti-Money Laundering Act (AMLA or GwG) in Switzerland
>
> – The European Market Infrastructure Regulation (EMIR) and Anti-Money Laundering Directives in the European Union'.[130]

The entity that will act as the FIFA Clearing House[131] has been set up in France.[132] Consequently, should the activities proposed by FIFA fall within the definitions of various financial services regulated by the EU (or by France specifically), the FIFA Clearing House entity would be required to comply with those laws.[133] As the FIFA Clearing House shall collect and distribute payments, the relevant regulated financial service that it may perform falls under Directive (EU) 2015/2366,[134] the revised directive on payment services in the internal market (PSD2). PSD2 is the main legislative instrument on payment services at an EU level. The services it covers include the execution of payment transactions[135] and

[129] 'Request for Proposal (RFP) Establishment and Operation of the FIFA Clearing House' (FIFA, 25 July 2019), https://digitalhub.fifa.com/m/2144c701011eec8b/original/nwa4pef272hssbgcefpo-pdf.pdf.

[130] ibid.

[131] With company registration number ('SIREN') SIREN: 908028715, Société, FIFA Clearing House, www.societe.com/societe/fifa-clearing-house-908028715.html8 October 2022.

[132] FIFA, 'French Banking Supervisory Authority Grants Licence to FIFA Clearing House' (*Fifa.com*, 29 September 2002), www.fifa.com/legal/media-releases/french-banking-supervisory-authority-grants-licence-to-fifa-clearing-house.

[133] In the RFP, FIFA suggested Regulation (EU) No 648/2012 of the European Parliament and of the Council of 4 July 2012 on OTC derivatives, central counterparties and trade repositories [2012] OJ L201/1–59 (European Market Infrastructure Regulation (EMIR)) as a potentially relevant regulatory requirement, presumably as that is a relevant regulation for central counterparties (CCPs) in clearing arrangements (EMIR Art 1). However, EMIR is limited in application to more complicated financial instruments and financial market participants. EMIR Art 1 states: 'This Regulation lays down clearing and bilateral risk-management requirements for over-the-counter ("OTC") derivative contracts, reporting requirements for derivative contracts and uniform requirements for the performance of activities of central counterparties ("CCPs") and trade repositories.'

The FIFA Clearing House does not involve OTC derivatives, and was unlikely to be structured such that the FIFA Clearing House would act either as a CCP or a trade repository. A CCP is defined in EMIR Art 2(1) as 'a legal person that interposes itself between the counterparties to the contracts traded on one or more financial markets, becoming the buyer to every seller and the seller to every buyer' and a trade repository by EMIR Art 2(2) as 'a legal person that centrally collects and maintains the records of derivatives'. These definitions do not apply to the FIFA Clearing House.

[134] Directive (EU) 2015/2366 of the European Parliament and of the Council of 25 November 2015 on payment services in the internal market, amending Directives 2002/65/EC, 2009/110/EC and 2013/36/EU and Regulation (EU) No 1093/2010, and repealing Directive 2007/64/EC [2015] OJ L337/35–127.

[135] Meaning 'an act, initiated by the payer or on his behalf or by the payee, of placing, transferring or withdrawing funds, irrespective of any underlying obligations between the payer and the payee' (PSD2 Art 4(5)).

acquiring payment transactions,[136] of which the activities contemplated by the FIFA Clearing House may include.[137]

Typically, it is prohibited to perform regulated financial services without an appropriate authorisation or exemption. In the case of payment services, Article 11 of PSD2 states that Member States shall require undertakings '… who intend to provide payment services, to obtain authorisation as a payment institution before commencing the provision of payment services.' In France, the prohibition on performing payment services without an appropriate authorisation is contained in Article L522-6 of the *Code Monétaire et Financier* (the French Monetary and Financial Code). Thus, the FIFA Clearing House entity was obliged to apply for and obtain regulatory authorisation from the applicable regulator in France before it could operate.[138] Once authorised, a system of regulatory oversight including 'effective, proportionate and dissuasive' penalties for breaches of the relevant regulatory obligations apply.[139]

One of the benefits of obtaining authorisation in an EU state is that authorised payment services providers are able to 'passport' their services into other Member States, meaning they can provide services throughout the EU without the need to obtain separate authorisations in each Member State. Appropriate regulatory authorisation of the FIFA Clearing House entity in France is sufficient for the FIFA Clearing House to provide payments services throughout the EU without further authorisations in other Member States. This position is naturally more complicated for payment services provided outside the EU, and thus FIFA must perform complicated cross-border analyses to determine whether the FIFA Clearing House encroaches on the regulatory perimeter of non-EU jurisdictions.

Once an entity such as the FIFA Clearing House is authorised by its supervisory regulator, the onerous compliance obligations set forth by PSD2 (as implemented into Member State law) will apply. These obligations include capital adequacy requirements,[140] obligations concerning the safeguarding of money,[141] and the management of operational and security risks.[142] PSD2 also covers specific conduct obligations in relation to the performance of payment transactions, a regime of liability for non-execution, defective or late execution

[136] Meaning 'a payment service provided by a payment service provider contracting with a payee to accept and process payment transactions, which results in a transfer of funds to the payee' (PSD2 Art 4(44)).

[137] It is these activities for which the FIFA Clearing House has been authorised by the French Prudential Supervision and Resolution Authority (Autorité de Contrôle Prudentiel et de Résolution, ACPR). See ACPR, 'Le Registre des Agents Financiers, Regafi, Identifiant REGAFI: 402628', www.regafi.fr/spip.php?type=simple&id_secteur=1&lang=fr&denomination=FIFA&page=af&id=451#zone_en_france.

[138] The regulation of payment services in France is performed by the ACPR, a branch of the Banque de France (the French central bank). See Article L522-6 I, Code Monétaire et Financier.

[139] PSD2, Art 103.

[140] ibid Arts 7–9.

[141] ibid Art 10.

[142] ibid Art 95.

of payment transactions,[143] and other matters, although some of these more burdensome compliance obligations can be disapplied where the payment service user is not a consumer[144] by agreement between the payment service provider (ie the FIFA Clearing House entity) and the payment service user (ie the relevant clubs) where they agree such disapplication.[145]

One aspect of PSD2 compliance that the FIFA Clearing House is unlikely to be able to avoid, which has the potential to have wider ramifications for football, is in respect of complaints and dispute resolution. Article 99 of PSD2 requires Member States to provide structures which 'allow payment service users and other interested parties including consumer associations, to submit complaints to the competent authorities with regard to payment service providers' alleged infringements of this Directive', and Article 102 requires Member States to ensure

> that payment service providers put in place and apply adequate and effective complaint resolution procedures for the settlement of complaints of payment service users concerning the rights and obligations arising under Titles III and IV of this Directive and shall monitor their performance in that regard.[146]

Payment service providers should reply to such complaints within 15 business days.[147] Finally, Article 102 compels a system of 'adequate, independent, impartial, transparent and effective ADR procedures for the settlement of disputes'. These provisions have the potential to create a system of oversight and disputes that are outside of FIFA's control; a position which has generally been anathema to SGBs.[148] However, as a balancing factor, Article 61(2) PSD2 states that 'Member States may provide that Article 102 does not apply where the payment service user is not a consumer', and so the degree to which the FIFA Clearing House will be open to complaints will be determined by whether or not the specific and applicable financial services alternative dispute resolution (ADR) system in either the jurisdiction into which services are received (ie by the club in question) or provided (ie the location of the FIFA Clearing House, France) is open to non-consumer complaints, subject to the jurisdiction rules of the particular ADR scheme; or whether the internal FIFA dispute resolution system, and appeal to the

143 ibid Art 89.

144 This is sometimes referred to as the 'corporate opt out'. Note that PSD2 allows for 'microenterprises' (which may include some smaller football clubs) to be treated as consumers.

145 The FIFA Clearing House entity presumably will seek such exclusions in order to reduce its compliance obligations. The FIFA Clearing House Regulations (October 2022 Edition) make reference to 'FCH Terms & Conditions', being 'the terms and conditions for a party to take part in a transaction involving the FIFA Clearing House'. The specific terms were not available to the author at the time of writing this chapter.

146 Although in practice a large proportion of the obligations in Titles III and IV of PSD2 are likely to be disapplied by the FIFA Clearing House pursuant to the corporate opt out.

147 PSD2 Art 101(2).

148 For detail, see Flanagan (n 17).

Court of Arbitration for Sport (CAS)[149] constitutes the 'adequate, independent, impartial, transparent and effective ADR' required by Article 102, PSD2. PSD2 allows for 'microenterprises'[150] to be treated as consumers,[151] although that is likely to exclude many football clubs, particularly the training clubs likely to rely on the FIFA Clearing House. Of course, given the cross-border nature of the relationship between the FIFA Clearing House and its users, additional analysis will need to be performed on a jurisdiction by jurisdiction basis.

Moreover, whether or not users of the FIFA Clearing House have access to a dedicated system of ADR outside of the private internal sports dispute system with a right of final appeal to the CAS, the FIFA Clearing House may struggle to oust claims before national courts in the way SGBs have traditionally done, and have jealously protected, in respect of their systems of compulsory private arbitration.[152] It is implied by the Recitals to PSD2 that payment service users may have a right for disputes to be heard in court.[153] For example, Recital 98, discussing ADR, describes a 'right of customers to bring action in the courts', Recital 100, discussing regulatory enforcement, is framed as being '[w]ithout prejudice to the right to bring action in the courts to ensure compliance with this Directive'.

Of course, the claims and complaints framework described above applies only to the FIFA Clearing House entity *qua* payment service provider, rather than to FIFA generally *qua* apex SGB of football, but it is possible, given the idiosyncratic nature of the FIFA Clearing House, that sport and financial services disputes may collide, and non-sporting ADR bodies or courts be called upon to adjudicate on subject matters that might ordinarily have stayed within the internal sports dispute resolution system.

[149] As facilitated by Article 18 of the FIFA Clearing House Regulations (October 2022 Edition).

[150] Defined as 'an enterprise, which at the time of conclusion of the payment service contract, is an enterprise as defined in Article 1 and Article 2(1) and (3) of the Annex to Recommendation 2003/361/EC'. Recommendation 2003/361/EC defines a microenterprise as 'an enterprise which employs fewer than 10 persons and whose annual turnover and/or annual balance sheet total does not exceed EUR 2 million'.

[151] It is not uncommon for financial services ADR bodies to treat microenterprises (including associations) as being in scope; for example, the Dutch financial services ADR body, *Klachteninstituut Financiële Dienstverlening* ('KIFID'), does accept complaints from microenterprises, KiFiD, 'About Kifid' (*KiFiD*, 2021), www.kifid.nl/about/, as does the UK Financial Ombudsman Service (FOS), Finance Ombudsman Service, 'Who We Can Help' (*FOS*, 2022), https://sme.financial-ombudsman.org.uk/complain/can-help. The system consumer ADR system in France, however, is 'highly fragmented', which 'tends to impair consumers' visibility and creates confusion', per A Biard, 'Impact of Directive 2013/11/EU on Consumer ADR Quality: Evidence from France and UK' (2018) *Journal of Consumer Policy* 42, 109–47.

[152] For a more detailed discussion of the effect of compulsory arbitration in sport, see A Duval, 'Not in My Name! Claudia Pechstein and the Post-Consensual Foundations of the Court of Arbitration for Sport' in H Ruiz Fabri, A Nunes Chaib, I Venzke, A von Bogdandy (eds), *International Judicial Legitimacy* (Nomos Verlag, 2020).

[153] At the very least, payment service users should have access to either ADR or the courts, as Recital 98 PSD2 states that, 'Member States should ensure that payment service providers put in place an effective complaints procedure that can be followed by their payment service users before the dispute is referred to be resolved in an ADR procedure or before a court'.

There are also second order effects of the authorisation of the FIFA Clearing House as a payment service provider. For example, a critical aspect of the operation of the FIFA Clearing House will be compliance with relevant anti-money laundering and counter terrorist financing laws, particularly the EU's suite of anti-money laundering directives, first introduced in the form of EU Council Directive 91/308/EEC on the prevention of the use of the financial system for the purpose of money laundering,[154] and most amended and revised from time to time (in recent times cumulatively in the form of the Fourth Money Laundering Directive ((EU) 2015/849) ('MLD4'), the Fifth Money Laundering Directive ((EU) 2018/843) ('MLD5'), and the Sixth Money Laundering Directive (EU) 2018/1673 ('MLD6'), taken together with the other EU money laundering directives the 'MLDs'); and further supplemented by the EU revised Wire Transfer Regulation (Regulation (EU) 2015/845) ('WTR').[155] The WTR ensures that the electronic transfer of monies is accompanied by transparent and meaningful information about the payer. The MLDs set out the anti-money laundering obligations that apply to 'financial institutions', which is defined to include payment service providers (Article 3(2)(a) MLD4). The MLDs institute a detailed, risk-based, system of anti-money laundering and counter terrorist financing measures, including an obligation to perform due diligence on its customers (ie clubs) and their beneficial owners.

These obligations take on further meaning in light of global geopolitics and the shifting boundaries between the sporting and the political. The ownership of professional football clubs has been described as 'a prominent issue with a heightened level of media attention, perhaps because it is a way for individuals (or nation-states) to buy respectability and enhance legitimacy and soft power'.[156] The EU legal order in which the FIFA Clearing House sits will agitate this dynamic by increasing scrutiny on club ownership: MLD4 extended due diligence requirements to include ultimate beneficial owners. Consequently, the FIFA Clearing House will need, directly or indirectly, to have performed appropriate due diligence not just on all football clubs, but on the beneficial owners of those clubs, to ensure that money passing through the international transfer system is not laundering the proceeds of criminal activity.[157] The introduction

[154] Council Directive 91/308/EEC of 10 June 1991 on prevention of the use of the financial system for the purpose of money laundering [1991] OJ L166/77–82.

[155] Regulation (EU) 2015/847 of the European Parliament and of the Council of 20 May 2015 on information accompanying transfers of funds and repealing Regulation (EC) No 1781/2006 [2015] OJ L141/1–18.

[156] H Gammelsæter and G Walters, 'Ownership and Governance in Men's Professional Football In Europe' in D Shilbury and L Ferkins (eds), *Routledge Handbook of Sport Governance*, 1st edn (Routledge, 2019).

[157] Article 15 of the FIFA Clearing House Regulations, October 2022 Edition, states 'The FIFA Clearing House has a legal obligation to monitor its business relationships and the transactions carried out during the existence of those relationships' (Art 15.1) and state that this may include a request for information on beneficial ownership from 'an individual, club, and/or member association' (Art 15.3).

of the FIFA Clearing House means that football cannot be a passive bystander in relation to illicit financial flows in football; a proactive and ongoing duty to prevent money laundering through the transfer system will apply.

Moreover, 'enhanced' due diligence measures must be performed where a beneficial owner is a 'politically exposed person' (a 'PEP') in light of the elevated risks associated with PEPs. So too must senior management within the relevant institution obliged to comply with the MLDs (in this case the FIFA Clearing House) approve the establishment or continuation of any business relationship involving PEP.[158]

The definition of a PEP is quite widely drawn, encompassing a variety of persons 'entrusted with prominent public functions'[159] – including politicians, judiciary, directors of international organisations, the management of state-owned enterprises, and so on.[160] Enhanced due diligence must also be performed in respect of the family members and close associates of PEPs.[161]

Thus, the FIFA Clearing House will be required to perform due diligence – sometimes referred to as 'know your customer' – measures to all persons to whom the FIFA Clearing House provides services, and indeed to ultimate beneficial owners. That means taking steps to understand the nature of the relevant party's financial flows, sources of wealth and so on, to ensure that it can identify and prevent the risk of the FIFA Clearing House, and therefore the international transfer market, being used to launder money. In respect of PEPs, those due diligence measures are 'enhanced'. Enhanced measures may include, for example:

> Identifying, and verifying the identity of, other shareholders who are not the customer's beneficial owner … [Building] a more complete customer profile, for example by carrying out open source or adverse media searches or commissioning a third party intelligence report … [Establishing] the source of the customer's wealth and the source of the customer's funds that are involved in the business relationship, to be reasonably satisfied that these are legitimate.[162]

In practical terms, this means that the FIFA Clearing House likely will not be able to provide services to – and thus must exclude from the regulatory benefits of the international transfer system such as training compensation and solidarity payments – any club whose owner presents a material money laundering risk. MLD6 sets out a list of predicate offences in relation to money laundering,

[158] MLD4 Art 20.

[159] ibid Art 2(9).

[160] ibid.

[161] ibid Art 23.

[162] Joint Committee of the European Supervisory Authorities, 'Final Guidelines: Joint Guidelines Under Articles 17 And 18(4) Of Directive (EU) 2015/849 On Simplified And Enhanced Customer Dure Diligence And The Factors Credit And Financial Institutions Should Consider When Assessing The Money Laundering And Terrorist Financing Risk Associated With Individual Business Relationships And Occasional Transactions' (JC/2017/37)' (26 June 2017), www.eba.europa.eu/documents/10180/1890686/Final+Guidelines+on+Risk+Factors+%28JC+2017+37%29.pdf.

which includes activities such as piracy, human trafficking, cybercrime, environmental crime, corruption, and tax crime.[163] Football is not unblemished by accusations of this nature, whether directly or in relation to club ownership.

Lindholm says that 'no clean division between sports and politics is possible'.[164] The FIFA Clearing House enshrines that supposition in law. Lindholm identifies 'difficult questions' faced by sport in addressing sanctions and geopolitical turmoil. The FIFA Clearing House, as a creature of EU law, will be required to follow the established EU order; applying European norms and legal standards to the world at large.

However the socio-political dimension may evolve, the regulatory framework within which the FIFA Clearing House sits, in and of itself, has the potential to take the *lex sportiva* in new directions.

III. THE INFLUENCE OF EU REGULATION AND REGULATORY INSTITUTIONS ON THE REGULATION OF FOOTBALL

The traditional conception of the influence of EU law on SGBs, and that which has seen the most detailed analysis, is in respect of the ways in which EU law and institutions (specifically the Commission and the CJEU) have shaped the regulatory autonomy of those SGBs. Undoubtedly the friction between SGBs and the appropriate application of EU competition law, in particular, has had an influence on policy and practice in football.

What we see in the FIFA DPRs and the likely structure of the FIFA Clearing House, however, shows that the influence of EU law on football is not limited to the provisions of the TFEU; nor supervisory scrutiny limited to the Commission and courts. Having moved from a position of resistance to a position of acceptance of the applicability of EU law, FIFA is now further influenced by EU regulations and directives.

The reasons for this influence are in likelihood not underpinned by a unitary principle of general application, but speak to both the breadth and depth of the activities FIFA has brought within its regulatory purview, and the pervasive influence of EU law. The latter point is well established insofar as it applies to the influence of EU generally.

Bradford identifies five elements underpinning the Brussels Effect: market size, regulatory capacity, stringent standards, inelastic targets, and non-divisibility (legal and economic).[165] For financial and data flows in football, the market size of the European game, and in particular the European market size of one of the most idiosyncratic parts of football, its player transfer market is significant – clubs

[163] MLD6 Art 2(1).

[164] J Lindholm, 'How Russia's Invasion of Ukraine Shook Sports' Foundation' (2022) *International Sports Law Journal* 22, 1–4.

[165] Bradford (n 5) chapter 2.

within the UEFA confederation being the largest market by volume and transaction value of player transfers.[166] The player transfer market, as structured by FIFA, entails the movement of money and personal data, and is most concentrated in Europe. The exacting regulatory standards applied to financial services and data protection in the EU are each overseen by a network of national supervisory authorities, overseen and co-ordinated at a transnational level, meaning regulatory capacity apt to oversee stringent standards.

Thus, unless FIFA were willing and able to take the impractical step of dividing the regulation of player transfers between EU and non-EU markets (for example, by applying the FIFA Clearing House only to transfers within the confines of the European Union, or restructuring its activities such that its activities would not fall within the ambit of PSD2), it has little choice but to comply with, and thereby spread beyond the boundaries of the Union, EU law.

The influences of EU law on sport discussed here amplify the existing extra-territorial effects of EU regulatory measures. The scope of the GDPR can in effect be extended worldwide; the scope of PSD2 is also capable of extension beyond the ordinary boundaries of the EU where there is some nexus to the EU in the relevant transaction or relationship. For example, PSD2 will apply to transactions in EU currencies where the payment service providers in the chain are located within the EU whether or not the payment service user is in the EU or not. So, for example, a club based in Brazil with a bank account in Portugal using the FIFA Clearing House in France to receive training compensation and solidarity payments in Euro would necessitate compliance by the FIFA Clearing House with PSD2, notwithstanding the club's location.

Perhaps it is simply that the FIFA DPRs follow a global trend in data protection awareness and the FIFA Clearing House falls into EU regulation because the particular policy objectives of FIFA in establishing the Clearing House happen to imply that its proposed activities will fall within the ambit of EU financial services law. Bradford explains that, on the part of the EU, the Brussels Effect 'can be unintentional'.[167] For FIFA, though, the move towards EU law may, in contrast to the historic trend of SGBs, be more deliberate. FIFA, despite being headquartered outside the EU, nevertheless adopts EU-inspired regulations. Moreover, in the case of the FIFA Clearing House, FIFA chose to locate the FIFA Clearing House within the EU, whether to avail itself of the benefits of being located within the internal market, or for other reasons.[168]

In the case of the FIFA Clearing House, the maturity of the regulatory systems in structures in the EU make it an attractive place to do business. The possibility of passporting payment services throughout the EU once authorised in one jurisdiction gives the EU a structural advantage as a place to perform

[166] See FIFA, 'FIFA Global Transfer Report 2021', Figure 29, 22 https://digitalhub.fifa.com/m/2b542d3b011270f/original/FIFA-Global-Transfer-Report-2021-2022-indd.pdf.

[167] Bradford, 'The Brussels Effect' (n 51).

[168] See section II.C.

financial services, just as, after the UK's exit from the EU, 'Amsterdam ousted London as the largest financial trading centre in Europe'.[169] The nature of the Single Market is such that undertakings in regulated spaces are able to act throughout the EU without the additional burden of maintaining authorisations in each jurisdiction. When further considering Europe as the locus of economic value in the football industry, locating the FIFA Clearing House within the EU is a pragmatic choice, notwithstanding the regulatory burdens that accompany that choice.

The leveraging of EU law also has a legitimising effect on FIFA's regulatory authority. Andrews and Harrington suggest that as a result of 'a myriad of claims of fraud, corruption, mismanagement, and money laundering by senior officials … many have lost trust in these bodies'.[170] FIFA, further to its 'FIFA 2.0: The Vision for the Future'[171] aimed to 'drive significant improvements to the governance of global football'; there is sanctuary in using established systems of regulation in order to drive those governance improvements.

There can be little doubt that the adoption by FIFA of the regulatory concepts of EU law precipitates an intended increase in standards: Minimum data protection standards are introduced where previously they were none, financial services laws intend to protect the users of the relevant financial system, anti-money laundering laws intend to reduce financial crime, and so on; a 'race to the top' mechanism redolent of that which has been suggested of globalism more generally.[172] That having been said, except to the degree FIFA was already subject to EU laws, the raising of standards need not have relied on EU laws and regulatory systems; those standards could have been entrenched voluntarily, or indeed by reference to the legal and regulatory systems of other parts of the world. Football has tended towards Eurocentricity; its wealth is concentrated in Europe, its apex regulator is in Europe; and its legal systems are defined – increasingly – by EU law, with oversight by EU regulators. Together this could be construed as a manifestation of European cultural imperialism.

Whether or not these developments can be depicted as an overreach of European systems of law, the regulatory initiatives described in this chapter were not primarily driven by EU authorities; rather, they are driven by FIFA, as it moves towards EU law, and towards a system of layered regulation.

[169] 'Brexit: London Loses Out As Europe's Top Share Trading Hub' (*BBC News*, 11 February 2021), www.bbc.co.uk/news/business-56017419.

[170] Andrews and Harrington (n 21).

[171] FIFA, 'FIFA President Infantino Unveils "FIFA 2.0: The Vision For The Future"' (*Fifa.com*, 2021), www.fifa.com/who-we-are/news/fifa-president-infantino-unveils-fifa-2-0-the-vision-for-the-future-2843428#:~:text=FIFA%20President%20Gianni%20Infantino%20has%20today%20unveiled%20%E2%80%9C,fans%20and%20players%20and%20build%20a%20stronger%20institution.

[172] See Bradford, 'The Brussels Effect' (n 51); D Spar and D Yoffie, 'A Race to the Bottom or Governance from the Top?' in A Prakash and JA Hart (eds), *Coping With Globalization* (Taylor Francis, 2000) 31, 31–51.

The activities envisaged by the FIFA DPRs and the FIFA Clearing House each potentially open the door to external regulators – data protection and financial services supervisory authorities respectively – although the degree of oversight exercised by those regulators will be limited to their own spheres of competence. Whilst there is a prospect of this having an influence on the future regulation of football, the limited competence and capacity[173] of the external regulators outside of their sphere of specialism should mean that the impact is limited and can be managed by FIFA.

The nature of external regulation means that disaffected subjects of the relevant ecosystems could seek recourse either via those regulators; so too could they seek recourse via domestic courts or tribunals. The specific rights that arise will depend on the instrument under which rights are created. In the present cases, PSD2 primarily imposes a system of ADR,[174] whereas the GDPR gives a clear right of action enforcement before the courts.[175] The FIFA DPRs imply rights of action before courts, but only 'in accordance with the Applicable Data Protection Laws' rather than pursuant to the FIFA DPRs directly.[176] In the data protection sphere, the rights of action of private persons have been described as having 'an important role in … enforcement … As a supplement to enforcement by public regulators',[177] and more generally 'private enforcement is seen as a tool to strengthen the overall enforcement'.[178] These specific rights of private enforcement follow a general trend in which 'the EU legislature started responding to the calls for the establishment of EU legislation to facilitate the private enforcement of EU law',[179] and this proliferation of private enforcement rights, including civil rights of action for damages, although complex in effect, means enforcement of the EU legal order operates on a multi-level basis, driving adoption.[180] In the case of each of the data protection and financial services regulatory regimes, EU law can be enforced by regulators *and* private persons.

[173] Public regulators and administrative bodies must prioritise cases based on resources, priorities, and their own statutory and internal regulatory frameworks. See, eg, van Rompuy's analysis of the European Commission's handling of non-priority antitrust complaints: B van Rompuy, 'The European Commission's Handling of Non-priority Antitrust Complaints: An Empirical Assessment' (2022) 45 *World Competition* 2, 265–94.

[174] For analysis, see A Janczuk-Gorywoda, 'Enforcing Smart: Exploiting Complementarity of Public and Private Enforcement in the Payment Services Directive' in OO Cherednychenko and M Andenas (eds), *Financial Regulation and Civil Liability in European Law* (Elgar, 2020) chapter 5, 115–37.

[175] See GDPR Arts 79, 80 and 82.

[176] FIFA DPRs Art 5.

[177] P Blok, 'The Role of Private Actors in Data Protection Law and Data Protection Practice' in M de Cock Buning and L Senden (eds), *Private Regulation and Enforcement in the EU: Finding the Right Balance from a Citizen's Perspective* (Hart Publishing, 2020).

[178] W Wurmnest and M Gömann, 'Comparing Private Enforcement of EU Competition and Data Protection Law' (2022) 13 *Journal of European Tort Law* 2, 154–82.

[179] F Wilman, *Private Enforcement of EU Law Before National Courts: The EU Legislative Framework* (Edward Elgar, 2015) 14.

[180] See ibid chapter 1.

Thus, as Wurmnest and Gömann state: 'Private enforcement is ... supposed to complement the efforts of the authorities ....by disclosing ... violations that might otherwise remain unpursued due to the authorities' lack of resources or prioritisation'.[181]

However, FIFA has an unusual position as both *regulator* and *regulated*. It may find itself subject to private enforcement measures pursuant to its obligations where it performs regulated activities; however, it is also able to manage its risk in that regard with its powers as a regulator, including by the imposition and enforcement of private dispute resolution systems. It is well documented that SGBs 'can, and do, promulgate their own regulations as having primacy' within a private system of arbitration; and within that system, as Duval has highlighted, the prospect of an SGB's rule being struck down for want of compliance with EU law has historically been vanishingly small.[182] Unsurprisingly, the FIFA DPRs and the FIFA Clearing House Regulations demur from giving a direct right of appeal to the ordinary courts in the event of a breach by FIFA of a provision of EU law, although equally neither appears to directly oust an appeal to the courts.[183]

Thus, private enforcement of the EU legal order may be possible, and that may in turn shape the *lex sportiva*, but the primary control of FIFA's private legal order will remain in FIFA's control; the effect of EU secondary legislation is more to influence (and, arguably, improve) the standards of football's internal regulatory system than to supplant it.

There is, consequently, the spectre of a fragmented regulatory approach, with courts or regulators interpretating legal obligations of FIFA in relation to its activities one way (whether directly or by decisions capable of application to the activities of FIFA in the field of data protection or payment services), and FIFA *qua* regulator (or a panel of arbitrators at the CAS) deciding another way. But the prospect seems somewhat remote. If such a conflict were to arise, it remains to be seen whether any harmonisation measures would be implemented, and if so by whom and how.

With the FIFA Clearing House in particular, there is a certain circularity to the adoption of EU law regulatory structures: The FIFA Clearing House is necessary in order to ensure the proper distribution of training compensation and solidarity payments. The proper distribution of training compensation and

[181] Wurmnest and Gömann (n 178) comparing and contrasting the positions in EU competition and data protection law.

[182] See analysis by A Duval, 'The Court of Arbitration for Sport and EU Law' (2015) 22 *Maastricht Journal of European and Comparative Law* 2.

[183] The FIFA DPRs, at Art 12, say that 'Any infringement of these Regulations may incur sanctions under the *Applicable Data Protection Laws*, the FIFA Statutes or any other FIFA Regulations' (emphasis added), although the nature of a 'sanctions' provision is such that it is unlikely to be construed as applying to the actions of FIFA qua regulator; the FIFA Clearing House Regulations (October 2022 Edition) meanwhile, state that 'Any final decision, as identified in these Regulations, may be appealed to CAS in accordance with the FIFA Statutes ...' (Art 18.1), with 'may' rather than 'must' capable of being interpreted as granting non-exclusive jurisdiction to CAS.

solidarity payments is necessary to defend the legitimacy of the restrictions inherent to the player transfer system. Defending the legitimacy of the restrictions inherent to the player transfer system is necessary to comply with EU law. In order for FIFA to manage the risks associated with the intersection of primary EU law (namely EU internal market law) and the regulatory system associated with the transfer market, FIFA has been driven towards a system of secondary EU law (namely payment services regulation).

Added to this is the fact that personal data processing via FIFA infrastructure,[184] and consequently engaging with the FIFA DPRs, is necessary for clubs engaging with the FIFA Clearing House. This presents a picture of a complex and growing web of inter-connecting internal and external regulatory measures and influences, with a line drawn through them by FIFA's foundational rules governing the transfer system found in the RSTP, and the increasing intricacy and sophistication of that system.

As FIFA is the author of the FIFA DPRs and of the FIFA Clearing House system, it can retreat from those structures. It may nevertheless intersect with EU data protection, or financial services, or other general EU law, but it has control over the degree to which it volunteers to those structures beyond what is required by law.

So, in football, who regulates the regulators? Whilst the expansive nature of EU law goes some way to introducing new measures of regulatory oversight, the answer remains: While it may do so 'in the shadow of EU law',[185] for the most part, football regulates itself.

[184] The FIFA Clearing House being reliant on TMS and the Electronic Player Passport, described as 'an electronic document containing consolidated registration information of a player throughout their career, including the relevant member association, their status (amateur or professional), the type of registration (permanent or loan), and the club(s) (including training category) with which they have been registered since the calendar year of their 12th birthday'. See FIFA Clearing House Regulations (October 2022 Edition) Art 8.

[185] A Duval, 'The FIFA Regulations on the Status and Transfer of Players: Transnational Law-Making in the Shadow of Bosman' in Duval and van Rompuy (n 36).

7

The Europeanisation of Clean Sport: How the Council of Europe and the European Union Shape the Proportionality of Ineligibility in the World Anti-Doping Code

JAN EXNER*

> Anti-doping rules 'could indeed prove excessive by virtue of (…) the severity of (…) penalties'.[1]

IN 2006, THE Court of Justice (ECJ) ruled that sanctions for doping must be proportionate to comply with the law of the European Union (EU).[2] Similarly, the European Court of Human Rights (ECtHR) decided in 2018 that whereabouts requirements must respect the principle of proportionality to comply with the European Convention on Human Rights (ECHR) of the Council of Europe (CoE).[3] Therefore, respect for the principle of proportionality under EU law and the ECHR is essential for anti-doping rules and sanctions, including ineligibility. In essence, ineligible athletes or other persons may not participate in any capacity in a competition or a sporting activity for a certain period of time. The prohibited competitions or activities include all

* I would like to thank the editors of this book and other participants at the conference 'The Europeanization of the Lex Sportiva: How European Law Shapes the Governance of Global Sports' held in Umeå, Sweden, between 18 and 19 November 2021, for their valuable comments on this chapter. I would also like to thank Michaela Valinová, a student at the Faculty of Law at Charles University, for her valuable help while researching the topic of this chapter. All errors are nevertheless exclusively my responsibility.

[1] CJEU, C-519/04 P *Meca-Medina and Majcen v Commission* [2006] EU:C:2006:492, para 48.

[2] ibid.

[3] ECtHR, 18 January 2018, *National Federation of Sportspersons' Associations and Unions (FNASS) and Others v France*, CE:ECHR:2018:0118JUD004815111. See also J-P Costa, 'Legal Opinion 2019 (expert opinion) on the World Anti-Doping Code' (2019) *World Anti-Doping Agency* 38, 3–5.

those authorised or organised by any signatory to the World Anti-Doping Code (WADC), its member organisations or a club, any professional league, any event organisation or any elite or national-level sporting activity funded by a government agency.[4] As such, ineligibility limits the freedom of action of both athletes and other persons and thus also the rights that they derive from the ECHR or EU law. Therefore, ineligibility must respect the European dimension of proportionality, which this chapter analyses from a legislative point of view.

The goal of this chapter is to analyse how the CoE and the EU shaped the proportionality of ineligibility in the review process leading to the current WADC in force as from 2021 (WADC 2021). The author hypothesises that the CoE and the EU would emphasise the proportionality of ineligibility. They share the goal of eradicating doping through robust rules and sanctions with the World Anti-Doping Agency (WADA) and other anti-doping organisations (ADOs). Nevertheless, while the fight against doping is the primary interest of WADA and other ADOs, the CoE and the EU emphasise the rights that stem from the ECHR and EU law. Therefore, they also accentuate the need for their limitations to be proportionate. Consequently, the author hypothesises that the CoE and the EU would advocate for more proportionality, shorter ineligibility, and greater leniency and flexibility in sanctioning athletes and other persons. Therefore, this chapter empirically evaluates the validity of this hypothesis, seeking the answer to the following two research questions: Did the CoE and the EU emphasise proportionality of ineligibility in the review process leading to WADC 2021? Does WADC 2021 reflect the positions of the CoE and the EU?

The empirical study of the transnational law-making process resulting in WADC 2021 is the main research object of this chapter. In 2017, WADA initiated a two-year-long review process with the view of adopting a new edition of the WADC. During three phases of consultations, WADA's stakeholders, including various sporting, governmental and non-governmental organisations, submitted a total of 1,718 comments and proposals regarding the WADC. The representatives of the CoE submitted 103 comments through its Sport Convention Division. The Chairs of the Working Party on Sport contributed with 17 comments on behalf of the EU. This chapter focuses on comments regarding the proportionality of the duration of ineligibility. Therefore, it analyses submissions concerning the absolute length of ineligibility or the margin of appreciation of ADOs or hearing panels to eliminate, reduce or suspend ineligibility based on the criteria defined in Article 10 of WADC 2021. On this narrower issue, the representatives of the CoE submitted 15 sets of suggestions, while those of the EU and its Member States had two sets of comments.[5]

[4] WADC 2021, Art 10.14.1, 10.14.2. See also WADC 2021, Comment to Art 10.14.1 for examples of prohibited conduct.

[5] WADA, 2021 Code Review – First Consultation Phase (in total 637 comments, CoE 28 comments – 2 on proportionality of ineligibility, EU 4 comments – 1 on proportionality of ineligibility), Second Consultation Phase (in total 603 comments, CoE 40 comments – 8 on proportionality of ineligibility, EU 8 comments – 1 on proportionality of ineligibility), Third Consultation Phase (in total 478 comments, CoE 35 comments – 5 on proportionality of ineligibility, EU 5 comments – none on

This chapter starts by highlighting the importance of the European dimension of proportionality for the conditional autonomy of the World Anti-Doping Program under the ECHR and EU law (section I). Second, it provides a context on the competences, policies and activities of the CoE and the EU in the area of anti-doping, focusing on their cooperation with WADA (section II). Consequently, the third and main part of this chapter examines the comments of the representatives of the CoE and the EU in the review process leading to WADC 2021, focusing on those concerning the proportionality of ineligibility. It initially provides their descriptive statistics. Consequently, it examines their content to assess whether they emphasised proportionality of ineligibility. Moreover, it analyses whether the interim versions and especially the final text of WADC 2021 reflect these comments (section III).

I. THE CONDITIONAL AUTONOMY OF THE WORLD ANTI-DOPING PROGRAM: EUROPEAN DIMENSION OF PROPORTIONALITY

The legal nature and autonomy of WADA and the WADC might seem to shelter them from the influence of the CoE and the ECHR, and the EU and its law respectively. WADA is a non-profit foundation established according to Swiss law.[6] Switzerland is a member of the CoE and has a set of bilateral agreements with the EU but is not a Member State (of the latter). Moreover, WADC 2021 provides that anti-doping rules are 'sport-specific rules and procedures', which are 'distinct in nature from criminal and civil proceedings' and which are 'not intended to be subject to or limited by any national requirements and legal standards applicable to such proceedings'.[7] Furthermore, WADC 2021 provides that it shall be interpreted as an independent and autonomous text and not by reference to the signatories or governments' existing laws or statutes.[8] Moreover, WADC 2021 stipulates that all courts, arbitral hearing panels, and other adjudicating bodies should 'be aware of and respect the distinct nature of the anti-doping rules in (WADC 2021) and the fact that those rules represent the consensus of a broad spectrum of stakeholders around the world with an interest in fair sport'.[9] Thus, WADA and other ADOs claim broad autonomy in governing the World Anti-Doping Program.

Nevertheless, in reality, the autonomy of WADA is not absolute but conditional upon compliance with national and international laws and general legal principles, including the principle of proportionality. However specific the anti-doping rules are, they are still 'regulations of an association which cannot

proportionality of ineligibility). These numbers include comments regarding the draft WADC 2021 itself, excluding the International Standards.

[6] WADA, Constitutive Instrument of Foundation, Art 1.

[7] WADC 2021, Part One: Doping Control.

[8] ibid Art 26.3.

[9] ibid Part One: Doping Control.

(directly or indirectly) replace fundamental and general legal principles like the doctrine of proportionality a priori for every thinkable case'.[10] The principle of proportionality is an internationally recognised general principle of constitutional law and human rights.[11] In particular, it is the main legal mechanism used to assess limitations to constitutionally and internationally guaranteed human rights.[12] It implies that restrictions must follow a legitimate purpose, there must be a rational connection between the purpose and the restriction and the latter must be necessary to achieve the purpose.[13] Moreover, the principle of proportionality is a general principle of sanctioning,[14] which stipulates that sanctions must be proportionate to the seriousness of the violation.[15] They must also be adjustable depending on the circumstances of cases due to the related principle of the individualisation or personalisation of sanctions.[16]

Moreover, the principle of proportionality applies to the WADC. WADA commissioned legal opinions on the conformity of selected provisions of editions of the WADC in force from 2004,[17] 2009,[18] 2015 (WADC 2015),[19] and 2021[20] with legal and human rights principles at the international and national level. All the authors recognised the need to respect the principle of proportionality

[10] CAS 2005/A/830 *Squizzato v Fédération Internationale de Natation* para 48. See also A Duval, et al, 'The World Anti-Doping Code 2015': ASSER International Sports Law Blog Symposium' (2016) *International Sports Law Journal* 16, 115.

[11] See amongst others A Barak, *Proportionality. Constitutional Rights and their Limitations* (Cambridge University Press, 2012); G Huscroft, BW Miller, G Webber, *Proportionality and the Rule of Law. Rights, Justification, Reasoning* (Cambridge University Press, 2016); VC Jackson, M Tushnet, *Proportionality. New Frontiers, New Challenges* (Cambridge University Press, 2018); M Kremnitzer, T Steiner, A Lang, *Proportionality in Action. Comparative and Empirical Perspectives on the Judicial Practice* (Cambridge University Press, 2020); J-R Sieckmann (ed), *Proportionality, Balancing, and Rights. Robert Alexy's Theory of Constitutional Rights* (Springer, 2021).

[12] See especially Barak (n 11).

[13] ibid.

[14] See amongst others A Von Hirsch, A Ashworth, *Proportionate Sentencing. Exploring the Principles.* (Oxford University Press, 2005).

[15] ibid; J-P Costa, 'Legal Opinion Regarding the Draft 3.0 Revision of the World Anti-Doping Code' (2013) *World Anti-Doping Agency* 8–9; J-P Costa, 'Legal Opinion for WADA Dated 27 April 2017 Regarding a Proposal of the International Olympic Committee for a Revision of the World Anti-Doping Code 2015' (2017) *World Anti-Doping Agency*, 3–5; G Kaufmann-Kohler, G Malinverni, A Rigozzi, 'Legal Opinion on the Conformity of Certain Provisions of the Draft World Anti-Doping Code with Commonly Accepted Principles of International Law' (2003) *World Anti-Doping Agency*, para 143, 43.

[16] Costa, 'Legal Opinion Regarding the Draft 3.0 Revision' (n 15) 8; Costa, 'Legal Opinion for WADA' (n 15) 3–5; C Rouiller, 'Legal Opinion on whether Article 10.2 of the World Anti-Doping Code is Compatible with the Fundamental Principles of Swiss Domestic Law' (2005) *World Anti-Doping Agency*, 32–33.

[17] Kaufmann-Kohler et al (n 15); Rouiller (n 16).

[18] G Kaufmann-Kohler, A Rigozzi, 'Legal Opinion on the Conformity of Article 10.6 of the 2007 Draft World Anti-Doping Code with the Fundamental Rights of Athletes' (2007) *World Anti-Doping Agency*; A Rigozzi, 'Conformity of the Exclusion of 'Team Athletes' from Organized Training during their Period of Ineligibility with Swiss Law' (2008) *World Anti-Doping Agency*.

[19] Costa 'Legal Opinion Regarding the Draft 3.0 Revision' (n 15); Costa 'Legal Opinion for WADA' (n 15).

[20] Costa (n 3).

in the WADC.[21] In particular, Jean-Paul Costa, the former President of the ECtHR, confirmed that the principle of proportionality applies to anti-doping rules stemming from WADC 2021.[22] In addition, the WADC 2021 itself provides that 'it has been drafted giving consideration to the principles of proportionality and human rights',[23] and that anti-doping rules 'are intended to be applied in a manner which respects the principles of proportionality and human rights'.[24] Moreover, the WADC 2021 abides by the rule of law, which seeks to ensure that all measures taken in the application of anti-doping programmes respect 'the principles of proportionality and human rights'.[25] Finally, the WADC 2021 explicitly refers to the principle of proportionality in the context of a variety of provisions.[26]

Additionally, the general legal principle of proportionality has a European dimension enshrined in the ECHR and EU law, which is relevant for WADA and other ADOs when they fall under the jurisdiction of members of the CoE, EU Member States, or both. This is the case particularly when they have a seat on the territory of a member or Member State, or when their rules apply to people falling under the laws of such states. The ECtHR and the ECJ confirmed that WADA and other ADOs must comply with the ECHR and EU law respectively, and have applied the proportionality principle to them.[27] Moreover, the purpose of WADC 2021 is to 'ensure harmonized, coordinated and effective anti-doping programmes at the international or national level with regard to the prevention

[21] Kaufmann-Kohler et al (n 15) para 80–83, 27–28; Rouiller (n 16) 29–31; Kaufmann-Kohler and Rigozzi (n 18) para 122–41, 42–48; Rigozzi (n 18) para 75–90, 21–24; Costa, 'Legal Opinion Regarding the Draft 3.0 Revision' (n 15) p 6, 8–9, 16, 19, 22, 24–26; Costa, 'Legal Opinion for WADA' (n 15) para 15–22, 3–5, para 24, p 5; Costa (n 3) 7, 12, 15–16, 19–20, 28. They relied especially on the ECHR, EU law and international conventions related to doping, such as the CoE's Anti-Doping Convention (1989) and the International Convention against Doping in Sport adopted by the United Nations Educational, Scientific and Cultural Organization (UNESCO) (2005). They also relied on the Universal Declaration of Human Rights (1948), the Council of Europe's European Social Charter (1961); the International Covenant on Civil and Political Rights of the United Nations (1966), the International Covenant on Economic, Social and Cultural Rights of the United Nations (1966), provisions on human rights in national constitutions and legislation, and general principles of law.

[22] Costa (n 3). He relied especially on the ECHR, EU law and international conventions related to doping, the CoE's Anti-Doping Convention (1989) and the International Convention against Doping in Sport adopted by UNESCO (2005). See also Minutes of the WADA Foundation Board Meeting, 18 May 2017, Mr Sieveking, 9.4, 41; Minutes of the WADA Foundation Board Meeting, 16 May 2019, Mr Muyters, 10.1, 35; Minutes of the WADA Foundation Board Meeting, 16 May 2019, Mr Sieveking, 10.1, 35; Minutes of the WADA Executive Committee Meeting, 23 September 2019, Mr Sieveking, 6.1, 29; Minutes of the WADA Executive Committee Meeting, 23 September 2019, Mr Young, 6.1, 29.

[23] WADC 2021, Purpose, Scope and Organization of the World Anti-Doping Program and the Code.

[24] ibid, Part One: Doping Control, Introduction.

[25] ibid, Purpose, Scope and Organization of the World Anti-Doping Program and the Code.

[26] ibid, Art 2.11.2 (Acts discouraging or retaliating against reporting to authorities), Art 5.5 (Non-Code consequences for violations of whereabouts requirements), Art 10.12 (Financial consequences), Art 14.3.7 (Optional public disclosure).

[27] *Meca-Medina* (n 1); *FNASS and Others v France* (n 3). See also Costa (n 3) 3–5.

of doping'.[28] It also seeks 'to advance the anti-doping effort through universal harmonization of core anti-doping elements'.[29] Since WADC 2021 must comply with the ECHR and EU law, the European dimension of proportionality gains global importance. Therefore, the role of the CoE and the EU in the fight against doping, particularly in shaping the proportionality of ineligibility in the WADC, deserves further analysis.

II. THE COUNCIL OF EUROPE, THE EUROPEAN UNION AND THE FIGHT AGAINST DOPING

The CoE and the EU play an important role in the governance of the World Anti-Doping Program and the enactment and implementation of the WADC. Before delving into their comments on WADC 2021, this section examines the competences and policies of the CoE and the EU in the fight against doping. It focuses on their role and function regarding WADA, particularly their participation in the review process of the WADC. First, it analyses anti-doping competences and policies of the CoE stemming particularly from the Enlarged Partial Agreement on Sport (EPAS), the European Sports Charter, the Anti-Doping Convention, the European Cultural Convention and the ECHR (section II.A). Second, it focuses on the EU's anti-doping competences and policies based especially on Articles 6(e) and 165 of the Treaty on the Functioning of the European Union (TFEU) (section II.B). Simultaneously, this section explores how the CoE and the EU co-operate in anti-doping efforts and activities with each other and with WADA and other ADOs.

A. The Council of Europe and Anti-Doping

The CoE's role in the field of sport, including anti-doping, stems from three main legal mechanisms: the EPAS, thematic conventions, and the ECHR. First, the EPAS is a platform for intergovernmental sports co-operation and dialogue between public authorities, sports federations and non-governmental organisations. It develops policies and standards to make sport more ethical, inclusive and safe.[30] Moreover, the EPAS promotes and monitors the effective implementation of the European Sports Charter. As such, it also guides the CoE's members to improve their existing legislation or other policies and to develop a comprehensive framework for sport.[31] Second, the CoE's toolkit for sport includes three thematic conventions: the Council of Europe Convention on the

[28] WADC 2021, Purpose, Scope and Organization of the World Anti-Doping Program and the Code.

[29] ibid.

[30] CoE, 'Enlarged Partial Agreement on Sport', www.coe.int/en/web/sport/epas.

[31] CoE, 'The European Sports Charter', www.coe.int/en/web/sport/european-sports-charter.

Manipulation of Sports Competitions from 2014 (Macolin Convention), the Council of Europe Convention on an Integrated Safety, Security and Service Approach at Football Matches and Other Sports Events from 2016 (Saint-Denis Convention), and the Anti-Doping Convention from 1989.

The Anti-Doping Convention is the main legal instrument of the CoE in the fight against doping, the CoE's first intervention in the domain of sport.[32] The members of the CoE, the other state parties to the European Cultural Convention, and other states adopted the Anti-Doping Convention in 1989 with an additional protocol in 2002.[33] Nowadays, 52 state parties[34] undertake, within the limits of their respective constitutional provisions, to take the steps necessary to apply the provisions of the Convention with a view to the reduction and eventual elimination of doping in sport.[35] The Anti-Doping Convention is primarily an instrument of cooperation between the state parties, WADA and other ADOs. It contains rules and principles on domestic coordination, measures to restrict the availability and use of banned doping agents and methods, laboratories, anti-doping education, cooperation with sports organisations, international cooperation, and the provision of information.[36] Importantly, the Anti-Doping Convention sets up the Monitoring Group of the Council of Europe Anti-Doping Convention ('T-DO') as its statutory body.[37]

The T-DO monitors the implementation of the Anti-Doping Convention, interprets its provisions and aids its state parties. It also reviews the provisions of the Convention and examines any necessary modifications. Moreover, the T-DO approves the list of pharmacological classes of doping agents and methods, and the criteria for the accreditation of laboratories. It also holds consultations with relevant sports organisations. Furthermore, the T-DO recommends to the state parties which measures they should take for the purposes of the Anti-Doping Convention and to keep relevant international organisations and the public informed about activities undertaken within its framework. Following the recommendation of the T-DO, the Committee of Ministers adopted the recommendation on general principles of fair procedure applicable to anti-doping proceedings in sport and related explanatory memorandum in 2022.[38] In addition, the T-DO makes recommendations to the Committee of Ministers concerning states that are not members of the CoE to be invited to accede to the Convention. Finally, it makes proposals for improving the effectiveness of

[32] CoE, 'Anti-Doping', www.coe.int/en/web/sport/anti-doping-convention.

[33] ibid.

[34] CoE, 'State Parties to the Anti-Doping Convention', www.coe.int/en/web/sport/state-parties-to-anti-doping-convention.

[35] CoE, Anti-Doping Convention, Art 1.

[36] ibid Arts 2–9.

[37] ibid Arts 10–11; CoE, The Council of Europe and Sport, Strategic Priorities for 2022–2025, SG/Inf(2022)2, 2.

[38] CoE, Recommendation CM/Rec(2022)14 of the Committee of Ministers to member States on general principles of fair procedure applicable to anti-doping proceedings in sport; Explanatory memorandum.

the Convention.[39] The T-DO organises advisory groups of experts in many areas of anti-doping.[40] In fulfilling its mission, it cooperates with WADA, the International Olympic Committee (IOC), the United Nations (UN) Educational, Scientific and Cultural Organization (UNESCO), and other sporting organisations and bodies of the CoE, including the ECtHR.[41] Importantly, it also ensures cooperation with the EU in anti-doping matters.[42]

Moreover, the T-DO cooperates with the Ad hoc European Committee for the World Anti-Doping Agency (CAHAMA). The CAHAMA is an intergovernmental committee established by a decision of the Committee of Ministers to coordinate positions of state parties to the European Cultural Convention. Historically, the work of the CoE on anti-doping stemmed from the European Cultural Convention adopted in 1954.[43] The 50 state parties[44] agreed to take appropriate measures to safeguard and encourage the development of its national contribution to the common cultural heritage of Europe.[45] The state parties coordinate their positions regarding WADA through CAHAMA, which has essentially three goals. First, it examines issues concerning relations between the CoE, its members and WADA, and decides on a common position. Second, it draws up, if necessary, opinions for the Committee of Ministers, including the budgetary elements.[46] Moreover, it periodically revises the mandates of two representatives of the CoE on the WADA Foundation Board.[47] In addition, the CoE participates in OneVoice, an intergovernmental coordination mechanism on issues related to WADA.[48] Consequently, the CoE submits its comments on the drafts of the WADC through its Sport Convention Division.[49]

The comments of the CoE also result from the case law of the ECtHR applying the ECHR in doping-related matters. The ECtHR considered rules concerning doping from the perspective of freedom of speech,[50] the right to a fair trial,[51] and the right to respect for a private and family life.[52] In particular,

[39] CoE, Anti-Doping Convention, Art 11.

[40] CoE, 'The Monitoring Group of the Anti-doping Convention (T-DO)', https://www.coe.int/en/web/sport/t-do.

[41] CoE, Anti-Doping (n 32).

[42] CoE, Strategic Priorities for 2022–2025 (n 37) 4.

[43] CoE, European Cultural Convention.

[44] CoE, 'State Parties to the European Cultural Convention', www.coe.int/en/web/sport/state-parties-european-cultural-convention.

[45] CoE, European Cultural Convention, Art 1.

[46] CoE, 'Ad hoc European Committee for the World Anti-Doping Agency (CAHAMA)', https://www.coe.int/en/web/sport/cahama.

[47] ibid; WADA, Constitutive Instrument of Foundation, Art 6.2; WADA, 'Foundation Board', www.wada-ama.org/en/who-we-are/governance/foundation-board.

[48] CoE, Anti-Doping (n 32).

[49] CoE, 'Sport', www.coe.int/en/web/sport; WADA, 2021 Code Review – First Consultation Phase, Second Consultation Phase, Third Consultation Phase, Council of Europe, Sport Convention Division (France), Public Authorities – Intergovernmental Organization.

[50] ECtHR, 28 June 2012 *Ressiot and Others v France*, CE:ECHR:2012:0628JUD001505407.

[51] ECtHR, 2 October 2018 *Mutu and Pechstein v Switzerland*, CE:ECHR:2018:1002JUD004057510.

[52] *FNASS and Others v France* (n 3). See also Costa (n 3) 3–5.

the ECtHR assessed the compliance of anti-doping rules with the ECHR in 2018 in *National Federation of Sportspersons' Associations and Unions ('FNASS') and Others v France*. In the latter case, the ECtHR considered whereabouts requirements stemming from WADC 2015 as implemented into French law. The ECtHR ruled that these requirements comply with the right to respect for private and family life protected by Article 8 of the ECHR. It reasoned that the constraints caused by anti-doping rules were necessary in a democratic society as they were proportionate in the interests of protecting the health and the rights and freedoms of others. Even though the ECtHR upheld the anti-doping rules, it clarified that they must respect the ECHR, especially the principle of proportionality.[53]

B. The European Union and Anti-Doping

The EU's scope of intervention in anti-doping matters includes coordination of the actions of Member States through incentive measures and recommendations, and the mobilisation of the EU's funding programmes. The legal basis of anti-doping policies and activities of the EU is Article 165 of the TFEU. It provides that the EU 'shall contribute to the promotion of European sporting issues, while taking account of the specific nature of sport, its structures based on voluntary activity and its social and educational function'.[54] The actions of the EU should aim at 'developing the European dimension in sport, by promoting fairness and openness in sporting competitions and cooperation between bodies responsible for sports, and by protecting the physical and moral integrity of sportsmen and sportswomen, especially the youngest sportsmen and sportswomen'.[55] Moreover, the EU and its Member States cooperate in sport-related matters with third countries and competent international organisations, explicitly including the CoE.[56] To achieve these objectives, the EU adopts incentive measures or recommendations. On the other hand, the EU cannot harmonise the laws and regulations of the Member States in the area of sport.[57]

Anti-doping has been a key part of the EU work plan for sport. In the period between 2017 and 2020, which covered the review process leading to WADC 2021, the integrity of sport, including fighting doping, was one of the priority themes for the Member States and the European Commission (Commission).[58]

[53] ibid. See also Costa (n 3) 3–5.
[54] TFEU, Art 165(1).
[55] ibid Art 165(2).
[56] ibid Art 165(3).
[57] ibid Art 165(4).
[58] Resolution of the Council and of the Representatives of the Governments of the Member States, meeting within the Council, on the European Union Work Plan for Sport (1 July 2017–31 December 2020), Part II: Developing further the European dimension in sport by establishing an EU work plan, para 12.

The Member States invited the Commission to support them and other relevant actors in their activities by 'providing the necessary expert input on anti-doping issues, in particular the compatibility with EU law of any forthcoming revision of the (WADC)'.[59] They have also asked the Council and its preparatory bodies to prepare expert input on anti-doping issues to be discussed within the Working Party for Sport as an EU contribution. Second, they have asked them to prepare the EU and its Member States' joint position for the meetings of CAHAMA and WADA supported when necessary by meetings of experts. The third requested input was for the Presidency to prepare a seminar on ways of preventing the use of doping by young people in professional and in grassroots sports.[60]

Experts on anti-doping matters prepared material for the discussions within the Working Party for Sport, which resulted in the contribution of the EU and its Member States to the review process that resulted in WADC 2021. In the first consultation phase, Viktoria Slavkova, the Chair of the Working Party on Sport and the Deputy Member of the WADA Foundation Board submitted the comments of the EU and its Member States on their behalf.[61] In the second consultation phase, Barbara Spindler-Oswald, the Chair of the Working Party on Sport contributed on behalf of the EU and its Member States.[62] Following the adoption of the WADC 2021, anti-doping also remains a key topic in the current EU Work Plan for Sport 2021–2024. The tasks of the EU again include the preparation and coordination of the position of the EU and its Member States for the meetings of the CAHAMA and WADA, particularly the WADA Foundation Board,[63] where the Member States have three representatives.[64] Moreover, the work plan for sport again calls upon the EU Expert Group on Anti-Doping to propose revisions to the WADC.[65]

As in the case of the CoE and the ECtHR, the EU's intervention in anti-doping matters emanates partly from the case law of the Court of Justice of the European Union (CJEU) in sport-related matters. The CJEU has in particular applied the free movement of persons and services,[66] and competition law

[59] ibid, Part IV: further steps, para 18.

[60] ibid, Annex 1: Key topics (para 12), requested outputs and corresponding working structures: Anti-Doping.

[61] WADA, 2021 Code Review – First Consultation Phase, Ministry of Youth and Sport, Viktoria Slavkova, Chair of Working Party on Sport, Deputy member of FB on behalf of EU (Bulgaria), Public Authorities – Government.

[62] ibid – Second Consultation Phase, EU and its Member States, Barbara Spindler-Oswald on behalf of the EU and its Member States, Chair of the Working Party on Sport (Austria), Public Authorities.

[63] Resolution of the Council and of the Representatives of the Governments of the Member States meeting within the Council on the European Union Work Plan for Sport (1 January 2021–30 June 2024), Annex 1: priority area: Protect integrity and values in sport, key topic: Anti-Doping, theme.

[64] WADA, Foundation Board (n 47).

[65] See also Commission, 'Anti-Doping', https://sport.ec.europa.eu/policies/sport-and-integrity/anti-doping.

[66] CJEU, C-36/74 *Walrave and Koch v Association Union Cycliste Internationale and Others*, EU:C:1974:140; CJEU, C-13/76 *Dona v Mantero*, EU:C:1976:115; CJEU, C-415/93 *Union royale*

to sport.[67] Regarding anti-doping, *Meca-Medina and Majcen v Commission* from 2006 is the flagship judgment. The ECJ ruled that EU law, particularly rules on competition and the freedom of movement of persons and services, apply to anti-doping rules. It further considered that the restrictive effects of the detection threshold of Nandrolone on professional athletes were inherent in the pursuit of legitimate anti-doping objectives and, importantly, that they were proportionate to them. The ECJ concluded that the restrictions did not go beyond what was necessary to ensure that sporting events take place and function properly.[68] Nevertheless, the ECJ warned ADOs that the anti-doping rules

> could indeed prove excessive by virtue of, first, the conditions laid down for establishing the dividing line between circumstances which amount to doping in respect of which penalties may be imposed and those which do not, and second, the severity of those penalties.[69]

Therefore, the ECJ ruled that anti-doping rules do not escape the scrutiny of EU law and that they must respect the principle of proportionality.[70]

III. THE COUNCIL OF EUROPE AND THE EUROPEAN UNION IN THE REVIEW PROCESS OF THE WORLD ANTI-DOPING CODE: PROPORTIONALITY OF INELIGIBILITY

Having examined the competences, policies and activities of the CoE and the EU in anti-doping, this section focuses on their involvement in the review process that resulted in WADC 2021. It particularly examines whether they emphasised the proportionality of ineligibility and whether the interim versions and the final text of WADC 2021 reflect their comments. This section

belge des sociétés de football association and Others v Bosman and Others, EU:C:1995:463; CJEU, C-51/96 and C-191/97 *Deliège*, EU:C:2000:199; CJEU, C-176/96 *Lehtonen and Castors Braine*, EU:C:2000:201; CJEU, C-438/00 *Deutscher Handballbund*, EU:C:2003:255; CJEU, C-265/03 *Simutenkov*, EU:C:2005:213; *Meca-Medina and Majcen* (n 1); CJEU, C-152/08 *Real Sociedad de Fútbol and Kahveci*, EU:C:2008:450; CJEU, C-325/08 *Olympique Lyonnais*, EU:C:2010:143; CJEU, C-22/18 *TopFit and Biffi*, EU:C:2019:497.

[67] CJEU, T-193/02 *Piau v Commission*, EU:T:2005:22 CJEU; *Meca-Medina and Majcen* (n 1); CJEU, C-49/07 *Motosykletistiki Omospondia Ellados NPID (MOTOE) v Elliniko Dimosio*, EU:C:2008:376; CJEU, T-93/18 *International Skating Union v Commission*, EU: T:2020:610.

[68] *Meca-Medina* (n 1) paras 35–60.

[69] ibid para 48.

[70] The General Court relied on the principles established by the ECJ in *Meca-Medina and Majcen* (n 1) while confirming the key role of the general legal principle of proportionality for the compliance of sporting sanctions with EU competition law in the case concerning eligibility rules of the International Skating Union (ISU'). See *International Skating Union v Commission* (n 67) para. 90–95. The ISU appealed the General Court's judgment to the ECJ, see CJEU, C-124/21 P *International Skating Union v Commission*.

analyses both the quantity and quality of the sets of comments of the representatives of the CoE and those of the EU and its Member States. Starting with the quantity, the number of comments is relevant since this indicates the relative level of interest in the topic. Providing more comments on proportionality would suggest that the CoE and the EU accentuate the issue in WADC 2021. On the other hand, a lower number of comments would indicate less interest in the topic. Therefore, Table 7.1 presents the descriptive statistics of the sets of comments that the representatives of the CoE and those of the EU and its Member States submitted in all three phases of the consultation process. It demonstrates that the CoE attempted to influence WADC 2021 and the proportionality of ineligibility considerably more than the EU and its Member States.

Table 7.1 Descriptive Statistics of the Comments of the Representatives of the CoE and the EU in the Review Process of the WADC

Consultation phase (period)[71]	Comments in total	CoE Comments in total	CoE Comments on the proportionality of ineligibility	EU Comments in total	EU Comments on the proportionality of ineligibility
1[72] (12 December 2017 – 31 March 2018)	637	28 (4.4 %)	2	4 (0.6 %)	1
2[73] (14 June 2018 – 14 September 2018)	603	40 (6.6 %)	8	8 (1.3 %)	1
3[74] (10 December 2018 – 4 March 2019)	478	35 (7.3 %)	5	5 (1 %)	–

Focusing on the proportionality of ineligibility, Table 7.2 illustrates how many comments the representatives of the CoE and the EU submitted on which areas of the draft Article 10 of WADC 2021. Their comments concerned areas including both pre-existing principles of WADC 2015 and the novelties introduced with WADC 2021, especially the new concepts of protected persons and recreational athletes and their sanctioning.

[71] WADA, 2021 Code Review Process, Schedule.
[72] WADA, 2021 Code Review – First Consultation: Questions to Discuss and Consider.
[73] ibid – Second Consultation Phase.
[74] ibid – Third Consultation Phase.

Table 7.2 Areas of the Comments of the Representatives of the CoE and the EU in the Review Process of the WADC

Area	CoE	EU
Standard period of ineligibility for presence, use or attempted use, or possession of a prohibited substance or method (Art 10.2 of WADC 2021)	2[75]	–
New sanctioning regime for the ingestion, use or possession of substances of abuse (Art 10.2.4 of WADC 2021)	4[76]	–
Standard period of ineligibility for other anti-doping rule violations (Art 10.3 of WADC 2021)	6[77]	–
Elimination or reduction of the standard period of ineligibility on grounds of fault-related reasons (Arts 10.5 and 10.6 of WADC 2021)	6[78]	–
The new concept of protected persons (Definitions)	4[79]	2[80]
The new concept of recreational athletes (Definitions)	3[81]	–

(continued)

[75] WADA, 2021 Code Review – Second Consultation Phase, Council of Europe, Sport Convention Division (France), Public Authorities – Intergovernmental Organization, 73; WADA, 2021 Code Review – Third Consultation Phase, Council of Europe, Sport Convention Division (France), Public Authorities – Intergovernmental Organization, 52.

[76] ibid – First Consultation Phase, Council of Europe, Sport Convention Division (France), Public Authorities – Intergovernmental Organization, 201; WADA, 2021 Code Review – Second Consultation Phase, Council of Europe, Sport Convention Division (France), Public Authorities – Intergovernmental Organization, 18, 173; WADA, 2021 Code Review – Third Consultation Phase, Council of Europe, Sport Convention Division (France), Public Authorities – Intergovernmental Organization (online), 52.

[77] ibid – First Consultation Phase, Council of Europe, Sport Convention Division (France), Public Authorities – Intergovernmental Organization, 3–4, 200–201; WADA, 2021 Code Review – Second Consultation Phase, Council of Europe, Sport Convention Division (France), Public Authorities – Intergovernmental Organization, 18–19, 78–79, 86.

[78] ibid – Second Consultation Phase, Council of Europe, Sport Convention Division (France), Public Authorities – Intergovernmental Organization, 19, 73, 85, 86; WADA, 2021 Code Review – Third Consultation Phase, Council of Europe, Sport Convention Division (France), Public Authorities – Intergovernmental Organization, 52, 60.

[79] ibid – Second Consultation Phase, Council of Europe, Sport Convention Division (France), Public Authorities – Intergovernmental Organization, 72–73, 165–66; WADA, 2021 Code Review – Third Consultation Phase, Council of Europe, Sport Convention Division (France), Public Authorities – Intergovernmental Organization, 8, 122–23.

[80] ibid – First Consultation Phase, Ministry of Youth and Sport, Viktoria Slavkova, Chair of Working Party on Sport, Deputy member of FB on behalf of EU (Bulgaria), Public Authorities – Government, 198–99; WADA, 2021 Code Review – Second Consultation Phase, EU and its Member States, Barbara Spindler-Oswald on behalf of the EU and its Member States, Chair of the Working Party on Sport (Austria), Public Authorities, 84–85.

[81] WADA, 2021 Code Review – First Consultation Phase, Council of Europe, Sport Convention Division (France), Public Authorities – Intergovernmental Organization, p. 200-201; WADA, 2021 Code Review – Second Consultation Phase, Council of Europe, Sport Convention Division (France), Public Authorities – Intergovernmental Organization, p. 173; WADA, 2021 Code Review – Third Consultation Phase, Council of Europe, Sport Convention Division (France), Public Authorities – Intergovernmental Organization, p. 7.

Table 7.2 *(Continued)*

Area	CoE	EU
The new sanctioning regime of protected persons and recreational athletes (Art. 10.6.1.3 of WADC 2021)	5[82]	–
Elimination, reduction or suspension of ineligibility or other consequences for reasons other than fault (Art. 10.7 and 10.8 of WADC 2021)	3[83]	–

Having presented the quantity, this section further focuses on the content of the comments of the representatives of the CoE and those of the EU and its Member States. The comments that the WADA stakeholders submitted in all three phases of the review process are publicly available.[84] Therefore, they are the basis for analysing how the CoE and the EU approached the topic of proportionality of ineligibility. Consequently, the interim versions of the draft WADC 2021 and especially its final text enable an analysis of whether they reflect the comments, or not. It would also be interesting to know how the drafting team considered specific comments of the representatives of the CoE, and those of the EU and its Member States. However, the transparency of the review process of WADC 2021 is unfortunately rather limited. The representatives of the drafting team presented some of their conclusions at the meetings of the WADA Foundation Board[85] or the Executive Committee.[86] Nevertheless, there are no minutes from the internal discussions of the drafting team.

Therefore, the following section examines the comments of the representatives of the CoE and those of the EU and its Member States, particularly whether they emphasised proportionality of ineligibility. Moreover, it uses interim versions of the draft WADC 2021 and its final text to assess whether they reflect the comments. The analysis follows the structure of Article 10 of the WADC. It starts with the standard period of ineligibility for presence, use or attempted use or possession of a prohibited substance or method (section III.A) and for other anti-doping rule violations (section III.B). Thereafter, it analyses the comments regarding the possible elimination or reduction in the period of ineligibility on the grounds of no significant fault or negligence (section III.C). It particularly

[82] WADA, 2021 Code Review – Second Consultation Phase, Council of Europe, Sport Convention Division (France), Public Authorities – Intergovernmental Organization, p. 85–86, 165–166, 173; WADA, 2021 Code Review – Third Consultation Phase, Council of Europe, Sport Convention Division (France), Public Authorities – Intergovernmental Organization, p. 7–8, 122.

[83] WADA, 2021 Code Review – First Consultation Phase, Council of Europe, Sport Convention Division (France), Public Authorities – Intergovernmental Organization, p. 201; WADA, 2021 Code Review – Second Consultation Phase, Council of Europe, Sport Convention Division (France), Public Authorities – Intergovernmental Organization, p. 91, 96.

[84] WADA, 2021 Code Review – First Consultation Phase; WADA, 2021 Code Review – Second Consultation Phase; WADA, 2021 Code Review – Third Consultation Phase.

[85] WADA, 'Foundation Board Meeting Minutes', www.wada-ama.org/en/resources/foundation-board-meeting-minutes.

[86] ibid.

examines two new categories of protected persons (section III.D) and recreational athletes (section III.E) and their sanctioning (section III.F). Finally, this section analyses recommendations regarding the possible elimination, reduction or suspension of the period of ineligibility based on reasons other than fault (section III.G).

A. Standard Ineligibility for Presence, Use or Attempted Use or Possession of a Prohibited Substance or Method

The representatives of the CoE unsuccessfully proposed a tightening of the burden on athletes to prove that their doping was not intentional. Athletes or other persons have to prove that the presence, use or attempted use or possession of a non-specified prohibited substance was not intentional to avoid the standard four-year period of ineligibility.[87] Ulrich Haas, one of the drafters of WADC 2021, notes that they do not have to establish the source of a prohibited substance to exclude intent, which is clear from the wording of the WADC and the case law of the Court of Arbitration for Sport (CAS).[88] Nevertheless, the comment concerning Article 10.2.1.1 of WADC 2021 provides that it is 'highly unlikely that (…) an athlete will be successful in proving that the athlete acted unintentionally without establishing the source of the prohibited substance'.[89] Therefore, the hearing panels should interpret the provision that it is 'highly unlikely' that athletes or other persons manage to prove a lack of intent without proving the source of the prohibited non-specified substance. Moreover, the representatives of the CoE proposed the inclusion of the comment directly in Article 10.2.1.1 of WADC 2021. They sought to make 'establishing the circumstances how the prohibited substance entered the system' a condition to prove the lack of intent in cases involving non-specified substances. They argued that such a step would help the uniform application of WADC 2021 and the related anti-doping rules.[90] However, the drafters of WADC 2021 did not reflect the proposal in the final text and the provision remained a non-binding interpretative comment.[91]

[87] WADC 2021, Art 10.2.1.1.

[88] U Haas, 'The Revision of the World Anti-Doping Code 2021' (2020) *CAS Bulletin. Budapest seminar October 2019*, 35, referring to CAS 2018/A/5580 *Blagovest Krasimirov Bozhinovski v Anti-Doping Centre of the Republic of Bulgaria & Bulgarian Olympic Committee*, CAS Bulletin 2019/02, 57; CAS 2016/A/4534 *Mauricio Fiol Villanueva v Fédération Internationale de Natation*, CAS Bulletin 2017/02, 42, 43; CAS 2019/A/6313 *Jarrion Lawson v IAAF*. See also CAS 2018/A/5768 *Dylan Scott v ITF*, para 137 et seq; CAS 2017/A/5178 *Tomasz Zieliński v IWF*, para 87 et seq.

[89] WADC 2021, Comment to Art 10.2.1.1.

[90] WADA, 2021 Code Review – Second Consultation Phase, Council of Europe, Sport Convention Division (France), Public Authorities – Intergovernmental Organization, 73; WADA, 2021 Code Review – Third Consultation Phase, Council of Europe, Sport Convention Division (France), Public Authorities – Intergovernmental Organization, 52.

[91] WADC 2021, Comment to Art 10.2.1.1.

Furthermore, the representatives of the CoE expressed their views on the special sanctioning regime for the new category of prohibited substances, substances of abuse. They include those prohibited substances which are 'frequently abused in society outside of the context of sport' and which are 'specifically identified as substances of abuse on the Prohibited List'.[92] The WADC 2021 consequently provides a universal three-month period of ineligibility if athletes establish that the ingestion or use of substances of abuse occurred out of competition and was unrelated to sport performance.[93] Moreover, ADOs may further reduce the ban to one month if the athlete or other person satisfactorily completes a treatment programme approved by the ADO with results management responsibility.[94] Nevertheless, such a period of ineligibility is not subject to any further fault-related reductions.[95] Second, if the ingestion, use or possession of substances of abuse occurred in-competition, but athletes can establish that its context was unrelated to sport performance, hearing panels shall not consider such a violation intentional, or as a basis for the finding of aggravating circumstances.[96]

The representatives of the CoE recommended not to include cocaine as a substance of abuse due to its alleged stimulating effect on sports performance and the danger of drug abuse in sport. They noted that some substances of abuse cannot improve athletic performance, for example, cannabinoids.[97] On the other hand, they argued that 'other substances that are proposed for inclusion in this definition, for example, cocaine, are inherently powerful stimulants and can significantly improve athletic performance when using in the competition period'.[98] Moreover, they claimed that

> the introduction of such stimulants in the definition of 'substances of abuse' and the imposition for their detection in any concentration of minimum term of ineligibility lasting (three) months can cause a significant increase in the use of cocaine and other similar substances to improve athletic performance.[99]

They particularly argued that 'the temptation will be high among speed-power and team sports athletes to use this type of stimulants before the start (even if

[92] ibid Art 4.2.3. See also WADA, 2021 Code Revision – Third Draft (Following the Third Consultation phase), Summary of Major Changes, para 23, 11; WADA, 2021 World Anti-Doping Code and International Standard Framework: Development and Implementation Guide for Stakeholders (hereinafter 'World Anti-Doping Code Development and Implementation Guide'), 11; Haas (n 75) 31–32.

[93] WADC 2021 Art. 10.2.4.1. See also ibid Art 7.4.1: Such a case may also be a reason for the elimination of a mandatory provisional suspension. See also ibid Art. 10.9.2: Such an anti-doping rule violation shall not be considered a violation for the purpose of sanctioning multiple violations.

[94] WADC 2021, Art 10.2.4.1, Comment to Art 10.2.4.1.

[95] ibid Art 10.2.4.1.

[96] ibid Art. 10.2.4.2.

[97] WADA, 2021 Code Review – Third Consultation Phase, Council of Europe, Sport Convention Division (France), Public Authorities – Intergovernmental Organization (online), 52.

[98] ibid.

[99] ibid.

the sample is positive, the sanction will be minimal)'.[100] Therefore, the representatives of the CoE proposed that cocaine not be included as a substance of abuse.

Should cocaine be considered a substance of abuse and have a special sanctioning regime, the representatives of the CoE suggested an alternative approach based on its alleged performance-enhancing effect. They argued that there should be 'a detection threshold for these types of stimulants, based on their real ability to improve athletic performance at a specific concentration, above which the detection of cocaine in a sample should be punished by the standard sanction for non-specified substances'.[101] The drafting team of WADC 2021 had initially tried to come up with a reporting limit for cocaine under which it had no performance-enhancing effect, but it did not succeed, largely due to the difficulties of analysing urine samples.[102] Consequently, the drafting team created the category of substances of abuse and left the decision of whether to include cocaine or not to the WADA Executive Committee. Based on the recommendation of the WADA List Committee, the 2024 Prohibited List identifies cocaine as a substance of abuse, alongside diamorphine (heroin), methylenedioxymethamphetamine (MDMA/ecstasy), and tetrahydrocannabinol (THC).[103] Therefore, WADA refused to adopt the suggestion of the CoE and applied to cocaine the special sanctioning regime of substances of abuse.

Having examined the substances of abuse, the representatives of the CoE further commented on the sanctioning of their ingestion, use or possession. They initially criticised a 'disproportionate sanctioning policy' for substances of abuse.[104] Consequently, in the second consultation phase, they supported reconsidering sanctions for the ingestion or use of substances of abuse out of competition unrelated to sports performance. They argued that 'from a psychological perspective, the motivation for taking recreational drugs is often completely at odds with the motivation for taking performance-enhancing substances'.[105] At one point, they recommended considering 'a uniform one-year or eighteen-month suspension'.[106] They argued that it 'would save a lot of time and money arguing over "fault", and particularly about mental health issues'.[107] Moreover, they proposed that 'sports could also be given the power to stipulate that an athlete must also undergo therapy or rehabilitation before they return to sport. But the sanction should still be stipulated according to the

[100] ibid.
[101] WADA, 2021 Code Review – Third Consultation Phase, Council of Europe, Sport Convention Division (France), Public Authorities – Intergovernmental Organization (online), 52.
[102] Minutes of the WADA Executive Committee Meeting, 15 May 2019, 10.1, 31.
[103] WADC 2021, WADA Prohibited List 2024.
[104] WADA, 2021 Code Review – First Consultation Phase, Council of Europe, Sport Convention Division (France), Public Authorities – Intergovernmental Organization, 201.
[105] WADA, 2021 Code Review – Second Consultation Phase, Council of Europe, Sport Convention Division (France), Public Authorities – Intergovernmental Organization, 18.
[106] ibid.
[107] ibid.

individual circumstances of the case'.[108] Nevertheless, such proposals seem to be contradictory. The sanction can be either uniform or based on a case-by-case assessment.

Moreover, the representatives of the CoE encouraged WADA to consider the conflicting opinions of some delegations. They could not 'support the suggestion of a uniform one-year or eighteen-month suspension'.[109] They argued that 'the sanction should still be stipulated according to the individual circumstances of the case'.[110] Moreover, they could not support sports organisations having the power to stipulate that an athlete must undergo therapy or rehabilitation before they return to sport. 'We could foresee many practical obstacles, and furthermore, athletes should be able to count on sanctions issued according to the Code is the full sanction, without any additional sanctions given by sports organisations.'[111] In the end, the drafters of WADC 2021 heard the calls for uniformity and set a uniform three- or one-month ineligibility period for the ingestion or use of substances of abuse out of competition unrelated to sport performance.[112] In addition, signatories can enact further code of conduct rules punishing the ingestion or use of substances of abuse for other than anti-doping purposes, but they cannot impose additional sanctions for situations already covered in WADC 2021.[113] Therefore, the drafters of WADC 2021 essentially did not reflect the comments of the representatives of the CoE.

B. Standard Ineligibility for Other Anti-Doping Rule Violations

In addition to the presence, use or attempted use, or possession of a prohibited substance or method, the representatives of the CoE addressed the standard ineligibility for other anti-doping rule violations and their proportionality. In particular, they asked for specifications on the degree of fault that is required to commit each anti-doping rule violation. They proposed an explicit reference to whether the violation needs to be 'intentional' or can also be 'negligent', reasoning with legal certainty and athletes' rights.[114] They specifically required clarifications in the case of evasion, refusal or failure to submit to sample collection.[115] They asked whether 'intention (as defined in article 10.2.3) must be proved to establish an (anti-doping rule violation) of evasion or refusal

[108] ibid.

[109] WADA, 2021 Code Review – Second Consultation Phase, Council of Europe, Sport Convention Division (France), Public Authorities – Intergovernmental Organization, 173.

[110] ibid.

[111] ibid.

[112] WADC 2021, Art 10.2.4.1.

[113] ibid Art 23.2.2, Comment to Art 23.2.2.

[114] WADA, 2021 Code Review – Second Consultation Phase, Council of Europe, Sport Convention Division (France), Public Authorities – Intergovernmental Organization, 18.

[115] ibid 19.

contrary to Article 2.3 (…)'.[116] Finally, Article 10.2.3 of WADC 2021 defines the term 'intentional', but only for the purpose of sanctioning the presence, use or attempted use, or possession of a prohibited substance or method.[117] Regarding the evasion, refusal or failure to submit to sample collection, the comment to Article 2.3 of WADC 2021 suggests how hearing panels should interpret the provision. It provides that 'a violation of failing to submit to sample collection may be based on either intentional or negligent conduct of the athlete, while "evading" or "refusing" sample collection contemplates intentional conduct by the athlete'.[118] Consequently, the period of ineligibility for failing to submit to sample collection shall be two instead of four years if 'the athlete can establish that the commission of the anti-doping rule violation was not intentional'.[119]

Moreover, only certain anti-doping rule violations in WADC 2021 explicitly specify whether they must be committed intentionally or whether negligence is sufficient. Tampering in particular includes 'intentional conduct which subverts the doping control process (…)'.[120] It covers any 'intentional interference or attempted interference with any aspect of doping control'.[121] Moreover, Article 2.9 of WADC 2021 prohibits 'assisting, encouraging, aiding, abetting, conspiring, covering up or any other type of intentional complicity'.[122] Furthermore, Article 2.11 of WADC 2021 prohibits 'any act which threatens or seeks to intimidate another person with the intent of discouraging the person' from good-faith reporting to authorities.[123] In addition, the comment to Article 10.6.2 of WADC 2021 suggests that 'intent is an element of (tampering, complicity, and acts discouraging or retaliating against reporting to authorities) as well as of trafficking and administration'.[124] Otherwise, there is no explicit reference to intent or negligence regarding other anti-doping rule violations.

Furthermore, the representatives of the CoE commented on the standard period of ineligibility for tampering, seeking a tightening of sanctions for fraudulent conduct. They initially highlighted the 'disproportionate sanctioning policy' for tampering.[125] They particularly noted that 'violations involving fraud are more serious than other violations because they involve an intention to deceive: but they all receive the same sanction'.[126] WADC 2021 defines tampering as an 'intentional conduct which subverts the doping control process, but which

[116] ibid 86.
[117] WADC 2021, Art 10.2.3.
[118] ibid Comment to Art 2.3.
[119] ibid Art 10.3.1.
[120] ibid Annex 1 (Definitions): Tampering.
[121] ibid.
[122] ibid Art 2.9.
[123] ibid Art. 2.11.
[124] ibid Comment to Art 10.6.2.
[125] WADA, 2021 Code Review – First Consultation Phase, Council of Europe, Sport Convention Division (France), Public Authorities – Intergovernmental Organization, 201.
[126] ibid 3–4.

would not otherwise be included in the definition of prohibited methods'.[127] Moreover, the definition provides examples of tampering, which include 'any fraudulent act upon the (ADO) or hearing body to affect results management or the imposition of consequences, and any other similar intentional interference or attempted interference with any aspect of doping control'.[128] Therefore, tampering essentially involves fraud.

Consequently, WADC 2021 provides the same standard ineligibility for all kinds of tampering, except for exceptional circumstances, violations committed by protected persons or recreational athletes, or aggravating circumstances. The standard sanction is four-year ineligibility.[129] If the athlete or other person can establish exceptional circumstances that justify a reduction of the period of ineligibility, the ban shall range from two to four years depending on the degree of fault.[130] Moreover, in a case involving a protected person or recreational athlete, the period of ineligibility shall range from a maximum of two years to a minimum of a reprimand and no period of ineligibility, again depending on the degree of fault.[131] On the other hand, tampering during the results management process is an aggravating circumstance that may lead to an increase in the basic period of ineligibility by up to two years, depending on the seriousness of the violation and the nature of the aggravating circumstances.[132] Therefore, fraudulent tampering during the results management process may lead to two extra years of ineligibility.

Moreover, the representatives of the CoE proposed milder standard ineligibility for whereabouts failures. They argued that ineligibility between one and two years is of 'dubious proportionality' and should be based solely on fault because the violation 'does not involve any doping' and athletes committing it 'are not dopers'. Moreover, they claimed that it should not be subject to financial consequences.[133] WADC 2021 provides that the period of ineligibility for whereabouts failures 'shall be two (2) years, subject to reduction down to a minimum of one (1) year, depending on the athlete's degree of fault'.[134] Therefore, athletes' fault plays an important role in determining the standard sanction for whereabouts failures. Nevertheless, the flexibility between two years and one year is not available to athletes where a pattern of last-minute whereabouts changes or other conduct raises a serious suspicion that they are trying to avoid being available for testing.[135] Moreover, whereabouts failures are not excluded

[127] WADC 2021, Art 2.5, Annex 1 (Definitions): Tampering.
[128] ibid, Annex 1 (Definitions): Tampering.
[129] ibid Art 10.3.1.
[130] ibid.
[131] ibid Art 10.3.1.
[132] ibid Art 10.4, Annex 1 (Definitions): Aggravating Circumstances.
[133] WADA, 2021 Code Review – First Consultation Phase, Council of Europe, Sport Convention Division (France), Public Authorities – Intergovernmental Organization, 200.
[134] WADC 2021, Art 10.3.2.
[135] ibid Art 10.3.2.

from the possibility of imposing financial consequences. Nevertheless, ADOs may impose financial sanctions only 'where the maximum period of ineligibility otherwise applicable has already been imposed', and they must explicitly respect 'the principle of proportionality'.[136]

Furthermore, the representatives of the CoE unsuccessfully argued in favour of a milder punishment for trafficking or administration. They claimed that the standard ineligibility starting with four years is reasonable if 'intent' is required. On the other hand, negligent violations should 'benefit from a more flexible sanction with the possibility to reduce the period of ineligibility below (four) years'.[137] Nevertheless, trafficking or administration can only be intentional. Therefore, there is no possibility of a reduction based on no significant fault or negligence.[138] Consequently, WADC 2021 provides that the standard period of ineligibility for trafficking or administration 'shall be a minimum of four (4) years up to lifetime ineligibility, depending on the seriousness of the violation'.[139] Moreover, an athlete's support staff committing trafficking or administering a non-specified substance involving a protected person shall receive lifetime ineligibility.[140] Therefore, there is no milder penalty for negligent trafficking or administration.

On top of that, the representatives of the CoE successfully argued in favour of converging sanctions for trafficking and administration on the one hand, and complicity on the other. They argued that the violations might overlap. 'But the sanctions are different: (trafficking) starts at (four) years, but (complicity) is capped at (four) years. This does not work.'[141] Consequently, the first draft of WADC 2021 lifted the cap of four years and proposed maximum lifetime ineligibility for complicity. The representatives of the CoE reacted that 'it seems advisable to at least maintain the current level of responsibility'.[142] Finally, the period of ineligibility for complicity 'shall be a minimum of two (2) years, up to lifetime ineligibility, depending on the seriousness of the violation'.[143] Lastly, the representatives of the CoE commented on the standard ineligibility for the new anti-doping rule violation, acts discouraging or retaliating against reporting to authorities. The representatives of the CoE asked for 'an unconditional exception' from such proposed ineligibility between two years and a lifetime.[144]

[136] ibid Art 10.12.
[137] WADA, 2021 Code Review – Second Consultation Phase, Council of Europe, Sport Convention Division (France), Public Authorities – Intergovernmental Organization, 78–79.
[138] WADC 2021, Comment to Art 10.6.2.
[139] ibid, Art 10.3.3.
[140] ibid.
[141] WADA, 2021 Code Review – First Consultation Phase, Council of Europe, Sport Convention Division (France), Public Authorities – Intergovernmental Organization, 200.
[142] WADA, 2021 Code Review – Second Consultation Phase, Council of Europe, Sport Convention Division (France), Public Authorities – Intergovernmental Organization, 79.
[143] WADC 2021, Art 10.3.4.
[144] WADA, 2021 Code Review – Second Consultation Phase, Council of Europe, Sport Convention Division (France), Public Authorities – Intergovernmental Organization, 79.

Nevertheless, in the end, WADC 2021 does not provide any such exception, and the standard ineligibility depends solely on 'the seriousness of the violation by the athlete or other person'.[145]

C. Fault-Related Elimination or Reduction of the Period of Ineligibility

In addition to the standard period of ineligibility, the representatives of the CoE, and this time also those of the EU commented on the possibility of its reduction on grounds of no significant fault or negligence. The representatives of the CoE particularly asked for clarifications 'as it is difficult to discern consistent principles in the case law'.[146] They concretely proposed to add notes specifying that the reduction of the period of ineligibility on grounds of no significant fault or negligence 'is possible only after admitting that the violation was committed unintentionally'.[147] In this regard, they referred to a practice of incorrect application of this item by a CAS sole arbitrator, who had recognised that an athlete had committed an intentional violation, but who reduced the sanction based on no significant fault or negligence.[148] Moreover, the representatives of the CoE asked for specifications in the particular case of evading, refusing or failing to submit to sample collection with regard to possible elimination or reduction of the basic period or ineligibility based on fault-related reasons.[149] 'Should (elimination or reduction) apply to intentional breaches of Article 2.3?'[150]

In WADC 2021, the elimination of the period of ineligibility on grounds of no fault or negligence or its reduction based on no significant fault or negligence is only possible when the violation was not intentional. First, no fault or negligence refers to

> the athlete or other person's establishing that he or she did not know or suspect, and could not reasonably have known or suspected even with the exercise of utmost caution, that he or she had used or been administered the prohibited substance or prohibited method or otherwise violated an anti-doping rule.[151]

Second, no significant fault or negligence means that the athlete or other person established 'that any fault or negligence, when viewed in the totality of the circumstances and taking into account the criteria for no fault or negligence, was not significant in relationship to the anti-doping rule violation'.[152] Therefore,

[145] WADC 2021, Art 10.3.6.
[146] WADA, 2021 Code Review – Second Consultation Phase, Council of Europe, Sport Convention Division (France), Public Authorities – Intergovernmental Organization, 86.
[147] ibid – Third Consultation Phase, Council of Europe, Sport Convention Division (France), Public Authorities – Intergovernmental Organization, 60.
[148] ibid.
[149] ibid – Second Consultation Phase, Council of Europe, Sport Convention Division (France), Public Authorities – Intergovernmental Organization, 19.
[150] ibid 86.
[151] WADC 2021, Annex 1 (Definitions): No Significant Fault or Negligence.
[152] ibid Annex 1 (Definitions): No Significant Fault or Negligence.

the definitions of no and no significant fault or negligence exclude the intent on the part of the athlete or other person.

Moreover, WADC 2021 keeps distinguishing between two categories of violations for the reduction of the standard period of ineligibility on grounds of no significant fault or negligence. First, Article 10.6.1 of WADC 2021 provides rules for the reduction of the standard ineligibility for the presence, use or attempted use or possession of a specified prohibited substance or contaminated product. Moreover, WADC 2021 extends such a possibility to specified methods or violations committed by protected persons or recreational athletes.[153] Such a reduction is possible only if the violation was not intentional, and the standard period of ineligibility is two years.[154] Second, Article 10.6.2 of WADC 2021 specifies the reduction in the case of all other violations.[155] Nevertheless, the comment to the provision provides that the reduction does not concern

> articles where intent is an element of the anti-doping rule violation (…) or an element of a particular sanction (…) or a range of ineligibility is already provided in an article based on the athlete or other person's degree of fault.[156]

Moreover, the intent is an explicit element of evading or refusing sample collection.[157] Therefore, reducing the period of ineligibility based on no significant fault or negligence is only possible for non-intentional violations, including negligent failure to submit to sample collection.[158]

In addition, the representatives of the CoE submitted comments related to the obligation of athletes to establish how a prohibited substance entered their body to claim no significant fault or negligence where there is a presence of a prohibited substance. They argued that 'it is possible to specify that which particular circumstances may be indicative of no significant fault or negligence even in case the athlete failed to establish the source of entering the prohibited substance his/her system (…)'.[159] However, WADC 2021 provides only one exception from such an obligation. In particular, protected persons and recreational athletes do not have to show how the prohibited substance entered their system.[160] All other athletes have to establish the source of the prohibited substance if they want to have the standard period of ineligibility reduced. There are no particular circumstances indicative of no significant fault or negligence without fulfilling such an obligation.

[153] ibid Art 10.6.1.
[154] ibid Art 10.2.2.
[155] ibid Art 10.6.2, Comment to Art 10.6.2.
[156] ibid Comment to Art 10.6.2.
[157] ibid Comment to Art 2.3.
[158] ibid Art 10.3.1, Comment to Art 10.6.2.
[159] WADA, 2021 Code Review – Second Consultation Phase, Council of Europe, Sport Convention Division (France), Public Authorities – Intergovernmental Organization, 73; WADA, 2021 Code Review – Third Consultation Phase, Council of Europe, Sport Convention Division (France), Public Authorities – Intergovernmental Organization, 52.
[160] WADC 2021, Annex 1 (Definitions): No Significant Fault or Negligence.

Alternatively, the representatives of the CoE proposed 'to specify which particular circumstances should not be interpreted as the basis for reducing the sanction period within the framework of this article'.[161] Regarding fault, WADC 2021 follows in the footsteps of WADC 2015 and provides that 'the circumstances considered must be specific and relevant to explain the athlete's or other person's departure from the expected standard of behavior'.[162] Consequently, WADC 2021 provides that

> for example, the fact that an athlete would lose the opportunity to earn large sums of money during a period of ineligibility, or the fact that the athlete only has a short time left in a career, or the timing of the sporting calendar, would not be relevant factors to be considered in reducing the period of ineligibility (…).[163]

As such, WADC 2021 specifies circumstances that should not be interpreted as a basis for reducing the sanction based on no significant fault or negligence.

Moreover, the comment to Article 10.5 of WADC 2021, which essentially follows the same provision in WADC 2015, provides circumstances that could result in a reduction of a sanction based on no significant fault or negligence. It provides that (Article 10.6.2 of WADC 2021) only applies 'in exceptional circumstances, for example, where an athlete could prove that, despite all due care, he or she was sabotaged by a competitor'.[164] Consequently, it provides circumstances, which cannot be grounds for eliminating the ineligibility based on no fault or negligence, but which could result in a reduced sanction on the grounds of no significant fault or negligence. These circumstances include a positive test resulting from a mislabelled or contaminated vitamin or nutritional supplement, the administration of a prohibited substance by the athlete's personal physician or trainer without disclosure to the athlete, and sabotage of the athlete's food or drink by a spouse, coach or other people within the athlete's circle of associates.[165] Therefore, WADC 2021 provides examples of circumstances which should and should not be interpreted as grounds for a reduction of the period of ineligibility on the grounds of no significant fault or negligence.

On top of that, the representatives of the CoE recommended specifying the length of the period of ineligibility be reduced based on no significant fault or negligence. They particularly argued that the provision should include 'a scale of different periods of ineligibility ranging from a warning to (two) years, depending on the degree of fault' as established in the *Cilic* case of the CAS.[166]

[161] WADA, 2021 Code Review – Second Consultation Phase, Council of Europe, Sport Convention Division (France), Public Authorities – Intergovernmental Organization, 73; WADA, 2021 Code Review – Third Consultation Phase, Council of Europe, Sport Convention Division (France), Public Authorities – Intergovernmental Organization, p. 52.

[162] WADC 2021, Annex 1 (Definitions): Fault.

[163] ibid.

[164] ibid Comment to Art 10.5.

[165] ibid.

[166] WADA, 2021 Code Review – Third Consultation Phase, Council of Europe, Sport Convention Division (France), Public Authorities – Intergovernmental Organization, 60, referring to CAS, 2013/A/3335 *International Tennis Federation v Martin Cilic.*

Moreover, they claimed that WADC 2021 should also define 'the criteria that has to be met to ascertain the degree of fault'.[167] The representatives of the CoE explained that

> the introduction of such scale, specifying criteria for its application, will preclude the imposition of fundamentally different periods of ineligibility (eg, 3 months vs. 20 months) for similar anti-doping rule violations by different ADOs, which is aligned with the main objective of (the WADC), namely justice and equality for all athletes.[168]

The CAS set the scale of fault or negligence and the corresponding duration of ineligibility also in the case of the Norwegian cross-country skier Therese Johaug: a significant degree of fault may lead to a sanction of 20–24 months; a normal degree of fault equals a sanction of 16–20 months; and a light degree of fault may lead to a sanction of 12–16 months.[169] Nevertheless, WADC 2021 does not contain such a scale or criteria, and leaves the appreciation to hearing panels.

Moreover, the representatives of the CoE suggested a specification of conditions for reducing the period of ineligibility in cases involving contaminated products. They argued that the comments included in the first draft of WADC 2021 softened the provision and could 'lead to an unwanted gateway for unclear legal situations'.[170] WADC 2015 provided a period of ineligibility between zero to two years depending on the athletes' or other persons' degree of fault if they were able to establish both no significant fault or negligence and that the detected prohibited substance came from a contaminated product.[171] Consequently, the accompanying comment provided that 'in assessing that athlete's degree of fault, it would, for example, be favorable for the athlete if the athlete had declared the product which was subsequently determined to be contaminated on his or her doping control form'.[172] The representatives of the CoE argued that 'the fact that it is a "contamination" of supplements and/or food, water, etc. is currently a commonly used (and not proven) claim by the athletes involved'.[173] Therefore, they suggested that the provision should 'provide a clear case scenario in which both the disciplinary bodies and the athletes, as well as the competent anti-doping organisations, can clearly differentiate between an attributed fault and a missing responsibility concerning the anti-doping rule violation'.[174]

[167] ibid.
[168] ibid.
[169] CAS 2017/A/5015 *Fédération Internationale de Ski v Therese Johaug & NOPC*, CAS 2017/A/5110 *Therese Johaug v NOPC*. See also Czech NOC Arbitration Commission, 2018-1, *Šefl*, para 9.16.
[170] WADA, 2021 Code Review – Second Consultation Phase, Council of Europe, Sport Convention Division (France), Public Authorities – Intergovernmental Organization, 85.
[171] WADC 2015, Art 10.5.1.2.
[172] ibid Comment to Art 10.5.1.2.
[173] WADA, 2021 Code Review – Second Consultation Phase, Council of Europe, Sport Convention Division (France), Public Authorities – Intergovernmental Organization, 85.
[174] ibid.

Finally, WADC 2021 has kept the content of the initial provision but substantially modified the accompanying comment. The comment specifies that 'athletes are on notice that they take nutritional supplements at their own risk'.[175] Consequently, it explains that 'the sanction reduction based on no significant fault or negligence has rarely been applied in contaminated product cases unless the athlete has exercised a high level of caution before taking the contaminated product'.[176] The comment is followed by a provision similar to the one in WADC 2015 regarding the declaration of the product which was subsequently determined to be contaminated on the doping control form.[177] Consequently, it states that

> this article should not be extended beyond products that have gone through some process of manufacturing. Where an adverse analytical finding results from environment contamination of a 'non-product' such as tap water or lake water in circumstances where no reasonable person would expect any risk of an anti-doping rule violation, typically there would be no fault or negligence under Article 10.5.[178]

Therefore, WADC 2021 provides athletes, ADOs and disciplinary bodies with extended guidance on when the sanction can be reduced on grounds of no significant fault or negligence in cases involving contaminated products.

D. Protected Persons

Regarding fault-related reductions in the period of ineligibility, comments of the representatives of both the CoE and the EU concerned a new category of protected persons. The representatives of the EU and its Member States considered in particular already in the first consultation phase that 'the rights of athletes, including minors, must be properly guaranteed in (WADC 2021)'.[179] In the second consultation phase, they emphasised 'the objective of the protection of minors to the primary consideration of the best interests of the minor for all actions and decisions concerning minors'.[180] Therefore, the representatives of the EU and its Member States encouraged WADA 'to consider if the sanctions in the Code are appropriate for minors'.[181] Consequently, they welcomed 'the

[175] ibid.
[176] ibid.
[177] ibid.
[178] WADC 2021, Comment to Art 10.6.1.2.
[179] WADA, 2021 Code Review – First Consultation Phase, Ministry of Youth and Sport, Viktoria Slavkova, Chair of Working Party on Sport, Deputy member of FB on behalf of EU (Bulgaria), Public Authorities – Government, 198–99.
[180] ibid – Second Consultation Phase, EU and its Member States, Barbara Spindler-Oswald on behalf of the EU and its Member States, Chair of the Working Party on Sport (Austria), Public Authorities, 84–85.
[181] ibid – First Consultation Phase, Ministry of Youth and Sport, Viktoria Slavkova, Chair of Working Party on Sport, Deputy member of FB on behalf of EU (Bulgaria), Public Authorities – Government, 198–99.

aim to implement more flexibility in the scale of the sanctions'.[182] Therefore, the representatives of the EU and its Member States supported more flexible sanctions for minors with the aim of protecting their interests.

Consequently, the representatives of the CoE and those of the EU and its Member States expressed their concern regarding the initial proposal to reduce the age limit for minors. WADC 2015 defined a minor as 'a natural person who has not reached the age of eighteen years'.[183] The representatives of the EU and its Member States suggested 'keeping the definition of minors as all human beings below the age of (eighteen), as defined in the UN Convention on the Rights of the Child'.[184] Moreover, the representatives of the CoE pointed out that 'reducing the age limit for minors to be treated as minors under (the WADC) violates the current UN Convention on the Rights of the Child'.[185] They explained further that

> although the proposal to reduce the age limit is based on an explicit proposal of the athletes, the legality of such a proposal is limited by applicable, supranational law. An implementation into national law is internationally extremely difficult or merely impossible to standardize.[186]

Therefore, the representatives of the CoE and those of the EU and its Member States recommended keeping the definition of minors as natural persons under the age of 18.

Finally, the drafters of WADC 2021 kept the original notion of a minor, but only for the purpose of the newly retitled public disclosure.[187] Moreover, they created a new category of protected persons that overlaps with the notion of a minor. The new concept includes three categories of athletes or other natural persons who were not of a certain age or did not have legal capacity at the time of the anti-doping rule violation. The first group contains athletes or other persons younger than 16.[188] The second category includes those athletes or other persons who have not reached the age of 18 and who are not included in any registered testing pool and have never competed in any international event in an open category, which excludes competitions that are limited to junior or age group categories.[189] The third category includes those athletes or other persons

[182] ibid – Second Consultation Phase, EU and its Member States, Barbara Spindler-Oswald on behalf of the EU and its Member States, Chair of the Working Party on Sport (Austria), Public Authorities, 84–85.

[183] WADC 2015, Annex 1 (Definitions): Minor.

[184] WADA, 2021 Code Review – Second Consultation Phase, EU and its Member States, Barbara Spindler-Oswald on behalf of the EU and its Member States, Chair of the Working Party on Sport (Austria), Public Authorities, 84–85.

[185] ibid – Second Consultation Phase, Council of Europe, Sport Convention Division (France), Public Authorities – Intergovernmental Organization, 165–66.

[186] ibid.

[187] WADC 2021, Appendix 1 (Definitions): Minor, Art 14.3.7.

[188] ibid Appendix 1 (Definitions): Protected Person.

[189] ibid Appendix 1 (Definitions): Protected Person, Comment to Protected Person.

who have been determined to lack legal capacity under applicable national legislation for reasons other than age.[190] Therefore, the final category would include, for example, a Paralympic athlete with a documented lack of legal capacity due to intellectual impairment.[191] As such, the drafters of WADC 2021 implemented the proposal of the representatives of the CoE to provide a special regime also to para-athletes.[192]

Similar to the definition of minors, the representatives of the CoE expressed concern about the compliance of the definition of protected persons with the Convention on the Rights of the Child. They particularly invoked Article 2, which prohibits 'discrimination of any kind, irrespective of the child's or his or her parent's or legal guardian's race, colour, sex, language, religion, political or other opinion, national, ethnic or social origin, property, disability, birth or other status'.[193] The representatives of the CoE feared that the definition of protected persons might violate this provision since 'age, as an indicator of a "status" of a child could constitute a discrimination'.[194] Consequently, they called for a legal expert's opinion, suggesting Costa.[195] He concluded that 'the threshold of 16 years is reasonable and does not seem disproportionate'.[196] Moreover, he argued that 'considering significant variation can be accepted for the purpose of criminal sanctions, this is even more acceptable for the non-criminal and lighter sanctions in the World Anti-Doping Code'.[197] Therefore, Costa concluded that 'the exception for certain athletes aged between 16 and 18 is proportionate and nondiscriminatory'.[198] Following the favourable opinion of Costa, later also confirmed by other authors,[199] the drafting team kept the definition of a protected person, which also appears in the final text of WADC 2021.

E. Recreational Athletes

In addition to protected persons, representatives of the CoE supported the introduction of a more flexible sanctioning regime for recreational athletes. They highlighted the fact that under WADC 2015, recreational athletes 'are held to

[190] ibid Appendix 1 (Definitions): Protected Person. See also World Anti-Doping Code Development and Implementation Guide (n 79) 19.

[191] ibid Appendix 1 (Definitions): Comment to Protected Person.

[192] WADA, 2021 Code Review – Second Consultation Phase, Council of Europe, Sport Convention Division (France), Public Authorities – Intergovernmental Organization, 72–73.

[193] Convention on the Rights of the Child 1989, Art 2.

[194] WADA, 2021 Code Review – Third Consultation Phase, Council of Europe, Sport Convention Division (France), Public Authorities – Intergovernmental Organization, 8, 122–23.

[195] ibid.

[196] Costa (n 3) 19.

[197] ibid 20.

[198] ibid.

[199] Haas (n 75) 36–37; A Kambhampati, S Star, 'Playing True? A Critique of the 2021 WADA Code' (2021) *International Sports Law Journal* 21, 231.

exactly the same standards as their elite-level counterparts'.[200] They specified that 'athletes who compete at a purely social level are now facing long bans from a sport for failing to check supplement products closely enough, or remember the specifics of bi-annual anti-doping "education" sessions that last barely an hour'.[201] In this regard, the representatives of the CoE pointed out that elite athletes and recreational athletes 'have little in common aside from the sport they compete in'.[202] Therefore, they proposed to consider whether 'graduated sanctions, that take account of relevant experience, competition level and infrastructure, should be introduced'.[203] As such, the representatives of the CoE supported the introduction of a sanctioning regime that takes into account the specificities of recreational athletes.

Consequently, the representatives of the CoE commented on the definition of recreational athletes. They particularly emphasised that 'the definition of recreational athletes should be carefully drafted, so that ADOs do not face difficulties trying to transpose/use it'.[204] In the end, WADC 2021 provides National Anti-Doping Organisations (NADOs) with the power to define which natural persons are recreational athletes under their authority.[205] Nevertheless, WADC 2021 restricts their appreciation by imposing three limitations. First, the definition may not include any person who was an international or national level athlete within a five-year period prior to committing any anti-doping rule violation. Second, WADC 2021 excludes any person who has represented any country in an international event in an open category in the past five years. Finally, the definition may not cover any person who has been included in any registered testing pool or other whereabouts information pool maintained by an international federation or a NADO within the past five years.[206] In this regard, WADA suggests that a recreational athlete may be

> any person who engages or participates in sport or fitness activities for recreational purposes but who would not otherwise compete in competitions or events organized, recognized, or hosted by a national federation, or by any affiliated or non-affiliated association, organisation, club, team, or league.[207]

Therefore, the concept of recreational athletes only applies to persons who participate in sport in lower categories than international and national level athletes.[208]

[200] WADA, 2021 Code Review – First Consultation Phase, Council of Europe, Sport Convention Division (France), Public Authorities – Intergovernmental Organization, 200–201.

[201] ibid.

[202] ibid.

[203] ibid.

[204] WADA, 2021 Code Review – Second Consultation Phase, Council of Europe, Sport Convention Division (France), Public Authorities – Intergovernmental Organization, 173.

[205] WADC 2021, Appendix 1 (Definitions): Recreational Athlete.

[206] WADC 2021, Appendix 1 (Definitions): Recreational Athlete; World Anti-Doping Code Development and Implementation Guide (n 79) 19.

[207] WADA, 2021 Model Rules for National Anti-Doping Organizations, Introduction, 7, Definitions, 74. For an example of NADO's regulations, see Regulations for Doping Control and Sanctions in Sports in the Czech Republic 2022, Introduction, 7, Definitions: Recreational Athlete, 65.

[208] Haas (n 75) 29.

Nevertheless, such a definition does not prevent all the difficulties in its transposition or use. On the one hand, the representatives of the CoE acknowledge that the new category of recreational athletes means that 'countries can operate an anti-doping system targeting only persons that engage in fitness activities at a non-competitive level, as is the case in Denmark, under which the sanctioning regime slightly differ from that in the WADC'.[209] On the other, there may be different definitions of recreational athletes in different countries, 'for example, because of different criteria for who might be a part of their whereabouts pools'.[210] Consequently, such different definitions can result in unequal treatment amongst recreational athletes on grounds of nationality, residence, licence membership of sport organisation, or presence in the country.[211] Moreover, the narrow definition creates inequalities between certain sports since it does not include some athletes that are considered to be amateurs by international federations.[212] Therefore, there remain practical difficulties in the transposition and use of the definition of recreational athletes.

F. Ineligibility for Protected Persons and Recreational Athletes

Having assessed the definition of protected persons and recreational athletes, the representatives of the CoE commented on the new sanctioning regime of such persons. In particular, they successfully opposed the initial idea to shift the burden of proof from minors to ADOs to establish intent in cases involving non-specified substances. According to the first draft of WADC 2021, an ADO had to establish that the violation was intentional so that a minor receives a four-year ban. Otherwise, the standard ineligibility would be two years. Nevertheless, the representatives of the CoE asked: 'Is it really acceptable to impose a 2-year-ban to a 17-year-old with a sample positive to multiple steroids where the ADO is not able to gather enough evidence to prove the intent and give a 4-year-ban?'[213] Conversely, they would welcome 'more flexibility in the range of applicable sanctions and reductions, but the quantum of sanctions shall remain identical for all athletes'.[214] Richard Young, the main drafter of WADC 2021, explained to the WADA Foundation Board that 'the team had received a lot of feedback on it and dropped it'.[215] He specified that 'some of the most interesting feedback

[209] WADA, 2021 Code Review – Third Consultation Phase, Council of Europe, Sport Convention Division (France), Public Authorities – Intergovernmental Organization, 7.

[210] Synrem, W, 'A guide to the main changes under the 2021 World Anti-Doping Code' (2020), Law In Sport.

[211] Haas (n 75) 29; Synrem (n 197).

[212] World Conference on Doping in Sport, Katowice, Poland, 5–7 November 2019, Intervention on behalf of the IIHF delivered by its legal director Ashley Ehlert, 2.

[213] WADA, 2021 Code Review – Second Consultation Phase, Council of Europe, Sport Convention Division (France), Public Authorities – Intergovernmental Organization, 165–66.

[214] ibid.

[215] Minutes of the WADA Foundation Board Meeting, 15 November 2018, 6.1.1, 20.

had come from the Council of Europe, which had always been a very strong supporter of minors' rights, and it had told the team that it had gone too far'.[216] Therefore, the representatives of the CoE contributed to the fact that minors must establish a lack of intent in cases involving non-specified substances to avoid the standard four-year ineligibility.

Moreover, the representatives of the CoE opposed the initial proposal to alleviate sanctions for minors and recreational athletes. Richard Young explained that 'in draft one, there had been a proposal that, when a minor established no significant fault, instead of the sanction being reduced by a half, the sanction could go all the way down to a warning'.[217] However, the representatives of the CoE refused this proposal. They asked:

> How can an athlete who is a minor/recreational athlete who: a) tests positive for a non-specified substance; and b) bears no significant fault (as opposed to no fault at all), receive only a reprimand and return immediately to competition without this posing a serious threat to protecting a level playing field?[218]

They argued that 'if the adverse analytical finding concerns a steroid, such a minor/recreational athlete could still be benefiting from the performance enhancing substance in his system'.[219] Therefore,

> allowing such an athlete (who acted with a certain degree of fault) an immediate return to competition would be detrimental to creating a level playing field and be manifestly unfair to his clean competitors. This cannot be the objective of the very Code which is designed to protect clean athletes.[220]

Thus, the representatives of the CoE did not support the idea of providing hearing panels with more flexibility while sanctioning the negligent doping of minors and recreational athletes.

Consequently, all minors do not benefit from milder sanctions as a direct consequence of the comment made by the representatives of the CoE. Richard Young admitted that he 'had been fairly impressed with the position of the Council of Europe'.[221] He noted that 'usually, the Council of Europe as a group was very supportive of the rights of minors'.[222] However, 'it thought that it went too far; the code drafting team had agreed and taken it out'.[223] Moreover, the representatives of the CoE suggested more flexibility in the range of applicable sanctions and reductions for recreational athletes, but the quantum of sanctions should stay identical for all athletes. They argued that 'the maximum applicable

[216] ibid.
[217] Minutes of the WADA Executive Committee Meeting, 14 November 2018, 6.1.1, 23.
[218] WADA, 2021 Code Review – Second Consultation Phase, Council of Europe, Sport Convention Division (France), Public Authorities – Intergovernmental Organization, 85–86, 166.
[219] ibid.
[220] ibid.
[221] Minutes of the WADA Executive Committee Meeting, 14 November 2018, 6.1.1, 23.
[222] ibid.
[223] ibid.

sanction in case of absence of significant fault or negligence should be 2 years'.[224] Therefore, the representatives of the CoE proposed more flexibility while sanctioning recreational athletes, but that the upper limit of sanctions should remain identical as in the case of other athletes.

In the end, protected persons, including some minors and recreational athletes, benefit from the initially proposed milder sanctions and the greater flexibility of hearing panels. Article 10.6.1.3 of WADC 2021 provides a special regime for cases where protected persons or recreational athletes commit an anti-doping rule violation not involving substances of abuse with no significant fault or negligence. In such cases, 'the period of ineligibility shall be, at a minimum, a reprimand and no period of ineligibility, and at a maximum, two (2) years ineligibility (…).'[225] Therefore, even though not all minors benefit from this amendment, those falling within the definition of protected persons do. This was, for example, the case with the Russian figure skater Kamila Valieva at the XXIV Olympic Winter Games in Beijing in 2022. Valieva was 15 years old at the time and therefore a protected person. The CAS panel noted that 'there is a lacuna, or a gap, in (…) (WADC 2021) (…)' concerning provisional suspensions of protected persons.[226] Consequently, her status as a protected person was one of the reasons why the CAS panel lifted the provisional suspension and let Valieva compete.[227] Therefore, protected persons benefit from milder sanctions and a greater sanctioning flexibility of hearing panels.

In addition, the representatives of the CoE successfully suggested that milder and more flexible sanctions should be imposed not only for presence, use or attempted use, or possession of a prohibited substance or method, but also for evading, refusing or failing to submit to sample collection.[228] They argued that 'indeed, a minor who is submitted to a first doping control might, in good faith, feel uncomfortable and refuse to be supervised during the collection of the sample'.[229] They claimed that

> otherwise, the new regime could lead to unfair differences in the sanctioning regime between a 15-year-old athlete sanctioned for 2 years for the use of anabolic steroids and another one sanctioned for 4 years because he felt uncomfortable having to submit to a first doping control.[230]

[224] WADA, 2021 Code Review – Second Consultation Phase, Council of Europe, Sport Convention Division (France), Public Authorities – Intergovernmental Organization, 173.

[225] WADC 2021, Art 10.6.1.3.

[226] CAS OG 22/08-CAS OG 22/09-CAS OG 22/10, *IOF, WADA, ISU v RUSADA*, Valieva, ROC, para 200.

[227] ibid para 202–18.

[228] WADA, 2021 Code Review – Second Consultation Phase, Council of Europe, Sport Convention Division (France), Public Authorities – Intergovernmental Organization, p. 165–166, 173; WADA, 2021 Code Review – Third Consultation Phase, Council of Europe, Sport Convention Division (France), Public Authorities – Intergovernmental Organization, 7, 8, 122.

[229] ibid – Second Consultation Phase, Council of Europe, Sport Convention Division (France), Public Authorities – Intergovernmental Organization, 165–66; WADA, 2021 Code Review – Third Consultation Phase, Council of Europe, Sport Convention Division (France), Public Authorities – Intergovernmental Organization, 8, 122.

[230] ibid – Third Consultation Phase, Council of Europe, Sport Convention Division (France), Public Authorities – Intergovernmental Organization, 8, 122.

In the end, Article 10.3.1 of WADC 2021 provides protected persons and recreational athletes with an exception from the standard four-year period of ineligibility for evading, refusing or failing to submit to sample collection, but also for tampering. 'The period of ineligibility shall be in a range between a maximum of two (2) years and, at a minimum, a reprimand and no period of ineligibility, depending on the protected person or recreational athletes' degree of fault.'[231] Therefore, the WADC 2021 reflects the comments of the representatives of the CoE and provides milder and more flexible sanctions for protected persons and recreational athletes also regarding an evasion, refusal or failure to submit to sample collection.

Finally, the representatives of the CoE successfully supported an optional public disclosure of violations committed by minors. WADC 2015 exempted minors from the mandatory public disclosure of anti-doping rule violations.[232] In the draft WADC 2021, the exception originally covered protected persons. The representatives of the CoE noted that 'the exception in the public disclosure disappears for minors who do not fall within the definition of "protected persons"'.[233] They further commented that such a situation 'is incompatible with our current national legislation and will certainly be a major issue if the draft does not evolve'.[234] Consequently, they recommended that public disclosure shall not be requested for all minors, irrespective of the fact that they fall or do not fall under the definition of 'protected persons'.[235] Finally, Article 14.3.7 of WADC 2021 provides that

> the mandatory public disclosure (…) shall not be required where the athlete or other person (…) is a minor, protected person or recreational athlete. Any optional public disclosure in a case involving a minor, protected person or recreational athlete shall be proportionate to the facts and circumstances of the case.[236]

Therefore, WADC 2021 includes an exemption from mandatory public disclosure for all minors, regardless of whether they fall under the definition of a protected person or not.

G. The Elimination, Reduction, or Suspension of the Period of Ineligibility or Other Consequences for Reasons Other than Fault

Finally, the representatives of the CoE commented on the possibility to eliminate, reduce or suspend the period of ineligibility or other consequences on

[231] WADC 2021, Art 10.3.1.
[232] ibid Art 14.3.6.
[233] WADA, 2021 Code Review – Third Consultation Phase, Council of Europe, Sport Convention Division (France), Public Authorities – Intergovernmental Organization, 7–8, 122.
[234] ibid.
[235] ibid.
[236] WADC 2021, Art 14.3.7.

grounds other than fault. Under WADC 2015, the elimination, reduction or suspension concerned ineligibility.[237] The first draft of WADC 2021 broadened such a possibility to all consequences of anti-doping rule violations. The representatives of the CoE initially highlighted the 'disproportionate sanctioning policy' for substantial assistance.[238] Moreover, they suggested that 'it is not clear what effect widening an ADOs powers to suspend any Consequence, and not just the period of ineligibility, is supposed to have, when the Article is read as a whole – it appears to be inconsistent'.[239] Moreover, 'if this change is adopted, Article 13.2 will need to be amended to allow appeals relating to all consequences, rather than just periods of ineligibility'.[240] In the end, WADC 2021 provides the possibility to eliminate, reduce or suspend any consequence,[241] but ADOs cannot suspend disqualification or mandatory public disclosure based on substantial assistance in discovering or establishing violations.[242] Moreover, appeals are extended to apply to all consequences of anti-doping rule violations.[243] Nevertheless, neither WADC 2021 nor any other document explains such a modification.

Moreover, the representatives of the CoE pleaded for an expansion of the possibility to reduce the period of ineligibility where there is an admission of an anti-doping rule violation in the absence of other evidence. They argued that 'an athlete that voluntarily admits to a possible rule violation, irrespective of later proof, should be entitled to a reduction without WADAs consent in an Art. 2.1-case'.[244] They further explained that 'the principle of a reduction is commonly applied because admittance will reduce the financial complications of a criminal procedure'.[245] Finally, they argued that 'the length of reduction should depend on at what time the admission was forwarded'.[246] Therefore, the representatives of the CoE supported broadening the possibility to reduce a period of ineligibility based on the admission of an anti-doping rule violation.

Nevertheless, WADC 2021 has kept the possibility of an admission of an anti-doping rule violation having the period of ineligibility reduced as provided in WADC 2015. An athlete or other person must voluntarily admit the violation before receiving the notice of a sample collection or the other admitted violation. Moreover, the admission must be the only reliable evidence of the

[237] WADC 2015, Art 10.6.
[238] WADA, 2021 Code Review – First Consultation Phase, Council of Europe, Sport Convention Division (France), Public Authorities – Intergovernmental Organization, 201.
[239] WADA, 2021 Code Review – Second Consultation Phase, Council of Europe, Sport Convention Division (France), Public Authorities – Intergovernmental Organization, 91.
[240] ibid.
[241] WADC 2021, Art 10.7.
[242] ibid Art 10.7.1.1.
[243] ibid Art 13.2.
[244] WADA, 2021 Code Review – Second Consultation Phase, Council of Europe, Sport Convention Division (France), Public Authorities – Intergovernmental Organization, 91.
[245] ibid.
[246] ibid.

violation. Consequently, 'the period of ineligibility may be reduced, but not below one-half of the period of ineligibility otherwise applicable'.[247] Moreover, the provision 'is intended to apply when an athlete or other person comes forward and admits to an anti-doping rule violation in circumstances where no anti-doping organisation is aware that an anti-doping rule violation might have been committed'.[248] Conversely, 'it is not intended to apply to circumstances where the admission occurs after the athlete or other person believes he or she is about to be caught'.[249] Moreover, 'the amount by which ineligibility is reduced should be based on the likelihood that the athlete or other person would have been caught had he or she not come forward voluntarily'.[250] Therefore, WADC 2021 does not reflect the CoE's proposal regarding a modification of the regime of a reduction of ineligibility based on the admission of guilt.

In addition, the representatives of the CoE addressed the possibility of a reduction of a sanction based on a prompt admission of a violation after being confronted with the violation. They particularly proposed that it should be specified whether, in the case of multiple grounds for reduction, athletes can rely on a prompt admission to receive a suspension below two years, which was the minimum limit in WADC 2015.[251] However, the drafters of WADC 2021 omitted the possibility of a reduction of the period of ineligibility down to a minimum of two years based on a prompt admission of an anti-doping rule violation from WADC 2021. WADA explains that 'Articles 10.6.3 (Prompt Admission) and Article 10.11.2 (Timely Admission) have been eliminated and replaced with a new Article 10.8. Both of the prior Articles have been a repeated source of questions and misinterpretations.'[252] Therefore, the new results management agreements replaced the possibility of reducing a sanction on the grounds of a prompt or timely admission. They include a one-year reduction for certain anti-doping rule violations based on an early admission and acceptance of a sanction and a case resolution agreement.[253]

IV. CONCLUSION

The CoE and the EU shaped the proportionality of ineligibility in WADC 2021 to a limited extent. This chapter hypothesised that representatives of the CoE and the EU would advocate for more proportionality, and thus shorter ineligibility, greater leniency and flexibility in sanctioning athletes and other persons.

[247] WADC 2021, Art 10.7.2; WADC 2015, Art 10.6.2.
[248] WADC 2021, Comment to Art 10.7.2; WADC 2015, Comment to Art 10.6.2.
[249] ibid.
[250] ibid.
[251] WADA, 2021 Code Review – Second Consultation Phase, Council of Europe, Sport Convention Division (France), Public Authorities – Intergovernmental Organization, 96.
[252] World Anti-Doping Code Development and Implementation Guide (n 79) 13.
[253] WADC 2021, Art 10.8.2.

Nevertheless, this turned out to be only partially true. The representatives of the CoE attempted to influence the proportionality of ineligibility in WADC 2021 significantly more than the representatives of the EU and its Member States. The CoE submitted 15, while the EU only had two sets of suggestions in this regard. Both sets of comments of the EU, which WADC 2021 reflects, recommended milder and more flexible sanctions for protected persons. On the other hand, only one-third of the comments of the CoE advocated milder sanctions. On the contrary, the representatives of the CoE pleaded for a tightening of sanctions in one third of their comments. The rest of the comments submitted by the CoE were neutral in this regard. Therefore, the CoE puts a similar emphasis on punishing dopers as it does on the proportionality of ineligibility, contrary to the original hypothesis. Finally, the text of WADC 2021 fully reflects both the sets of comments submitted by the EU and one third of the comments submitted by the CoE. It reflects the other third of the CoE's comments partially and disregards the final third.

Future research further exploring the role of the CoE and the EU in influencing the proportionality of ineligibility for doping would be desirable. In particular, it should explore the reasons behind the involvement of the CoE and the EU in the review process of the WADC, especially why the CoE intervenes in the process to a significantly greater extent than the EU. Moreover, it could examine why the CoE emphasises a tightening of sanctions in certain areas while pleading for greater proportionality in others. In addition, it should focus on how WADA reflects the comments of the representatives of the CoE and the EU and why. In this regard, the increased transparency of the review process of the WADC, particularly the discussions and conclusions of the drafting team, is desirable. It would help the researchers and the public to better understand how WADA and the review process work. Moreover, increased transparency would also strengthen WADA's good governance and athletes' confidence in the effective fight against doping which also protects their rights. In September 2023, WADA started gathering feedback on WADC 2021 to have the new edition of the WADC effective from 2027.[254] As the review process is now back on track, the time is ripe for more transparency.

[254] WADA, WADA launches first phase of 2027 World Anti-Doping Code and International Standards Update Process (online): https://www.wada-ama.org/en/news/wada-launches-first-phase-2027-world-anti-doping-code-and-international-standards-update.

Part II

The Integration of European Checks into the *Lex Sportiva*

8

False Friends: Proportionality and Good Governance in Sports Regulation

MISLAV MATAIJA*

I. INTRODUCTION

THE IMPORTANCE OF European Union (EU) law in scrutinising the practices of sporting bodies is well-known. By first establishing the principle that the measures of those bodies are subject to the disciplines of freedom of movement despite the freedom of association (*Walrave & Koch*[1]), and then progressively moving away from the notion of a 'sporting exception' towards a broadly conceived proportionality assessment (*Bosman*,[2] *Meca Medina*,[3] *MOTOE*,[4] among others), EU internal market law has become a meaningful constraint.[5] Some even see it as a beacon of hope: if not the EU, who will rein in the various abuses and corruption in the sporting world?

The proportionality assessment that is the core of both EU internal market and competition law has had a significant impact, as shown by the *Bosman* case, or more recently the *ISU*[6] case. In this chapter, however, I explore not how courts and regulators apply the notion of proportionality, but how it has been 'translated' by the sporting world into the related, but different idea of 'good

* Member of the Legal Service, European Commission. All views are personal and do not necessarily reflect those of the European Commission.

[1] Case 36/74 *BNO Walrave and LJN Koch v Association Union cycliste internationale, Koninklijke Nederlandsche Wielren Unie and Federación Española Ciclismo* [1974] ECLI:EU:C:1974:140.

[2] Case C-415/93 *Union royale belge des sociétés de football association ASBL v Jean-Marc Bosman, Royal club liégeois SA v Jean-Marc Bosman and others and Union des associations européennes de football (UEFA) v Jean-Marc Bosman* [1995] ECLI:EU:C:1995:463.

[3] Case C-519/04P *David Meca-Medina and Igor Majcen v Commission of the European Communities* [2006] ECLI:EU:C:2006:492.

[4] Case C-49/07 *Motosykletistiki Omospondia Ellados NPID (MOTOE) v Elliniko Dimosio* [2008] ECLI:EU:C:2008:376.

[5] I explored this in my book *Private Regulation and the Internal Market: Sports, Legal Services, and Standard Setting in EU Economic Law* (Oxford University Press, 2016).

[6] Case T-93/18 *International Skating Union (ISU) v European Commission* [2020] ECLI:EU:T:2020:610. Currently under appeal before the Court of Justice as C-124/21 P.

governance'. For example, in the 'Arrangement for Cooperation' between the Commission and the Union of European Football Associations (UEFA), UEFA commits to follow 'good governance principles' and to apply 'appropriate and proportionate measures'; similar requirements are then proposed by UEFA to national associations in its ten 'good governance' principles.

Instead of pushing back against the very idea of legal control over their measures (as done in the past), sporting bodies may have moved on to a different strategy: co-opting, normalising and, perhaps, pacifying the requirements of good governance as part of their own legal DNA. In the view of sporting bodies, however, good governance is likely to be a way of avoiding or diminishing, rather than reinforcing, legal scrutiny.

This chapter will first describe and contrast the notions of proportionality and good governance, while also explaining the connection between them. It will then explore what may be the ultimate step of a rhetorical or legal strategy based on good governance: a possible 'proceduralisation' of legal scrutiny, a less demanding standard of review over the measures of sporting bodies as long as a certain level of good governance is ensured. It will be argued that such a strategy would raise significant problems.

The story of the sporting world's conflicts and engagement with EU law is by now well-known. While there has traditionally been little appetite to re-regulate the sporting world through EU measures, decisions of the Court of Justice of the EU (CJEU) and the Commission's competition enforcement have made significant inroads into the autonomy of sporting bodies. Consequently, what was once seen as an area of pure private autonomy because 'sport is special' is today, by and large, accepted to be constrained by EU free movement, competition, and indeed constitutional principles. This means, by definition, some sort of supervisory role for EU institutions and national courts applying EU law. *Ad hoc* enforcement and judicial decisions have, to some extent, cleared the ground for more ambitious policy work. However, Article 165 of the Treaty on the Functioning of the European Union (TFEU), the Treaty provision which expressly addresses sport, puts limits on the EU's legislative role. Hence, to the extent that the EU has a more systematic sport policy, it has so far been mostly limited to a supporting role, while encouraging sporting bodies to act in accordance with 'good governance' principles and in pursuit of certain desirable policy objectives.

The sporting world has understood that EU sports law does not grant it full-on autonomy. Instead of a conflictual attitude, it has astutely sought to engage proactively with the EU.[7] A result of this process is that sporting bodies are, in some sense, seen as 'partners', recognised as legitimate regulators, and bestowed with so-called 'conditional autonomy', not to be understood as an exclusion from legal scrutiny but, at best, as a measure of deference. The price to be paid

[7] B García and S Weatherill, 'Engaging with the EU in Order to Minimize Its Impact: Sport and the Negotiation of the Treaty of Lisbon' (2012) 19 *Journal of European Public Policy* 2, 238–56.

for this 'conditional autonomy' is good governance. From the point of view of the sporting world, such efforts may help to pre-empt more extensive legal interventions. In return for implementing 'good governance' reforms, sporting bodies expect to continue largely governing our own affairs. The payback for political decision-makers is, perhaps, getting some of the credit for such reform efforts, while not having to undertake risky and unpopular decisions conflicting with the sporting world.

The period in which this dialogue between the EU institutions and the sporting world has been developing is also a period which has seen major corruption scandals in the sporting world, such as the various *Fédération internationale de football association* (FIFA) and UEFA corruption, bribery and fraud allegations; the Russian doping scandal; the International Association of Athletics Federation (IAAF) doping cover-ups and bribery; various match-fixing scandals, etc. The drive for good governance reforms by sporting bodies can also be seen as an attempt on their part to bolster their public image and signal a sort of new beginning.

In the process, 'good governance' has become something of a shorthand, or panacea for all the different ways in which the structures and practices of the sporting world fall short of legal requirements.[8] In the context of EU law, 'good governance' has become enmeshed with the key concept of proportionality. Whether in competition law or in free movement law, the central legal question is whether a particular measure taken by a sporting association is an appropriate and necessary response to a legitimate regulatory objective. The various sub-questions asked in that context overlap with the concerns of 'good governance'. If one squints, it may therefore seem that good governance and proportionality are interchangeable. The sporting world would likely welcome such a view, because it would mean that implementing good governance reforms also sorts out the proportionality concerns. To some extent, EU policy documents support such a reading. Translated in legal terms, a governance-based approach to sporting bodies may involve less demanding scrutiny over measures taken by well-governed bodies or in the context of well-designed and inclusive procedures. This approach would not be legally unprecedented, as this chapter will further explore.

[8] See, eg, Council of the EU, Resolution of the Council and of the representatives of the Governments of the Member States meeting within the Council on the key features of a European Sport Model, 30 November 2021(14430/21): 'Good governance in sport is a prerequisite for the autonomy and self-regulation of sport organisations and federations, in compliance with the principles of democracy, transparency, integrity, solidarity, gender equality, openness, accountability and social responsibility.' (Recital 15); 'At a time when modernisation of sport is bringing new financial opportunities from the economic potential of sport, it is of overriding importance that values-based organised sport preserves the integrity of sport, adheres to good governance principles, respects national, EU and international law and maintains the level-playing field necessary to effectively implement the solidarity values between all actors.' (Recital 20); calling upon the sporting world to 'ensure that effective internal and external mechanisms are in place to ensure compliance with good governance principles and respect of fundamental and human rights as well as with appropriate monitoring, reporting and sanctions mechanisms.' (Recital 43).

The following sections will look more closely at what good governance, as implemented in the measures of sporting associations, means. This will then be contrasted with the principle of proportionality as developed in the case law.

II. GOOD GOVERNANCE IN *LEX SPORTIVA*

The concept of good governance is proliferating in the world of sport regulation. Chronologically, the first major modern initiative are the International Olympic Committee's (IOC) Basic Universal Principles of Good Governance, approved by the XIII Olympic Congress in 2009. Leveraging the breadth of the Olympic Movement's umbrella, all member associations are required to adopt those principles by the IOC's Code of Ethics. It is worth listing them in some detail, as they are a good example of what the sporting world understands by 'good governance'. The IOC's principles are set out as follows:

- Vision, mission and strategy: values and objectives that should form part of the association's 'mission', for example, promotion of sport, organisation of competitions, solidarity, fairness, etc.
- Structures, regulations and democratic process: transparent rules on governing bodies and processes, their tasks, rules on elections, limited terms of office, allocation of tasks, representativeness, conflicts of interests, review of decisions affecting individual members, etc.
- Competence, integrity and ethical standards: competence and professionalism, powers of signature, risk management, financial monitoring, existence of ethical rules, etc.
- Accountability, transparency and control: accountability of all bodies to members 'and in certain cases, stakeholders', accountability of management to the executive body, and employees to management; transparency, accounting rules, internal controls, training, etc.
- Solidarity and development: fair allocation of revenues, principally to the sport, equitable distribution, development issues, etc.
- Athletes' involvement: right of athletes to participate, and their protection, including anti-doping, health, fairness and fair play.
- Relations with governments: coordination, cooperation but also (perhaps most of all) – preservation of the autonomy of sport.

Individual sports have pursued similar initiatives. To take the example of football, UEFA, the European football association, has adopted 'good governance' reforms itself, and has attempted to disseminate them to member (national) associations.[9] On UEFA's level, it has modified its statutes to, among other things,

[9] 'A Guide To UEFA's Good Governance Reform' (*LawInSport*, 17 January 2019), www.lawinsport.com/topics/features/item/a-guide-to-uefa-s-good-governance-reform#references.

make ethics and good governance a statutory objective, limit the terms of high officials, introduce club and league representation on the Executive Committee, etc. It has also published 'Good Governance Principles for UEFA Member Associations', which are not binding but are linked to incentive payments.[10]

Such good governance initiatives have been met with substantial praise in the political world, notably at the EU level. In 2014, Androulla Vassiliou, Commissioner for Education, Culture, Multilingualism and Youth, said that 'the Commission will cooperate with UEFA in its efforts to promote a more transparent and fair football'.[11] In 2017, then-Commissioner for Education, Culture, Youth and Sport, Tibor Navracsics, welcomed UEFA's initiative, stating that UEFA 'is taking seriously' the commitment to 'embed the culture of good governance in their activities'.[12]

Such endorsements of good governance reforms are, of course, welcomed and actively sought by the sporting world. Kruessmann describes this as a 'horizontal legitimacy-building strategy':

> By concluding memoranda of understanding, e.g. between the IOC and the UN or between FIFA and the CoE, [sports governing bodies], depending on their level of regional or universal exposure, co-opted their potential critics and tried to acquire legitimacy by involving them into the so-called reform processes.[13]

Case in point, the 2022 'Arrangement for Cooperation between the European Commission and UEFA',[14] the third in a row of such arrangements, is a more formal document adopted as part of a Commission Decision. It has as one of its objectives to 'support the efforts to improve good governance in sport' and describes the key features of the 'European Sport Model' as including 'autonomy of sport governing structures, which is conditioned on good governance' (Annex, point 3.6.1). It uses relatively strong language in saying that good governance, including 'accountability, democracy, inclusivity, integrity, participation and

[10] The principles are: clear strategy; statutes (including fixed terms for officials, gender representation); stakeholder involvement (recognition, consultation); promotion of ethical values; integrity and good governance (inclusion as objectives, either disciplinary regulations or codes of ethics); professionalism of committee structures (setting out responsibilities, composition, appointments, qualifications); administration (protection of the administration from undue political influence, transparent hiring, need for regulations on certain ethical principles); accountability (rights of signature, insurance, tendering, budgets); transparency in financial matters and corporate documents (financial controls, audits, publication of key documents and organisational structures); compliance (including on policies like health and safety, equality, protection of minors,match0fixing, doping …); and volunteer programmes. See www.uefa.com/insideuefa/news/024a-0f8e64c32833-1f4730cdd722-1000--uefa-good-governance-principles-for-associations/.

[11] See https://ec.europa.eu/commission/presscorner/detail/en/SPEECH_14_706.

[12] See M Chaplin, 'European Commissioner Welcomes UEFA Reforms' (*UEFA.com*, 6 April 2017), www.uefa.com/insideuefa/about-uefa/news/0238-0f8e4fe1f2cc-77d21b664e65-1000--european-commissioner-welcomes-uefa-reforms/?referrer=%2Finsideuefa%2Fabout-uefa%2Forganisation%2Fcongress%2Fnews%2Fnewsid%3D2455627.

[13] T Kruessmann, 'Extending Integrity to Third Parties: In Search of a New Model for Anti-Corruption in Sports'" (2019) 18 *The International Sports Law Journal* 18, 3, 136, at 138.

[14] Decision C(2022) 3721 on the adoption of the Arrangement for Cooperation between the European Commission and the Union of European Football Associations (UEFA) and Annex.

transparency' is a 'necessary condition' for self-regulation and the autonomy of sport (Annex, point 3.6.4). At the same time, the Arrangement provides some support, at least implicitly, for issues close to UEFA's heart. For example, it refers to the 'pyramidal structure' and 'open system of promotion and relegation', which may be read as a criticism of breakaway leagues like the Super League,[15] and supports 'policies to increase financial sustainability' (by which UEFA surely understands its Financial Fair Play policies).

The European Commission had itself sponsored the publication of a set of 'Principles for the Good Governance in Sport',[16] coupled with a 'pledge' to which numerous sports organisations have signed up.[17] Similar initiatives have been developed, or are in the works, in the Council of Europe[18] and the United Nations Educational, Scientific and Cultural Organization (UNESCO),[19] to name just two institutions. Similarly, states have required sporting bodies to adopt good governance codes, either directly by law or as a condition to access public funding.[20]

With the proliferation of good governance, there has also been a rise in benchmarking and indicators.[21] The Association of Summer Olympic International Federations (ASOIF) has published three governance reviews, scoring sporting bodies on the basis of 50 indicators divided across principles of transparency, integrity, democracy, control mechanisms and development and solidarity. Public organisations have also entered the fray. For example, the Parliamentary Assembly of the Council of Europe has called for an 'independent sports ethics rating system'.[22]

While recent, the good governance trend in sport has generated academic literature, which has both highlighted its potential and criticised it. It has been argued that there is a lack of clarity about the actual meaning of good governance, its rationale, or its actual impact: 'the proliferation of good governance codifications and policies can better be understood as a tendency to prescribe medicines without a clear diagnosis and without knowledge about possible side

[15] On this, see pending case C-333/21, *European Super League Company*.

[16] EU Work Plan for Sport 2011–2014, 'Expert Group 'Good Governance', Deliverable 2: Principles of Good Governance in Sport'. See https://ec.europa.eu/assets/eac/sport/library/policy_documents/xg-gg-201307-dlvrbl2-sept2013.pdf.

[17] See www.eusport.org/goodgovernance/GGS_outputs/GGS_Documents/good_governance_pledge.

[18] In 2018, the Parliamentary Assembly (PACE) adopted a Resolution on the path towards a framework for modern sports governance (Resolution 2199 (2018)).

[19] UNESCO's International Charter for Physical Education, Physical Activity and Sport is a 'rights-based reference that orients and supports policy- and decision-making in sport'; see in particular Article 10 (version of 2015).

[20] S De Dycker, 'Good Governance in Sport: Comparative Law Aspects'. (2019) 19 *The International Sports Law Journal* 1, 116, at 119–22.

[21] R Pielke Jr et al, 'An Evaluation of Good Governance in US Olympic Sport National Governing Bodies'' (2020) 20 *European Sport Management Quarterly* 4, 480, at 486. Pielke et al list a number of benchmarking initiatives which, as he points out, all coincide with major governance failures in the world of sport.

[22] Resolution 2199 (2018) (n 18), para 12.

effects'.[23] Another fundamental criticism is that 'good governance' reforms are likely to remain a self-serving exercise as long as the main motivation for adopting them is to 'protect and preserve the autonomy of sport'.[24] Various authors have highlighted the gap between the adoption of good governance indicators and their actual implementation in practice, which is not well captured by indicators and scoring. After studying US Olympic sporting bodies, Pielke et al, for example, discuss the actual results of implementing the IOC's broad principles in the practices of various sporting bodies, which differ enormously in terms of size and resources.[25] They 'arrive at strongly mixed views on the usefulness and appropriateness of such indicators as a practical tool for improving governance and organisational practices'. According to them, measurement problems, the simplifications involved in scoring, the use of proxies, and other difficulties make such indicators highly imprecise. At the same time, the indicators were unable to capture instances of pervasive corruption, leading to very high scores for organisations such as FIFA or US Gymnastics at times when this would not have been expected by a layman observer.[26] Indeed, among the top-rated associations in ASOIF's most recent review are FIFA and *Union Cycliste Internationale* (UCI)[27] – which shows that even highly-rated good governance reforms do not shield organisations from corruption and integrity concerns.[28]

Scholars have suggested that the drawbacks of self-regulation could be addressed through independent, external enforcement mechanisms, or with the involvement of public actors. While acknowledging the fact that, under current good governance schemes such as ASOIF's Key Governance Principles (KGPs), there is no independent external compliance monitoring mechanism and that non-compliant federations do not face sanctions, Geeraert has highlighted the potential of 'soft' mechanisms such as persuasion or naming-and-shaming in improving the governance of sporting bodies. Ultimately, however, even Geeraert's proposals put significant emphasis on the need for public actors, such as sporting bodies' host countries or international organisations, to impose minimum standards for self-regulation or 'exert coercive pressure'.[29]

[23] A Geeraert, 'Introduction: The Need for Critical Reflection on Good Governance in Sport' in A Geeraert and F van Eekeren (eds), *Good Governance in Sport: Critical Reflections* (Routledge, 2022), 4.

[24] Pielke et al (n 21) 496.

[25] ibid 482.

[26] ibid 494.

[27] See www.velonews.com/news/uci-chief-denies-cycling-imperiled-as-olympic-sport/.

[28] M Maduro and JHH Weiler, '"Integrity", "Independence" and the Internal Reform of FIFA: A View from the Trenches' in Geeraert and van Eekeren (n 23); see also M van Bottenburg, 'A Relational and Processual Perspective on Good Governance in Sport: Tackling the Deeper Problem', ibid, 32.

[29] A Geeraert, '"The Limits and Opportunities of Self-Regulation: Achieving International Sport Federations' Compliance with Good Governance Standards"' (2019) 19 *European Sport Management Quarterly* 4, 520, at 534. Similarly, A Geeraert, 'Football is War: the'EU's Limits and Opportunities to Control FIFA'. (2015) 1 *Global Affairs* 2, 139–47.

Three features of good governance in sport as it is now understood, as discussed in the literature, are particularly relevant for our topic.

First, its 'contemporary codifications emerged under the rubric of "corporate governance" in the corporate sector ... initially aimed at protecting shareholder investment'.[30] Indeed, governance reforms and codes have been principally driven not by a rising awareness of the public role of sporting bodies, but by the 'emergence of commercialisation culture in sport organisations';[31] the key objective of good governance is, seen in this light, effectiveness. It is telling in that regard that the Expert Group associated with the EU Work Plan for Sport puts effectiveness ahead of proportionality in its definition of good governance:

> The framework and culture within which a sports body sets policy, delivers its strategic objectives, engages with stakeholders, monitors performance, evaluates and manages risk and reports to its constituents on its activities and progress including the delivery of effective, sustainable and proportionate sports policy and regulation.[32]

Second, good governance is largely focused 'on the internal characteristics of organisations while ignoring the influence of the social context in general and inter-organisational power relations in particular'.[33] In other words, good governance is to a large extent inward-focused.

Third, it is perceived as an end unto itself, and not as an instrument for the pursuit of specific public values or substantive objectives, such as health or social cohesion. Van Eekeren notes, for example, that 'sport organisations and researchers often refer to good governance as a means of creating public values. However, in the implementation stage, the approach to good governance as an end winds up being used in most cases'.[34]

III. PROPORTIONALITY IN EU SPORTS LAW

From the perspective of EU law, as applied to sport, the good governance discussion is closely related to a key element of EU internal market and constitutional law: proportionality.

It is, of course, a huge simplification to describe EU law as simply requiring 'proportionality' of sporting bodies. In fact, there are (at least) two sets of rules which are relevant in relation to the sporting world: free movement and

[30] A Geeraert, 'Introduction: The Need for Critical Reflection on Good Governance in Sport', in: Geeraert and van Eekeren (n 23) 3.

[31] V Girginov, 'A Relationship Perspective on Organisational Culture and Good Governance in Sport' in Geeraert and van Eekeren (n 23) 86, citing D Shilbury, L Ferkins and L Smythe, 'Sport Governance Encounters: Insights from Lived Experience"' (2013) 16 *Sport Management Review* 3, 349–63.

[32] EU Work Plan for Sport 2011–2014 (n 16) 5.

[33] van Bottenburg (n 28) 30.

[34] F van Eekeren, 'The Value of a Public Value Perspective on Good Governance in Sport' in Geeraert and van Eekeren (n 23) 48.

competition. Under the free movement rules, the relevant question is whether the rules or practices at issue are discriminatory or restrictive of the free movement of goods, persons, services, establishment or capital. Under the competition rules, the question is whether there is an agreement, or decision of an association of undertakings, that restricts competition, or an abuse of market dominance.

Under either set of rules, finding that there is some restrictive effect on economic activity is not the end of the story, because there are possibilities of justification. The free movement rules provide for justification on a limited list of grounds (public policy, public healthy, public security), as well as by invoking an objective that can be described as an 'overriding reason in the public interest'. The CJEU explained in *Bosman* that all of these justifications can be invoked not just by states, but also by 'private' regulators like sporting bodies.[35] Whatever the legitimate objective is, the main hurdle is proportionality, in the broad sense: the measure has to be appropriate and necessary to achieve that objective.

As for the competition rules, they provide for a set of (largely) economic efficiency-driven considerations in Article 101(3) TFEU, as well as so-called 'objective justification' under Article 102 TFEU on abuses of dominance. However, the case law starting with (in the sport context) *Meca-Medina* has also developed a so-called 'inherent restriction' test, which is similar to the proportionality test under free movement.

Both sets of rules have been applied to a wide variety of measures of sporting bodies, and often at the same time. The reason why proportionality tends to become the main issue in these cases is that it is usually not too difficult to find a restriction. As long as the measures of sporting bodies go beyond so-called 'purely sporting' issues (for example, the number of allowed substitutes in a match), they are likely to have a restrictive effect on the activities of, usually, players or clubs. At the same time, it is rarely possible to dismiss out of hand the claims of sporting bodies that their measures are connected to a legitimate objective, such as preserving the integrity of sport. Hence, most of the action tends to revolve around the question of whether the sporting body has acted in a proportionate manner when engaging in the restrictive action.

This means asking whether the specific measure taken by the sporting body, also in light of the decision-making processes and safeguards surrounding it, is suitable for achieving its objective in a consistent, coherent and systematic way, and whether it goes further than is necessary.[36] Under the competition rules, the question is, similarly, whether the anti-competitive effects of the measure are 'inherent' in the attainment of legitimate objectives and proportionate to it.[37]

In both iterations, the proportionality requirement will typically be applied so as to change the way sport is regulated, and not simply to condemn regulation as such. As Duval explains, 'the use of the control of proportionality can

[35] *Bosman* (n 2) para 86.

[36] Case C-66/18 *Commission v Hungary* [2020] ECLI:EU:C:2020:792, para. 178. See also C-333/14 *Scotch Whisky* [2015] EU:C:2015:845, para 53.

[37] Cases C 309/99 *Wouters* [2002] E U:C:2 002:98, para 97; *Meca-Medina* (n 3) para 42.

lead to re-assessment and contestation of a regulation, without necessarily leading to a de-regulation'; it could even be said that the obligation to justify aims to 'compensate for the democratic deficit of the *lex sportiva*'.[38] For this reason, it is clear that proportionality and good governance are linked. This connection can be traced in Commission policy documents at least as far back as the 2007 White Paper on Sport.[39] The White Paper sets the template for most later expressions of EU sports policy: it emphasises the primary role of the sporting bodies and states that 'most challenges can be addressed through self-regulation respectful of good governance principles, provided that EU law is respected'. This signals deference to sporting bodies, dependent on respecting two closely linked benchmarks: 'good governance', and 'EU law'. Separately, the White Paper discussed the possible future application of the competition and free movement rules, based on a case-by-case approach (an element that the sporting world tends not to look favourably on).[40] A 2011 document sets out even more clearly that good governance is 'a condition for the autonomy and self-regulation of sport organisations'.[41]

The link between the two notions can also be traced in the application of both free movement and competition rules. Indeed, competition and internal market enforcement often turns on issues that form part of the 'good governance' toolkit. The Commission's competition enforcement has led sporting bodies to increase transparency in internal decision making,[42] or to preserve recourse to national courts.[43] But such motives appear frequently in the case law as well.

[38] A Duval, *La Lex Sportiva Face au Droit de l'Union Européenne: Guerre et Paix dans l'Espace Juridique Transnational* (PhD thesis, European University Institute, 2015).

[39] European Commission, *White Paper on Sport* (2007) COM/2007/0391 final.

[40] On this, the accompanying staff working document 'The EU and Sport: Background and Context' provides further detailed information.

[41] European Commission, *Communication from the Commission to the European Parliament, the Council, the European Economic and Social Committee and the Committee of the Regions, Developing the European Dimension in Sport* (2011) COM/2011/0012 final 10. More broadly, see J Alm (ed), *Action for Good Governance in International Sports Organisations* (Play the Game/Danish Institute for Sports Studies Report, 2013). Interestingly, the same trade-off is recognised by sports organisations as well, if perhaps with a difference in emphasis. See, eg, T Bach, vice-president of the International Olympic Committee, 'European Union, Sport and Athletes – Quo Vadis' at the 'European Evening of Sport' (Brussels, 27 February 2013), www.dosb.de/fileadmin/fm-dosb/arbeitsfelder/Internationales/Rede_Bach_Europa _Bruessel_engl_270213BXL_final_pdf.pdf '… "autonomy" is indispensable for the existence of sport and is necessary for the dissemination of sporting values … On the other hand, sport should ensure a decision-making process characterised by the rules of good governance' (4).

[42] Notice published pursuant to Article 19(3) of Council Regulation 17 concerning Cases COMP/35.163 – Notification of FIA Regulations, COMP/36.638 – Notification by FIA/FOA of agreements relating to the FIA Formula One World Championship, COMP/36.776 – GTR/FIA [2001] OJ C169/5. See the press releases IP/01/1523 'Commission Closes its Investigation into Formula One and other Four-Wheel Motor Sports' (30 October 2001) and IP/03/1491 'Commission Ends Monitoring of FIA/Formula One Compliance with 2001 Settlement' (31 October 2003), claiming that FIA fulfilled the terms of the settlement to 'limit its role to that of a sports regulator, to guarantee access to motor sport to any racing organization meeting the requisite safety criteria and to no longer prevent teams and circuit owners not to participate in other races'.

[43] See the press release IP/02/824 'Commission Closes Investigations into FIFA Regulations on International Football Transfers' (5 June 2002). FIFA also changed its rules in order to create 'an

One example is *MOTOE*, where the CJEU based its approach on the prevention of conflicts of interests. When applying Articles 102 and 106 TFEU (the latter dealing with exclusive rights granted by the State), the CJEU suggests that it is very difficult to justify cases in which a single sporting body is both a regulator of, and a participant in, the market for the organisation of sporting events, at least in the absence of any 'restrictions, obligations and review'.[44] Case law in the area of free movement has taken up similar ideas. For example, in *Commission v Italy* (trade fairs), the very fact of a competitor being involved in controlling the access of new entrants led to a breach of the fundamental freedoms. A long line of free movement case law similarly requires authorisation requirements to be 'clearly defined, transparent, non-discriminatory, reviewable and capable of ensuring … effective access to the relevant market' – again, imbuing the proportionality test with a distinctly procedural flavour.[45]

This point was taken up more recently in *ISU*, a Commission competition decision on restrictions imposed on breakaway competitions in ice-skating, largely confirmed by the General Court.[46] When setting out a legal test for appropriate authorisation criteria for competing competitions, the General Court relied on free movement case law on authorisation procedures, mentioned above.[47]

The case law, therefore, suggests that, quite apart from the impact on economic activities *in concreto*, EU internal market rules can be employed as a sort of governance toolkit.[48] For example, the General Court held in *Piau* (a case dealing with FIFA's rules on football players' agents) that the rule-making power over economic activities claimed by FIFA is 'open to question', as a possible violation of 'civil and economic liberties'.[49] In *Meca-Medina*, the CJEU accepted the notion that doping sanctions and procedures, if disproportionate,

effective, quick and objective arbitration body with members chosen in equal numbers by players and clubs and with an independent chairman … FIFPro [the main players' union] will also nominate representatives for the new Arbitration Tribunal for Football, to which decisions of the Dispute Resolution Chamber can be appealed.' Staff working document, 'The EU and Sport: Background and Context' at 74.

[44] *MOTOE* (n 4) para 48. For an analysis, see S Miettinen, 'Policing the Boundaries Between Regulation and Commercial Exploitation: Lessons from the MOTOE Case' (2008) *The International Sports Law Journal* 3–4, 13–19. See also A Di Marco, 'Conflicts of Interest in Sport: A Comparative Analysis of International and European Remedie"' (2020) *European Journal of Comparative Law and Governance* 7.2, 201–24.

[45] Case C-205/99 *Analir* [2001] ECLI :EU:C:2 001:107, para 38. See, more broadly, S Prechal, 'Free Movement and Procedural Requirements: Proportionality Reconsidered' (2008) 35 *Legal Issues of Economic Integration* 3, 201–16.

[46] *ISU v Commission* (n 6) paras 70–71.

[47] ibid para 88. These issues are also discussed in the well-publicised *Superleague* case, pending at the Court in parallel with the appeal against the General Court's decision in *ISU*.

[48] This exercise need not be performed by courts or enforcers themselves. They can, however, open up possibilities for further elaboration of good governance principles as 'catalysts', to use Scott's and Sturm's terminology. J Scott and S Sturm, 'Courts as Catalysts: Rethinking the Judicial Role in New Governance' (2007) *Columbia Journal of European Law* 13, 565.

[49] Case T-193/02 *Piau v Commission* [2005] ECLI:EU:T:2005: 22, paras 76–78.

could infringe competition law, without bothering too much with the question of how exactly competition, and what sort of competition, would be affected.

These links have been noticed by legal scholars. Duval, for example, describes the proportionality principle as a 'procedural tool' that 'opens up spaces of argumentation and negotiation', including a 'recognition of the institutional peculiarities of the sports world'.[50] Others go a step further, placing proportionality and good governance on an equal footing, which may be taken to suggest that measures adopted based on a sound process should not be subject to a full proportionality analysis. A good example is Parrish's argument that:

> [T]he CJEU and the Commission will generally accept the legitimacy of sports bodies enacting rules designed to secure sports specific objectives as long as these rules do not transgress the boundaries of proportionality. This approach conditions sporting autonomy on the acceptance of good governance in sport ... adherence to good governance, procedural fairness and the harmonisation of standards between internal sporting federations are principles the *lex sportiva* aspires to transplant universally in sport ... The view expressed by the European Court in *Meca-Medina* therefore reflects the standards the sporting movement themselves seek to achieve. The European Court is merely patrolling the outer limits of the *lex sportiva*.[51]

Later on, Parrish states that

> [t]he jurisprudence of the Court reveals that EU sports law is respectful of claims to sporting autonomy and the recognition of the specific nature of sport. However, it conditions this autonomy on respect for the lex sportiva's own principles of proportionality and good governance.[52]

At first sight, this does not seem to go further than the Commission said itself, as cited above: autonomy is conditioned on good governance. Importantly, however, Parrish – along with many others – presents 'proportionality' and 'good governance' as substitutable or at least very closely connected; he also portrays the body of law developed by and for the sporting world as having internalised both principles.

IV. TOWARDS A 'PROCEDURALISATION' OF PROPORTIONALITY?

The suggestion that compliance with 'good governance' requirements is relevant within the four corners of a proportionality test leads us to a more speculative question. Can the implementation of 'good governance' reforms, whether superficial or real, have an impact on the application of EU law, and especially the principle of proportionality? Would a given restrictive measure of a sporting

[50] A Duval, 'Lex Sportiva: A Playground for Transnational Law' (2013) 19 *European Law Journal* 6, 822, 840.

[51] R Parrish, 'Lex Sportiva and EU Sports Law' (2012) 36 *European Law Review* 6, 716, 725.

[52] ibid 733.

body, such as the exclusion of an athlete or a club from a competition, be viewed more favourably by a court or a competition regulator if the governance mechanisms used to arrive at it are 'good'? Conversely, will poor governance doom a measure that might, on substance, seem like a proportionate response to a legitimate regulatory concern?

A 'procedural' approach seems especially relevant in the context of private regulators such as sporting bodies. It can be connected to theoretical approaches based on 'reflexive law', which suggest that self-regulation could be subject to a 'principle of constitutionalized autonomy', which falls short of detailed substantive review and seeks instead to structure the self-regulator's interactions with non-members, as well as its 'internal organisation and processes' to ensure that constitutional values are upheld.[53] The Global Administrative Law project, which seeks to identify administrative law-type mechanisms for control over global governance, including private actors, can be seen as a weaker version of that argument.[54]

It is helpful, however, to zoom in on what precisely a procedural approach would look like in legal practice. This debate is well developed, in rather explicit terms, in the context of the scrutiny of *State* measures by supranational courts, notably the European Court of Human Rights (ECtHR). In what follows, this chapter therefore uses that strand of case law and literature as a case study of what such an approach might mean in the context of sport governance.

As Arnardóttir describes it, the ECtHR has been known to 'emphasise the quality of national decision-making processes as an element that influences its own review of the proportionality or reasonableness of a contested measure'.[55] She describes how the ECtHR has shifted from 'substantive' (a case-by-case assessment of the substantive justifiability of human rights impacts in individual cases anchored in the regulatory objectives) to 'procedural' review (a more general assessment of the decision-making practices used, possibly leading to deference to national bodies), in several steps. By developing a doctrine of 'margin of appreciation' for national bodies, creating the pilot judgment procedure, extending a measure of deference to other international organisations with robust human rights safeguards in *Bosphorus Airlines*,[56] and later, first, to 'responsible courts' and then to 'responsible legislators', the ECtHR has arrived at a review model which focuses primarily 'on a) legislative choices, b)

[53] J Black, 'Constitutionalising Self-Regulation' (1996) *MLR* 59, 24, 53.

[54] RB Stewart, 'Remedying Disregard in Global Regulatory Governance: Accountability, Participation, and Responsiveness' (2014) 108 *American Journal of International Law* 2, 211–70; N Krisch and B Kingsbury, 'Introduction: Global Governance and Global Administrative Law in the International Legal Order' (2006) 17 *European Journal of International Law* 1, 1–13.

[55] OM Arnardóttir, 'Organised Retreat? The Move from "Substantive" to "Procedural" Review in the ECtHR's Case Law on the Margin of Appreciation' (European Society of International Law (ESIL) 2015 Annual Conference (Oslo)) 6–7.

[56] *Bosphorus Hava Yollari Turizm Ve Ticaret Anonim Şirketi v Ireland* (2005) App no 45036/98 (ECtHR, 30 June 2005).

the quality of parliamentary review, and c) the persuasiveness of abstract justifications for general measures'.[57]

Two examples of this approach are *Animal Defenders* and *MGN*. In *Animal Defenders*, a case concerning a ban on political advertising, the Court's proportionality analysis focused on the quality of the process that led to the law's adoption, as well the subsequent domestic judicial review. The Court concluded:

> The Court, for its part, attaches considerable weight to these exacting and pertinent reviews, by both parliamentary and judicial bodies, of the complex regulatory regime governing political broadcasting in the United Kingdom and to their view that the general measure was necessary to prevent the distortion of crucial public interest debates and, thereby, the undermining of the democratic process.[58]

This was not the entirety of the analysis. It was, however, quite important, as shown by the fact that it is what the Court looked at first. The discussion on the substantive justifiability of the prohibition, in a sense, confirmed the positive findings concerning the procedure, not *vice versa*.

MGN, a case concerning the requirement to pay lawyers' success fees and the balance between the freedom of expression and the right to access a court, shows that the 'procedural' turn can lead to quite the opposite result. Here, the Court relied on the UK Government's own consultation processes, highlighting flaws in the functioning of the law in question, to find a violation of the Convention:

> [T[he Court considers that the depth and nature of the flaws in the system, highlighted in convincing detail by the public consultation process, and accepted in important respects by the Ministry of Justice, are such that the Court can conclude that the impugned scheme exceeded even the broad margin of appreciation to be accorded to the State in respect of general measures pursuing social and economic interests.[59]

That approach does not entirely collapse proportionality into procedure. The objective is not to defer to any decision that might be made by a 'well-governed' body, or to condemn measures purely on the basis of procedural reasons. However, procedural factors are taken into account, and can weigh on either side of the balance.[60] As examples of such factors, Sathanapally gives:

> 1. The effort and time taken to make the decision: Was the decision made after due consideration, or hastily? 2. Reason-giving: Did deliberation proceed on the basis of publicregarding reasons, rather than self-interested motives? 3. Information: Was the

[57] Arnardóttir (n 55) 18–19.

[58] *Animal Defenders International v The United Kingdom* (2013) App no 45036/98 (ECtHR, 22 April 2013) para 116.

[59] *MGN Ltd v The United Kingdom* (2011) App no 39401/04 (ECtHR, 18 January 2011) para 217.

[60] A Sathanapally, 'The Modest Promise of "Procedural Review" in Fundamental Rights Cases' in J Gerards (ed), *Procedural Review in European Fundamental Rights Cases* (Cambridge University Press, 2017) 40, 47–48.

> relevant information available to decisionmakers in their deliberation? 4. Diversity: Was there deliberation that encompassed or invited a diverse range of viewpoints? 5. Openness to change: Were decision-makers open to changing their viewpoints in the course of deliberation; that is, was the deliberation genuine, or only symbolic?[61]

The CJEU has also developed similar approaches in certain cases. Apart from the sport cases mentioned above, it has centred its analysis of the legality of EU instruments on procedural arguments related to the decision-making process. This enabled it to avoid entering into the merits of the legislators' decisions. Such approaches are more difficult to find with respect to the measures of Member States, but they exist. Beijer, for example, gives several examples of judgments where the CJEU has imposed requirements like the right to be heard, protection of the rights of defence, the existence of judicial review, accessibility and reasonableness of national procedures, etc.[62] Unlike the ECtHR's approach in *Animal Defenders*, however, there is rarely a suggestion that the quality of domestic procedures is the primary concern. Instead, it is an additional hurdle to be passed by national rules.

For example, towards the end of its proportionality analysis in *Dynamic Medien*, the Court acknowledges that different procedures can be used by different Member States to achieve legitimate objectives, as long as they are 'readily accessible, can be completed within a reasonable period, and, if it leads to a refusal, the decision of refusal must be open to challenge before the courts'.[63] This is not unlike the requirement, in *Hartlauer*, that procedures involving prior authorisation for market access must be 'based on objective, non-discriminatory criteria known in advance, in such a way as adequately to circumscribe the exercise of the national authorities' discretion'.[64] And indeed, as already mentioned, the very same test was used in the *ISU* judgment, making a double leap: from free movement to competition, and from state measures to the decisions of private (sporting) bodies.[65]

The main justification for including process considerations in judicial review is that it allows courts to avoid second-guessing substantive political choices, for which legislators and executive bodies are thought to be better placed.[66] Of course, this consideration does not apply in the same way to private regulators as to states. On the one hand, the institutional logic of deferring to the decisions of public regulators and legislatures may not hold with respect to private transnational bodies, such as sporting bodies, and the legitimacy of their decisions

[61] ibid 59.

[62] M Beijer, 'Procedural Fundamental Rights Review by the Court of Justice of the European Union' in Gerards (n 60) 177.

[63] C-244/06 *Dynamic Medien Vertriebs GmbH v Avides Media AG*[2008] EU:C:2008:85, para 50.

[64] C-169/07 *Hartlauer Handelsgesellschaft mbH v Wiener Landesregierung and Oberösterreichische Landesregierung* [2009] EU:C:2009:141, para 64.

[65] *ISU v Commission* (n 46) para 88.

[66] K Lenaerts, 'The European Court of Justice and Process-oriented Review' (2012) 31 *Yearbook of European Law* 1, 3–16.

will not be seen in the same way. On the other, transnational regulators, even private ones, may be less exposed to certain biases than state bodies; in particular, they may be less inclined to favour local interests[67] (although, perhaps, still biased in favouring certain own constituencies, not defined in territorial terms).

In any event, even in the context of state measures, there is little evidence of the CJEU actually deferring to Member States' choices on the basis of sound procedures. Nevertheless, it may be attractive, especially from the point of view of the sporting world, to transpose this kind of process-based review to the measures of sporting bodies. In that context, it would have the additional benefit of reinforcing the autonomy of sport, or private autonomy more generally. Because using economic law as a sort of quasi-administrative law to control the measures of sporting bodies is already controversial, focusing that review on the quality of the process instead of on the substantive decisions may not just give due regard to the expertise of private regulators, but also strengthen the legitimacy of judicial review.

There are, however, important reasons why that approach may not be desirable. First, the good governance discourse originates, in part, in corporate governance notions;[68] proportionality, on the other hand, is a constitutional notion designed with regulators in mind. This need not mean much in itself. But the different intellectual history matters. Corporate governance and, by extension, 'good governance' is primarily targeted at increasing market value by improving the internal functioning of the organisation and making it accountable to shareholders. Proportionality is, at root, designed to limit the discretion of public authorities and other regulators, in order to protect those affected by their actions. In other words, good governance looks inwards while proportionality looks outwards. It is of course true that good governance reforms involve reaching out to external stakeholders, building appropriate relationships with governments, and taking into account various societal interests. These are, however, far from the centre of attention. An organisation that complies with good governance criteria could still, in an entirely democratic and transparent way, take measures that harm outsiders. State measures are subject to more meaningful disciplines designed to prevent such outcomes, especially in the context of a supranational legal system like that of the EU, focused on battling the exclusion of outsiders, such as nationals of other states.[69]

Second, deferring to the judgments of an institution that is supposedly 'better placed' should not be based on rigid assumptions of the superiority of, say, legislators, but on a comparative analysis of the different institutions

[67] MP Maduro, '*We the Court: The European Court of Justice and the European Economic Constitution* (Bloomsbury Publishing, 1998).

[68] See section II.

[69] Maduro (n 67).

based on some benchmark, such as representation.[70] It is not obvious that this comparison would work in the same way between a court and a sporting body as it would between a court and a legislator. While sporting bodies typically have a strong claim of representativeness of at least one set of actors in their sport (for example, UEFA assembles all European national football federations, which in turn can claim to be representative of clubs in their territory), there are frequent complaints that other actors within the sporting world (such as individual athletes) are not sufficiently represented. This does not even touch upon the question of third parties affected in various ways by the measures of sporting bodies, which are at best listened to as 'external stakeholders'. This is not to say that a review of the measures of sporting bodies should not encompass procedural concerns or governance drawbacks. However, even taking as a given that there are sometimes good reasons for eschewing substantive review and making instead a 'procedural turn' in order, for example, to defer to the policy choices of legislatures, it does not follow that the same is true with respect to sporting bodies, whether transnational or local.

Third, the notion of the unity of the State in international law is an important feature of process-based review by supranational courts. This allows the supranational court to consider not just the inner workings of a single institution, like an executive body, but the ability of the broader domestic constitutional framework to keep such deficiencies in check. The difficulties posed by a particular measure, or even procedural drawbacks in its adoption, could still be rectified, for example, by domestic review by independent courts. In some contexts, like in the European Union, such domestic checks and balances could be presumed to exist, barring exceptional cases, based on notions such as 'mutual trust' and the fact that all national courts are, in some sense, partners in the implementation of Union law. But this step cannot be so easily taken with respect to a sporting body, especially an international one, which is typically designed so as to be isolated from any national legal system, and with judicial review principally through internal bodies and arbitration. Of course, such internal judicial bodies can be considered as part of a broader equation, which might also have the knock-on effect of assessing the quality of their own design and functioning.[71] But that only speaks in favour of an approach that is more closely modulated to the context.

Fourth, the proceduralisation of proportionality implies repeat players. To take the example of *Bosphorus*: the ECtHR defers to the EU legal system, as a general matter, based on its guarantees of fundamental rights protection. But

[70] NK Komesar, *Imperfect Alternatives: Choosing Institutions in Law, Economics, and Public Policy* (University of Chicago Press, 1994).

[71] See, as an example of the types of issues that this could give rise to, the *Mutu and Pechstein* case, concerning the independence and impartiality of the Court of Arbitration for Sport (CAS) in light of the right to a fair trial. *Mutu and Pechstein v Switzerland* (2018) App nos 40575/10 and 67474/10 (ECtHR, 2 October 2018).

the 'as long as' logic on which the deference is based implies a regular review of the actual implementation of those guarantees, possibly reverting to stricter review if need be. Similarly, whether national courts provide an effective guarantee against executive abuses can only be assessed over time. Sporting bodies, however, appear before supranational courts only sporadically. Any softening of judicial review based on their alleged good governance could, therefore, be based only on a snapshot, not on a video. For that reason alone, it would be much more difficult to form an informed view of how 'good' the governance actually is.

Fifth, the highly diverse and constantly changing set-up of sporting bodies would be a challenge in developing any coherent doctrine of deference based on good governance. To take two extreme examples: one sporting body may be set up as a non-profit, granted special status under national law, and actively supervised by public authorities; another could be a for-profit off-shore company, answering only to its shareholders. While these differences could of course be taken into account, they would imply that any modification of the proportionality test based on good governance would have to be a complex case-by-case assessment. It could not be based simply on a generic label such as 'autonomy of sports governing bodies'.

V. CONCLUDING REMARKS

From the point of view of sporting bodies, the main objective of implementing good governance is the preservation of autonomy, while proportionality is suspicious of autonomy; hence, to a certain degree, the insistence in EU policy documents on the 'conditional' autonomy of sport. Proportionality, even understood in procedural terms, involves making sure that each individual measure is appropriate, necessary and coherent. The scrutiny can perhaps be more or less intrusive on a case-by-case basis, but it does not allow for free passes.

From the EU's perspective, linking good governance with autonomy is perhaps understandable: EU policy-makers want to achieve a measure of progress without too much heavy lifting, relatively risk-free and in the absence of a clear legislative competence. It is therefore natural to give sporting bodies free rein to some extent, as long as there is at least the appearance of receiving something in return. However, as decisions of the CJEU have shown time and again, such political bargains can be thrown off-course by a case-by-case, proportionality-based legal assessment. Promises of autonomy may turn out to be less solid than they seem. This shows that, while the quality of the governance and process employed by sporting bodies certainly deserves to be a central part of both 'good governance' efforts and a legal proportionality test, one should not be mistaken for the other.

The superficial approach to 'good governance', which too often amounts to a formalisation of decision-making rules and the publication of a set of carefully worded general documents on a sporting body's website, risks swallowing up the various legal and political controversies raised in sport. It becomes a sort of easy answer to everything. Corruption, doping, human rights violations, improper treatment of individual athletes, exclusion of competitors … all can be solved, according to this mantra, if we only implement the right 'good governance' reforms. Both from the point of view of the sporting world, and from the point of view of sport policy-makers, this fiction is helpful. It lends sporting bodies a layer of credibility, and allows them to keep making a claim for legal and political autonomy. For policy-makers, it is a way of avoiding the difficult, legally troublesome and possibly unpopular work of addressing these problems head-on, by relying on sporting bodies.

The risk, however, is that 'good governance' also swallows up the core external legal requirements imposed on sporting bodies. Indeed, certain policy documents give the impression that good governance and compliance with EU law, including proportionality, are interchangeable, or that EU law will be less likely to intervene if good governance reforms are in place. It is helpful to be reminded of the fact that the two concepts are different, especially because the way in which they are blended may be a deliberate choice. It is also important to consider how a deference to well-governed organisations would translate in the context of a proportionality analysis. This chapter has explained, using the case law of the CJEU and the ECtHR as examples, that even where such deference can be found, it rests on assumptions that do not necessarily hold in the context of sporting bodies.

9

Sport Beyond the Market? Sport, Law and Society in the European Union

AURÉLIE VILLANUEVA*

Does EU law approach sport beyond market regulation? This chapter argues that in its approach to sport, EU law embraces an understanding of sport in its societal function. It is by unfolding the relationship between sport and society in the EU legal order that the chapter sheds light on the building blocks of the EU societal narrative in the field of sport.

Football is the most emblematic example of how an after-work social activity has transformed into an industry. What do such transformations entail for the relationship between sport and society? The increasing professionalisation and globalisation of sport has led to its inevitable commodification.[1] Guilianotti and Walsh qualify as hyper-commodification the greater professionalisation and global migration of players, the corporatisation of clubs, the proliferation of merchandising and a general redefinition of the competitive structures as ethos of the sport.[2] While grassroot sport activities remain important, the gap between local amateur and transnational professional sport has increased. In particular, the economic resources and capacities of amateur and professional clubs are becoming polarised.

The EU has witnessed the transformation of the sport sector all while supervising the Member States' support to clubs, distortions of competition in the sale of broadcasting rights for sport events and any restrictions of the fundamental freedoms.[3] While the EU covers sport activities via internal market law, its approach to sport is not limited to market law *stricto sensu*. The EU has

* PhD researcher at the Law Department of the European University Institute, Florence, Italy.

Paper presented at the conference 'The Europeanization of the Lex Sportiva: How European Law Shapes the Governance of Global Sports' organised by the Swedish Network for European Legal Studies, Umeå 17–18 November 2021. I am grateful to the participants and editors for their valuable comments on earlier drafts.

[1] A J Walsh and R Giulianotti, 'This Sporting Mammon: A Normative Critique of the Commodification of Sport' (2001) 28 *Journal of the Philosophy of Sport* 53, 58.

[2] ibid 53.

[3] S Weatherill, *Principles and Practice in EU Sports Law* (Oxford University Press, 2017).

developed its sport policy and participates in discussions at the transnational level thereby positioning itself as an actor in sport governance rather than as a mere market regulator. In this capacity, the EU is developing a narrative linked to the values of sport and the role of sport for society.

The chapter does not aim to discuss what society is, what it is made up of, nor what a European society might look like.[4] It highlights the interconnections between the notions of society and sport in EU law and policy documents. In this context, the distinction between social and societal aspects of sport is relevant, and in the scope of this chapter, the former refers to considerations regarding employment conditions and working relations in EU law, which are attached to the sphere of the internal market.[5] While the latter relates to the sphere beyond the market, where society is the object that is looked at when one looks beyond the market. Although the distinction between social and societal serves to clarify the terminology relied on in the chapter, it is not claimed that the spheres of the social and societal are separate and irreconcilable. On the contrary, many social concerns are part of the societal narrative developed by the EU, and in policy documents, law and political declarations, the terms are used interchangeably.

The chapter investigates whether EU law relates to the notion of sport beyond the market and whether it connects the notion of sport to other notions such as society, cohesion or identity. However, without engaging with the substance of such concepts, the focus is on putting them in relation to each other. By highlighting the societal dimension of sport in the case law of the European Court of Justice (ECJ), policy documents and selected legal provisions, the chapter aims to show that the EU is developing a societal narrative which has the potential to counterbalance the hyper-commodification of sport.

The first section of the chapter sketches the relationship between sport and the EU, starting with the ECJ (section I), which was the first actor to deal with sport in the EU legal order. The ECJ determined when EU law applies to sport and its implications. The case law of the ECJ also sheds light on the distinctive aspects of sport, in particular sport values such as the training of young players. It shows that the ECJ recognised the societal implications of sport at an early stage.

The second part continues with the evolution of sport policy in the EU (section II). The narratives of heads of states and of the Commission illustrate an ideal where sport is inseparable from society and even becomes a tool to achieve societal objectives such as cohesion.

The third part of the chapter examines how law accommodates sport and society by relying on the provisions concerning events that are important to society contained in the EU Audiovisual Media Services Directive

[4] For a discussion on this see H-W Micklitz, 'Discussion Society, Private Law and Economic Constitution in the EU' in G Grégoire and X Miny (eds), *The Idea of Economic Constitution in Europe* (Brill, 2022); L Azoulai, 'The Law of European Society' (2022) 59 *CMLR* 203.

[5] European Commission, *White Paper on Sport* COM(2007) 391 final, 19.

(AVMSD) (section III).[6] It starts by reconstructing the definition of events of major importance to society which leads to the finding that the provision covers a large range of sport events, from local to international events, as well as cultural events, showing they all have a place in the legal balance found between sport and society.

Before concluding, the fourth and last part discusses the gap between, on the one hand, sport and the economy and, on the other, sport and society. It asks whether the EU can be an actor in the decommodification of sport. It concludes that that is the case to the extent that the EU is able to develop a narrative to counterbalance the economic rationale which is the basis of the commodification of sport (section IV).

I. THE SOCIETAL RECOGNITION OF SPORT IN THE LAW OF THE MARKET

The ECJ has long had to arbitrate between the autonomous organisation of sport in the transnational legal order and the economic effects of sport within the EU internal market. With the limited competence of the EU in the field of sport until the Treaty of Lisbon, sport activities could nevertheless fall within the scope of the EU's competence to police and regulate its internal market. In articulating the relationship between sport and law, the ECJ had to firstly situate the relevance of the global legal order of sport within the EU legal order.[7] In doing so it relied on the economic impact of such rules on the internal market and distinguished them from purely sporting rules which embody the societal function of sport.[8]

Sport had not yet been included in the Treaties when the ECJ dealt with the application of EU law in a sporting context for the first time in 1974. Walrave and Koch, two Dutch cyclists, challenged a rule established by the UCI, the international cyclist association, according to which the coach had to be of the same nationality as the cyclist. Asked about the compatibility of this rule with EU

[6] Directive 97/36/EC of the European Parliament and of the Council of 30 June 1997 amending Council Directive 89/552/EEC on the coordination of certain provisions laid down by law, regulation or administrative action in Member States concerning the pursuit of television broadcasting activities [1997] OJ L202/60–70; Now Directive (EU) 2018/1808 amending Directive 2010/13/EU on the coordination of certain provisions laid down by law, regulation or administrative action in Member States concerning the provision of audiovisual media services (Audiovisual Media Services Directive) in view of changing market realities [2018] OJ L303/69–92 (hereinafter referred to as AVMSD).

[7] The chapter refers to the global sport legal order or global sporting rules to designate the body of private law rules adopted by national and international sport bodies and which form a legal order beyond the state. See A Duval, *La Lex Sportiva Face Au Droit de l'Union Européenne: Guerre et Paix Dans l'espace Juridique Transnational* (European University Institute, 2015) 11–14.

[8] Case 36/74 *Warlrave and Koch v Union Cycliste Internationale* ECLI:EU:C:1974:140, 8–9; Case 13/76 *Donà v Mantero* ECLI:EU:C:1976:115, 14; Case C-415/93 *Bosman* ECLI:EU:C:1995:463, 106; B García, A Vermeersch and S Weatherill, 'A New Horizon in European Sports Law: The Application of the EU State Aid Rules Meets the Specific Nature of Sport' (2017) 13 *European Competition Journal* 28, 29.

non-discrimination principles, the ECJ established that the practice of sport falls under the scope of EU law insofar as it constitutes an economic activity.[9] The ECJ added that the prohibition on non-discrimination on the basis of nationality 'does not affect the composition of sport teams, in particular national teams, the formation of which is a question of purely sporting interest and as such has nothing to do with economic activity'.[10] It thus established a general rule whereby sport falls under the scope of the Treaty if it has an economic impact and carved out an exception for issues of purely sporting interest.

The reference to rules of purely sporting interest relates to the claim of autonomy of transnational sport rules, also known as *lex sportiva*.[11] The ECJ does so without discussing conflicts of law or the legal nature of the rules enacted by international sport bodies, it relies instead on a common benchmark in EU law, the one of economic activity, to justify and limit the application of EU law to sport activities at the same time.

The ECJ later confirmed its approach and the distinction between rules of economic effects and rules relating to the purely sporting nature of the activities carried out.[12] It recognised that nationality conditions imposed on players can be justified by rules of purely sporting nature such as the aim to organise matches between national teams.[13] In the first cases, which related to nationality conditions, the ECJ implicitly recognised the specific character of sport, however, it did not yet explicitly engage with arguments linked to the societal implications of sport.

In 1995, the ECJ found in *Bosman*, a case concerning rules on the transfer of football players and nationality quotas for club competitions, that such rules are not limited to their proper objective, since they have greater implications than the transfer of individual players from one club to another.[14] Thereby such rules could not be relied upon to exclude the whole of a sporting activity from the scope of EU law.[15] The ECJ relied on its approach regarding the economic nature and economic spill over of sporting rules to define the scope of application of EU law to, in this case, the movement of professional football players.

At the hearing in the *Bosman* case, the German Government submitted that sport is not to be qualified as an economic activity. Instead, it argued that sport has similarities with culture and that the EU must respect the national and regional diversity of the culture of the Member States, in accordance with Article 167(1) of the Treaty on the Functioning of the European Union (TFEU).[16]

[9] *Warlrave and Koch*, ibid 4.
[10] ibid 8–9.
[11] Duval (n 7); R Parrish and S Miettinen, *The Sporting Exception in European Union Law* (Asser Press, 2008).
[12] *Donà v Mantero* (n 8).
[13] ibid 14.
[14] *Bosman* (n 8) 76.
[15] ibid; Weatherill (n 3) 112.
[16] *Bosman* (n 8) 72.

The ECJ refused to assimilate sport with culture under Article 167(1) TFEU as it argued that the question referred related to the free movement of workers and not the scope of the EU's powers under Article 167 TFEU.[17] Even if Article 167(1) TFEU does not act to shield cultural activities from the application of internal market law, since it also applies the criteria of economic activity, extending the scope of Article 167(1) TFEU would have been a symbolic recognition of the societal relevance of sport within the EU legal order.

In *Bosman*, the ECJ nevertheless took another route to shed light on the societal significance of sport. The ECJ noted that sporting activities have a considerable social importance and recognised the legitimate 'aims of maintaining a balance between clubs by preserving a certain degree of equality and uncertainty as to results and of encouraging recruitment and training of young players'.[18] This acknowledgement of the societal role of sport and the recognition of such legitimate objectives by the ECJ constitutes an account of sport's societal importance and locates it beyond a mere economic activity bluntly captured by EU free movement law.

Ten years later, in *Meca-Medina*, two swimmers banned from competition because they had failed drug tests submitted a complaint to the Commission arguing that the ban imposed by the international swimming federation breached EU competition law.[19] In its assessment, the Commission distinguished purely sporting rules and economic activity deriving from sports, in other words between 'the sporting activity which fulfils a social, integrating and cultural role that must be preserved' and therefore shielded from the application of competition law and 'a series of economic activities generated by the sporting activity' triggering the application of the Treaty provisions.[20] This distinction was rejected by the ECJ, establishing that 'rules of sporting organisation which have economic effects are subject to review and that their legality under competition law can be decided only on a case-by-case basis'.[21] The ECJ thereby refined its reasoning towards rules of sporting nature and established that it shall not provide a general exemption but be determined according to the specific effects of the rules or policies concerned.

The *Bernard* case concerned compatibility with the free movement of workers of the rule requiring young players to pay damages to the club that has trained them when joining another club after the training scheme.[22] In its scrutiny, the ECJ referred to Article 165 TFEU and the relevance of considering the 'specific characteristics of sport in general, and football in particular and of their social

[17] ibid 78.

[18] *Bosman* (n 8) 106.

[19] Case C-519/04 P *Meca-Medina v Commission* ECLI:EU:C:2006:492. For a detailed account of sport in competition law, see Weatherill (n 3) 104–23.

[20] K Lefever, *New Media and Sport: International Legal Aspects* (TMC Asser Press, 2012) 33.

[21] García, Vermeersch and Weatherill (n 8) 29.

[22] Case C-325/08 *Bernard* ECLI:EU:C:2010:143; Lefever (n 20) 46.

and educational function'.[23] Article 165 TFEU had been introduced in the Treaty of Lisbon and although it is argued that it did not change the legal status quo,[24] it does represent a symbolic recognition of sport in the EU legal order.

In *Bernard*, the ECJ recalled what it had established in *Bosman* that 'the considerable social importance of sporting activities and in particular football in the European Union, the objective of encouraging the recruitment and training of young players must be accepted as legitimate'.[25] It echoes the ideals depicted by the European Commission and the heads of state in policy documents and political declarations which will be explored in the second part of this chapter.[26]

Through its jurisprudence, the ECJ has included global sporting rules within the scope of EU internal market law. Accordingly, the two legal orders become intertwined rather than independent, reflecting a complex relationship between EU law and sport. Yet, in this legal relationship, sport is always linked to society. Hence, the ECJ has contributed to an institutional narrative recognising the preeminent role of sport in society also set out in policy documents and the political declarations of the other EU institutions.

II. THE IDEAL OF SPORT IN EUROPEAN SOCIETY

While the ECJ interacted with sport from the 1970s through free movement law, the EU as a whole was not equipped with a competence in the field of sport until the Treaty of Lisbon. It was thereby from that moment onwards that the EU was legitimised in developing sport policies and that an ideal of sport and society became identifiable in policy documents.

The Treaty of Lisbon introduced a supporting competence in Article 6(e) of the TFEU and Article 165 TFEU which establishes in its first and most emblematic paragraph that 'The Union shall contribute to the promotion of European sporting issues, while taking account of the specific nature of sport, its structures based on voluntary activity and its social and educational function'. The provision highlights the link between sport and society as well as a European dimension for sport with the wording 'European' sporting issues, supporting the new competence of the EU in the field of sport. The Lisbon Treaty represents a symbolic step in the relationship between sport and law since it formalises its integration in the EU Treaties. Today, it is the Directorate General for Youth, Sport, Education and Culture (DG EAC) that coordinates the Commission's actions in the field of sport. According to its website, DG EAC is 'responsible for the development of evidence-based policy in the field of sport, as well as

[23] *Bernard* (n 22) 40.

[24] Duval (n 7) 219–20.

[25] *Bernard* (n 22) 39.

[26] White Paper on Sport (n 5) 2; Treaty of Amsterdam amending the Treaty on European Union, Declaration on sport [1997] OJ C340/136.

fostering cooperation, and managing initiatives in support of physical activity and sport across Europe, notably through the Erasmus+ programme'.[27] Following the 2011 Communication on Sport, the Commission adopts three-year-long Work Plans.[28] The Council then adopts a Resolution on each new Work Plan.[29] According to the 2017–2020 Work Plan and 2017 Council Resolution, the key priorities for the Member States and the European Commission are: the integrity of sport (good governance, the fight against doping, the specificity of sport); the economic dimension of sport (innovation and the Digital Single Market); and sport and society (social inclusion, education, health, media).[30] The specificity of sport, which includes the scope of application of EU law, remains a priority. The latest Work Plan follows the same objectives and adds the strengthening of the recovery and the crisis resilience of the sport sector during and in the aftermath of the COVID-19 pandemic.[31]

One of the more emblematic policy documents in the field of sport is the Commission White Paper on Sports published in 2007, where the Commission writes the following:

> Sport is a growing social and economic phenomenon which makes an important contribution to the European Union's strategic objectives of solidarity and prosperity. The Olympic ideal of developing sport to promote peace and understanding among nations and cultures as well as the education of young people was born in Europe and has been fostered by the International Olympic Committee and the European Olympic Committees.[32]

The reference to the Olympic ideal sends a strong message regarding the Member States' common cultural heritage in the field of sport. It places sport and its traditions at the heart of society but also highlights its role as an institution with fundamental functions and values such as education, peace and inter-cultural dialogue. At the same time, the passage does not overlook the economic importance of sport, especially its role for (economic) prosperity, nor the international dimension of sport governance. It provides a clear picture of sport in the EU and the intermingling between sport and society.

[27] See https://ec.europa.eu/sport/policy_en.

[28] Commission Communication, *Developing the European Dimension in Sport* COM(2011) 0012 Final. At the time of writing, there have been four Work Plans: 2011–2014, 2014–2017, 2017–2020 and 2021–2024.

[29] Resolution of the Council on a European Union Work Plan for Sport for 2011–2014 [2011] OJ C162/1–6. Resolution of the Council on the European Union Work Plan for Sport (2014–2017) [2014] OJ C183/12–17.

[30] Resolution of the Council on the European Union Work Plan for Sport (1 July 2017–31 December 2020) [2017] OJ C189/5–14, 12.

[31] Resolution of the Council on the European Union Work Plan for Sport (1 January 2021–30 June 2024) [2020] OJ C419/1–11, 9.

[32] White Paper on Sport (n 5) 2. See on this S Weatherill, 'The White Paper on Sport as an Exercise in "Better Regulation"' in S Weatherill (ed), *European Sports Law: Collected Papers*, 2nd edn (TMC Asser Press, 2014). See also Commission Communication Developing the European Dimension in Sport (n 28).

The Commission policy documents have elaborated different roles for sport in society: A health promotion function, since sport contributes to good health and helps fight a number of diseases;[33] an educational function, transmitting skills and values such as teamwork and fair play; a social function as a tool to combat racism and discrimination, and to foster inclusion; a recreational role, for the active and passive participants in sports activities; and a cultural role, as it creates a sense of belonging and identity. From such categories, it is clear that sport is not portrayed as disconnected from society, on the contrary, it is said to contribute to its functioning, development and the good health of citizens.[34]

As highlighted in the 2007 White Paper, sport serves a cohesive and identity-building function. The organisation of sport and competitions at the national level is considered part of

> the historical and cultural background of the European approach to sport and corresponds to the wishes of European citizens. In particular, national teams play an essential role not only in terms of identity but also to secure solidarity with grassroots sport.[35]

This statement suggests a European dimension for sports engaging European citizens and based on the common cultural heritage of the Member States. The ideal pictured is one where the European approach to sport and national sports coexist and are mutually reinforcing. In addition, solidarity between professional and amateur sport is underlined. De Witte and Zglinski identify financial solidarity as a particularity of the European model of football.[36]

Furthermore, in its cohesive function, sport is an instrument for the integration of non-nationals, such as migrants, and supports inter-cultural dialogue.[37] The role of sport as a force for integration and identity was already recognised in the context of the 1995 revision of the Treaty on European Union through the Amsterdam Treaty where the Amsterdam Declaration on Sport was annexed to the Treaty, stating: 'The Conference emphasises the social significance of sport, in particular its role in forging identity and bringing people together.'[38] It is undeniable that the EU sport policy attributes an important societal role to sport and celebrates the values attached to it.

The ideal of sport that is depicted in the policy documents goes beyond the territory of the EU as the White Paper mentions the role for sport in the EU's external relations where sport is depicted as a tool to promote education, health, inter-cultural dialogue, development and peace.[39] The external dimension of

[33] White Paper on Sport (n 5) 3.

[34] ibid; Commission Communication Developing the European Dimension in Sport (n 28) 4.

[35] White Paper on Sport (n 5) 14.

[36] F de Witte and J Zglinski, 'The Idea of Europe in Football' (2021) 17 *LSE Law, Society and Economy Working Papers* 19.

[37] White Paper on Sport (n 5) 7.

[38] Treaty of Amsterdam amending the Treaty on European Union, Declaration on sport [1997] OJ C340/136.

[39] White Paper on Sport (n 5) 9.

sport in the EU is also concrete where the Commission refers to its commitment towards a multi-level structured dialogue with different actors such as European sports federations, Olympic Committees or international organisations.[40] The EU thereby demonstrates its determination to collaborate and participate at the international level in sport governance. Sport is also embraced as a diplomatic instrument in its external relations with third countries, as the Eramus+ sport programme shows.

Erasmus+ is traditionally known to cover education but today its priorities are education, training, youth and sport. Erasmus+ supports the objectives of the Work Plan for Sport and the development of the European dimension in sport. The programme has three key actions: learning mobility of individuals, cooperation among organisations and institutions and support to policy development and cooperation. One of the programme's specific objectives is to 'promote learning mobility of sport staff, as well as cooperation, quality, inclusion, creativity and innovation at the level of sport organisations and sport policies'.[41] Aside from mobility, the programme covers two actions in the field of sport aimed at capacity building and support for non-profit events.

Capacity-building projects in the field of sport aim to support international cooperation projects based on multilateral partnerships between sport organisations in EU Member States as well as third countries which are either part of or not part of the Erasmus+ programme. The participation of third countries not part of the programme is a specific objective of this action and is meant to support sport activities and policies as a 'vehicle to promote values as well as an education tool to promote the personal and social development of individuals and build more cohesive communities'.[42] The action has specific aims such as raising the capacity of grassroots sport organisations; promoting social inclusion through sport; promoting positive values through sport; and fostering cooperation across different regions of the world through joint initiatives.[43]

Non-profit sport events support the organisation of sport events with a European dimension in fields such as volunteering in sport, social inclusion through sport, the fight against discrimination in sport, encouraging participation in sport and physical activity.[44] The objective is to increase the visibility of the Erasmus+ sport actions as well as to raise awareness on the role of sport in promoting social inclusion, equal opportunities and health-enhancing physical activities.[45]

EU sport policy through funding policies such as Erasmus+ highlights the importance given to grassroot initiatives and community building, not only

[40] ibid 18.
[41] Commission, Erasmus+ Programme Guide 2022 (Version 2) 6.
[42] ibid 16.
[43] ibid 325.
[44] ibid 332.
[45] ibid 16.

mobility. It also illustrates the internationalisation of sport policy with the possibility of building international consortia to take part in actions under the programme. Sport is presented as a way to foster a sense of European society and promote the values of sport from the local to the supra-national level.

The ideal of sport depicted in the EU's policy documents is one where sport plays a key role in society at different levels. Sport is portrayed as a living practice involving actors at a multiplicity of levels and therefore subjected to multi-level governance. It is also seen as connected to national identity, and as reinforcing the sense of belonging, and as such it becomes a tool to integrate foreigners. It is based on this understanding, which involves a national outlook, that the EU can claim that sport can have the same cohesive function outside the EU. The coordination of such a function, and of sports in general at the international level, is how the EU justifies the involvement of the Commission through supporting actions and policy initiatives.

III. THE SOCIETAL ROLE OF SPORT IN THE AUDIOVISUAL MEDIA SERVICES DIRECTIVE

In the previous sections, I have demonstrated that there is a common narrative in the approach to sport and society in the EU's policy documents and to the approach to the application of EU law to sport in the case law of the ECJ. The intersection between EU law and societal interests in the sporting context is further illustrated by a close analysis of the Audiovisual Media Services Directive (AVMSD).

Article 14 of the AVMSD leaves to the

> Member States the prerogative to prohibit the exclusive broadcasting of events which they deem to be of major importance for society, where such broadcasts would deprive a substantial proportion of the public of the possibility to follow those events on free-to-air television.[46]

The provision on events of major importance for society was introduced in the 1997 amendment of the AVMSD in the context of the rise of pay TV. The concern that triggered the amendment at that time was that events of societal relevance traditionally broadcast on free television would be broadcast on pay TV instead and thereby exclude the part of the population unable to afford a subscription.[47]

The Member States took their national concerns to the European fora and mobilised for an EU level regulation of the audiovisual sector that would cover

[46] AVMSD Art 14(1).

[47] J Weinand, *Implementing the EU Audiovisual Media Services Directive: Selected Issues in the Regulation of AVMS by National Media Authorities of France, Germany and the UK* (Nomos, 2018) 90.

this issue.[48] Accordingly, the Member States' societal concerns were reflected in the EU Directive.

The text does not define events of major importance for society. Recital 49 mentions as examples the Olympic Games, the football World Cup and the European football championship. This leaves considerable discretion to the Member States. The Recitals in the Directive indicate four criteria considered to be reliable indicators of the importance of events for society:

(i) a special general resonance within the Member State, and not simply a significance to those who ordinarily follow the sport or activity concerned;
(ii) a generally recognised, distinct cultural importance for the population in the Member State, in particular as a catalyst of cultural identity;
(iii) involvement of the national team in the event concerned in the context of a competition or tournament of international importance; and
(iv) the fact that the event has traditionally been broadcast on free television and has commanded large television audiences.[49]

The criteria refer to several key notions such as society, sport, culture, identity and tradition. Reference to identity, culture and tradition echoes the societal role of sport recognised in policy documents published by the EU institutions. There is also a considerable connection to the state in the reference to the cohesive and identity-building function of sport. In short, the understanding of sport and society laid down in the Recitals in the Directive resonates with a societal ideal of sport.

The Directive provides no further guidance as regards the nature of events (sporting or non-sporting) and refers to 'international, European and national events', thereby the provision leaves a wide scope for the definition of events of major importance for society to the Member States. Five out of 11 Member States, including the UK, that have notified a list to the Commission have included a definition of events of major importance for society in their notification, such definitions, however, all follow the criteria of the Commission.[50] Nevertheless, the definitions differ as regards the scope of the event, namely if it only covers sporting events or also includes other events. Denmark makes explicit that the article only refers to sporting events while Italy refers to events of a sporting and non-sporting nature and Austria, Belgium and the UK refer only to events. A closer look at the content of the Member States' lists illustrates what the respective Member States consider as events of major importance.

Two events are listed by all the Member States that have notified a list, namely, the summer and winter Olympic Games (bar Ireland that excludes the summer

[48] BJ Drijber, 'The Revised Television Without Frontiers Directive: Is It Fit for the next Century?' (1999) 36 *CMLR* 87, 89–91.

[49] AVMSD Recitals 49 and 52.

[50] The lists of major events for society published by the Member States can be consulted at https://ec.europa.eu/digital-single-market/en/avmsd-list-major-events.

Olympics) and football (11 Member States list the *Fédération internationale de football association* (FIFA) World Cup and seven of them matches of their national championships). Athletics, in particular the World Championships but also European and national competitions, are listed by five out of 11 Member States. Events in rugby, handball and tennis are listed by four Member States. Skiing, cycling and cultural events are listed by three Member States and basketball, horse-riding, volleyball and water polo events are listed by two Member States. Finally, some events are only listed by one Member State such as ice hockey by Finland, moto GP by Italy, cricket, golf and the Commonwealth Games (multisport) by the UK, camogie and hurling by Ireland and swimming events by Hungary.

What is striking is that only three Member States list non-sporting events that are of a cultural nature, namely, in the Italian list we find the Sanremo Italian Music Festival; the New Year concert at La Fenice in Venice and the opening night of the opera season at La Scala in Milan. The Austrian authorities list the Vienna Philharmonic Orchestra's New Year Concert and the Vienna Opera Ball and the UK lists the final of the Queen Elizabeth Music Competition.

The list of major events that have been notified include both large scale international competitions and events relevant mostly at the national level, reflecting the specific national culture and identity of the countries concerned. This illustrates well the duality of sport's impact today, turned towards the international and based largely on global competitions while at the same time remaining close to local societies. Including both international and local events in the lists is significant as they might not have the same impact for broadcasters. It is a sign that the Member States consider them to be equally relevant for their societies.

The provision on events of major importance for society sends a message as to the balance between sport, society and law in the internal market. Considerable leeway is given to the Member States in implementing Article 14 AVMSD. When the provision was designed, the sale of broadcasting rights was already a great source of revenue for sport federations, and it is even more so today. The provision strikes a delicate balance between the freedom of owners of pay TV channels, sport governing bodies as rights-holders, and the overriding interest in ensuring the general public adequate access to major sporting events.[51] Accordingly, due to its economic implications for the rights-holders, the interpretation of Article 14 AVMSD was brought before the ECJ.

Two actions were brought by FIFA and the Union of European Football Associations (UEFA) concerning the decisions of the European Commission finding compatible with the internal market the list of events of major importance notified by Belgium and the UK.[52] In the decision, the Commission accepted the inclusion by Belgium of all the matches of the final stages of the World Cup as

[51] Drijber (n 48) 117.

[52] Case C-204/11 P *FIFA* and Case C-205/11 P *FIFA*. C-204/11 P *FIFA v Commission* ECLI:EU:C:2013:477 appeal of T-385/04 *FIFA v Commission* ECLI:EU:T:2011:42; Case C-205/11P *FIFA v Commission* ECLI:EU:C:2013:478 appeal of T-68/08 *FIFA v Commission* ECLI:EU:T:2011:44;

being of major importance in the sense of the Directive. FIFA argued that the Member States could list only 'prime' or 'gala' matches, namely the final, the semi-finals and the matches involving the Belgian national team. Accordingly, FIFA claimed the list should not have included the other matches of the World Cup (non-gala matches).[53] Similarly, the dispute in *UEFA v Commission* revolved around the UK's list of events which included the UEFA EURO tournament in its entirety.[54] The ECJ examined the different grounds and rejected the appeals brought by FIFA and UEFA.

The ECJ established that the free movement restrictions occurring as a result of Article 14 AVMSD are justified by the objective of protecting the right to information and ensuring wide public access to television coverage of those events.[55] Further, the Court concluded that Member States have a broad discretion in determining the events which are of major importance.[56] It argued that the Directive did not aim to achieve a harmonised European list of events, but instead was mindful of the 'social and cultural differences that exist within the European Union in so far as concerns their importance for the general public', which is why each Member State can draw up its own list according to its own criteria.[57]

The ECJ highlighted the need to respect the different traditions of the Member States, which may involve a different interpretation and application of the Directive. In this regard, the role of the ECJ was to preserve the margin of appreciation given to the Member States by the Directive to ensure that they can implement the provisions for events of major importance in accordance with their national culture and identity. When faced with cases on the interpretation of the Directive, the ECJ followed the intent of the law and deferred to the compromise between market and societal interests reached by the Member States. In the relationship between market and society that emerges out of the provision on events of major importance for society, the Member States' societal concerns were consolidated into EU law.

IV. THE DECOMMODIFICATION OF SPORT THROUGH THE SOCIETAL NARRATIVE

Sport is a multidimensional phenomenon. It lies at the heart of the lives of children practising in school and afterschool, amateurs, semi-professionals devoting their free time to it and professionals who can make a profitable living out of it.

Case C-201/11 P *UEFA v Commission* ECLI:EU:C:2013:519 appeal of Case T-55/08 *UEFA v Commission* ECLI:EU:T:2011:43.

[53] Case C-204/11 P *FIFA* (n 52) 7.

[54] Case C-201/11 P *UEFA* (n 52); Case T-55/08 *UEFA* (n 52).

[55] Case C-204/11 P *FIFA* (n 52) 11.

[56] ibid 13.

[57] Case C-204/11 P *FIFA* (n 52) 14–15.

Yet, sport is also put under pressure by professionalisation and commodification which impact the dynamic between sport and society.

The professionalisation of sport, which entails the creation of a dedicated, paid pool of players and other stakeholders such as teams, coaches management, referees, sponsorship and so forth, revolves around the economic relationship between the stakeholders.[58] Guilianotti and Walsh qualify as hyper-commodification the greater professionalisation and global migration of players, the corporatisation of clubs, the proliferation of merchandise and a general redefinition of the competitive structures as ethos of the sport.[59] While grassroot sport activities remain important, the gap between local amateur and transnational professional sport has increased.

The pressure of commodification in the sport sector does not only concern those who actively participate in sport, but also those who participate passively, by watching sport. With technological changes, it is not only possible to watch a game at a stadium, but a game can also be watched at home or at the pub through live broadcasting, as well as in the car or on public transport on any digital device connected to the Internet. Yet, the audiovisual sector is managed by market forces relying on the willingness of sports fans to pay subscriptions to have access to live sport events. As Weatherill explains, wealth maximisation is not the main concern of sport which plays an important and valuable social, educational and cultural role.[60] How can the recognition of the societal function of sport work as a counterbalance to the commodification of sport in the EU?

EU law grasps sports through its competence to regulate markets but also participates in de-commodifying sport by recognising its societal role. The ECJ acknowledges the organic character of sport when identifying rules and practices of purely sporting interest and legitimate objectives for sporting regulation, such as sporting integrity or the training of young players. This duality reflects the recognition of the societal implications of sport whereby it is not only a commodity but is attributed a societal role. Sport as a social activity is of importance for society generally and contributes to collective identity building.[61] The pressure put on sport by professionalisation, commodification and globalisation has increased the tension between sport and society. The fact that sport is increasingly transnational justifies the regulatory intervention of the EU and points to the EU as a suitable actor in the decommodification of sport.

[58] S Archer, 'Commodification and Juridification in Football: Reflections on the Study of Law and Society' (2014) 21 *Southwestern Journal of International Law* 9, 12.

[59] Walsh and Giulianotti (n 1) 53.

[60] S Weatherill, 'Sport as Culture in EC Law' in R Craufurd Smith (ed), *Culture and European Union Law* (Oxford University Press, 2004) 151.

[61] N Blain, 'Beyond "Media Culture": Sport as a Dispersed Symbolic Activity' in A Bernstein and N Blain (eds), *Sport, Media, Culture: Global and Local Dimensions* (Taylor & Francis Group, 2002) 233; See also L Crolley and D Hand, *Football and European Identity: Historical Narratives through the Press* (Routledge, 2006).

A clear example of the recognition of the societal importance of sport currently running counter to commodification is embodied in the provisions on major events for society. Not only does this materialise in the AVMSD, but the objectives of the provisions also benefit from the support granted by the case law of the ECJ. EU sport policy also seems to be heading in this direction since it attributes several non-economic roles to sport and openly develops an EU sport model based on a number of societal non-economic values.[62] In particular, the role of sport for cohesion and culture ties it intimately to society. In the same vein, the Erasmus+ programme encourages mobility and exchanges to catalyse the societal benefits of sport by supporting grassroot initiatives and capacity building. Solidarity and redistributive mechanisms within sport are also promoted as pillars of the European sports model.[63]

What can also be taken into account in the discussion regarding whether the recognition of the societal function of sport in EU law and policy documents can play a role towards the decommodification of sport is the case of the European Super League. When the project was announced in April 2021, public officials reacted strongly. Margaritis Schinas, Vice-President of the European Commission, tweeted on 19 April 2021:

> We must defend a values-driven European model of sport based on diversity and inclusion. There is no scope for reserving it for the few rich and powerful clubs who want to severe links with everything associations stand for: national leagues, promotion and relegation and support to grassroots amateur football. Universality, inclusion and diversity are key elements of European sport and our European way of life.[64]

On the same day, the twitter account of the Italian Government expressed its support for the football associations opposing the European Super League arguing for the preservation of national competitions, meritocratic values and the social function of sport.[65] Boris Johnson and Emmanuel Macron also positioned themselves against the European Super League.[66] After much debate in the news and social media, the European Super League was challenged at the Commercial Court of Madrid which referred questions to the ECJ regarding the validity of the European Super League in light of EU competition law.[67]

At the hearing at the ECJ, which was retransmitted online, many of the Member States intervening referred to the Commission policy documents on the European dimension in sport. They identified a number of principles such

[62] White Paper on Sport (n 5) 3; Commission Communication Developing the European Dimension in Sport (n 28) 4.

[63] de Witte and Zglinski (n 36) 19.

[64] See https://twitter.com/margschinas/status/1383908874101530625.

[65] See https://twitter.com/Palazzo_Chigi/status/1384159234468716548?ref_src=twsrc%5Etfw.

[66] See https://sport.sky.it/calcio/2021/04/19/mario-draghi-superlega-europea-calcio?social=twitter_skysport_link_null.

[67] Case C-333/21 *European Super League Company SL v UEFA and FIFA*, case lodged on 27 May 2021, pending in front of the ECJ.

as the pyramidal structure of football, the openness of competition, financial solidarity and redistribution, as fundamental parts of the European sports model. The Member States thereby relied on a common conception of the European sports model which enshrines non-economic values. The European Super Leagues is a relevant example of the commodification of football and how both professionalisation and commodification result in wealth concentration for a few elite clubs which can cause deep unease for supporters, commentators, amateurs, smaller clubs and other excluded stakeholders.[68] The fact that the case was referred to the ECJ and that legal arguments were grounded on EU law supports the view that the EU could play a role in the decommodification of sport.

From the arguments presented at the hearing and the Opinion of Advocate General Rantos, it becomes clear that both EU competition law and the European sport model were used as legal tools to try to counter the commodification of football in Europe in the European Super League case. In particular, the Advocate General noted that Article 165 is a horizontal provision that is to be accounted for in the application of EU law, especially competition law.[69] He also explained that the rationale behind the introduction of Article 165 is rooted jointly in the fact that sport is a significant economic activity and in the special social character of that economic activity.[70] The first part of the Opinion regarding Article 165 TFEU, the European Sport Model and the challenge to the European Sport Model highlights the economic and societal duality explored in this chapter.[71] Irrespective of the outcome of the case, it is significant that in a case before the ECJ the social function of sport and the societal implication of such activities are discussed and contrasted based on the economic rationale and wealth concentration that illustrates the commodification of football.

This section has shown how EU law emphasises the societal functions of sport, distancing it from a purely market rationale thereby ensuring a balance between the non-economic and the economic aspects of sport. It seems that the EU has the potential to contribute to the decommodification of sport. This could go as far as the EU committing itself to new societal mechanisms linked to sport and reshaping the relationship between sport and society beyond the national level.

V. CONCLUSION

Does EU law approach sport beyond the market? Yes, there is a societal dimension to sport in EU law. It is found in policy documents, political declarations

[68] Archer (n 58) 21.

[69] Case C-333/21 *European Superleague Company SL v FIFA and UEFA* Opinion of Advocate General Rantos ECLI:EU:C:2022:993, 35.

[70] ibid 34.

[71] ibid 27–38.

and Treaty provisions. Even the ECJ's case law has progressively embraced sport in its societal dimension. The EU's approach to sport has different facets, which appear through the exploration of the relationship between sport and society in legal and policy documents of the EU.

The relationship between sport and society, as promoted by the European Commission in policy documents and supported by heads of states in political declarations and Treaty amendments, reflects an ideal of sport which emphasises its societal relevance. The EU's sport policy is focused primarily on the role of sport in fulfilling fundamental societal objectives such as cohesion or education. In striking a balance between the EU legal order and global sports law, the ECJ has insisted on sport's societal role. This is especially true where the ECJ identifies sector-specific legitimate objectives justifying restrictions of economic freedoms, be it under free movement or competition rules. In other contexts, Member States' societal concerns are transposed directly into EU legislation, as is the case regarding the rules on major events for society in the AVMSD. This demonstrates once again, and contrary to what is often thought, that the EU has been rather willing to strengthen the societal dimension of sport and to contribute to its societal impact.

10

EU Competition Law and Sport: Checks and Balances 'à l'européenne'

RUSA AGAFONOVA*

ORGANISED SPORT HAS undergone a long evolution since the creation of the first sports governing bodies (SGBs) in the late nineteenth century and many factors have shaped the system of sports governance as we know it today. Originally, the core characteristics of the so-called European model of sport, such as the broad private autonomy of sports associations and its traditional reluctance towards commercialisation, were anchored in the ideals inspired by the Football Association and Pierre de Coubertin's vision of the Olympic Movement.[1] Later, phenomena such as a very simple and liberal legal regulation of private associations,[2] the presence of reputable commercial arbitration forums, a leading financial market, and successful international diplomacy, have transformed Switzerland into the epicentre of global sports management or, as Chappelet has called it, a 'global sport administration hub'.[3] Just like the English sports culture and the Frenchman de Coubertin's progressive vision at the end of the nineteenth century, the Swiss legal order plays a crucial role in international sport today even though many segments of the industry and a growing number of SGBs are now located outside Switzerland.[4] Nevertheless, the considerable security provided by Swiss legislation has not only ensured a thriving sports ecosystem, but has also enabled the SGBs to have a significant control over their activities but has deprived many of them of the incentive to revise their regulations and practices.[5] Meanwhile, in more than one century of existence many changes

* PhD candidate at the University of Zurich.

[1] See more in S Szymanski and AS Zimbalist, *National Pastime: How Americans Play Baseball and the Rest of the World Plays Soccer* (Brookings Institution Press, 2005).

[2] M Baddeley, 'The Extraordinary Autonomy of Sports Bodies under Swiss Law: Lessons to be Drawn' (2020) 20 *International Sports Law Journal* 4.

[3] J-L Chappelet, 'Switzerland's Century-Long Rise as the Hub of Global Sport Administration' (2021) 38 *International Journal of the History of Sport* 6, 569.

[4] ibid 583–84.

[5] Baddeley (n 2) 4.

have occurred: the organisation of sport has become more sophisticated; SGBs have grown in size and influence; associations and arbitral tribunals have developed a private legal order specific to their community (commonly known as '*lex sportiva*');[6] and sport has become a major industry generating billions of dollars through various markets worldwide.[7]

As a consequence, it has resulted in the unpreparedness and even obsoleteness of many SGBs in the new economic realities.[8] Moreover, in the absence of any *proactive* steps on behalf of sports organisations, more and more regulations and decisions have been challenged before the courts in and outside Switzerland.

In recent decades, EU competition law has become a helpful *corrective* tool to rein in anticompetitive policies of SGBs.[9] Given a strong intertwinement of their regulatory and commercial functions, sports associations have a rather vulnerable position in the eyes of antitrust.[10] However, in the presence of two different legal orders and given the sport-specific considerations, it remains unclear how to make full use of EU competition law in regard to the Swiss-based sports ecosystem. In practice, the EU and the Swiss legal orders often find themselves at opposite poles when it comes to their stance towards the governance of sport, significantly restricting the ability to invoke EU competition law against SGBs. In the absence of a perfect procedural mechanism, a party whose rights have been affected has a choice between multiple imperfect strategies. It is useful to identify each of these options in order to determine their respective pros and cons from the standpoint of a complainant as well as to find out how the most prospective procedures can be developed and implemented in the regular practice of sports stakeholders.

This contribution is aimed at presenting the main pillars of the organisation of sports (section I) and a judicial review of the decisions of SGBs (section II), explaining the growing role of EU competition law in sports governance (section III), and identifying how to implement EU antitrust requirements in the system of sport-related justice while reconciling the two independent legal orders – the Swiss-built *lex sportiva* and EU law – in a harmonious way (sections IV and V).

[6] A Duval, '*Lex Sportiva*: A Playground for Transnational Law' (2013) 19 *European Law Journal* 6, 827–28.

[7] Baddeley (n 2) 5–6.

[8] A Geeraert, J Alm and M Groll, 'Good Governance in International Sport Organizations: An Analysis of the 35 Olympic Sport Governing Bodies' (2014) 6 *International Journal of Sport Policy and Politics* 3, 282.

[9] B Van Rompuy, 'The Role of EU Competition Law in Tackling Abuse of Regulatory Power by Sports Associations' (2015) 22 *Maastricht Journal of European and Comparative Law* 2, 207.

[10] ibid 199.

I. THE ORGANISATION OF SPORT

A. Sports Governing Bodies

The description of the European sports model, a structure traditionally underpinning the organisation of most sporting disciplines worldwide, inevitably starts with the introduction of a pyramid, which includes the SGBs on several 'integrated and interdependent'[11] levels and comprises regional, national, continental and international associations. The legal basis which ensures sufficient integration between them is membership: an entity belonging to a lower part of the structure holds membership in the superior organisation, recognises the governing role of the latter, accepts and complies with the statutes, rules and regulations of the upper association. In exchange, it becomes formally integrated in the sports system, obtains the recognition necessary to access the official calendar of sports events, organise competitions, etc.[12] At the apex of the pyramid stand the supreme SGBs – international federations, which regulate their respective sports disciplines worldwide. For reasons of consistency and uniformity, there is always only one officially recognised SGB per sport per territorial unit ('*Ein-Platz-Prinzip*'), making every such organisation de facto monopolist in their respective area.

The functional cohesion between the levels is secured by the rule of promotion and relegation giving competitions organised from the grassroots to the elite level a functional interconnectivity. By designing open leagues and by providing participants with the possibility of promotion to a higher-ranking level based on sporting merit, the European model has established a selection system.[13] On the other hand, the (vertical) solidarity mechanism has been implemented with a view to ensuring an equitable redistribution of revenue generated by high-profile events at the grassroots level and the participants of the 'sport for all' movement, thus creating strong economic bonds between the levels.[14]

The pyramid structure is highly centralised,[15] hierarchised and enjoys wide autonomy.[16] From the very beginning, the central tenet of organised sport in

[11] J Nafziger, 'A Comparison of the European and North American Models of Sports Organization (2008) 8(3–4) *International Sports Law Journal* 100.

[12] Baddeley (n 2) 4–5.

[13] See, notably, the statement by FIFA and the six confederations available at www.fifa.com/about-fifa/associations/news/statement-by-fifa-and-the-six-confederations.

[14] Nafziger (n 11) 101.

[15] A Geeraert, M Mrkonjic and J-L Chappelet, 'A Rationalist Perspective on the Autonomy of International Sport Governing Bodies: Towards a Pragmatic Autonomy in the Steering of Sports' (2015) 7 *International Journal of Sport Policy and Politics* 4, 481.

[16] A Geeraert and H Bruyninckx, 'You'll Never Walk Alone Again. The Governance Turn in Professional Sport' in J Mittag and S Guldenpfennig (eds), *Sportpolitik im Spannungsfeld von Autonomie und Regulierung: Grundlagen, Akteure und Konfliktfelder* (Klartext Verlag, 2014) p 2.

the modern era has been autonomy vis-à-vis states and governments, so-called 'political autonomy'.[17] In accordance with Pierre de Coubertin's concept, still valid for the International Olympic Committee (IOC) today, members should represent the Olympic Movement in their country (not the other way round) and must be independent of their governments.[18] Today, the concept of SGBs' autonomy comprises not only freedom from political interference, but also legal and financial independence.[19] In this regard, the choice of the country (and, by extension, the national law) in which a sports organisation is domiciled becomes crucial.[20]

The many benefits that Swiss legislation grants sports associations (as subjects of private law) explain – alongside political and financial stability and a favourable taxation regime – why three quarters of all international SGBs are located or have their headquarters in Switzerland[21] and are set up in the form of associations incorporated under Swiss law.[22]

Swiss association law, as a part of the Swiss Civil Code (SCC),[23] imposes few mandatory requirements and gives remarkable flexibility in terms of organisational and functional set-up.[24] To establish an association, it is sufficient that the assembly of founding members evidence it in writing (articles of association), mentioning its purpose, resources and structure.[25] While the purpose should be non-profit, Swiss law does not prohibit associations from running annex commercial activities necessary to finance the main non-commercial purpose.[26]

There are normally only two mandatory bodies of an association, a general assembly as the legislative governing body which is run by the voting of members (Article 64 SCC) and a committee as the executive body (Article 69 SCC). Beyond these mandatory requirements, associations are free to define their organisational set-up. As Baddeley notes, international governing bodies tend to take advantage of the possibility to design a more sophisticated framework with a complex organisational chart as well as providing detailed rights and obligations for its members.[27] This is exemplified notably by the IOC and *Fédération Internationale de Football Association* (FIFA), the most powerful sports organisations both politically and economically.

In addition to the minimal legal requirements for establishing an association, the Swiss legislator has also limited the possibilities for *ex ante* and *ex post*

[17] Geeraert et al (n 15) 477–78.
[18] J-L Chappelet, *Autonomy of Sport in Europe* (Council of Europe Publishing, 2010) 11.
[19] ibid.
[20] D Oswald, *Associations, fondations et autres formes de personnes morales au service du sport*, (Peter Lang. 2010) 155.
[21] Chappelet (n 3) 583.
[22] Baddeley (n 2) 5.
[23] SCC Art 60–79.
[24] ibid Art 63 clearly favours this flexibility.
[25] ibid Art 60 para 2.
[26] Baddeley (n 2) 4.
[27] ibid.

reviews of an association's policies. There is generally no preliminary control of the association's rules, so they can only be judicially reviewed indirectly, within the framework of a legal challenge against a decision rendered by the association on the basis of its regulations.[28] In this regard, one of the few mandatory rules provided by the Swiss Civil Code is the right of members to challenge associations' decisions before the courts.[29] But even when an individual decision is submitted for judicial review, private autonomy is again likely to outweigh other considerations.[30]

B. The Court of Arbitration for Sport

In 1984, the IOC established the Court of Arbitration for Sport (CAS), a specialised arbitral institution 'devoted to resolving disputes directly or indirectly related to sport' through a flexible, quick and inexpensive procedure.[31] With the 1994 reform, in order to distance itself from the functioning of the CAS, the IOC established the International Council of Arbitration for Sport (ICAS) and transferred to it the powers to manage the administration and financing of the arbitral institution. The same year, the Code of Sports-related Arbitration (the CAS Code) entered into force and became the main procedural document of the organisation. The CAS only has jurisdiction over sport-related disputes[32] covered by a valid arbitration agreement. Disputes brought to it are either of a commercial nature and are heard by the CAS acting as a court of sole instance in the Ordinary Arbitration Division, or of disciplinary nature and are decided first by the competent internal body of an SGB and, if necessary, can be later appealed before the CAS Appeals Arbitration Division.[33]

Lausanne is where the CAS has its headquarters and is the seat of every arbitration, so that Swiss law becomes automatically *lex arbitri* for all the proceedings before it.[34] The procedural issues, inherent to arbitration before the CAS, such as the arbitrability of disputes and grounds for challenging arbitral awards, are covered by the Swiss Private International Act (PILA), often praised as short and comprehensive which is useful for foreign practitioners who might otherwise be unfamiliar with Swiss law.[35]

[28] ibid 4.

[29] SCC Art. 75.

[30] Baddeley (n 2). 7.

[31] History of the CAS, available at www.tas-cas.org/en/general-information/history-of-the-cas.html.

[32] CAS Code Art. R27.

[33] ibid Art S3.

[34] M Coccia, 'International Sports Justice: The Court of Arbitration for Sport' in M Colucci and KL Jones (eds), *International and Comparative Sports Justice* (European Sports Law and Policy Bulletin, Issue 1-2013) 28–30.

[35] G Kaufmann-Kohler and A Rigozzi, *International Arbitration: Law and Practice in Switzerland*, (Oxford University Press, 2015) 29.

The popularity of CAS arbitration among the SGBs is undeniable. In 1991, the International Equestrian Federation (FEI) became the first global organisation to insert in its statutes an arbitration clause referring to the exclusive jurisdiction of the CAS in all the disputes arising from the decisions of its disciplinary bodies, the so-called 'CAS clause'. Since then, the majority of the sports federations have followed its example.[36] The adoption of the first World Anti-Doping Code in 2003 equally boosted the caseload of the Lausanne-based institution.[37]

Athletes and entities opposing SGBs in CAS proceedings, have, in contrast, on several occasions called into question the legitimacy of this dispute resolution mechanism denouncing the disadvantaged position in which they find themselves while opposing a sports organisation. First, athletes have sometimes no direct legal relationship with the sports association referring the disputes to CAS (an arbitration agreement by reference).[38] Most importantly, given the absence of alternatives available to athletes when they adhere to SGBs' regulations in view of competing in official events, they are most likely to submit themselves to these rules, including the CAS clause. The forced character of such consent – and the validity of arbitration clauses granting exclusive jurisdiction to the CAS – has been the central issue of multiple landmark disputes in sports law.[39]

However, in the eyes of the Swiss Federal Tribunal,[40] the German Federal Tribunal[41] and the European Court of Human Rights (ECtHR),[42] the sport-specific advantages, such as uniformity in the application of rules and deep expertise of arbitrators, favour athletes in the first place and outweigh the drawbacks.

In *Mutu and Pechstein v Switzerland*, the ECtHR recognised that:

> in the specific case of sports arbitration, [...] it is certainly of interest for the settlement of disputes arising in a professional sports context, especially those with an international dimension, to refer them to a specialised body which is able to give a ruling swiftly and inexpensively. High-level international sports events are held in various countries by organisations based in different States, and they are open to athletes from all over the world. Recourse to a single and specialised international arbitral tribunal facilitates a certain procedural uniformity and strengthens legal certainty.[43]

[36] Coccia (n 34) 24.

[37] J Lindholm, *The Court of Arbitration for Sport and Its Jurisprudence: An Empirical Inquiry into Lex Sportiva* (TMC Asser Press, 2019) 63.

[38] Kaufmann-Kohler and Rigozzi (n 35) 119–20.

[39] Judgment of the SFT 4A_428/2011, *World Anti-Doping Agency v Flemish Tennis Federation*, 13 February 2012, para 3.2.3; Judgment of the SFT, 4P.172/2006, *Cañas v Commission*, 22 March 2007; *Mutu and Pechstein v Switzerland* (2018) App nos 40575/10 and 67474/10 (ECtHR, 2 October 2018).

[40] Judgment of the SFT ATF 129 III 445, pt. 3.3.3.2.

[41] Judgment of the German Federal Tribunal KZR 6/15, *Pechstein/International Skating Union*, 7 June 2016, para 32.

[42] *Mutu and Pechstein v Switzerland* (n 39) para 98.

[43] ibid. The General Court of the Court of Justice of the European Union (CJEU) later referred to this decision, see Case T-93/18 *International Skating Union v Commission* [2020] ECLI:EU:T:2020:610, para 156.

While it is difficult to deny the multiple benefits of CAS arbitration, its organisation remains a stumbling block on the way to legitimacy. The CAS arbitrators (425 as of 21 November 2022) are appointed by the ICAS at the proposal of the IOC, the international federations (hereafter: IFs) and the national Olympic committees (hereafter: NOCs) for a renewable four-year term among 'personalities with a legal training and who possess recognised competence with regard to sport'. In the view of their narrow specialisation, the sports industry professionals can perform different roles (arbitrator, counsel, mediator) at different times. Whereas the CAS explicitly prohibits its arbitrators and mediators from acting as counsel or experts for a party before the CAS (the so-called 'double hatting'),[44] you cannot exclude a sense of community among them moulded by years of work in a highly specialised field.[45]

There are indications that are statistically supported of certain amount of 'institutionalism' or 'internal networks' within the CAS.[46] Despite a long and ever-expanding list of CAS arbitrators, it appears that, in practice, there is a much smaller group of individuals who are appointed to hear cases. Having analysed 2,195 instances where an arbitrator was appointed, Lindholm has demonstrated that only 232 unique individual arbitrators have been appointed to sit on a CAS panel at least once.[47] In addition, the CAS's so-called 'super-arbitrators', (ie) the 17 most frequently nominated arbitrators (only seven per cent of the appointed and four per cent of the appointable arbitrators) have received 45 per cent of all the appointments.[48] The same empirical research has shown that Swiss arbitrators are appointed to CAS panels disproportionately more frequently, roughly three times more frequently, compared to arbitrators of any other nationality.[49] One of the most probable explanations lies in the preference of Swiss-based SGBs to nominate local experts who often have experience of working for SGBs and who possess the respective network connections ('corporate arbitration based on sporting solidarities').[50]

C. A Dynamic Model

The traditional pyramidal organisational chart is constantly being reviewed. Although institutions such as the World Anti-Doping Agency and International Testing Agency are not included in the hierarchical structure,

[44] CAS Code Art S18(3).

[45] S Besson, A Rigozzi and W McAuliffe, 'International Sports Arbitration' (2017) *The European Arbitration Review* 7–8.

[46] L Franck, *La Lex Sportiva: Recherche Sur Le Droit Transnational* (Martinus Nijhoff Publishers, 2007) 262.

[47] Lindholm (n 37) 222.

[48] ibid 223.

[49] ibid.

[50] Latty (n 46) 262.

they are inextricably linked to the functioning of sport today. It is also important to mention that new business structures, such as breakaway leagues and independent promoters, although still litigating with SGBs over their place under the sporting sun, are playing a more important role in the organisation of sport. Traditional international federations have been experiencing an 'erosion of their hierarchical powers'[51] in recent years. While this trend can be interpreted as positive, it remains unclear, whether it would result in a more open, diverse, and inclusive system. The growth and diversification of the European sports model does not automatically bring balance and democratisation. The traditional structure characterised by a monopoly of SGBs in their respective sports disciplines can be successfully reshaped into an oligopoly, ie a market in which several entities retain market power but are interdependent in their pricing and output policies.[52] For example, this scenario may happen when there is a coexisting SGB and a powerful third-party promoter or a breakaway league. However, even in this case, SGBs generally retain the key position in policy-making and maintain their internal networks. As a result, without appropriate accountability mechanisms, the mere existence of a more diversified organisational model cannot guarantee the legitimacy of sports governance.[53]

II. ACCESS TO JUSTICE AND JUDICIAL REVIEW

The fact that CAS arbitration is governed by Swiss law, notably by the PILA, has important consequences for sports governing structures in many ways. *Lex arbitri* determines, among other things, the procedure for judicial review of arbitral awards.

In accordance with Article 191 PILA, the only authority competent to set aside arbitral awards is the Swiss Federal Court (SFT),[54] the supreme judicial body of Switzerland. The number of appeals before the SFT has been growing steadily since 1989, with a particular increase after 2009.[55] CAS arbitration has played a paramount role in this trend:[56] by 2009, every third challenge of an

[51] Geeraert et al (n 15) 473.

[52] See G Monti, 'Oligopoly Markets' in G Monti, *EC Competition Law* (Cambridge University Press (Law in Context), 2007) 308–345.

[53] For eg, the equestrian sport is governed by the FEI but there are several major promoters organising elite competitions under their own auspices. In 2017, the Belgian Competition Authority found that the FEI granted to two promoters a special regime enabling them to make participation in the competitions conditional on the financial contributions of the teams rather than on sporting merit, thus, violating EU competition law.

[54] Swiss Federal Tribunal Act Art 77, para 1(a).

[55] F Dasser and P Wójtowicz, 'Swiss International Arbitral Awards Before the Federal Supreme Court Statistical Data 1989–2019' (2021) 39 *ASA Bulletin* 1, 11–12.

[56] The fraction of cases involving the awards issued by other sports arbitral tribunals is insignificant.

arbitral award brought before the SFT (and during the period between 2009 and 2019 almost every second challenge) concerned a sport-related case.[57]

For the reasons explained, the possibilities of annulment (theoretical and practical) are very limited, which makes every challenge of a CAS award 'a "one shot" appeal',[58] but the whole procedure is simplified and speedy compared to litigation. In practice, the prospects of a challenge are poor: only around seven per cent of applications for the annulment of a CAS decision are successful (wholly or partially).[59]

First of all, there is no 'appeal' *stricto sensu*, ie the SFT has no full power of review as to the findings of fact and law. Article 190, para 2 PILA gives an exhaustive (and very limited) list of – mainly procedural – grounds for setting aside arbitral awards, comprising: (a) improper tribunal constitution; (b) lack of jurisdiction; (c) *ultra* or *infra petita* decisions; (d) violation of fundamental procedural rights; and (e) breach of public policy. The two latter grounds are the most frequently used.[60] That said, in spite of its popularity, violation of public policy is by far the least efficient (with a 0.9 per cent success rate).[61] The SFT has upheld only two sport-related appeals lodged on this ground.[62]

Despite slim chances for setting aside an award, the mere availability of judicial review is vital for the legitimacy of the CAS. For the ECtHR, 'a non-State mechanism of conflict resolution at first and/or second instance, with the possibility of appeal, albeit limited, before a state court at last instance, could be an appropriate solution in this field'.[63]

But whereas you might admit the appropriateness of the solution to limit judicial review to a 'one shot appeal', it is difficult to deny the scarcity of tools for this appeal. Delegating to the Swiss supreme judicial body the exclusive competence for reviewing arbitral awards, already heavily influenced by other elements favouring SGBs and the CAS, might just reinforce the effect of exclusivity. A limited list of grounds for setting aside arbitral awards combined with a traditionally non-interventionist approach towards international arbitration (and, consequently, with a narrow interpretation of these grounds) by the SFT results in very few possible configurations regarding the outcome of a case. Whereas it obviously benefits the uniformity of the SFT's case law, it might also hinder an alternative look at the legal questions inherent in the changing sports

[57] Dasser and Wójtowicz (n 55) 11–12.

[58] A Rigozzi, *Challenging Awards of the Court of Arbitration for Sport* (2010) 1 *Journal of International Dispute Settlement* 1, 217–65.

[59] Dasser and Wójtowicz (n 55) 15–16. That said, there is only a nominal difference in the success rate between appeals in sports-related cases and other disputes – staying at the level of 'the Magic Seven'.

[60] ibid 17.

[61] ibid 19.

[62] Judgments of the SFT ATF 138 III 322, *Francelino da Silva Matuzalem v FIFA*, 27 March 2012, and ATF 136 III 345, *Club Atlético de Madrid SAD v Sport Lisboa E Benfica – Futebol SAD, and FIFA*, 13 April 2010.

[63] *Mutu and Pechstein v Switzerland* (n 39) para 98.

environment, and, thus, give another advantage to the Swiss-based SGBs. This concern seems fair considering that CAS arbitration was conceived as a dispute resolution mechanism to handle *international* sport-related disputes.

Furthermore, certain legal notions vary even between different jurisdictions in the same region. One of these is the above-mentioned notion of public policy. The SFT qualifies itself as 'ungraspable',[64] and, for this reason, sticks to a pragmatic approach, as 'the Swiss judge does not live in a no man's land but in a country attached to a given civilisation where certain values are privileged as opposed to others',[65] and states:

> Even though the public policy reservation is broadly acknowledged [...], it behoves nonetheless the Swiss judge to interpret art. 190 (2) (e) PILA when relied upon as a ground for appeal and to determine what the Swiss legislator had in mind when it adopted this undetermined legal concept. It is not sure that the same principles would be considered as fundamental on the entire planet [...], as the diversity of civilisations may perfectly well justify fundamental principles of different or event opposed nature [...]. Thus, the Swiss lawmakers, when choosing the terms 'public policy', necessarily had in mind the system of values prevailing in the part of the world where the country of which they are entrusted with adopting the laws is located, as well as the founding principles of the civilisations to which this country belongs. The Swiss judge's work, when deciding an appeal in the field of international arbitration, is therefore to seek the principles flowing from that system of values and to verify if the award under review is consistent with them.[66]

Substantive public policy remains a debatable subject matter when it comes to reviewing international arbitral awards, in particular in connection with the application of EU competition law. Given the historical influence of the latter on the SGBs, the question of how much the concept of public policy (in the sense of Article 190, para 2e) overlaps with EU law deserves to be developed further.

III. EU COMPETITION LAW

The European Union and, to some extent, the Council of Europe, are allegedly the only regional organisations that have a tangible impact on international sports governance.[67] EU law (and in particular EU competition law) is of utmost significance for the legal autonomy of SGBs.[68] On the one hand, it grants them regulatory autonomy; on the other, it makes this autonomy conditional upon

[64] Judgment of the SFT ATF 132 III 389, pt 2.1., 2.2.3.

[65] ibid pt 2.2.2.

[66] ibid. The decision was issued in French; an English translation is available at www.swissarbitrationdecisions.com.

[67] Geeraert et al (n 15) 475.

[68] Geeraert et al (n 15) 476; Van Rompuy (n 9) 207–208.

compliance with EU law provisions.[69] The element of conditionality has become particularly important. Today, SGBs almost always conduct economic activities (eg, selling tickets to their competitions, broadcasting rights, etc), are thus qualified as undertakings and must therefore comply with EU competition law as a condition for safeguarding their privileged position.[70] In addition, the sports model with its '*Ein-Platz Prinzip*' and membership basis, attracts increased antitrust scrutiny.[71]

The two articles constituting the core of EU competition law, Article 101 (agreements restricting competition) and Article 102 (abuse of dominance position) of the Treaty on the Functioning of the European Union (TFEU), are relevant in this regard.

The former provision prohibits 'all agreements between undertakings, decisions by associations of undertakings and concerted practices which may affect trade between Member States, and which have as their object or effect the prevention, restriction or distortion of competition within the internal market'.[72] It may, nevertheless, be inapplicable in certain cases in the presence of demonstrated efficiency gains.[73] The latter Article outlaws 'any abuse by one or more undertakings of a dominant position within the internal market or in a substantial part of it [...] in so far as it may affect trade between Member States'.[74]

Both Articles target anticompetitive behaviour which may affect trade between Member States, ie which is 'capable of having a minimum level of cross-border effects' within the Union.[75] As for the impact of these provisions, it goes far beyond the EU's borders and has repercussions on the non-European sporting landscape.

Since international and European sports federations must comply with EU competition law, non-European national SGBs, in conformity with their membership obligations vis-à-vis international federations, should act in accordance with the governing policies and thus, comply with EU antitrust

[69] S Weatherill, 'Article 82 EC and Sporting "Conflict of Interest": The Judgment in MOTOE' (2009) 9(1–2) *International Sports Law Journal* 5. The supervised autonomy of sports organisations has been recognised by the Council of Europe through the European Sports Charter and by the European Council through the 2000 'Nice Declaration on sport'. The latter states: 'with due regard for national and Community legislation [...], it is the task of sporting organizations to organize and promote their particular sports'.

[70] S Weatherill, *Principles and Perspectives in EU Sports Law* (Oxford University Press, 2017) 3; Weatherill (n 69) 5.

[71] *International Skating Union v Commission* (n 43); Case C-49/07 *MOTOE* ECLI:EU:C:2008:376; Case C-519/04 P *David Meca-Medina and Igor Majcen v Commission* ECLI:EU:C:2006:492; Case T-193/02 *Laurent Piau v Commission* ECLI:EU:T:2005:22.

[72] TFEU Art 101(1).

[73] ibid Art 101(3).

[74] ibid Art 102.

[75] Commission Notice – Guidelines on the effect on trade concept contained in Articles 81 and 82 of the Treaty, pts 8, 13.

rules *par ricochet*.[76] The uniformity of the policies and activities of the SGBs at the different levels of the pyramid is vital for the very organisation of sport. In addition, any national sports authority refusing to comply with the directives of the global regulator runs the risk of being sanctioned by the latter, losing temporarily or permanently its status of a recognised SGB by suspension or expulsion.[77] As a result, a decision rendered by the European Commission will affect not only the initial addressee of a decision (for example, an international SGB), but can indirectly have significant regulatory effect on a US national sports association, otherwise mostly exempted from the US antitrust rules by the Ted Stevens Olympic and Amateur Sports Act (in the case of amateur sports)[78] and by the non-statutory labour exemption of collective bargaining agreements (in the case of the professional leagues).[79]

It is important to remember that most sports industries depend on the EU internal market. This circumstance multiplies the possibility of bringing an antitrust lawsuit against a non-EU undertaking. The extraterritorial effect of EU competition law on sports management and business processes makes it even more influential.[80]

Finally, any government interference in the affairs of one of its national SGBs will be also regarded as a violation of sports autonomy and may trigger the suspension of the membership of the said national SGB. The EU is immune to this rule because it does not have any SGBs in its jurisdiction, and therefore, it cannot be influenced by the considerations of membership or sanctions.[81]

That said, EU case law shows that, despite the strong bargaining power of the EU vis-à-vis the sports governance system, it would be fair to underline the rather prudent approach adopted by its bodies in handling sport-related matters.

A. *Meca-Medina*

The 2006 *Meca-Medina and Majcen v Commission*[82] case started with a complaint filed by two swimmers against a suspension imposed on them by

[76] S Weatherill, *Saving Football from Itself: Why and How to Re-make EU Sports Law* (Cambridge Yearbook of European Legal Studies. Cambridge University Press, 2022) 14.

[77] For example, Art 14 para 1(a) and para (2) Art 16 and 17 of the FIFA Statutes, Edition of May 2021.

[78] 36 US Code Chapter 2205 – United States Olympic Committee, 'Ted Stevens Olympic And Amateur Sports Act'.

[79] L O'Leary, *Employment and Labour Relations Law in the Premier League, NBA and International Rugby Union* (TMC Asser Press, 2017) 102–103.

[80] Weatherill (n 76) 14. See further A Bradford, *The Brussels Effect: How the European Union Rules the World* (Oxford University Press, 2020; G Monti, *The Global Reach of EU Competition Law* in M Cremona and J Scott (eds), *EU Law Beyond EU Borders: The Extraterritorial Reach of EU Law* (Oxford University Press, 2019).

[81] Weatherill (n 76) 14.

[82] *Meca-Medina and Majcen v Commission* (n 71).

the International Swimming Federation ('FINA') as a sanction for the violation of the anti-doping rules (FINA's ban was confirmed by the CAS). The athletes claimed that the SGB's rules infringed Article 101(1) TFEU (what was Article 81(1) of the Treaty establishing the European Community) and restricted the swimmers' economic freedoms.

The judgment outlined the core principles of the intervention of EU competition law in international sports governance. First, it showed that internal decisions of SGBs and the arbitral procedure of the CAS were autonomous but not immune to a review by EU authorities, and that the sporting activities with their economic dimension fell under the scope of EU law. Second, the focus in *Meca-Medina* was drawn to *the contextual assessment* of the contested sporting rules.[83] This implied that the special features of sport should be taken into consideration and that the compatibility of rules with EU competition law should be assessed on a case-by-case basis, with due regard to the rationale behind the restrictions and to the scale of the restrictive effects.[84] According to the Court, a restrictive practice is not illegal if it can be justified by a legitimate objective, and if the consequential effects restricting competition are inherent in the pursuit of this objective and are proportionate to it.[85]

This approach seems to be a truly Solomonic solution since, while shutting the door to the full regulatory autonomy of SGBs, it opens another door to a new form of autonomy, the one in which governing organisations can explain what is actually to be found behind their activities. The consequences of this position are far-reaching for global sports governance since the vast majority of rules issued by SGBs have an economic dimension and are covered by EU antitrust law. Therefore, the outcome of every particular regulation depends on the ability to establish a legitimate objective and to choose a proportionate measure to attain it. In *Meca-Medina*, the Court found that FINA anti-doping rules did not infringe EU competition law because they were necessary for the proper organisation of the sport, provided for proportionate requirements and sanctions, and were based on a fair procedure. In conformity with this logic, had some of those elements been missing, the case would have resulted in an adverse outcome.

B. *MOTOE*

There was an adverse outcome in the *MOTOE* case in 2008.[86] *Elliniki Leskhi Aftokinitou kai Periigiseon* ('ELPA') is the Greek national SGB for motorcycling, endowed by Greek law with the exclusive power to license promoters of

[83] Weatherill (n 76) 8.
[84] *Meca-Medina and Majcen v Commission* (n 71) para 42.
[85] ibid para 42.
[86] *MOTOE* (n 71).

motorcycling events, while it also organises its own races. When an application submitted by MOTOE, a promoter, was refused by ELPA, MOTOE brought an action before a Greek court on the grounds of what is today Article 102 TFEU.

The Court of Justice of the European Union (CJEU) rendered a preliminary ruling finding that a statutory rule enabling an SGB to act as a gatekeeper and hold commercial functions in the same market and without any review, was in violation of EU competition law. Following the contextual assessment, the Court accentuated the public character of the monopoly retained by the SGB, concluding that it created a complementary burden of precaution and additional obligations for the monopolist regarding possible abuses of its power.[87] In the absence of the duty to give a statement of reasons in the case of a refusal to grant a licence, the SGB was enabled to issue arbitrary decisions, while the lack of any available legal remedies against such decisions reinforced the arbitrariness of the result.[88]

If in *Meca-Medina* the focus was drawn to the rules, in *MOTOE*, the Court shifted it towards the subject, ie the SGB itself. In the latter case, the Court outlined the core elements of 'good governance', serving as pre-requisites for the legitimacy of the SGB's activities: it referred to such notions as transparency, objectivity, and judicial review. This originally nationwide case resulted in a statement to the international sports community, and started a more complex discussion about the importance of good governance in sport.

C. The ISU's Eligibility Rules

The global impact of EU antitrust law is exemplified in the more international case of *the International Skating Union (ISU)'s Eligibility Rules*,[89] which entails a considerable development of certain aspects initiated in *MOTOE*. In June 2014, two Dutch speed skaters lodged a complaint against the ISU's 2014 Eligibility Rules with the European Commission.[90] The Eligibility Rules of the Swiss-based international federation provided for a lifetime disqualification for competitors, staff and officials if they participated in competitions not authorised by the ISU. Authorisations were granted to organisers on the basis of a pre-authorisation system ensuring their compliance with standards of conduct for speed skating elaborated and safeguarded by the ISU. The skaters challenged the Rules as they prevented them from taking part in a commercial speed skating event organised by a South Korean promoter in Dubai and, therefore, deprived them of the possibility to fully exploit their sporting talent and to receive additional financial earnings.

[87] ibid paras 49 and 50.

[88] ibid para 52.

[89] European Commission, Case AT.40208 – *International Skating Union's Eligibility Rules*, Decision of 8 December 2017.

[90] Rules 102 and 103 of the ISU 2014 Constitution and General Regulations.

Despite the objections of the SGB, the Commission found that, since the contested Rules were applied by an international federation and, thus, were implemented in every country where the ISU was active through its national associations, its rules and decisions could potentially harm the worldwide market for the organisation of sports events.[91] Likewise, since an international competition, such as the one organised by the South Korean promoter, presumed the participation of athletes irrespective of their nationality, the Commission also saw in the Eligibility Rules a threat to athletes' ability to provide services cross-border. As a result, neither the place of registration of the promoter, nor the place of the event hindered the fulfilment of the effect on trade conditions.[92] Therefore, in December 2017, the European Commission rendered a decision[93] finding the ISU's Eligibility Rules to be in breach of Article 101 TFEU as a decision of an association of undertakings restricting competition by object, thus allocating them to the category of the most harmful anticompetitive practices, injurious to the proper functioning of normal competition by their very nature.[94]

During the long proceedings, the ISU changed its Eligibility Rules twice, adjusting them to be more in line with the Commission's expectations. For this reason, it is important to recognise the impact of the antitrust mechanism on SGBs' policies. With a combined legal and economic analysis, the case-by-case approach applied in the framework of the competition law test allows the specificities of the sports market at hand to be taken into account, and to expand the scope of possible adjustments caused by the evolution of the market and new challenges before the industry.

IV. ALTERNATIVE AVENUES FOR THE APPLICATION OF EU COMPETITION LAW TO SPORT

Nevertheless, whereas EU antitrust law seems apt to strike the right balance between the interests of SGBs and the freedoms of other stakeholders, the procedural aspects might represent a stumbling block on the way towards the functionable enforcement of Articles 101 and 102 TFEU. Taking into consideration the length of proceedings and the fact that it is impossible for the Commission to deal with all the complaints that are lodged, public enforcement on its own is clearly insufficient to handle all sport-related cases. In this regard, all the procedural options for the application of EU competition law to sport should be analysed in order to compare their respective viability and efficiency. It is possible to identify multiple – both practical and theoretical – avenues for the application of competition law to the SGBs' policies and decisions.

[91] *International Skating Union's Eligibility Rules*, Decision (n 89) para 311.
[92] ibid para 314.
[93] ibid.
[94] Case C-226/11 *Expedia* ECLI:EU:C:2012:795, para 36.

A. The Annulment of Arbitral Awards by the SFT on the Basis of EU Competition Law Violations

Firstly, as mentioned above, it is possible to rely on the SFT's procedure for annulment of arbitral awards by including EU antitrust rules as a part of substantive public policy in the sense of Article 190, paragraph 2e PILA. However, the SFT discarded this possibility by referring to its narrow interpretation of the notion. According to the SFT, substantive public policy covers only those fundamental principles of material law, violation of which is no longer consistent with the determining legal order and system of values;[95] among such principles are prohibition of abuse of rights, prohibition of discriminatory[96] or confiscatory measures,[97] and principle of good faith.[98] In contrast, the SFT refuses to include EU antitrust provisions (irrespective of the degree of violation[99]) in the category of substantive public policy as the provisions does not reflect 'the essential and broadly recognised values, which, according to the concepts prevailing in Switzerland, would have to be found in any legal order'.[100]

In the opinion of SFT, there are too many discrepancies between competition law regimes to identify one general and universal set of principles which could match the characteristics of public policy:

> [I]t would be presumptuous to take the view that European or Swiss concepts in the field of competition law should evidently be imposed to all the states of the planet as a panacea, because such concepts are tied to a certain type of economy and to a certain regime (art. 1 Lcart). [...] In reality, the differences between the various laws on competition are too acute – specially between Switzerland and the European Union – to allow a finding that a transnational or international rule public policy would have to be found there.[101]

This point is questionable, since the antitrust laws of Switzerland and of the EU are largely similar, notably with regard to the provisions on the abuse of a dominant position,[102] as the Swiss Cartel Act was adopted with the view of being as 'euro-compatible' as possible and fulfilling the internal market requirements.[103]

[95] Judgment of the SFT 4P_71/2002 of 22 October 2002, pt 3.2.
[96] Judgment of the SFT ATF 147 III 49 of 25 October 2020.
[97] Judgment of the SFT 4A_668/2016 of 24 July 2017, pt 4.1.
[98] Judgment of the SFT 4A_600/2008 of 20 February 2009, pt 4.1.
[99] Judgment of the SFT ATF 144 III 120 of 20 February 2018, pt 5.2.
[100] Judgments of the SFT ATF 132 III 389 pt 2.2.3; 4P.119/1998, pt 1b/bb; ATF 128 III 234 pt 4c.
[101] Judgment of the SFT 4P.278/2005 of 8 March 2006, pt 3.1. The judgment was issued in French; an English translation is available at www.swissarbitrationdecisions.com.
[102] F Maiani, *Lost in Translation: Euro-Compatibility, Legal Security, and the Autonomous Implementation of EU Law in Switzerland* (2013) 1 *European Law Reporter* 33–34.
[103] P Këllezi, 'L'évolution de la loi suisse sur les cartels: entre intégration au marché européen et réglementation des marchés' in H Schneider and A Kellerhals (eds), *25 Jahre Kartellgesetz – ein kritischer Ausblick* (EIZ Publishing, 2022) 94. Organisation for Economic Co-operation and Development, 'Competition Law and Policy in Switzerland' (OECD Policy Brief, March 2006) p 2, available at www.oecd.org/competition/36386974.pdf. See also A Epiney, 'How does the European

Likewise, the Swiss competition authority regularly refers to EU decisions, especially in niche sectors such as sport.[104] At the same time, despite the existing discrepancies between the laws on competition of different jurisdictions, the main antitrust principles could potentially fall under the concept of 'widely prevailing values'.[105]

Second, the SFT interprets the reference to the internal market literally, ie as a clear indication of the geographical scope of the EU antitrust provisions.

> The Court itself narrowed the scope of its conclusion by pointing out that art. 81 EC is qualified as public policy because it is a 'fundamental provision, indispensable to carry out the missions entrusted to the Community and, particularly, to the smooth functioning of the internal market'.[106]

The preference given to a literal reading of teleological interpretations (according to which the Swiss Cartel Act as it exists today was adopted with the economic purpose of facilitating the integration of the Swiss economy into the EU internal market) is aligned with the SFT's approach but narrows the scope of the notions even further.[107] Thus, as already pointed out in section II, challenging an anti-competitive decision before the SFT on the grounds of violation of public policy seems highly unlikely to result in a successful outcome.

B. Non-Enforcement of Arbitral Awards

The second option to challenge the compatibility of a specific CAS decision with EU competition law appears at the enforcement stage of an arbitral award. Contrary to the SFT, the European Court of Justice recognises EU competition law as a part of public policy in the sense of the New York Convention on the Recognition and Enforcement of Foreign Arbitral Awards of 1958 because of its 'essential' role in the accomplishment of the Union's tasks and in the functioning of the internal market.[108] Therefore, the enforcement of CAS awards can be challenged before national courts in the EU on the grounds of violation

Union Law Influence Swiss Law and Policies?' in S Nahrath and F Varone (Hrsg), *Rediscovering Public Law and Public Administration in Comparative Policy Analysis: A Tribute to Peter Knoepfel* (Bern, 2009) 179–96; S Rab, I Stempler and G Brei, *EU and Swiss Competition Law: Navigating the Boundaries* in (2012) 2 *SZW/RSDA* 136–44. CAS 98/200 *AEK Athens and SK Slavia Prague v UEFA*, award of 20 August 1999, para 11.

[104] M Dietrich, F Hoffet, R Stäuber and S Gohari Ramin, *Neue Praxis zur Geschäftsverweigerung im Schweizer Kartellrecht* (30 October 2020), available at www.homburger.ch/de/insights/neue-praxis-geschaeftsverweigerung-schweizer-kartellrecht.

[105] *AEK Athens and SK Slavia Prague v UEFA* (n 103) para 11.

[106] Decision of the SFT 4P.278/2005 of March 8, 2006, pt 3.1. referring to Case C-126/97 *Eco Swiss China Time Ltd v Benetton International NV* ECLI:EU:C:1999:269, [1999] ECR I-3055, para 36.The decision of the SFT was issued in French; an English translation is available at www.swissarbitrationdecisions.com.

[107] Maiani (n 102) 32.

[108] *Eco Swiss China Time Ltd v Benetton International* (n 106) paras 36–39.

of public policy if these awards breach antitrust provisions.[109] Nevertheless, in practice, this option is not very useful since CAS awards are predominantly self-enforced.[110] Besides, in this case, athletes would be obliged to file a separate application in every state in which they are going to compete, making the process too burdensome.

C. EU Competition Law Enforcement

The third scenario is available in the form of antitrust enforcement. Like most competition law systems, EU antitrust is based on two pillars: public and private enforcement. Both mechanisms are used in the sports sector but serve different strategies.

i. Public Enforcement

Public enforcement is undertaken by state authorities which are vested with special powers and use special procedures (market enquiries, requests, interviews, investigations, etc)[111] to detect, prosecute and penalise antitrust infringements. Among these authorities are the European Commission and the national competition authorities (NCAs), which together form the European Competition Network (ECN). The Commission is better placed to deal with agreements and practices affecting competition in three or more Member States, or with cases in which the Union interest requires it (for example, for competition policy-making purposes or to ensure effective enforcement).[112]

The procedure is initiated either on a complaint or on the initiative of an authority. Once the procedure has been initiated, the authority first undertakes an investigation in order to gather the relevant information on the potential infringement. At the end of the investigative phase, a case might be closed, settled, resolved by commitments, or it might transition to a formal

[109] *International Skating Union's Eligibility Rules*, Decision (n 89) para 284.

[110] See M Maisonneuve, *L'arbitrage des litiges sportifs* (LGDJ, 2011) 403–407. M Orth, 'Verstoßen exklusive Sportschiedsklauseln mit Schiedsort Schweiz gegen europäisches Kartellrecht?' (2018) *ZWeR* 4, 385. *cf*, the SV Wilhelmshaven case before the Highest Regional Court of Bremen (OLG Bremen, 30.12.2014–2 U 67/14) as well as the Diarra case before the Hainaut Commercial Tribunal – Charleroi division (Jugement du Tribunal de Commerce du Hainaut, division Charleroi, 19.01.2017, A/16/00141) are the rare examples of successful challenges of the CAS's awards in the light of Art 45 TFEU. Similarly, through the Pechstein decision rendered by the Highest Regional Court of Munich (OLG München, 15.01. 2015 – Az. U 1110/14 Kart), the athlete managed to challenge the arbitral award on the basis of Art 102 TFEU.

[111] Articles 17–22 of the Council Regulation (EC) No 1/2003 of 16 December 2002 on the implementation of the rules on competition laid down in Articles 81 and 82 of the Treaty [2003] OJ L1/1.

[112] A Jones, 'Competition Law Enforcement' in D Chalmers and A Arnull (eds), *The Oxford Handbook of European Union Law* (Oxford University Press, 2015) 660.

proceeding.[113] Following the formal procedure, the authority either makes a final decision ordering the termination of the infringement or issues binding commitments (without making an infringement finding). The key objective of public enforcement usually lies in creating a deterrent effect.[114] For this reason, if the authority finds a violation of Articles 101 or 102 TFEU, it imposes behavioural and/or structural remedies as well as fines.[115]

If a party decides to challenge the final decision of the Commission, it can proceed in conformity with Article 263 TFEU. In this case, the Court of Justice can review such a decision on the grounds of the lack of competence, infringement of essential procedural requirements or provisions of the Treaty, or misuse of powers. In addition, the Court has the unlimited jurisdiction to review fines, including the power to assess the evidence, annul the contested decision and alter the amount of the fine.[116]

In Europe, public enforcement has traditionally dominated.[117] In the sports sector, the Commission rendered decisions on FIA's regulations and commercial agreements in 2001,[118] the joint selling of media rights to the FA Premier League in 2006[119] and the ISU's Eligibility Rules in 2017.[120] All three cases comprised complex EU-wide issues, had far-reaching political implications on sport, and thus, required assessment and response from the most influential institution. For instance, the investigation in the FIA case resulted in the commitments decision which integrally modified the SGB's structure and organisation.

That said, the major weakness of public enforcement is the so-called 'enforcement gap' provoked by its understandable inability to handle all attention-worthy cases.[121] For instance, the dispute between the International Federation of Basketball (FIBA) and the professional basketball league in Europe (Euroleague) remains unresolved since 2016, hindering the efficient functioning of basketball competitions.

In February 2016, Euroleague filed a complaint with the Commission accusing FIBA and FIBA Europe of violating Article 102 TFEU by putting basketball

[113] ibid 648.

[114] K Hüschelrath and S Peyer, 'Public and Private Enforcement of Competition Law: A Differentiated Approach' (2013) 36 *World Competition* 4, 588.

[115] ibid.

[116] Article 261 TFEU and Article 31 of the Regulation 1/2003 (n 111).

[117] AP Komninos, 'Public and Private Antitrust Enforcement in Europe: Complement? Overlap?' (2006) 3 *The Competition Law Review* 1, 6.

[118] Notice published pursuant to Article 19(3) of Council Regulation No 17 concerning Cases COMP/35.163 Notification of FIA Regulations, COMP/36.638 – Notification by FIA/FOA of agreements relating to the FIA Formula One World Championship, COMP/36.776 – GTR/FIA & others.

[119] Commission Decision of 22 March 2006 relating to a proceeding pursuant to Article 81 of the EC Treaty (Case COMP/38.173 – Joint selling of the media rights to the FA Premier League) (notified under document number C(2006) 868).

[120] *International Skating Union's Eligibility Rules*, Decision (n 89).

[121] Komninos (n 117) 11.

clubs, players and officials under undue pressure with the intention to coerce them into participating in FIBA's new club competition, the Basketball Champions League (to the detriment of the Euroleague's tournaments).[122] Two months later, FIBA lodged a counter-complaint (based on the same provision) denouncing Euroleague's abusive practices: the non-release of players to compete in international games, the 'syndication agreement' between the most powerful clubs, unfair discrimination of smaller clubs, and the arbitrary selection mechanism for Euroleague and Eurocup.[123]

The Commission left the complaints without response, and the situation deteriorated. In the summer of 2016, Euroleague requested (and obtained) a preliminary injunction before the Regional Court in Munich to prohibit FIBA from penalising national associations for non-sanctioning the affiliated clubs for participating in Euroleague's competitions.[124] On the other hand, the game calendar for the season 2017/18 revealed by Euroleague in July 2017 did not provide any windows for national team matches (which are organised by FIBA). In November 2017, 31 members of the European Parliament brought the issue back onto the political stage urging the Commission to address the governance crisis in basketball and to resolve the non-release-of-players controversy.[125] Finally, in 2020, ULEB (the association of the 11 major European Basketball Leagues) signed a joint defence agreement with FIBA, officially joining FIBA's 2016 complaint with the European Commission.[126]

It is unclear when the conflict will be resolved, and if it will be resolved through public antitrust enforcement. However, even in the event of a possible intervention by the Commission, the procedure might take another couple of years to conclude.[127]

With the decentralisation of the competition law enforcement system in the EU introduced by Regulation 1/2003,[128] the NCAs also play a significant role in the investigation of anticompetitive practices of the national and, to a lesser degree, international sports organisations.[129] In comparison to the European

[122] 'Euroleague Opts for Legal Action over Dialogue' (FIBA.basketball, 20 February 2016), www.fiba.basketball/news/euroleague-opts-for-legal-action-over-dialogue.

[123] 'FIBA Files Complaint against Euroleague' (FIBA.basketball, 5 April 2016), www.fiba.basketball/news/fiba-files-complaint-against-euroleague. 'FIBA Filed a Complaint to the EC vs Euroleague' (*Eurohoops*, 5 April 2016), www.eurohoops.net/en/fiba/220198/fiba-filed-a-complaint-to-the-ec-vs-euroleague.

[124] LG München I, 23.06.2016–1 HK O 8126/16.

[125] 'Members of the European Parliament Request a Solution to FIBA-Euroleague Conflict (*Eurohoops*, 17 November 2017), www.eurohoops.net/en/fiba/556090/members-european-parliament-request-solution-fiba-euroleague-conflict/.

[126] 'ULEB Files Competition Complaint before European Commission against Euroleague Organiser ECA' (*ULEB*, 30 September 2020), www.uleb.com/news/uleb-files-competition-complaint-before-european-commission-against-euroleague-organizer-eca.

[127] The ISU's Eligibility Rules, the Commission initiated proceedings in 2015 and rendered the final decision at the end of 2017.

[128] Regulation No 1/2003 (n 111).

[129] Van Rompuy (n 9) 202–206.

Commission, NCAs are often better placed to ensure an effective enforcement, particularly in terms of the deadlines of proceedings. That said, there are two possible drawbacks with this option.

The first weakness has to do with the fact that the decisions made by the NCAs are not binding in nature beyond the borders of each respective Member State. This is a particularly regrettable flaw when an investigation targets infringements by international SGBs. Should a challenged rule be found to violate competition law, it would be made inapplicable only in the Member State in which the rule is overturned.

In particular, it became an issue in the case of the *Bundeskartellamt*'s investigation into Rule 40.3 of the Olympic Charter and the respective Guidelines on Advertising by members of Team Deutschland implemented by the German Olympic Committee (DOSB)[130] Within the framework of the investigation, the German Competition Authority found that the restrictions on advertising by unofficial Olympic sponsors established by the abovementioned regulations were inherent to the prevention of ambush marketing during the Olympic Games but many of the requirements implemented by the DOSB were not proportionate to this objective.[131] Therefore, the *Bundeskartellamt* preliminarily assessed the rules provided in the DOSB Guidelines 2016 as violating Article 102 TFEU and its German equivalent (Section 19 GWB).[132] At a later stage of the investigation, the IOC and the DOSB offered final commitments amending the problematic provisions (that were accepted by the NCA), but the commitments only applied to the members of the German Olympic team[133] leaving members representing other national Olympic committees under the old and much stricter regulatory regimes.

In other words, in comparison to the powers of the European Commission, NCAs have a certain legal and political impotence when dealing with the international organisations: while being able to force SGBs to refrain from an anticompetitive practice in one state, NCAs lack jurisdiction to exercise a more direct global impact.

Following the *Bundeskartellamt's* case on Rule 40, however, the decision helped to launch a process for further changes: in the summer of 2019, the IOC amended Rule 40 considerably softening the advertising restrictions for all Olympic athletes around the globe. That said, national Olympic committees have the right to apply the new rule as they deem necessary and enjoy a considerable leeway.[134]

[130] *Bundeskartellamt*, Decision pursuant to Section 32b GWB Public version, B-226/17, 25 February 2019. The version in English is available at www.bundeskartellamt.de/SharedDocs/Entscheidung/EN/Entscheidungen/Missbrauchsaufsicht/2019/B2-26-17.pdf?__blob=publicationFile&v=2.

[131] ibid paras 106–120.

[132] ibid para 127.

[133] ibid para 150.

[134] See more R Agafonova, 'WISLaw Blog Symposium – Rule 40 of the Olympic Charter: The Wind of Changes or a New Commercial Race' (*Asser International Sports Law Blog*, 29 June 2021),

Secondly, the limits of the geographical reach of NCAs might create a risk of unequal treatment between subjects from different Member States in relation to a particular policy implemented by an SGB. While it is true that given that EU competition law is directly applicable in all Member States, and that national competition laws in Member States are shaped after it, and decisions rendered by different NCAs on the same facts are supposed to be consistent, it can take a long time for all the NCAs to investigate a similar case within their jurisdictions and for the policy in question to be harmonised within all national sports organisations.

ii. Private Enforcement

Historically, private enforcement has been a rare phenomenon in Europe (unlike the United States).[135] Alongside its direct corrective function, this mechanism is also designed to relieve pressure on public enforcement agencies.[136]

Private enforcement litigation is initiated by individual plaintiffs before a court either as a stand-alone or a follow-on action to remedy an infringement of competition law. In other words, it is a form of 'corrective justice'[137] primarily serving the restorative-compensatory objective.[138] Potential remedies include damages, restitution, injunction, nullity or interim relief. Private enforcement entails a number of advantages. While a national judge has no investigative tools, the injunctions ordered by civil courts may be more efficient than public enforcement: it may be easier to obtain a preliminary injunction from a national judge than from the European Commission, a national judge can (unlike the Commission) issue orders imposing positive measures on undertakings.[139]

The focus is, however, placed on the action for damages. In the *ISU v Commission* case, the General Court stated that it is a sufficient and effective remedy for the harm caused by an SGB's anticompetitive decisions or practices.[140]

> In the present case, while it is true that the arbitration rules do not permit skaters to bring an action before a national court for annulment of an ineligibility decision which infringes Article 101(1) TFEU, the fact remains that skaters may bring, if they so wish […], an action for damages before a national court. Furthermore, organisers who are third parties may also bring an action for damages where they consider that a decision refusing authorisation infringes Article 101(1) TFEU.[141]

www.asser.nl/SportsLaw/Blog/post/rule-40-of-the-olympic-charter-the-wind-of-changes-or-a-new-commercial-race-by-rusa-agafonova.

[135] Jones (n 112) 664.

[136] ibid 662.

[137] ibid.

[138] Komninos (n 117) 9.

[139] ibid.

[140] *International Skating Union v Commission* (n 43) para 157.

[141] ibid para 159.

However, while monetary compensation can indeed compensate certain losses incurred due to unfair suspension or another illegal sanction, from the point of view of an athlete, damages, irrespective of the ground on which they are claimed, are 'a less important arrow'.[142] As Beloff fairly points out, although damages are almost an inalienable part of civil actions in the field of sport, 'the remedy uppermost in the claimant's mind' is usually an injunction or declaratory relief.[143]

However, the practical effect of private enforcement is greater than just a corrective function. Komninos underlines that private antitrust enforcement is an example of private interests contributing to the safeguarding of the public interest.[144] In the same vein, Van Rompuy argues that the mere possibility for athletes and other stakeholders to resort to EU competition law enforcement may deter sports associations from abusing their regulatory powers.[145] As the Court of Justice has acknowledged in multiple cases, the right to claim damages strengthens the working of the EU competition rules and discourages anti-competitive agreements or practices, thus making a significant contribution to maintaining effective competition in the EU:

> The right of any individual to claim compensation for such a loss actually strengthens the working of the EU competition rules, since it discourages agreements or practices, frequently covert, which are liable to restrict or distort competition, thereby making a significant contribution to the maintenance of effective competition in the European Union.[146]

Moreover, in the *ISU v Commission* judgment, the General Court emphasised the absolute autonomy of EU law vis-à-vis the CAS, and stressed that a national judge does not have any obligation to take account of the CAS's assessment of the case:

> In such cases, the national court is not bound by the CAS's assessment of the compatibility of the ineligibility decision or the refusal of authorisation with EU competition law and, where appropriate, may submit a request for a preliminary ruling to the Court of Justice under Article 267 TFEU.[147]

In sum, actions for damages could also be a deterrent for SGBs. This part of the judgment is important because, first, it can be interpreted as sending a strong political message to the 'Swiss sports administration hub' reminding it

142 M Beloff QC, T Kerr QC and M Demetriou Marie QC, *Sports Law* (Bloomsbury Publishing, 2012) 289.

143 ibid.

144 Komninos (n 117) 10.

145 Van Rompuy (n 9) 208.

146 *International Skating Union v Commission* (n 43) para 158. See also: Case C-453/99 *Courage and Crehan* ECLI:EU:C:2001:465, [2001] ECR I-6297, 6323, paras 26–27; Case C-557/12 *Kone and Others* ECLI:EU:C:2014:1317 [2014] para 23; Joined Cases C-295/04 to C-298/04 *Manfredi and Others* ECLI:EU:C:2006:461, [2006] ECR I-6619, para 91.

147 *International Skating Union v Commission* (n 43) para 159.

of the limits of the autonomy of SGBs. Secondly, it mirrors the logic of the SFT: whereas the latter insists on the term 'public policy' being interpreted according to the concepts inherent in the Swiss legal order, the Court of Justice makes the questions of EU antitrust the *domaine réservé* of the EU legal order.

D. The CAS Applying EU Competition Law

Under Swiss law, competition law disputes are arbitrable.[148] The application of EU antitrust provisions by CAS panels is currently a rare but interesting and prospective alternative. There are very few published CAS awards implementing EU competition law.[149] Duval sees in it a strategic decision of parties and their (predominantly Swiss) counsels to avoid the less familiar area of law.[150]

As opposed to the SFT, CAS panels assign competition rules to the category of public policy.[151] However, this finding has a limited effect and is not deemed sufficient to prevail over the CAS jurisdictional rules since 'antitrust complaints may always be lodged with a competition authority or a state court if an arbitral tribunal declines jurisdiction'.[152]

Opfermann notes that arbitral agreements are generally 'neutral towards competition law'.[153] Arbitral tribunals with a seat in Switzerland, including the CAS, are competent to handle disputes comprising competition law questions if they deem it necessary[154] and are asked to do so by the parties.[155] If an arbitrator unlawfully denies jurisdiction, the arbitral award can be challenged under Article 190(2)(b) PILA:[156]

> [P]ublic policy within the meaning of art. 190 (2) (e) PILA should be distinguished from public policy as to how the Arbitral Tribunal applied the law [...] In other words, the arbitrator's public policy is not the public policy of the appeal judge.

[148] Judgment of the SFT ATF 118 II 193, 28 April 1992.

[149] The most complete antitrust analysis was undertaken by a CAS panel in the case CAS 98/200 *AEK Athens and SK Slavia Prague / Union of European Football Associations (UEFA)*, award of 20 August 1999.

[150] A Duval, *La Lex Sportiva Face au Droit de l'Union Européenne: Guerre et Paix dans l'Espace Juridique Transnational* (Doctoral Thesis, Florence, 2015) 425.

[151] CAS 2013/A/3254 PT *Liga Prima Indonesia Sportindo (LPIS) and others v FIFA and others*, award of 2 May 2014, para 6.11; CAS 98/200 *AEK Athens and SK Slavia Prague v UEFA*, award of 20 August 1999, para 11.

[152] CAS 2013/A/3254 *PT Liga Prima Indonesia Sportindo (LPIS) and others v FIFA and others*, award of 2 May 2014, para 6.11.

[153] G Opfermann, *Schiedsvereinbarungen zum CAS: Eine Untersuchung aus der Perspektive des Kartellrechts* (Mohr Siebeck, 2021) 414.

[154] CAS 2019/A/6345 *Club Raja Casablanca v FIFA*, award of 16 December 2019, para 41; CAS 2007/A/1287 *Danubio FC v FIFA & FC Internazionale Milano S.p.A.*, award of 28 November 2007, paras 9–11.

[155] A Heinemann, 'Private Kartellrechtsdurchsetzung in der Schweiz' in F Weitbrecht (Hrsg), *Handbuch Private Kartellrechtsdurchsetzung* (München, 2019) paras 89–90.

[156] Judgments of the Swiss Federal Tribunal 4P.119/1998, quoted above, cons. 1a; ATF 118 II 193, pt 5.

> Thus, there is no contradiction between holding that the Arbitral Tribunal would violate art. 190 (2) (b) PILA (in connection with art. 187 (1) PILA) by denying jurisdiction to examine the application of a foreign mandatory law, such as European [...] competition laws, when asked to do so by a party, whilst also refusing to review the way in which an Arbitral Tribunal applied the same law because it does not belong to the realm of public policy as defined at art. 190 (2) (e) PILA.[157]

The option chosen by the CAS to apply EU antitrust law to sports cases seems viable and even attractive because one of the key advantages of arbitration is the possibility to provide in-depth expertise depending on the needs in a particular dispute.[158] Given the highly technical and complex profile of antitrust law, especially when combined with numerable specificities of a sports organisation, there might be a need for very specific knowledge and experience. The CAS's list of arbitrators already includes several high-profile experts in competition law, and thus the adequacy of 'private justice' in this regard seems warranted.

That said, this option should be taken with a pinch of salt. Even with a high level of expertise in antitrust issues, it is legitimate to question how this expertise is applied in practice by the CAS arbitrators. In conditions in which the independence of the institution from the Olympic Movement continues to raise occasional concerns,[159] you might expect from the CAS decisions favourable to SGBs, regardless of the applied field of expertise.

However, the major problem of the present situation is the absence of any guarantees that the proceedings will respect the substantive and procedural standards inherent in the EU enforcement mechanism,[160] since neither the CAS nor the Swiss Federal Tribunal are entitled to make a preliminary reference to the Court of Justice.[161] This principle aligns with the autonomous and *private* nature of arbitration and corresponds to the generally limited intervention of public authorities in arbitral proceedings. For instance, when applying Swiss competition law, arbitral tribunals with their seat in Switzerland are not obliged to consult the Swiss Competition Commission.[162]

Theoretically, a competition authority can participate in arbitral proceedings as amicus curiae or a 'non-disputing party', ie as a third party that intervenes to a certain degree in the proceedings with the view to assisting the arbitral tribunal regarding some of the aspects of a case.[163] The CAS Code provides for this

[157] Judgments of the Swiss Federal Tribunal 4P.278/2005 of 8 March 2006, pt 3.3; ATF 120 II 155 of 19 April 1994, p 6a. The decisions were issued in French and German respectively; English translations are available at www.swissarbitrationdecisions.com.

[158] Kaufmann-Kohler and Rigozzi (n 35) 13–14.

[159] See partly dissenting, partly concurring Joint Opinion of Judges Keller and Serghides concerning the Judgment of the ECHR, *Mutu and Pechstein v Switzerland* (n 39).

[160] *International Skating Union's Eligibility Rules*, Decision (n 89) para 283.

[161] ibid.

[162] Heinemann (n 155) para 97.

[163] A Stanimir and C Marinn, 'The Opportunity to Be Heard: Accommodating Amicus Curiae Participation in Investment Treaty Arbitration' in MA Fernandez Ballesteros and D Arias (eds), *Liber Amicorum Bernardo Cremades* (La Ley, 2010) 50.

possibility but only if a third party 'is bound by the arbitration agreement or if it and the other parties agree in writing'.[164] In international investment arbitration, the Commission has intervened as amicus curiae on many occasions.[165] Naturally, sports arbitration differs considerably in terms of the nature of the parties to disputes, the scope of disputes and the stakes behind them. However, particularly high-profile cases with considerable political implications for European sport might eventually be of interest to the European Commission.

Another difficulty is caused by the requirement of the CAS Code that an individual be personally affected by an identifiable *decision* for an appeal to be admissible.[166] While it is sometimes the case that athletes are subjected to an individual decision restricting their rights in violation of Articles 101 and/or 102 TFEU, usually SGBs proceed by adopting regulations, memoranda of understanding with other entities, resolutions, etc.[167] Thus, the range of anticompetitive acts undertaken by SGBs appealable before the CAS is also significantly reduced on jurisdictional grounds.

V. FROM AUTONOMY TO CHECKS AND BALANCES

Sports organisations need to be recognised by the European authorities in order to remain as legitimate bodies. Moreover, when facing existential threats, such as the appearance of an aggressive competitor, SGBs tend to cede some attributes of their autonomy and to engage with the EU on its terms[168] in order to retain governance control ('pragmatic autonomy').[169] For example, UEFA reinforced its partnership with the European Commission and the Council of Europe[170] in the context of the Superleague case in 2021.[171] A cooperative relationship with the EU authorities would allow SGBs to maintain significant control over their respective markets, provided that they channel sufficient efforts into sporting and social activities promoted by the European Union.[172]

[164] Rule R41.4 of the CAS Code.

[165] Among the most recent cases are *UP and C.D Holding Internationale (formerly Le Cheque Dejeuner) v Hungary*, ICSID Case No ARB/13/35; A.M.F. *Aircraftleasing Meier & Fischer GmbH & Co. KG v Czech Republic*, PCA Case No 2017-15; *Addiko Bank AG and Addiko Bank d.d. v Republic of Croatia*, ICSID Case No ARB/17/37.

[166] Article R47 of the CAS Code. CAS 2013/A/3254 *PT Liga Prima Indonesia Sportindo (LPIS) and others v FIFA, AFC, PSSI and Johar Arfin Husin*, award of 2 May 2014, paras 6.6 and 6.7.

[167] CAS 2013/A/3254 *PT LPIS*, ibid para 7.4.

[168] Weatherill (n 70) 124.

[169] Geeraert et al (n 15) 481–82.

[170] UEFA and the European institutions, available at www.uefa.com/insideuefa/stakeholders/european-union/.

[171] 'European Commission and UEFA Strengthen Partnership with New Cooperation Agreement up to 2025' (*European Commission*, 6 October 2022), https://ec.europa.eu/commission/presscorner/detail/en/AC_22_6010.

[172] Weatherill (n 76) 19.

In addition, new global challenges faced by the sports community can only be tackled if SGBs are integrated in and compliant with a truly transnational legal framework rather than if they stay shielded by the legal regime of one single state and remain insensitive to the needs of other stakeholders. It is impossible to disagree with Baddeley who writes:

> In view of the development of the regulations of the international sports governing bodies, it appears necessary to reverse the tendency of the last 20 years to ever increase the autonomy of the sports governing bodies if the essential rights of weaker parties in litigations of the sporting world and more generally of the participants in organised sports are to remain protected. A change of the established practices is all the more urgent that new questions arise f.ex. about e-sports, match fixing, corruption, data protection and gender discrimination and must be dealt with by the sports governing bodies. More intricate aspects of personality rights will become apparent and need adequate answers.[173]

The Swiss legal order creates optimal conditions accommodating SGBs and often shielding them from outer threats, such as legal claims, financial crises or shifts in the political environment. However, even such a steadfast system cannot remain isolated and pursue ambitious global interests at the same time. Therefore, traditional governance models should be revisited. For Chappelet:

> sports organisations must work with states to develop a new model of sports autonomy falling somewhere between the ideal of complete autonomy and an undesirable superficial autonomy; [...] a halfway point between liberalism and interventionism, what might be described as a 'negotiated autonomy', [...] characterised by strong negotiated co-operation mutual understanding and respect, as well as regular consultations.[174]

The reconciliation of *lex sportiva* and the Swiss legal order with EU competition law is a long, legal and largely/primarily political story, which correlates with the realities of sports economics and its massive development. There is a temptation to oppose the interests of SGBs often backed by the Swiss legal order to the principles and goals of EU law. Notwithstanding, it is more accurate to conceptualise them as coexisting elements which, while remaining fully separate, overlap in multiple points and interrelate in the form of checks and balances,[175] ideally reaching the zone *between liberalism and interventionism*.

There are different options available in order to integrate an EU antitrust review into the system of sports governance depending on the choice of strategy adopted by the claimant/appellant in each case. That said, the most effective strategy that can be undertaken by SGBs in terms of antitrust scrutiny remains the reformation of the governance setup: by making the decision-making process inclusive of all the stakeholders, amending regulations and policies

[173] Baddeley (n 2) 16.
[174] Chappelet (n 18) 52.
[175] Weatherill (n 70) 123.

in compliance with the requirements of objectivity, transparency, and non-discrimination, and by giving necessary guarantees of accountability to their stakeholders and general public. The need for deeper reforms might become more evident (and urgent) after the upcoming judgments of the European Court of Justice, the appeal in *ISU v Commission*[176] and the preliminary ruling in *European Superleague Company, S.L. v UEFA and FIFA*.[177]

VI. CONCLUSION

The international system of sports governance, based predominantly on Swiss law, secured by a powerful sports arbitration system and subject to very limited judicial control, and EU competition law supervision, designed to safeguard much broader interests than sport and to ensure the viability of market mechanisms, serve very different objectives. However, when the power of the free market reached the realms of organised sport, the two systems became inextricably linked. Even with the refusal of Swiss judges to include EU competition law in their review of CAS awards, the EU antitrust system is powerful enough to counterweigh the flaws of associations' regulations and to mitigate the defects of CAS decisions, thus, indirectly shaping sports governance. The right to file an action for damages caused by the anticompetitive practices of an SGB contributes to a gradual reform of the traditional governance structures of sport 'from below upwards'. A wider application of EU antitrust provisions in the framework of CAS arbitration would also be interesting for most stakeholders, since it would keep the proceedings within the private realm and protect the main attributes of sports justice: narrow expertise, speed of proceedings, and efficient enforcement. In the long run, however, you would hope to see a more sustainable and cooperative approach by sports organisations regarding their policy-making process and the policies themselves. It concerns, first of all, the inclusion of a broader circle of stakeholders in the adoption of said policies as well as the provision of sufficient accountability mechanisms to stakeholders and the general public. A particular importance should be attributed to the cooperation between SGBs and the EU authorities: this strategy may contribute to the overall legitimacy of sports policies, reinforce the reputation of sports organisations and, very importantly, protect SGBs from EU law lawsuits. In addition, through a systematic compliance with the criteria of objectivity, transparency, and non-discrimination in their policies, SGBs will ensure that their autonomy is safeguarded not only by the Swiss legal order, but also by EU law.

[176] Case C-124/21 P, *International Skating Union v Commission*.
[177] Case C-333/21, *European Superleague Company*.

11

Is the Lex Sportiva *on Track for Intersex Person's Rights? The World Athletics' Regulations Concerning Female Athletes with Differences of Sex Development in the Light of the ECHR*

AUDREY BOISGONTIER[1]

I. INTRODUCTION

IN FEBRUARY 2021, the South African athlete Caster Semenya submitted her case before the European Court of Human Rights (ECtHR).[2] The applicant challenged the decision of the Swiss Federal Tribunal (SFT) allowing World Athletics (previously known as the International Association of Athletics Federations, IAAF) to regulate her participation in the female category in athletics events by applying the 'DSD Regulations'.[3] The Federation indeed requires

[1] PhD Candidate at the Centre for the Study and Research on Fundamental Rights (CREDOF), Paris Nanterre University, France. I would like to thank Stéphanie Hennette-Vauchez for her helpful comments and suggestions on this text, as well as Antoine Duval, Alexander Krüger and Johan Lindholm.

[2] Registrar of the Court, Notification of *Semenya v Switzerland*, ECHR 148 (2021), 17 May 2021. Since the finalisation of this paper, the Semenya case has been decided: the Court found that the athlete was a victim of discrimination since Switzerland did not afford her sufficient procedural safeguards, leading to a violation of articles 13 and 14 (combined with article 8) of the Convention (*Semenya v Switzerland* (2023) App no 10934/21 (ECtHR, 11 July 2023).

[3] International Association of Athletics Federations (IAAF), *Eligibility Regulations for the Female Classification (Athletes with Difference of Sex Development)*, 23 April 2018, followed by the version 2.0 published on 1 May 2019 (hereinafter 'IAAF Eligibility Regulations'). Since the beginning of the procedure, a new version of the Regulation has been published (World Athletics, *Eligibility Regulations for the Female Classification (Athletes with Differences of Sex Development)*, 30 November 2021).

that female athletes with 'Differences of Sex Development'[4] (DSD) (ie intersex[5]), naturally producing levels of testosterone considered as above the normal male range – such as Semenya – should reduce these with medical treatment to be allowed to compete in international events.[6] The goal of this regulation is to ensure a 'fair and meaningful'[7] competition, since World Athletics considers that having too high testosterone levels is a source of abnormal sports performances and compromises equality between female athletes.[8] According to the applicant, the implementation of the regulation violates her fundamental rights, including the right to human dignity, the right to bodily and mental integrity, and the right not to be discriminated on the grounds of sex.[9] The ECtHR will therefore have to rule whether Switzerland[10] correctly interpreted the – private – regulations of World Athletics in light of the European Convention on Human Rights (ECHR). This case emphasises the potential conflicts existing between *lex sportiva* that refers to the set of rules shaping a 'transnational legal order of sport',[11] and the European human rights law principles, in particular regarding gender equality.

This chapter aims to demonstrate that this ongoing case is not only an opportunity for the Strasbourg Court to expand its jurisprudence related to self-determination and gender equality, but also to shape *lex sportiva* as a more inclusive framework. Indeed, I argue that the ECtHR, through its jurisprudence

[4] The Regulation defines DSD as 'congenital conditions that cause atypical development of their chromosomal, gonadal, and/or anatomic sex'; it applies in particular to the following DSDs: '5α-reductase type 2 deficiency; partial androgen insensitivity syndrome (PAIS); 17β-hydroxysteroid dehydrogenase type 3 (17β- HSD3) deficiency; ovotesticular DSD; any other genetic disorder involving disordered gonadal steroidogenesis' (IAAF Eligibility Regulations 2019 (n 3)9, para 2.2(a)(i).

[5] Intersex individuals are persons 'who cannot be classified according to the medical norms of so-called male and female bodies with regard to their chromosomal, gonadal or anatomical sex' (Commissioner for Human Rights, *Human Rights and Intersex People*, Council of Europe, 12 May 2015, CommDH/IssuePaper(2015)). If every individual has sexual variations, some are considered as not feminine or masculine enough and therefore cannot fit into one of the two categories, even though these physical variations are natural, such as having a higher level of testosterone.

[6] Athletes with complete androgen insensitivity syndrome (CAIS) are not affected by the regulation, since they eliminate the physiological effect of testosterone. An athlete with partial androgen insensitivity syndrome (PAIS) will be affected only if she is sufficiently sensitive to this hormone.

[7] IAAF Eligibility Regulations 2019 (n 3) 1.

[8] ibid 2: 'These Regulations exist solely to ensure fair and meaningful competition within the female classification, for the benefit of the broad class of female athletes'.

[9] *Semenya v Switzerland* (2021) App no 10934/21 (ECtHR, communicated case,18 February 2021).

[10] The case is brought against Switzerland since the procedure of appeal of CAS awards (based in Lausanne) is before the Swiss Federal Tribunal.

[11] A Duval, 'What Lex Sportiva Tells You About Transnational Law' (TMC Asser Institute, 2019) 8, https://papers.ssrn.com/abstract=3400656. If the term *lex sportiva* is indeed closely linked to the *lex mercatoria* concept, the notion is however far from being univocal, as some authors are only referring to the jurisprudence of the Court of Arbitration for Sport (CAS) (F Latty, *La Lex Sportiva: Recherche sur Le droit transnational* (Martinus Nijhoff Publishers, 2007) 32); on the complexity of the notion and its different uses, see also J Lindholm, *The Court of Arbitration for Sport and Its Jurisprudence* (Springer, 2019) 8.

developed in areas such as bodily integrity,[12] gender stereotypes,[13] or even non-discrimination,[14] can challenge the regulations of sports governing bodies' (SGBs) such as World Athletics. If we can agree that sport relies mainly upon physical characteristics of the body, it does not necessarily mean that this feature should overrule athletes' rights: the criteria, such as testosterone, used to define sex categories in sport according to binarism are not optimal to ensure sports values of fairness, respect, and non-discrimination,[15] and I believe even violate female athletes' fundamental rights. In this sense, the following developments suggest that the implementation of ECHR principles could oblige *lex sportiva* to converge more closely with human rights, and SGBs to withdraw or at least modify their regulations on the eligibility of athletes in the female category based on testosterone levels. Therefore, the Caster Semenya case becomes 'a question of what sport is willing to accept and what degree of difference we are willing to allow in sport',[16] a particularly key question bearing in mind the recent growing debate related to the participation of trans persons[17] – especially trans women – in sport.[18]

The analysis is structured in two parts: firstly, I start by looking at the roots of the so-called 'DSD Regulations' from a historical perspective, to critically examine how the implementation of this Regulation is in line with the long process of constant control over female athletes' bodies that raises several human rights

[12] *AP, Garçon and Nicot v France* (2017) App nos 79885/12, 52471/13, 52596/1 (ECtHR, 6 April 2017) para 135; *X and Y v Romania* (2021) App nos 2145/16, 20607/16 (ECtHR, 19 January 2021) para 168.

[13] *Konstantin Markin v Russia* (2012) ECHR 2012-III 1 77.

[14] *Vallianatos and others v Greece* (2013) ECHR 2013-VI 1 125, para 77.

[15] The Olympic Charter mentions as part of the fundamental principles of Olympism that 'the practice of sport is a human right' and that 'every individual must have the possibility of practising sport, without discrimination of any kind and in the Olympic spirit, which requires mutual understanding with a spirit of friendship, solidarity and fair play' (International Olympic Committee, 'Olympic Charter', 17 July 2020, 11). World Athletics specifies itself that 'athletics is no longer just about high performance, gold medals and records, but also about "sport for all" and about ensuring that the maximum number of citizens are able to participate in athletics", worldathletics.org/about-iaaf.

[16] S Patel, 'Gaps in the Protection of Athletes Gender Rights in Sport – a Regulatory Riddle' (2021) *The International Sports Law Journal*.

[17] Unlike cisgender individuals, trans persons have a gender identity and/or expression that do not fit with the sex assigned to them at birth.

[18] The controversy has grown as some trans women have started to participate in and win international competitions, such as the New Zealand weightlifter Laurel Hubbard, the first openly trans woman to compete in the Olympic Games in 2021. The policies including trans athletes in female competitions are often contested for being unfair for cisgender female athletes, since the former would have a biological advantage regarding their male physical characteristics (for eg, a group of 38 medical experts recently published a position paper criticising the International Olympic Committee's framework for ignoring scientific and medical aspects related to trans women's performances, see F Pigozzi et al, 'Joint Position Statement of the International Federation of Sports Medicine (FIMS) and European Federation of Sports Medicine Associations (EFSMA) on the IOC Framework on Fairness, Inclusion and Non-Discrimination Based on Gender Identity and Sex Variations' (2022) 8 *BMJ Open Sport & Exercise Medicine* e001273), leading some federations to adopt rules restricting the participation of trans women in female competitions (see n 97).

issues, albeit largely disregarded by SGBs, such as World Athletics (section II). Secondly, by using an analytical approach, I subsequently focus on how the use of the ECHR's principles by the ECtHR in the case of Caster Semenya may (or may not) shape the governance of athletics by infusing more gender equality into *lex sportiva* (section III).

II. THE CONTROL OF FEMALE BODIES IN OLYMPIC SPORTS AND THE DSD REGULATIONS: A CONTINUUM

A. From Physical Characteristics to Testosterone Levels

i. Who are 'Real' Women/Who is a Real Woman? Sex-Testing against Gender Fraud

The establishment of a female-only category in sport has mainly been justified by the need to ensure women's visibility at a professional level and therefore some sort of fairness, since their performance would necessarily be inferior to that of men. If it is indisputable that athletes who were assigned as male at birth in general perform better at the elite level than athletes assigned as female,[19] it is important that it does not conceal the misogynistic motivations behind the creation of the female category by sports authorities and the will to control the bodies and performances of female athletes.[20] Since – at least[21] – the first participation of women at the Olympic Games in 1900, women have had to face gender stereotypes:[22] female athletes were only able to compete in certain events, such as tennis or figure skating, considered to be compatible with their femininity

[19] This assertion is still valid today. For eg, the world record in the 800m male category with a time of 1'40.91 has been held by David Rudisha since 2012; for the same event, in the female category, the world record is held by Jarmila Kratochvílová with a time of 1'53.28 (Caster Semenya's record is 1'54.25 from 2018).

[20] P Liotard, 'From Apartheid to Segregation in Sports. The Transgressive Body of Caster Mokgadi Semenya' in S Montañola and A Olivesi (eds), *Gender Testing in Sport: Ethics, Cases and Controversies* (Routledge, 2016) 19.

[21] It is even possible to go back in time to the ancient Olympic Games in Greece. Women were excluded from the event both as participants and also as spectators, at the risk of 'being thrown from a precipitous mountain'. This exclusion was mainly due to the religious significance of the Ancient Olympics, being held in honour of Heracles, the 'great hero-warrior'. It was believed that the presence of women would have been a threat to the strength of the 'warriors' power'. In order to avoid any transgression, such as the one committed by the woman athlete and trainer Kallipáteira, the judges of the Games (Hellanodicae) decided to pass a decree stating that athletes should compete naked (See J Mouratidis, 'Heracles at Olympia and the Exclusion of Women from the Ancient Olympic Games' (1984) 11 *Journal of Sport History* 41, 50ff).

[22] Their inclusion was not without challenges, particularly from Pierre de Coubertin, former President of the International Olympic Committee (IOC), who was against it. He did not see the point of organising a 'small female Olympiad next to the major male Olympiad', at the risk of being 'impractical, uninteresting, unattractive', in short, 'incorrect' (P de Coubertin, 'Les femmes aux Jeux Olympiques' (1912) 79 *Revue Olympique* 109, 111).

and harmless for their fertility.[23] It was not until 1928 that a female category was introduced in athletics events, and women were soon subjected to rules determining their eligibility to compete as female. The first formal rule of this kind was known as the 'gender verification' test or 'sex testing':[24] the primary justification for its implementation was the need to avoid gender fraud, that is a man who pretends to be a woman in order to win a competition.[25] The first tests conducted based on this rule focused on physical appearance. Thus, during the 1966 European Athletics Championships, all athletes competing in the women's category had to submit to so-called 'nude parades' in front of a panel of doctors.[26] In the same year, female competitors had to undergo gynaecological examinations of their genitals during the British Empire and Commonwealth Games.[27] However, these medical examinations were considered too humiliating, and in 1968 the International Olympic Committee (IOC) decided to use chromosomal tests instead in order to identify the presence of the X chromosome (the 'Barr body test'),[28] and later in 1992, the Y chromosome (PCR amplification of the SRY gene).[29] Even though these tests were less invasive (since they consist of taking a smear of cells from the mouth), they were not more reliable in determining the gender of the athletes.[30] For example, the 'Barr body test' is supposed to reveal the Barr corpuscle, visible only in individuals with two X chromosomes (ie women). However, certain chromosomal variations, such as Klinefelter's syndrome, reveal the existence of an extra X chromosome: a male athlete could therefore have an XXY karyotype and thus obtain a positive result in the Barr body test, and in theory, compete in the female category.[31]

These first attempts to verify the sex of female athletes highlight the difficulties (or even the impossibility) for the sporting and medical authorities to establish a single criterion that would allow individuals to be distinguished into two and only two categories. SGBs, therefore, moved to a different criterion than the appearance of genitals or karyotype and focused instead on hormonal sex, particularly testosterone levels.[32]

[23] Y Ripa, 'Women and the Olympic Games' (*Encyclopédie d'histoire numérique de l'Europe*, 22 June 2020), https://ehne.fr/en/encyclopedia/themes/gender-and-europe/gendered-body/women-and-olympic-games.

[24] JL Rupert, 'Genitals to Genes: The History and Biology of Gender Verification in the Olympics' (2011) 28 *Canadian Bulletin of Medical History* 339, 340.

[25] A Bohuon, 'Sport et bicatégorisation par sexe : test de féminité et ambiguïtés du discours médical' (2008) 27 *Nouvelles Questions Féministes* 80, 81; Rupert (n 24) 340.

[26] A Ljungqvist and JL Simpson, 'Medical Examination for Health of All Athletes Replacing the Need for Gender Verification in International Sports: The International Amateur Athletic Federation Plan' (1992) 267 *Journal of the American Medical Association* 850, 850.

[27] ibid.

[28] Bohuon (n 25) 83; Ljungqvist and Simpson (n 26) 851.

[29] Rupert (n 24) 356.

[30] Bohuon (n 25) 83.

[31] Ljungqvist and Simpson (n 26) 851.

[32] It should be noted, however, that chromosomal tests have not been completely abandoned. For example, the Federation Internationale de Natation (FINA) mentioned in its latest 'policy on eligibility for the men's and women's competition categories' that 'all athletes must certify their chromosomal

ii. Who are the "Normal" Women? The Pathologisation of Hyperandrogenism

SGBs claim to have abandoned femininity testing in favour of regulations to reconcile the physical characteristics – in this case, androgen levels – of athletes with the objective of fairness in sports competitions.[33] However, I would argue that these regulations are part of a broader policy of control over women's bodies, and inevitably lead to a renewal of 'gender verification' tests and that have fuelled the logic of the surveillance of women's bodies since their very first participation in athletics events.

Indeed, World Athletics considers that testosterone is directly linked to advantages in 'size, strength and power',[34] and therefore uses it as a criterion to separate the male category from the female category, the latter being labelled a 'protected class'.[35] Accordingly, the Athletics Federation published Regulations in 2011 (the 'Hyperandrogenism Regulations') requiring females with hyperandrogenism[36] to reduce their testosterone levels through medical treatment if they were above the normal male range (10 nmol/L).[37] These Regulations also mentioned 'indicators' of increased testosterone production that needed to be monitored by the 'Expert Medical Panel': increased muscle mass, male-like hair, clitoromegaly, etc.[38] The first female athlete to challenge this regulation before the Court of Arbitration for Sport (CAS) was Dutee Chand, an Indian sprinter excluded from female competitions for having a too high testosterone level. At that time, the CAS found that the use of testosterone levels was indeed a relevant criterion to separate male from female athletes, but that scientific evidence was insufficient to prove the actual advantage of having a higher level of testosterone than endosex[39] females.[40] The CAS, therefore, suspended the Regulations for

sex with their Member Federation in order to be eligible for FINA competitions' (FINA, 'Policy on Eligibility for the Men's and Women's Competition Categories', 20 June 2022, p 6).

[33] K Karkazis and RM Jordan-Young, 'The Powers of Testosterone: Obscuring Race and Regional Bias in the Regulation of Women Athletes' (2018) 30 *Feminist Formations* 1, 16. For eg, World Athletics wrote in the 2011 Hyperandrogenism Regulations that 'these Regulations replace the IAAF's previous Gender Verification Policy and the IAAF has now abandoned all reference to the terminology "gender verification" and "gender policy" in its Rules' (IAAF, *Regulations Governing Eligibility of Females with Hyperandrogenism to Compete in Women's Competition*, 1 May 2011, para 1.4) (hereinafter 'IAAF Hyperandrogenism Regulations').

[34] IAAF Hyperandrogenism Regulations, ibid', para 1.2.1(b).

[35] Sebastian Coe, the President of World Athletics, recently said that 'gender cannot trump biology'; he made this statement in the context of the controversial performances of transgender swimmer Lia Thomas, the first trans athlete who won a National Collegiate Athletic Association swimming title in the woman category in the United States (R Myers, 'Lord Coe: Future of Women's Sport is "Very Fragile"' *The Times* (21 March 2022), thetimes.co.uk/article/lord-coe-future-of-women-s-sport-is-very-fragile-h79qkhrw3).

[36] Hyperandrogenism refers to a naturally higher production of androgenic hormones.

[37] IAAF Hyperandrogenism Regulations (n 33).

[38] ibid 20 (Appendix 2).

[39] Endosex, as opposed to intersex, refers to a person whose sexual characteristics at birth fit the typical and expected physical norms of female and male bodies.

[40] CAS, *Dutee Chand v Athletics Federation of India (AFI) & International Association of Athletics Federations (IAAF)*, 24 July 2015, 2014/A/3759, para 534.

two years. At the time, the case did not go any further since World Athletics announced new Regulations under which 100m and 200m events – Dutee Chand's favourite events – were no longer affected. World Athletics withdrew the 2011 Hyperandrogenism Regulations and adopted instead a new set of rules in 2018, 'the DSD Regulations'.[41] One of the major changes concerns testosterone levels, since the threshold to be barred from competing in female competitions is no longer set at 10 nmol/L but at 5 nmol/L, that is 'the highest level that a healthy woman with ovaries would have'.[42] Thus, according to World Athletics, this new testosterone level reduced the scope of application of the Regulations only to women with XY chromosomes (since no individuals with XX karyotype can exceed this threshold).[43] The Federation is therefore not only using hormonal sex (ie testosterone levels) to distinguish female from male athletes, but is combining it with chromosomal sex since the DSD Regulations are 'not about biological females' but 'biological males with 5-ARD (and other 46 XY DSDs), how their bodies respond to testosterone, and the performance advantages of that response when they compete against biological females'.[44]

Once again, however, the measurement of testosterone levels does not provide an infallible answer regarding distinguishing between male and female categories. Even if the Regulations claim that they do not question 'the sex or the gender identity of any athlete',[45] the rule follows a similar logic to the one adopted by 'gender verification' tests and shows that the way sex categories are implemented is a result of a long process of control of female athletes' bodies by SGBs.[46] Indeed, while the fight against 'gender fraud' was initially aimed at preventing male athletes from competing among women, it also had the consequence of defining the normal female body. By controlling the testosterone levels of athletes with variations in sexual development, sports authorities seek to limit the 'masculinisation' of female competitions: hyperandrogenism is directly associated with a characteristic that is considered too masculine to allow these athletes to compete in female competitions. Indeed, the application of World Athletics' rules is not systematic: when an athlete seems 'suspicious', either because of her physical appearance or her sporting performance, she may be required to undergo medical tests to continue competing. It was Semenya's 'deep voice and flat chest' that caught the attention of the sporting authorities when she won the 800m race at the World Championships in Berlin.[47] It is therefore

[41] IAAF Eligibility Regulations (n 3).

[42] World Athletics, 'IAAF Publishes Briefing Notes and Q&A on Female Eligibility Regulations' (Press Release), https://worldathletics.org/news/press-release/questions-answers-iaaf-female-eligibility-reg.

[43] CAS, *Mokgadi Caster Semenya, Athletics South Africa and International Association of Athletics Federations*, 30 April 2019, 2018/O/5794 & 2018/O/5798, para 610; SFT, 25 August 2020, 4A_248/2019 & 4A_398/2019, para B.c.c.a.

[44] CAS 2018/O/5794 & CAS 2018/O/5798, para 292.

[45] IAAF Eligibility Regulations 2019 (n 3) para 1.1.5.

[46] Patel (n 16) 29.

[47] L Eckert, *Intersexualization: The Clinic and the Colony* (Routledge/Taylor & Francis Group, 2017) 1.

a question of 'verifying' the sex of an athlete based on a suspicious physical appearance which, in turn, is based on gender stereotypes.

Thus, if sports authorities seem to control only the athlete's performance, they are also, in the end, delimiting what is expected of a female body for it to be allowed to participate in women's competitions, and producing gender norms. Only 'real' women are allowed to compete with other 'truly' female athletes. The DSD Regulations are therefore more a 'rebranding' of gender verification testing than a new way of thinking about sports categories.[48] Despite the unreliability of these tests and the difficulty sports authorities face in capturing the full range of athletes' bodies within a binary classification, SGBs persist in maintaining a dichotomy between male and female categories to pursue the objective of fairness.

B. The DSD Regulations: Fairness before Human Rights

Even before the DSD Regulations came into force, Caster Semenya initiated proceedings before the CAS to challenge them[49] since the Regulations concerned events in which she regularly participated, such as the 800m race. The arbitrators confirmed the validity of the DSD Regulations,[50] and the award was later confirmed on appeal by the SFT.[51] While World Athletics argued that 'the DSD Regulations do not give rise to any improper discrimination',[52] the CAS nuanced this assertion. Applying the World Athletics' Constitution and Rules, the Olympic Charter, and Monegasque law,[53] the Panel found that the DSD Regulations and their implementation might raise difficulties concerning their compliance with the fundamental rights of athletes. According to the CAS, the DSD Regulations are prima facie discriminatory both on grounds of legal sex (since they only apply to athletes who are not legal males) and innate biological characteristics (since they only apply to athletes who do not have a 46 XX karyotype and/or have DSD).[54] The CAS also expressed 'grave concerns' concerning the ability of athletes to maintain their testosterone levels below the 5 nmol/L thresholds.[55]

[48] Karkazis and Jordan-Young (n 33) 15.

[49] The request for arbitration with the CAS was made on 18 June 2018 against the IAAF, while the DSD Regulations came into force on 1 November 2018.

[50] CAS, *Mokgadi Caster Semenya & Athletics South Africa v IAAF*, 30 April 2019, 2018/O/5794 & 5798.

[51] SFT, 25 August 2020, no4A_248/2019. Since the CAS is officially seated in Lausanne, decisions might be appealed only to the Swiss Federal Court.

[52] CAS 2018/O/5794 *Mokgadi Caster Semenya v IAAF* and CAS 2018/O/5798 *Athletics South Africa v IAAF*, 30 April 2018, para 294.

[53] ibid para 424.

[54] ibid para 547.

[55] ibid para 620.

These concerns about the compatibility of the DSD Regulations with human rights – including the right to freedom from torture and other cruel, inhuman, or degrading treatment or punishment, the right to respect for the dignity, bodily integrity, and bodily autonomy of the person, or the right to sexual and reproductive health – have been shared by several human rights bodies.[56] For example, in his report, the Special Rapporteur on the right of everyone to the enjoyment of the highest attainable standard of physical and mental health, recommended sporting organisations to 'implement policies in accordance with human rights norms and refrain from introducing policies that force, coerce or otherwise pressure women athletes into undergoing unnecessary, irreversible and harmful medical procedures in order to participate as women in competitive sport'.[57] In a letter to World Athletics' President, Sebastian Coe, three Rapporteurs from UN bodies expressed their concerns and asked World Athletics to withdraw the DSD Regulations.[58] More recently, the Human Rights Council expressed the same concerns by adopting a resolution on the 'Elimination of discrimination against women and girls in sport',[59] which was followed by the publication of a Human Rights Watch report denouncing the human rights violation faced by women athletes because of the 'sex testing' policies.[60]

However, despite these numerous statements from human rights bodies, sports institutions as well as the SFT have always found that fairness must be given greater weight than the protection of human rights, and that the DSD Regulations are hence compatible with those principles. The CAS estimates that the DSD Regulations are necessary to ensure fairness and protect female athletes against the 'significant performance advantage' that female athletes with a higher testosterone level have.[61] The Panel, therefore, concluded that using hormone levels as a criterion to separate athletes into the men and women categories was legitimate to ensure fair competition. Indeed, since it is 'human biology, not legal status or gender identity, that ultimately determines which individuals possess the physical traits which give rise to that insuperable advantage', it is then necessary to refer to biological characteristics such as testosterone levels to define which athletes have a physical advantage.[62]

[56] Human Rights Council, *Report of the United Nations High Commissioner for Human Rights*, 15 June 2020, A/HRC/44/26 and examples below.

[57] Human Rights Council, *Report of the Special Rapporteur on the Right of Everyone to the Enjoyment of the Highest Attainable Standard of Physical and Mental Health*, 4 April 2016, A/HRC/32/33, para 57.

[58] UN Letter to Mr. Coe, 18 September 2018, OL OTH 62/2018, ohchr.org/Documents/Issues/Health/Letter_IAAF_Sept2018.pdf.

[59] Human Rights Council, *Elimination of Discrimination Against Women and Girls in Sport*, 4 April 2019, A/HRC/RES/40/5.

[60] Human Rights Watch, '"They're Chasing Us Away from Sport" Human Rights Violations in Sex Testing of Elite Women Athletes' (2020), hrw.org/sites/default/files/media_2020/12/lgbt_athletes1120_web.pdf.

[61] CAS 2018/O/5794 & CAS 2018/O/5798, para 580.

[62] ibid para 558.

According to the CAS, the performance advantage of athletes with a 46 XY DSD condition is so great that it is necessary to lower their testosterone level 'to maintain fair competition in female athletics'.[63] The DSD Regulations are reasonable for the same reasons that they are necessary: ensuring fair competition for female athletes by giving an equal chance to endosex women to successfully compete in sporting competitions.[64] Finally, according to the Panel, the scientific evidence at the time did not establish that the intake of oral contraceptives to lower testosterone had significant negative side effects: the DSD Regulations were therefore proportionate.[65] The Panel noted that the same side effects are 'experienced by the many thousands, if not millions, of other XX women, who take oral contraceptives'.[66]

These conclusions have been endorsed by the SFT, which delivered its final judgment in August 2020.[67] Under a narrow jurisdiction and based on the factual findings of the contested award,[68] the Tribunal found that the sovereign appreciation made by the CAS concerning the DSD Regulations was compatible with the principles of Swiss public policy. In fact, the examination by the Tribunal is limited to the award's compatibility with public order,[69] ie the fundamental values that are the basis of every legal order.[70] The Swiss Court adopts a very restrictive interpretation of Swiss public policy: for the award to be set aside it must be manifestly 'untenable', 'seriously disregard' legal principles, or 'shockingly offend the sense of justice and equity'.[71] The SFT also specifies that violations of the ECHR cannot be directly invoked to challenge the CAS award, but only to interpret the notion of public policy.[72] In the present case, the SFT rejected Caster Semenya's appeal and concluded that the award was not contrary to public policy as the decision did not violate the prohibition of discrimination, her personality rights or human dignity. Instead, the Swiss judges recognised the 'insurmountable advantage' of having a high level of testosterone,[73] and the need to ensure fairness in sport despite the violation of intersex athletes' bodily integrity by imposing these testosterone regulations.[74] Both the CAS and the SFT recognised that the DSD Regulations are prima facie discriminatory but also that female athletes with a higher level of testosterone competing in the female category would be a threat to fairness. This discrimination was therefore

[63] ibid para 580.
[64] ibid para 583.
[65] ibid para 599.
[66] ibid para 598.
[67] SFT, 25 August 2020, 4A_248/2019 & 4A_398/2019.
[68] ibid para 5.2.2.
[69] ibid para 5.2.1; an appeal against a CAS award can be brought before the SFT only for a limited number of grounds: lack of jurisdiction, breach of procedural rules, and public policy.
[70] ibid para 9.1.
[71] ibid.
[72] ibid para 9.2.
[73] ibid para B.c.e.
[74] ibid para 10.2.

deemed necessary, reasonable, and proportionate since the testosterone level is presented as the main factor for sex differences in athletic performance.

This scientific assessment and the way to balance it with human rights principles, such as the right to bodily integrity or the protection from discrimination, is therefore at the very heart of the reasoning. I argue, however, that neither the sports authorities nor the CAS or the SFT handled this balancing in a way that permits the protection of athletes' fundamental rights, and that the uncertainties related to the correlation between high testosterone levels and strong sports performances should rather strengthen consideration for human rights arguments.

Indeed, since their first implementation, regulations related to female athletes with a DSD are mainly focused on the scientific reasoning establishing a high level of testosterone as a threat to fair female competitions, leaving little room for the protection of athletes' fundamental rights.[75] The focus on scientific evidence has, for example, positioned the CAS panels' 'decisions as "objective", taken within the realm of science and outside of human rights politics'.[76] According to World Athletics, the DSD Regulations 'are based on a strong scientific, legal and ethical foundation'.[77] This statement is, however, far from accurate: from the Dutee Chand case to the challenge made by Caster Semenya, the arbitral and legal procedures have demonstrated that this scientific argument, at the heart of the SGB's reasoning, is contested. Thus, when the athlete Dutee Chand challenged the 2011 rules in force at that time,[78] the CAS first suspended the Regulations, considering that the Federation did not provide sufficient evidence to show that athletes with hyperandrogenism had a significant advantage compared to other female athletes.[79] Two years later, World Athletics provided two new scientific studies in order to demonstrate further the correlation between testosterone levels and athlete's performances.[80] Even if they were not examined by the CAS (since the Federation later announced the adoption of a new regulation that did not exclude Dutee Chand from competition anymore[81]), this new scientific evidence was already criticised at the time by some authors.[82] It is interesting to

[75] Patel (n 16).

[76] L Holzer, 'What Does It Mean to Be a Woman in Sports? An Analysis of the Jurisprudence of the Court of Arbitration for Sport' (2020) 20 *Human Rights Law Review*, 394.

[77] CAS 2018/O/5794 & CAS 2018/O/5798, para 286.

[78] See text at section II.A.ii.

[79] *Chand v AFI & IAAF* (n 40) para 548.

[80] E Eklund, B Berglund, F Labrie et al, 'Serum Androgen Profile and Physical Performance in Women Olympic Athletes' (2017) 51 *British Journal of Sports Medicine* 1301; S Bermon and PYves Garnier, 'Serum Androgen Levels and their Relation to Performance in Track and Field: Mass Spectrometry Results from 2127 Observations in Male and Female Elite Athletes' (2017) 51 *British Journal of Sports Medicine* 1309.

[81] The new regulation did not apply to 100m and 200m events, see IAFF Eligibility Regulations 2018 (n 3).

[82] See, eg, P Sönksen et al, 'Hyperandrogenism Controversy in Elite Women's Sport: An Examination and Critique of Recent Evidence' (2018) 52 *British Journal of Sports Medicine*.

note that a lack of consensus also exists concerning the similar IOC regulation related to trans female athletes' eligibility, which also uses testosterone levels as a threshold.[83] The World Medical Association expressed severe doubts concerning the 2018 DSD Regulations just before the CAS released its Semenya decision. The Association asked for 'the immediate withdrawal of the regulations' since they are 'contrary to international medical ethics and human rights standards'.[84] Some medical professionals also criticised the Regulations, 'for being based on ethical and scientific flaws'.[85] While the CAS pointed out the 'scientific complexity' of the case[86] and some difficulties regarding the 'scientificity' of the Regulations,[87] the Panel mainly based its award upon scientific evidence and the expert testimonies provided at the hearing. It concludes that the study made by Stéphane Bermon and Pierre-Yves Garnier in 2017 (ie the contested study provided during the Chand case) was admissible.[88] The scientific evidence underlying the paper is, however, doubtful, leading the British Journal of Sports Medicine to publish a 'correction' to the original paper from 2017.[89] Stephane Bermon and Pierre-Yves Garnier, both employees of World Athletics, admitted that 'there is no confirmatory evidence for causality' between high-level testosterone and improved athletic performance in women,[90] and 'recognise that statements in the paper could have been misleading by implying a causal inference'.[91] In a previous article published in 2018, they already admitted that the analysis made in their first study was exploratory and not confirmatory.[92]

Given this lack of consensus concerning testosterone, the DSD Regulations are 'motivated by a misguided sense of fairness',[93] a notion that should rely

[83] Patel (n 16).

[84] The World Medical Association, 'WMA Urges Physicians not to Implement IAAF Rules on Classifying Women Athletes' (25 April 2019), wma.net/news-post/wma-urges-physicians-not-to-implement-iaaf-rules-on-classifying-women-athletes/.

[85] Holzer (n 76) 411.

[86] CAS 2018/O/5794 & CAS 2018/O/5798, para 582.

[87] ibid: see, eg, 'the Panel does have concerns as to the maximum level of 5 nmol/L and the practical ability of female athletes with 46 XY DSD to ensure that their levels of testosterone do not exceed that level' (para 617); 'The evidence of actual (in contrast to theoretical) significant athletic advantage by a sufficient number of 46 XY DSD athletes in the 1500m and 1 mile events could be described as sparse' (para 623).

[88] Bermon and Garnier (n 80), mentioned in CAS 2018/O/5794 & CAS 2018/O/5798, at para 516.

[89] S Bermon and PY Garnier, 'Correction: Serum Androgen Levels and their Relation to Performance in Track and Field: Mass Spectrometry Results from 2127 Observations in Male and Female Elite Athletes' (2021) 55(17) *British Journal of Sports Medicine* e7.

[90] As an example, Caster Semenya's performances in the 800m events do not seem unattainable for other athletes. Thus, during the last 2020 Olympic Games in Tokyo, the American athlete Athing Mu won the gold medal with a time of 1'55.21, while Caster Semenya won the same race in 2016 with a time of 1'55.28.

[91] Bermon and Garnier (n 89).

[92] S Bermon, AL Hirschberg, et al, 'Serum Androgen Levels are Positively Correlated with Athletic Performance and Competition Results in Elite Female Athletes' (2018) 52(23) *British Journal of Sports Medicine*.

[93] P Sonksen et al, 'Medical and Ethical Concerns Regarding Women With Hyperandrogenism and Elite Sport' (2015) 100 *The Journal of Clinical Endocrinology & Metabolism* 825, 825.

more on non-discrimination and reflect the right to participate for all 'regardless of economic, social, religious, racial/ethnic, and linguistic background or sexual orientation'.[94] This understanding of fairness might be adopted by the ECtHR, using ECHR principles to place human rights at the heart of this notion, and more broadly, at the centre of *lex sportiva*.

III. MOVING TOWARDS THE RESPECT OF INTERSEX ATHLETES' FUNDAMENTAL RIGHTS? APPLYING ECHR PRINCIPLES TO THE DSD REGULATIONS

A. *Lex Sportiva* and the ECHR

Lex sportiva is mainly the product of SGBs, ie private entities not directly subjected to European human rights law in the same way as states.[95] According to the 'vertical effect', since only the latter can become party to the ECHR, they should be the only ones legally bound by the Treaty. This situation places 'non-state actors such as sport bodies outside of the legal regime and creates a gap in the protection of athletes' rights'.[96] Indeed, following this mechanism, SGBs' decisions are not supposed to be bound by ECHR principles, including recent jurisprudential developments related to the right to bodily integrity[97] or non-discrimination.[98] However, the ECHR is not fully alien to *lex sportiva*.[99] The CAS itself progressively recognised the indirect applicability of the Convention,[100] and through the concept of the 'indirect horizontal effect' of the European judge, indirect obligations might be imposed on non-state actors such as SGBs.[101]

This indirect application can lead to tensions when it comes to confronting ECHR principles with regulations made by private sports entities. The difference in reasoning and interests between the two systems (*lex sportiva* and the ECHR) is particularly visible when it comes to the sex of

[94] ibid 826.

[95] As World Athletics has pointed out before, the CAS is 'a private body, not a state body. It is therefore not subject to human rights instruments such as the UNDHR or the ECHR' (CAS 2018/O/5794 & CAS 2018/O/5798, para 293).

[96] Patel (n 16).

[97] *AP, Garçon and Nicot v France* (n 12).

[98] *Vallianatos and others v Greece* (n 14).

[99] Thus, the EctHR has already had to deal with cases concerning a CAS Award. See, eg, *Platini v Switzerland* (2020) App no 526/18 (EctHR, 2020); *Mutu and Pechstein v Switzerland* (2018) App nos 40575/10, 67474/10 (EctHR, 2 October 2018).

[100] A Duval, 'Lost in Translation? The European Convention on Human Rights at the Court of Arbitration for Sport' (2022) 22 *The International Sports Law Journal* 132, 134.

[101] A Di Marco, 'Human Rights in the Olympic Movement: The Application of International and European Standards to the Lex Sportiva' (2022) 40 *Netherlands Quarterly of Human Rights* 244, 255. As underlined by Antoine Duval, this applicability of the ECHR to SGBs is quite justified regarding their functioning 'equivalent to public authorities' (Duval (n 100) 134).

individuals. While the body – or material dimension of sex[102] – is becoming less relevant in the human rights law jurisprudence (gender identity, and therefore legal sex, does not have to match with genitals anymore for example[103]), sports authorities continue to focus their attention on physical characteristics in order to separate females from males in competitions, which makes sport one of the few activities 'where sex segregation is accepted, required and controlled'.[104] Thus, while the IOC updated its guidelines which now provide that transgender athletes do not have to undergo hormonal treatment – and reduce their testosterone levels – to compete,[105] most of the SGBs maintain regulations related to the eligibility of trans athletes involving their hormone levels. Indeed, since the IOC's framework is not legally binding on other SGBs, each sports federation can enact its own rules on the matter. For example, the International Swimming Federation (FINA) recently published a policy that allows trans athletes to compete in the female category if they have not experienced any part of male puberty beyond a certain stage or before the age of 12, and maintained their testosterone levels below 2.5 nmol/L.[106] For its part, World Athletics allows transgender male athletes to participate in the male category without any restrictions,[107] while transgender female athletes are still subject to hormonal treatment and must maintain their testosterone levels below a certain limit (5 nmol/L) to compete in the female category.[108] This difference in treatment is justified by the need to 'guarantee fairness and safety within the sport':[109] by decreasing their testosterone levels from the male range to the female range,[110] transgender female athletes are reducing their physical abilities and therefore their performances to not 'discourage' other athletes from this category.[111]

The same tensions are visible when athletes do not fit – according to SGBs – within the two sex categories. The legal sex assigned at birth and recognised by

[102] J Butler, *Bodies that Matter: On the Discursive Limits of 'Sex'* (Routledge, 1993).

[103] *AP, Garçon and Nicot v France* (n 12).

[104] Patel (n 16).

[105] International Olympic Committee, *IOC Framework on Fairness, Inclusion and Non-Discrimination on the Basis of Gender Identity and Sex Variations*, 16 November 2021.

[106] FINA Policy (n 32) para F.4.

[107] A transgender male athlete only has to 'provide a written and signed declaration, in a form satisfactory to the Medical Manager, that his gender identity is male' (World Athletics, *Eligibility Regulations For Transgender Athletes*, 1 October 2019, para 3.1).

[108] However, the Regulations mention that the easiest way to decrease testosterone levels for a transgender female athlete is 'with gonad-removing surgery (an orchidectomy, which may or may not be part of genital reconstruction surgery, ie, vaginoplasty), followed by oestrogen replacement therapy' (ibid para 1.13).

[109] Ibid para 1.2.2(b).

[110] ibid para 1.13: according to the Federation, the normal range of testosterone levels in a male is 7.7 to 29.4 nmol/L, while in a female it is 0.06 to 1.68 nmol/L.

[111] ibid para 1.2.1(a).

the legal order is superseded by *lex sportiva's* own 'sport sex':[112] while athletes with DSD who are assigned as female by the state at birth (and are therefore administratively members of the female category), SGBs are invoking their physical characteristics to prevent them from competing in the category fitting their legal status. There is subsequently a gap between, on the one hand, the will of the ECtHR to consider sex/gender identity as part of the right to private life, and therefore exempt from any state authority prerogatives and, on the other, the attention paid to the material dimension of sex by SGBs due to the importance of the body in this field.[113]

The reasoning of SGBs (and the CAS) might, however, be challenged by the ECtHR since Caster Semenya contested the SFT decision before the Strasbourg Court,[114] which could lead to the 'humanrightisation' of the situation of athletes with DSD. What can we expect from the ECtHR? Will it agree on the need to limit testosterone levels to ensure fairness in sports competitions? If not, will the International Federation have to reconsider the 'binary sex paradigm'?[115] How can female athletes' rights and non-discrimination law be balanced with sports interests?

B. How May the ECHR Apply *Lex Sportiva* to Intersex Athletes?

In May 2021, the ECtHR communicated the application of Caster Semenya to the Swiss Government and published its questions to the parties.[116] The applicant argued that there had been a violation, inter alia, of Articles 3 and 8 of the Convention, separately and combined with Article 14.[117] The following developments thus offer an analytical approach for the ECHR to consider whether the implementation of the DSD Regulations, and more broadly, regulations of SGBs related to intersex athletes, might be in conflict with human rights principles.[118] Therefore, ruling in favour of Caster Semenya could involve many changes regarding the apprehension of SGBs of gender equality. It could oblige SGBs to reconsider their regulations related to athletes with DSD and make them apply sports standards to and promote values – such as fairness and inclusiveness – for all athletes recognised as women, regardless of their physical characteristics.

[112] According to World Athletics, 'the right to participate in the female class cannot simply depend on whether an athlete is recognised in national law as female' (ibid para 458).

[113] The CAS found, for eg, that 'there are some contexts where biology has to trump identity' (CAS 2018/O/5794 & CAS 2018/O/5798, para 289).

[114] *Semenya v Switzerland* (n 9).

[115] C Lee, 'The Binary World of Sports' (2017) VII *The National Law Review*.

[116] Registrar of the Court, Notification of *Semenya v Switzerland* (n 2).

[117] Articles 6 (right to a fair trial) and 13 (right to an effective remedy) will not be discussed here, since they concern procedural aspects.

[118] As mentioned above, World Athletics is not the only sports federation that has adopted a regulation on intersex athletes. See, eg, FINA Policy (n 32).

i. Prohibition of Torture and the Right to Respect for Private Life

The Court will first have to decide whether medical examinations and treatments, including the obligation to take oral contraceptives to lower natural testosterone levels, lead to a violation of the human dignity, physical and mental integrity, and social and gender identity of the applicant under Article 3 (prohibition of torture and inhuman or degrading treatment or punishment) and Article 8 (right to respect for private life) of the Convention. Although the claims examined by the judges to state a potential breach of the ECHR are the same under Articles 3 and 8, the logic applied is slightly different between the two articles: while the former is non-derogable and requires a high threshold of seriousness to lead to a violation, the latter is subject to derogations including if the disposal is in accordance with the law or necessary in a democratic society.

Regardless of whether it concerns Article 3 or 8, the Court will have to decide if the allegations of violations amount to interference with the applicant's rights, 'or to a failure by Switzerland to comply with its positive obligations to protect the applicant against treatment contrary to these provisions by private entities (in particular the "IAAF")'.[119] Positive obligations relate to the duty of state parties to take measures to ensure that individuals are not subjected to a violation of their rights, including when the infringement is a result of actions of private parties. For example, in the *Platini* case, the Court decided that since the measure did not emerge from the State but a private law association, it could only examine whether the State had complied with its positive obligation (and not whether there had been an interference with the right).[120] The Court also reminds state parties that positive obligations 'may require the adoption of measures to respect the private life even in relationships between individuals'.[121]

Concerning the first claim, the violation of Article 3, the Court does not specify a list of criteria used to define the high threshold of seriousness needed to lead to a violation of the Convention. However, through the analysis of case law related to the prohibition of torture, it can be noted that the judges usually focus on the duration of the treatment, its effects, or the age and sex of the victim.[122] The Court also clarifies that the threshold required to qualify a particular treatment as torture or inhuman treatment is evolving. Some acts that were not considered as such are becoming so in the light of the current case law, due to the increasing standard of protection of human rights.[123] Further, those treatments might also impact mental integrity and are not limited to physical abuse.[124]

[119] *Semenya v Switzerland* (n 9).
[120] *Platini v Switzerland* (n 99) para 59.
[121] ibid para 60.
[122] See, eg, *VC v Slovaquie* (2011) ECHR 2011-V 1 381, para 100; *Jalloh v Allemagne* (2006) ECHT 2006-IX 1 281, para 67.
[123] *Selmouni v France* (1999) ECHR 1999-V 1 149, para 101.
[124] *Muršić v Croatia* (2016) App no 7334/13 (EctHR, 20 October 2016) para 97.

Arguably, the whole implementation process of the DSD Regulations entails a violation of the human dignity, physical and mental integrity of athletes. Regarding physical integrity, athletes are threatened at two levels: during the examination phase designed to reveal their hyperandrogenism, and when medical treatments are imposed to reduce their testosterone levels. Indeed, in addition to blood samples to measure the level of testosterone in the blood, the current Regulations provide the possibility of a full medical examination including, for example, a psychological evaluation or a gynaecological examination.[125] The DSD Regulations prescribe hormonal treatment (such as oral contraceptives) to reduce testosterone levels. In this regard, the SFT recognised that the imposed use of hormonal treatment 'seriously infringes' the athletes' right to physical integrity, is not medically necessary, and is imposed without the free and informed consent of the athletes.[126] These unnecessary medical interventions may furthermore harm the athletes' right to sexual and reproductive health, by affecting 'hormones and reproductive anatomy and capacity'.[127] Moreover, they also have side effects,[128] impacting the athlete's performance (Caster Semenya has, for example, lost almost two seconds off her time in the 800m after starting hormonal treatment[129]) and mental health. Female athletes with DSD are targeted for their physical appearance or behaviour and thus stigmatised as 'suspicious' women even before being subject to the Regulations.[130] The implementation of the DSD Regulations had stigmatising and humiliating consequences for Caster Semenya: her intersex variations have been revealed to the general public, and her identity as a woman has been denied multiple times. She claims, for example, that the testosterone-suppressing medication had 'an enormous effect on her mental state' and undermined 'her self-confidence'. She further explained in front of the CAS that it was 'deeply hurtful' not to be considered as a woman by World Athletics,[131] and the arbitrators recognised that a medical examination to determine the extent of her 'virilisation' can be 'highly intrusive' and 'result in psychological harm'.[132]

[125] IAAF Eligibility Regulations 2019 (n 3) 17.

[126] SFT, 25 August 2020, no4A_248/2019, para 10.2.

[127] *Report of the Special Rapporteur on Torture and other Cruel, Inhuman or Degrading Treatment or Punishment*, *Juan E Méndez*, 1 February 2013, A/HRC/22/53, para 34 (d).

[128] Karkazis and Jordan-Young (n 33) 30; NA Xavier and JB McGill, 'Hyperandrogenism and Intersex Controversies in Women's Olympics' (2012) 97(11) *The Journal of Clinical Endocrinology & Metabolism* 3906.

[129] When Caster Semenya won the 800m event at the World Championships in Berlin on 19 August 2009, her time was 1 min 55s 45. She then began hormone treatment in accordance with World Athletics' Regulations; her times in the same event in 2011 (World Athletics Championships in Daegu) and 2012 (London Olympics) were 1 min 56s 35 and 1 min 57s 23 respectively. After stopping her hormone treatment, she won the 800m at the 2016 Rio Summer Olympics with a time of 1 min 55s 28.

[130] See text at section II.A.ii.

[131] CAS, 2018/O/5794 & CAS 2018/O/5798, para 78 et seq.

[132] ibid para 600.

On the assumption that these allegations do not reach the intensity level required by Article 3, it is, however, relevant to show that the DSD Regulations may lead to even more severe treatments that could be prohibited under the Convention. Indeed, the Regulations not only lead to the imposition of a hormonal treatment such as through the ingestion of oral contraceptive pills, but may also lead athletes to undergo surgery such as gonadectomy.[133] The 2019 Regulations states, 'for the avoidance of doubt', that surgery is not required under any circumstances to enable hyperandrogenic athletes to compete in the relevant competitions.[134] However, where hormonal treatments are not sufficient to maintain testosterone levels below the maximum threshold, and surgery (such as gonadectomy) is presented by the medical profession as the most effective means of achieving this objective, it cannot be ruled out.[135] In such circumstances, the athlete's free and informed consent may be called into question if this type of surgery is the only alternative offered allowing them to participate in competitions. For example, a 2013 study shows that four young elite female athletes were informed by the medical team that 'gonadectomy would most likely decrease their performance level but allow them to continue elite sport in the female category'.[136] They, therefore, agreed to undergo surgery (ie partial clitoridectomy, bilateral gonadectomy, feminising vaginoplasty, oestrogen replacement therapy) even though no health risks were diagnosed, and were allowed to compete in the female category by World Athletics[137] – who offered to pay for the procedures – the following year.[138] Therefore, given that the eligibility of these athletes to compete in the female category was dependent upon their consent to the removal of gonads and the additional feminising procedures, 'the line between consent and coercion is blurred in this instance'.[139] The testimony of the Ugandan athlete Annet Negesa is also relevant in the context of this assessment. In 2012, after her high blood level of testosterone was discovered, World Athletics sent her to a specialised fertility centre. She underwent an orchiectomy (the removal of her internal testicles) without having given prior consent to the operation, of which she was not informed.[140] The situation of Annet Negesa is not an isolated case, several testimonies have been published in a 2020 report by Human Rights Watch.[141] Just as the Special Rapporteur on

[133] R Jordan-Young, P Sonksen and K Karkazis, 'Sex, Health, and Athletes' (2018) 348 *British Medical Journal* g2926.

[134] ibid para 2.4.

[135] '"They're Chasing Us Away from Sport"' (n 60) 74.

[136] P Fénichel et al, 'Molecular Diagnosis of 5α-Reductase Deficiency in 4 Elite Young Female Athletes Through Hormonal Screening for Hyperandrogenism' (2013) 98 *The Journal of Clinical Endocrinology & Metabolism* E1057.

[137] ibid.

[138] Sonksen et al (n 93) 826.

[139] ibid.

[140] She was told by the medical team that she would only undergo 'a simple surgery – like an injection', see '"They're Chasing Us Away from Sport"' (n 60) 2.

[141] ibid.

torture and other cruel, inhuman, or degrading treatment or punishment did in 2013,[142] the European judge might condemn the recourse to involuntary medical treatments or surgeries on intersex persons promoted by World Athletics in its DSD Regulations.

The judge will consider the same allegations to determine whether there is a violation of Article 8 of the Convention. First, the Court will decide whether the applicant's claim falls within the scope of Article 8 (in the present case, the right to respect for private life), of which there should be little doubt. The concept has been indeed defined broadly, and includes 'not only a person's physical and psychological integrity, but can sometimes also embrace aspects of an individual's physical and social identity'.[143] In particular, it covers personal identity,[144] forced medical treatment,[145] and the right to self-determination.[146] Thereafter the Court will examine whether there has been an interference with this right or whether the State's positive obligations to protect the right have been engaged.[147] The European judge recognises that the States enjoy a certain margin of appreciation in this regard. However, in the Semenya case, this margin may be restricted since the case concerns 'a particularly important facet of an individual's existence or identity'.[148] In addition, this margin of appreciation might be restricted if the Court found European consensus within state parties. Even though only a few of them have adopted laws to prohibit – at least theoretically – medical treatment to 'normalise' intersex persons' bodies,[149] the way the European consensus is used by the ECtHR varies, and the judges 'might choose not to wait for the majority of the States of the Council of Europe to develop a shared approach to the issue at hand' – such as they did in the LGBT's rights area.[150] Finally, since Switzerland is the only state with the prerogative to review CAS awards and is therefore 'speaking for a worldwide community',[151] its margin of appreciation is expected to be narrow.

[142] Report of the Special Rapporteur (n 127).
[143] *AP, Garçon and Nicot v France* (n 12) para 92.
[144] *Vavřička and others v the Czech Republic* (2021) App no 47621/13 (EctHR, 8 April 2021) para 261.
[145] *Acmanne and others v Belgium* (1984) App no 10435/83 (Commission decision, 10 December 1984) 255.
[146] *Pretty v the United Kingdom* (2002) App no 2346/02 (EctHR, 29 April 2002) para 61.
[147] See above n 9.
[148] *Dickson v the United Kingdom* (2007) ECHR 2007-V 1 99, para 78.
[149] Including Malta (Gender Identity, Gender Expression & Sex Characteristics Act, 14 April 2015, Chapter 540), Portugal (*Direito à autodeterminação da identidade de género e expressão de género e à proteção das características sexuais de cada pessoa*, Lei no38/2018, Artigo 5), and Greece (Medically Assisted Reproduction Reforms Act, 19 July 2022, Articles 17 to 20).
[150] A Margaria, 'Trans Men Giving Birth and Reflections on Fatherhood' (2020) *International Journal of Law, Policy and The Family* 225, 243.
[151] M Krech, '"Sport Sex" before the European Court of Human Rights' (*Völkerrechtsblog*, 22 March 2021) voelkerrechtsblog.org/sport-sex-before-the-european-court-of-human-rights; in this regard, Antoine Duval points out that SFT decisions 'are defining the life of every athlete worldwide and have a clear transnational dimension and effect' (Duval (n 100) 149).

The Court will eventually have to decide whether the alleged violation is 'in accordance with the law' and 'necessary in a democratic society'.[152] However, since the DSD Regulations are not based on national law, Switzerland will have to defend a regulation adopted by a private entity based in Monaco.[153] Among the objectives that make the interference 'in a democratic society' legitimate, we can find 'public safety' or 'the protection of the rights and freedoms of others'. Can the DSD Regulations be justified on the basis of one of these objectives? Are the Regulations, and therefore the medical examinations and treatments imposed, really needed to ensure the right of other female athletes to participate in fair competitions? Besides the lack of evidence demonstrating the 'insurmountable advantage' of female athletes with a DSD over their competitors,[154] I argue that it is difficult to find a fair balance between the general interest and the applicant's interests.

Indeed, it is possible to stress here, as the SFT did, that if examinations are never imposed on athletes, the taking of hormonal contraceptives is nevertheless 'not based on completely free and informed consent'.[155] The athletes are therefore facing an 'impossible choice'[156] between, on the one hand, stopping their sporting activities and, on the other, being submitted to the medical examinations and treatments imposed by World Athletics.[157] An analogy can be made here with the *Mutu and Pechstein* case:[158] since the applicant had to choose 'between accepting the arbitration clause and thus earning her living by practising her sport professionally, or not accepting it and being obliged to refrain completely from earning a living from her sport at that level', the judges decided that her acceptance of CAS jurisdiction was not free and unequivocal.[159] To reach such a conclusion, the ECtHR might also draw on its jurisprudence related to trans persons' rights, recognising that asking for proof of sex reassignment surgery (sterilisation) to modify their civil status is violating their right to respect their physical integrity under Article 8 of the ECHR.[160] The Court decided that making the recognition of trans persons' gender identity conditional on sterilisation surgery or medical treatment placed them before 'an impossible

[152] According to the second paragraph of Article 8, 'there shall be no interference by a public authority with the exercise of this right except such as is in accordance with the law and is necessary in a democratic society in the interests of national security, public safety or the economic wellbeing of the country, for the prevention of disorder or crime, for the protection of health or morals, or for the protection of the rights and freedoms of others'.

[153] Krech (n 151).

[154] Sonksen et al (n 93).

[155] SFT, 25 August 2020, no4A_248/2019, para 10.2.

[156] K Karkazis and M Carpenter, 'Impossible "Choices": The Inherent Harms of Regulating Women's Testosterone in Sport' (2018) 15 *Journal of Bioethical Inquiry* 579.

[157] The Regulation specifies that an athlete 'must cooperate fully and in good faith' even to a 'medical physical examination' at the risk of being 'declared ineligible to compete in the female classification' (IAAF Eligibility Regulations 2019 (n 3) para 3.5).

[158] *Mutu and Pechstein v Switzerland* App nos 40575/10 and 67474/10 (EctHR, 2 October 2018).

[159] ibid para 113 and 114.

[160] *AP, Garçon and Nicot v France* (n 12) para 135; *X and Y v Romania* (n 12) para 168.

dilemma'.[161] In that case, a trans person had to choose between undergoing sterilisation surgery or treatment and being able to change their gender markers in civil-status documents or fully exercise their right to bodily integrity by refusing the surgery but waiving recognition of their gender identity. Female athletes with higher testosterone levels face the same dilemma:[162] to compete in the category that corresponds to their assigned gender identity, they must undergo the medical treatment imposed by the Federation. Therefore, even if the Court might find that the interests of other female athletes must be protected (ie participation in fair and equal competitions), the implementation of the DSD Regulations is disproportionately restricting Caster Semenya's fundamental rights, including her right to bodily integrity.

Once again, we could also argue that the ruling has deep consequences on the self-confidence of athletes and the perception of their identity, and therefore, on their right to respect for private life. Athletes can face social stigma and psychological repercussions for having their sex characteristics revealed to their surroundings or media.[163] Apart from Caster Semenya's case, we can in this context mention the situation of María José Martínez-Patiño, a Spanish athlete banned from athletics competitions in 1986 for having an XY karyotype according to the sex test in place at that time (a buccal smear test). Her experience shows very precisely how sex testing – from the original assessment of genitals to the DSD Regulations – can have serious consequences on athletes' personal lives. Years later, she explained that when her story leaked to the press, she 'felt ashamed and embarrassed' and 'lost [her] friends, fiancé, hope and energy'.[164] Sex testing can therefore be extremely damaging for female athletes, both for their own personal identity and the pursuit of their professional careers.

ii. Prohibition of Discrimination

Finally, the potential violation of Article 14 will be examined in conjunction with Article 3 and/or Article 8 of the Convention. The Court will have to decide

[161] *AP, Garçon and Nicot v France* (n 12) para 132.

[162] It can be noted that some SGBs have already adapted their regulations related to trans athletes to tackle this 'human rights issue' (as the former IOC Medical Commission Chairman Arne Ljungqvist said, see 'IOC Rules Transgender Athletes Can Take Part in Olympics Without Ssurgery' *The Guardian* (25 January 2016), www.theguardian.com/sport/2016/jan/25/ioc-rules-transgender-athletes-can-take-part-in-olympics-without-surgery). In 2015, the IOC decided, for eg, that to compete in a category other than the one related to their sex assigned at birth, trans athletes do not have to undergo sex reassignment surgery anymore. The 2003 'Stockholm Consensus on Sex Reassignment in Sports' published by the IOC required surgical anatomical changes 'including external genitalia changes and gonadectomy', but the IOC policy has been later updated in 2015, considering that 'to require surgical anatomical changes as a pre-condition to participation is not necessary to preserve fair competition and may be inconsistent with developing legislation and notions of human rights' (IOC Consensus Meeting on Sex Reassignment and Hyperandrogenism, November 2015, para E).

[163] '"They're Chasing Us Away from Sport"' (n 60) 9.

[164] MJ Martínez-Patiño, 'Personal Account: A Woman Tried and Tested' (2005) 366 *The Lancet* S38.

whether the DSD Regulations discriminate against the applicant as a 'woman with a naturally high level of testosterone'. This allegation of discrimination is particularly relevant, considering that 'sport is the field par excellence in which discrimination against intersex people has been made most visible'.[165] While the SFT found that the principle of non-discrimination, in the context of its interpretation of Swiss public policy, only applies to the relationship between private persons and the State to protect the former from illegitimate interventions from public authorities ('vertical effect'),[166] the jurisprudence of the ECtHR concerning the prohibition of discrimination is much wider. In particular, the principle does have a 'horizontal effect' and also applies in purely private situations.[167]

In the present case, the judge will first explore on which criteria the unequal treatment was based. The ground of sex will be relevant since the DSD Regulations only apply to female athletes with certain sex characteristics (in his report, the Commissioner for Human Rights argued that 'the ground of sex/gender should be authoritatively interpreted to include sex characteristics as prohibited grounds of discrimination'),[168] and the Court will look at sex characteristics in the specific context of competitive sport for the first time.[169] Thereafter, the judge will analyse whether the applicant has been treated differently than another group of persons placed in a relevantly similar situation, that is other athletes without a DSD competing in either female or male categories. Indeed, only female athletes with a DSD are directly affected by the Regulations, and no regulation of this type has ever existed for male athletes with a higher level of testosterone than the normal range. The Strasbourg Court might also use other grounds such as the athletes' health status since it already decided that a distinction made on this account should be covered by the term 'other status' in the text of Article 14 of the Convention.[170] This ground could refer to either testosterone levels or the karyotype of the athlete.

Finally, the Court will decide whether the differences in treatment lack objective and reasonable justification. The judge will explore whether the differences are based on public interest and strike a fair balance between the protection of the interests of the community and respect for the rights and freedoms safeguarded by the Convention.[171] The Court will therefore apply a proportionality test to decide whether the difference in treatment can be justified. Is there a legitimate aim for the difference in treatment? Is this difference *stricto sensu* proportionate? It is quite clear that the DSD Regulations aim to ensure fairness in athletics competitions; if this objective seems legitimate,

[165] Commissioner for Human Rights Issue Paper (n 5) 44.
[166] SFT, 25 August 2020, 4A_248/2019 & 4A_398/2019, para 9.4.
[167] *Pla and Puncernau v Andorra* (2004) ECHR 2004-VIII 179, para 59.
[168] Commissioner for Human Rights Issue Paper (n 5) 9.
[169] Krech (n 151).
[170] *Kiyutin v Russia* (2011) ECHR 2011-II 29, para 57.
[171] *Zarb Adami v Malta* (2006) ECHR 2006-VIII 1 305, para 73.

it requires a reasonable relationship of proportionality between the means employed and the aim sought to be realised.[172] Once again, the margin of appreciation of the State should be reduced, not to mention that according to the Court's jurisprudence, differences in treatment on the ground of sex may be justified only by very weighty reasons.[173] Did the applicant suffer from discrimination based on gender stereotypes? As Caster Semenya has argued, the implementation of the DSD Regulations allows women to compete in the female category only if they have physical characteristics that fit the traditional understanding of a woman's body.[174] The applicant faced gender stereotypes both on her appearance and performance: she was considered 'too masculine' for a female athlete, as well as 'too strong' regarding her naturally higher testosterone levels, a hormone usually associated with male characteristics. This focus on testosterone reinforces the idea of a perfect biological dichotomy between the sexes: men produce testosterone, and women produce oestrogen. Hyperandrogenism is therefore a concept applied only to women. Having too much testosterone for a woman is a pathology, while the level of this hormone in men will never be questioned.

Both the CAS and the SFT found that discriminatory treatment was necessary to maintain sex categories and ensure fairness. However, why use testosterone levels while a lot of innate characteristics might seem unfair as well? Why choose testosterone as a significant marker of superiority and as an advantage, while many other genetic variations[175] and criteria have an impact on athletes' performances, and are sometimes even celebrated?[176] How is having hyperandrogenism different from other (natural) physical or even social advantages that do not require a specific regulation? For example, a study comparing the performances of British athletes and Indian athletes showed that the latter spend about one-third less time on Olympic Games preparation.[177] Another example of a natural physical condition that induces an advantage concerns Eero Mäntyranta, a Finnish cross-country skier who has a rare genetic mutation of the EPOR gene, leading to an augmented production of red blood cells, and therefore an increased oxygen transport capacity.[178] Those situations have been seen as a threat to fairness by the International Ski Federation (FIS), which regulated the maximum level of haemoglobin concentration in the blood of athletes

[172] See, eg, *Molla Sali v Greece* (2018) App no 20452/14 (ECtHR, 19 December 2018) para 135.

[173] See, eg, *Konstantin Markin v Russia* (n 13) para 127.

[174] SFT, 25 August 2020, no4A_248/2019, para 11.1.

[175] S Camporesi, 'A Question of "Fairness": Why Ethics Should Factor in the Court of Arbitration for Sport's Decision on the IAAF Hyperandrogenism Regulations' (2019) 53 *British Journal of Sports Medicine* 797.

[176] Sonksen et al (n 93) 825.

[177] Holzer (n 76) 402.

[178] S Camporesi and M Hämäläinen, 'A Local Criterion of Fairness in Sport: Comparing the Property Advantages of Caster Semenya and Eero Mäntyranta with Implications for the Construction of Categories in Sport' (2021) 35 *Bioethics* 262, 264.

in 1997.[179] However, the FIS has not used a universal limit for all skiers since 2013. Instead, the Federation uses a personal limit: if an athlete has a haemoglobin level that differs greatly from the historical values, that athlete might be banned from a competition.[180]

It is possible to argue that discriminatory treatments based on testosterone are not simply made to ensure fairness, but to avoid 'that certain women transgress gender norms by producing testosterone through so-called "male" reproductive organs'.[181] And even if there is a significant gap between the performances of athletes competing in the female category compared to the male category in most athletics events (and sports in general),[182] it does not mean that sex categorisation is the ultimate answer to achieving fairness. Thus, it is possible to hypothesise that this distinction is maintaining the gap between female and male athletes (but also less opportunity, fewer women in sports, state programmes, etc[183]), if not *creating* the gap itself.[184]

IV. CONCLUSION: DE-GENDERING SPORTS CATEGORIES?

Confronting the DSD Regulations with the ECHR principles, I have demonstrated that the European judge has the opportunity to at least protect female athletes' fundamental rights, regardless of their physical characteristics: even if the ECtHR ends up finding that sex categories are necessary to ensure fairness, it is expected that the judge will at least conclude that the DSD Regulation and the use of testosterone levels are not proportionate considering the harm caused to the athletes concerned. The DSD Regulations cannot stay in place without violating the right to bodily integrity and non-discrimination from female athletes subject to them. It surely questions the relevance of sex categories in sports and the absurdity of the actual system. While World Athletics claims that its Regulations do not challenge athletes' sex or gender identity, the Federation considers that female athletes with a DSD are 'biologically male athletes'.[185] Therefore, despite having been assigned as female by the legal system when they were born, athletes with DSD are not allowed to compete in the female category because of their physical characteristics. There is,

[179] The German skier Evi Sachenbacher-Stehle was inter alia banned from the 2006 Turin Winter Olympics for having a too-high haemoglobin level in her blood (ibid 266).

[180] Camporesi and Hämäläinen (n 178) 266.

[181] Holzer (n 76) 403.

[182] Caster Semenya would not be able to qualify for male competitions even if she won a gold medal in female competitions.

[183] V Thibault et al, 'Women and Men in Sport Performance: The Gender Gap Has Not Evolved since 1983' (2010) 9 *Journal of sports science & medicine* 214.

[184] LA Wackwitz, 'Verifying the Myth: Olympic Sex Testing and the Category "Woman"' (2003) 26 *Women's Studies International Forum* 553.

[185] CAS, 2018/O/5794 & CAS 2018/O/5798, para 462.

moreover, a need to reconsider sports sex categories, since some legal systems now recognise non-binary gender options.[186]

Caster Semenya's case is not only of importance for *lex sportiva*. Indeed, like sports law, European human rights law relies on a strict division of individuals between men and women, using sex categories within a binary system. The situation of intersex athletes thus reveals the inconsistencies of both legal and sports authorities in maintaining sex binary categories. While it might upend World Athletics' rules, it could also lead the Strasbourg judges to further expand their jurisprudence related to gender equality, non-discrimination, or gender stereotypes outside the traditional scope of sexual binarism. The Caster Semenya case could also be an opportunity for the ECtHR to infuse more intersectionality in its reasoning. Indeed, even if the Court does not mention it in the questions communicated to the parties, it would be relevant to raise discrimination on the ground of race to highlight the 'western gaze'[187] of the case. It is possible to argue that the Regulations create an equality gap between women from Western countries and racialised women, since the vast majority of the athletes who have been tested since the 2000s and are publicly known are from non-European countries.[188] The World Athletics' rules produce a difference in treatment between white and racialised women, since they rely on norms and representations based on Western criteria. The alleged unfair advantage of hyperandrogenic athletes also reflects a racist bias that black bodies are stronger, more resilient, and athletic.[189] Indeed, while the criteria used (testosterone levels but also physical virilisation indices) are presented as objective data, standards of femininity vary according to location and time. For example, you could cite the measurement of hair density, formerly used by anthropologists as a method for determining race.[190] These elements are also reminiscent of the historical stigmatisation of black bodies (especially genitalia). In this regard, the United Nations High Commissioner for Human Rights published a report that highlights the 'intersection of race and gender discrimination in sport'.[191] Lastly, according to Doctor Stéphane Bermon, working for World Athletics, women from non-European countries would be less likely to have undergone sex confirming surgery at birth,[192] medical practices that have been denounced

[186] Eg, Malta (Gender Identity, Gender Expression & Sex Characteristics Act, Chapter 540, 14 April 2015), Iceland (Act on Gender Autonomy No 80 /2019, 18 June 2019), Argentina (Decreto 476/2021, 20 July 2021).

[187] Holzer (n 76) 401.

[188] Eg, Maximilla Imali, Linda Kageha, Evangeline Makena (Kenya), Beatrice Masilingi, Christine Mboma (Namibia), Annet Negesa (Ouganda), Francine Niyonsaba (Burundi), Caster Semenya (South Africa), Aminatou Seyni (Federal Republic of Nigeria), Margaret Nyairera Wambui, Jackline Wambui (Kenya).

[189] Karkazis and Jordan-Young (n 33) 22.

[190] ibid 26.

[191] Human Rights Council Report (n 56).

[192] Karkazis and Jordan-Young (n 33) 22.

by human rights bodies. Therefore, these women with variations of sex development have an unfair advantage since they have not been 'treated' at birth, unlike most intersex persons in Western countries.[193] The medical treatment imposed by SGBs in order to allegedly preserve their health can thus be likened to 'violent colonial interventions' to save 'women from their own [...] communities'.[194]

The situation of athletes with intersex variations clearly shows that the distinction of individuals within a binary system – in sports but also in the legal order – must be reconsidered and challenged. The 'reductionist definition of female sex' that results from this binarism leads to the exclusion of all women that do not fit into the typical female athlete profile drawn up by sports rules,[195] producing a far-removed effect from the stated aim of inclusiveness. A decision in favour of Caster Semenya from the ECtHR would not only be a success for intersex athletes, but it might also send a strong message of protection for every human's body. The desire to reduce the complexity and variety of human bodies into a binary framework leads to violence and discrimination, hence the ECtHR's decision is 'not just about the right to participate in sport' but also 'about the right to be human'.[196]

[193] ibid.

[194] ibid 27.

[195] Holzer (n 76) 410.

[196] In the words of Caster Semenya before the CAS, see.CAS 2018/O/5794 & CAS 2018/O/5798, para 82.

Part III

Engaging Critically with a Eurocentric *Lex Sportiva*

12

Lex Sportiva *and New Materialism: Towards Investigations into Sports Law's Dark Materials?*

ALEXANDER KRÜGER[1]

I. A CUT WITH THE SUBTLE KNIFE: A PATHWAY BETWEEN TRANSNATIONAL SPORTS LAW SCHOLARSHIP AND NEW MATERIALISM

THIS CHAPTER EXPLORES a previously unexplored path between transnational sports law scholarship and new materialism. The aim is to contribute to the uncovering of the material processes of the production of the transnational private legal regime governing global sports (*lex sportiva*). The aim is pursued here by reading the preceding contributions in this volume and their common theoretical framework against the backdrop of a new materialist theory.[2] Starting with the chapters and their theoretical framework and extending them by pointing to inherent ties to the kinetic-material conditions, I argue that (the) *lex sportiva* can be viewed as a posthuman legal regime produced not only by human but also nonhuman agencies. I seek to demonstrate that new materialist theories can generate new questions, a rethinking of transnational sports law and serve as a means for an immanent critique of *lex*

[1] Doctoral student, Umeå University. Email: alexander.kruger@umu.se. I would like to thank the co-editors Antoine Duval and Johan Lindholm for their generous and useful comments and the authors for their contributions.

[2] CN Gamble, JS Hanan and T Nail, 'What Is New Materialism?' (2019) 24 *Angelaki* 111, 24; J Käll, 'The Potential for New Materialist Justice via Nordic Feminist Perspectives of Law' (2021) 3 *Nordic Journal on Law and Society*; E Jones, *Feminist Theory and International Law: Posthuman Perspectives* (Routledge, 2023) 11 and 21; T Nail, *Marx in Motion: Reading Marx as Our Contemporary* (Oxford University Press, 2020). My use of the term 'new materialism' is broad and encompasses various posthuman approaches. From section III, the focus is on a performative new materialism which does not sideline global inequalities but rather recognises the importance of Marx (together with Lucretius and Woolf) as important intellectual precursors. 'Marx was the first to herald a "new materialism" that gave historical-ontological primacy to the stochastic motion of matter opposed to its discrete interpretation in Democritus, Newton, and others' (Nail, ibid).'

sportiva with potentially transformative emancipatory effects.[3] I hope to convey the contours of a materialist, posthuman approach to transnational sports law scholarship which has the potential of challenging binaries and exclusionary humanism (for example, class, race and gender), the western thought focus on the white male subject, and anthropocentric hierarchies (human and nonhuman or environment).[4] My conclusion is that new materialism can be put into a productive conversation with transnational sports law scholarship.[5]

The chapter is structured as follows: Section I outlines key aspects of new materialism and its relationship to legal scholarship.[6] Section II explores opening up the impure perspective of *lex sportiva* to new materialism. Section III introduces a performative new materialism and contains a reading of the chapters in this volume, deploying an analytical framework of *flow, fold* and *field of circulation*. I argue that, by exploring legal entanglement, the contributions have a function of transparency similar to that of Robinson Island. The chapters serve as 'islands' where it is possible, because of their focus on bringing the legal entanglement into light, to see the kinetic-material processes of the production of *lex sportiva*.[7] Section IV puts forward the notion of *posthuman sports law* as a critical new materialist research agenda for sports law scholarship.

Contemporary international sport governance finds itself *in media res*. Climate and ecological emergencies, gender and wealth inequalities, the COVID-19 pandemic highlight that there is no outside, only an inside. '[W]hile the crises disproportionately affect the working class, the dispossessed, and the racially marginalized, they have become opportunities for the transnational capitalist class to profit and consolidate their wealth and control.'[8] In a world of turbulence and increasingly visible human-nonhuman entanglement, what has been taken for granted no longer remains natural

[3] Nail (n 2) 51; M Davies, *Law Unlimited* (Routledge, 2017) 16–19 and 129–43.

[4] Nail (n 2) 51; Davies (n 3) 16–19.

[5] The conversation implies a move from restricted jurisprudence towards general legal theory. Davies (n 3) 20–40; C Douzinas and A Gearey, *Critical Jurisprudence: The Political Philosophy of Justice* (Hart Publishing, 2005) 3–43; J Käll, *Converging Human and Digital Bodies. Posthumanism, Property, Law* (PhD Thesis, Gothenburg University, 2017) 40–41, 51–55.

[6] Käll (n 5); G Stenseke Arup, 'Entangled Law: A Study of the Entanglement of Wolves, Humans, and Law in the Landscape' (PhD Thesis, Karlstads universitet, 2021); Jones (n 2) 21. I concur with the warnings against conflating new materialisms.

[7] Robinson Crusoe, on his island, was able to see '[…] the close entanglement of weather patterns, geological events, crop cycles, mineral compositions, his own life process, and much else – all as aspects of the same form of motion'. Nail (n 2) 185.

[8] C Chen, 'Naming the Ghost of Capitalism in Sport Management' (2022) 22 *European Sport Management Quarterly* 663; A Philippopoulos-Mihalopoulos, *Spatial Justice: Body, Lawscape, Atmosphere* (Routledge, 2015) 1; T Nail, *Being and Motion* (Oxford University Press, 2019) 67–76; J Hohmann, 'Diffuse Subjects and Dispersed Power: New Materialist Insights and Cautionary Lessons for International Law' (2021) 34 *Leiden Journal of International Law* 585.

or unchangeable. The current era necessitates collaborative action departing from colonialist, anthropocentric, patriarchal, and capitalist ways.[9] Legal scholars as well as scholars in sports sciences have suggested that it is time to turn to new materialism and posthumanism.[10] Sports law scholarship should be no exception in this regard.[11] What then is new materialism? Gamble et al clarify that new materialism – an important trend in humanities and social sciences – lacks a single definition.[12] Instead, new materialism has been considered as an umbrella term encompassing various theoretical endeavours and also as a sub-genre of posthumanism.[13] Today, it is a flourishing, dynamic, and criticised field.[14] In short, new materialism 'signals a cross-disciplinary challenge to longstanding assumptions about humans and the non- or other-than-human material world'.[15] It has a common theoretical commitment to '*problematize* the anthropocentric and constructivist orientations of most twentieth-century theory in way that encourages closer attention to the sciences by the humanities'. The motivation for the latter is the neglect or diminishment 'of matter in dominant Euro-Western tradition as a passive substance intrinsically devoid of meaning'.[16] New materialism could be conceived as a methodology:

> for the non-dualistic study of the world within, beside and among us, the world that precedes, includes and exceeds us. The effects of putting one's scholarly trust in dualisms such as matter–meaning, body–mind and nature–culture are reductivizing [...]. Neo-materialist researchers want to know how dualisms emerge [...]. [H]ow conclusions are drawn.[17]

[9] Stenseke Arup (n 6) 16–19; Chen (n 8); T Nail, *What's the Matter with Life? Life in the Posthuman Condition'* (Edinburgh University Press, 2023); Nail (n 8) 72.

[10] H Thorpe, J Brice and M Clark, *Feminist New Materialisms, Sport and Fitness: A Lively Entanglement* (Springer International Publishing, 2020) 2; See, eg, J Käll, *Posthuman Property and Law: Commodification and Control through Information, Smart Spaces and Artificial Intelligence* (Routledge, 2022); Jones (n 2); Hohmann (n 8).

[11] Chen (n 8) 665. See also Duval in chapter two of this volume for a call for critical enquiries.

[12] Gamble, Hanan and Nail (n 2) 111.

[13] Stenseke Arup (n 6) 116–31 and n 459; see Käll (n 5) for the relationship between new materialisms and posthumanism. Jones (n 2) 15.

[14] An exhaustive account of new, or renewed, materialism, a genealogy, even typology exceeds this work. See T Lemke, *The Government of Things: Foucault and the New Materialism's* (NYU Press, 2021) 2; Gamble, Hanan and Nail (n 2); R Dolphijn and I van der Tuin, 'Pushing Dualism to an Extreme: On the Philosophical Impetus of a New Materialism' (2011) 44 Continental Philosophy Review 383; Stenseke Arup (n 6) 116–31; R Dolphijn and I van der Tuin, *New Materialism: Interviews & Cartographies* (Open Humanities Press, 2012); D Coole and S Frost, *Introducing the New Materialisms* (Duke University Press, 2010.

[15] Gamble, Hanan and Nail (n 2) 1–17.

[16] ibid; Nail (n 2) 1–17.

[17] I van der Tuin, 'Neo/New Materialism' in R Braidotti and M Hlavajova (eds), *Posthuman Glossary* (Bloomsbury Academic, 2018) 277–79.

We live in a world of continuous motion of indeterminate relational processes characterised by entangled matter, but what does that have to do with law?[18] Nail writes:

> Without a doubt, contemporary reality is shaped by multiple human structures, but these structures are in turn conditioned by other real, nonanthropic material structures that precede and constitute them. The two then work on each other in turn, *really co-constituting each other*.[19]

Law, especially beyond the state, is no exception in this sense. Just as international law is inherently tied to the material conditions of the world,[20] so is my understanding of transnational sports law, a structure constructed by humans *existentially conditioned* on and *causally determined* by *historically preceding* material relations. While transnational sports law is *produced* by material relations, it also *produces* material structures.[21] Fast forwarding,[22] perspectives grounded in materialisms arrived with the new materialist/posthuman turn – a reaction to the cultural or linguistic turns – in legal scholarship at the very latest around the mid-2010s. New materialism is now considered a 'fairly well-established field'.[23] In the wake of the arrival of new materialist and posthuman ideas, the legal dimension has been reconceptualised in different ways, such as entangled law, ecolaw, lawscape, bodies, post-humanitarian law, and posthumanist jurisprudence.[24] Jones recently mapped out four approaches in posthuman legal theory: work that focuses on agency and vibrancy of matter; law and space connections; nonhuman subjects in law; and objects and law; covering a wide array of subjects.[25] The take-up of new materialist/posthuman ideas in scholarship devoted to international law is scarce, consisting of a few general interventions and some involvement in specific fields.[26] While legal theorists have explored the new materialist and posthumanist theories through the

[18] Nail (n 8); T Nail, *Theory of the Object* (Edinburgh University Press, 2021) 220–36; Gamble, Hanan and Nail (n 2).

[19] Nail (n 8) 19.

[20] Jones (n 2) 44.

[21] Nail (n 8); T Nail, 'What Is the Philosophy of Movement?' (2022) *Mobility Humanities*; Jones (n 2) 9; Davies (n 3) 44.

[22] Davies (n 3) 41–55. While research grouped together under the terms 'anti-formalist' or 'counter narratives' 'situate normative worlds in material social practices [...]'they do not always build on a theorised materialism. Socio-legal, feminist, Marxist, and critical legal scholars see law as at least in part embedded in material social life. Through the 'postmodern' period oriented towards the ideational and conceptual instead of the physical and material but not intrinsically antitethical materialism; Dolphijn and Tuin, *New Materialism: Interviews & Cartographies* (n 14) 19–37.

[23] Jones (n 2) 16; Käll (n 2); See R Braidotti, E Jones and G Klumbytė (eds), *More Posthuman Glossary* (Bloomsbury Academic, 2023).

[24] Stenseke Arup (n 6); M Davies, 'Ecolaw' in Braidotti, Jones and Klumbytė (n 23); Philippopoulos-Mihalopoulos (n 8); Käll (n 5); M Arvidsson, 'Post-Humanitarian Law' in Braidotti, Jones and Klumbytė (n 23); For more examples see Braidotti, Jones and Klumbytė (n 23).

[25] Jones (n 2) 16–20.

[26] Such as laws of armed conflict, international environmental law, and human rights law. ibid 21–24; See also Käll (n 2).

critical and socio-legal 'entry point' and others[27] have aligned their version of posthuman(-itarian) law with transnational law, sports law has not been the focus of new materialist or posthuman legal scholars. Scholars interested in the intersection between sports law and new materialist thought thus find themselves facing unexplored territory.

II. THE OPEN-ENDED *LEX SPORTIVA*

This section discusses how the common theoretical framework for *lex sportiva* explored in this volume can be opened up to new materialist theory. Through the discussion I seek to contribute to a critical project of the twenty first century of 'bending law towards a less abstract and more materially integrated understanding of the world'.[28] The contributions in this volume draw on and add to the development of an 'impure'[29] concept of (the) *lex sportiva* and have moved beyond 'Sports and the Law' theory with its roots in state positivism.[30] Instead, (the) *lex sportiva* is understood as 'a complex transnational legal regime enmeshing private Sport Governing Bodies [...] and their rules governing specific competitions [...], specific sports [...], or specific sporting issues [...] with a variety of public institutions and their laws'.[31] Duval, drawing on the idea of transnational law and transnational legal pluralism, has developed this concept and advocated for a 'methodological, pluralist and process-oriented perspective' to

> capture the intricacy of *lex sportiva* whereas a purist lens [which emphasises the autonomy of the private regime] would hide (or at least understate) its embeddedness in an ensemble of public rules and institutions at the national, European and International level [...].

Focus is on the '[...] plurality and relativity of transnational authorities, norms and processes that collaborate to *make* law'.[32] Understanding (the) *lex sportiva* as a complex and entangled transnational *legal* regime of sports means

[27] Arvidsson (n 24).

[28] M Davies, 'Re-Forming Property to Address Eco-Social Fragmentation and Rift' in A Grear and others (eds), *Posthuman Legalities* (Edward Elgar Publishing. 2021) 14.; See P Zumbansen, 'Transnational Law as Socio-Legal Theory and Critique: Prospects for "Law and Society" in a Divided World' (2019) 67 *Buffalo Law Review* 909, 957.

[29] A Duval, 'What Lex Sportiva Tells You about Transnational Law' in P Zumbansen (ed), *The Many Lives of Transnational Law: Critical Engagements with Jessup's Bold Proposal*, 1st edn (Cambridge University Press, 2020).

[30] F Latty, 'Transnational Sports Law' in RCR Siekmann and J Soek (eds), *Lex Sportiva: What is Sports Law?* (TMC Asser Press; Springer 2012).

[31] A Duval, *Transnational Sports Law: The Living Lex Sportiva* (Social Science Research Network, 2020).

[32] Duval (n 29); See also Zumbansen (n 28); P Zumbansen, 'Transnational Legal Pluralism' (2010) 1 *Transnational Legal Theory* 141.

departing from two main uses and concepts.[33] The impure approach emphasises, in contrast to the other views, the regime's entangled conditions in practice.

While scholarship devoted to the impure *lex sportiva*, this volume included, challenges some of the organising dualisms of jurisprudence (such as private/public, state/non-state or society, and law/non-law) engaging with connections rather than separations, other binaries have up until now largely been left untouched. Such is the case with, for example, the division between culture and nature, subject and object, and mind and matter.[34] In what follows, I argue, however, that the impure *lex sportiva* is 'open-ended'[35] and further explorations into this open-endedness can serve to challenge any remaining exclusionary humanist and anthropocentric hierarchies. I provide three intertwined reasons to support the image of the impure *lex sportiva* as open-ended. First, the concept's purpose is to shift focus from questions of 'autonomy' to the complexity and entanglement of current sports law practice to gain an enhanced understanding of transnational sports law, in which normative direction remains largely open.[36] This normative openness extends to new materialist and posthuman ethical approaches. Second, juxtaposing the impure *lex sportiva* with other concepts *could* invoke an exclusionary hierarchy, implying an exclusion of inquiries based on other conceptions. However, Duval explicitly stated that this is not the purpose.[37] The intention was rather, as I read it, to open up for scholarly inquiries into (the) *lex sportiva* based on various theoretical foundations. The third reason for referring to the concept as open-ended is that it and its uses (see section III) do not only leave open the question of where but also *what* to navigate, and thus, I argue, pave the way for a (new) materialist understanding of (the) *lex sportiva*.[38]

Sally Falk Moore's work from 1973 is illuminating in this sense. In *Semi-Autonomous Social Field as an Appropriate Subject of Study* she uses the dress industry in New York as an example to study how semi-autonomous social fields, similar to sports, work. The emphasis is on showing how the 'operation of the social field, is to a significant extent self-regulating, self-enforcing, and self-propelling within a certain legal, political, economic, and social environment'.[39]

[33] J Lindholm, *The Court of Arbitration for Sport and Its Jurisprudence: An Empirical Inquiry into Lex Sportiva* (Asser Press, Springer 2019); Duval (n 29); K Foster, 'Global Sports Law Revisited' (2019) 17 *The Entertainment and Sports Law Journal*.

[34] Davies (n 24) 90. It is easy to agree with Davies who states that: 'What is missing from twentieth-century accounts of legal co-creation within human society is an account of the co-becomings of human and nonhuman normativities.'

[35] By 'open-ended' I mean that the use (see section III), and the concept as such, have porous boundaries which invite us to explore *lex sportiva* from new materialist perspectives.

[36] See however: Duval (n 31) 21–22; A Duval, 'Taking Feminism beyond the State: FIFA as a Transnational Battleground for Feminist Legal Critique' (2022) 20 *International Journal of Constitutional Law* 277.

[37] Duval (n 29).

[38] See Nail (n 8) 129–44.

[39] S Falk Moore, 'Law and Social Change: The Semi-Autonomous Social Field as an Appropriate Subject of Study' (1973) 7 *Law & Society Review* 719.

However, it also shows that these fields are not only 'social' but material.[40] Stenseke Arup comments: 'The infrastructure of the city, the technologies available for producing dresses, the alcohol in the whiskey used as bribes, all co-produced the dress-making community itself. Her social fields were always already ecological, acknowledging materialities beyond the social.' To Stenseke Arup (even) legal pluralists have focused too much on the 'social' and the 'legal', and thus there is a need to account for other materialities in legal studies. He thus suggests a reconceptualisation of the semi-autonomous social fields as *entangled bodies co-producing law in the landscape* (emphasis added).[41] My suggestion is that insights from work done to fuse legal pluralism with new materialism in this vein can enrich our understanding of impure *lex sportiva.*

Duval has elaborated an understanding of the impure *lex sportiva* as a complex assemblage,[42] which returns in this volume. Drawing on Saskia Sassen's concept of assemblage, it is argued that *lex sportiva* should be understood as a transnational glocal assemblage of a plurality of legal components.[43] While scholars develop their own understanding of the assemblage, they remain indebted to its creators; Sassen's assemblages are influenced by the theoretical constructs of Deleuze and Guattari.[44] Deleuze's and Guattari's concept and theory of assemblage are in turn precursors to new materialism/posthumanism which emerged from poststructuralist theories.[45] The impure *lex sportiva* is thus bound together with new materialisms/posthumanism through a genealogical relationship going back to Deleuze and Guattari's work on assemblage. Drawing on Deleuze and Guattari's understanding of the assemblage *the concept* of impure *lex sportiva* could be understood as 'concrete assemblages, like the configurations of a machine [...]' *in itself.*[46] The impure *lex sportiva* is not a discrete unity 'cut off from influences and agencies of the material world' but is rather to be understood as a multiplicity, as a set of relations.[47] Along these lines the concept of *lex sportiva* consists of a range of relations. As an assemblage, the impure *lex sportiva* lacks essence. In this context, this means that neither *the concept nor the legal regime* is complete or closed off with eternally defined

[40] Stenseke Arup (n 6) 180–84.

[41] ibid 133–36 and 159–90.

[42] See nn 80 and 81; Duval (n 31); Duval (n 29).

[43] Antoine Duval, in chapters one and two of this volume. Sassen's concept helps to trancend the national/global and the public/private binary. S Sassen, 'Neither Global nor National: Novel Assemblages of Territory, Authority and Rights' (2008) 1 *Ethics & Global Politics* 61.

[44] See Antoine Duval, in chapter two of this volume.

[45] T Nail, 'Kinopolitics: Borders in Motion' in R Braidotti and S Bignall (eds), *Posthuman Ecologies: Complexity and Process after Deleuze* (Rowman & Littlefield International, 2019) 188; Dolphijn and Tuin, *New Materialism: Interviews & Cartographies* (n 14); see also T Nail, 'What Is an Assemblage?' (2017) 46 *SubStance* 21.

[46] G Deleuze and F Guattari, *What Is Philosophy?* (Columbia University Press, 1994) 20.

[47] Nail (n 45) 186; The concept of a bird '[...] is found not in its genus or species but in the composition of its postures, colors, and songs [...] A concept is a heterogenesis–that is to say, an ordering of its components by zones of neighborhood' Deleuze and Guattari (n 46) 36.

features. Rather, *lex sportiva* is dependent on and shaped by a vast network of material, social, and historical processes. Consequently, there is no definitive *lex sportiva* but only an ongoing process of becoming, a collection of contingent features. The *lex sportiva* assemblage of norms, actors and processes, would be comprised of human but also nonhuman assemblages mixing and affecting each other driven by a collective agency of matter.[48]

In this vein, Sullivan relies on *transnational legal assemblage* which he uses to analyse the UN 1267 Al-Qaida sanctions regime. To him: 'Plurality and contingency of power, material and institutional heterogeneity, distributed, emergent agency and spatio-temporal complexity are all important features of the assemblage analytic.' It is because of this that the assemblage offers new ways of understanding how law is 'constituted, negotiated and contested' in the context of transnational legal ordering.[49] '[M]aterialist ontology, distribution of agency and spatio-temporal complexity' makes it difficult to swallow for a legal theorist but provides an analytical advantage in the transnational legal challenging legal formalism and the way (inter)national norms are produced.[50]

The impure *lex sportiva* shifts focus from autonomy, 'conditional autonomy'[51] or 'autonomies'[52] of sports in relation to states, the EU or other normative orders to entanglement and co-production brings a higher degree of complexity to the fore.[53] Duval warns against romanticising autonomous *lex sportiva* detached from states and their laws and urges us to consider its legal entanglement.[54] Considering *lex sportiva's* materialities beyond textual aspects such as state law or sporting rules, challenges dualisms where categories making up the binary are opposed, such as mind and matter or body, nature and culture.[55] This reductive 'classificatory negation' obscures the affirmative relationship between categories, towards essentialism, and establishes hierarchies that devalue what is different.[56] By traversing inside/outside distinctions, tracing the flows of matter through the folds and fields of (the) *lex sportiva*, I suggest that new materialist insights complement the impure approach and is the pathway to non-reductionistic

[48] Nail (n 45) 185–88.

[49] G Sullivan, 'Transnational Legal Assemblages and Global Security Law: Topologies and Temporalities of the List' (2014) 5 *Transnational Legal Theory* 81, 84–95. The transnational legal assemblage is distinguished from the concept of transnational legal ordering and transnational legal pluralism precisely through the analytical focus on materiality and heterogeneity.

[50] ibid; See Zumbansen (n 28) 935–57.

[51] S Weatherill, 'Saving Football from Itself: Why and How to Re-Make EU Sports Law' (2022) *Cambridge Yearbook of European Legal Studies* 1, 8; S Weatherill, *Principles and Practice in EU Sports Law* (Oxford University Press, 2017).

[52] See HE Meier and B García, 'Beyond Sports Autonomy: A Case for Collaborative Sport Governance Approaches' (2021) 13 *International Journal of Sport Policy and Politics* 501 for a critical review of the concept of autonomy.

[53] Stenseke Arup (n 6) 159–90.

[54] Duval (n 31).

[55] Käll (n 2) 6–8.

[56] Guattari and Deleuze (n 46); Dolphijn and van der Tuin, *New Materialism: Interviews & Cartographies* (n 14) 359.

and non-anthropocentric, non-exclusionary humanist transnational sports law analysis with emancipatory potential.[57]

III. TRANSNATIONAL SPORTS LAW BATHED IN LIGHT

The primary focus of this volume is on legal entanglement, more specifically on how European legal concepts, idea(l)s, norms, and so on interact and intra-act with what is formally considered social norms and institutions in *lex sportiva*; and what this means for the governance of global sport. While the contributions highlight different forms of legal entanglement, the thesis here is that the chapters shed light on how the (semi-)-autonomous *lex sportiva* is materially produced. By drawing on various elements of legal entanglement pertaining to each chapter, this section aims to point out an inevitable connection between this volume and underlying kinetic-material processes of *lex sportiva* through a new materialist reading. While further exploration and theorisation of the concept assemblage in a posthumanist direction in the context of transnational sports law would be productive, this section seeks to expand the new materialist or posthuman legal conceptual toolbox by utilising the analytical framework of *flow*, *fold* and *field of circulation* based on a performative new materialism. Let us now turn to a brief outline of the latter.[58]

A. The Secret of the God Particle: Notes on a Performative New Materialism

Twenty years ago, 'popular press fetishized' the discovery of the God particle, also known as the Higgs boson. However, the important finding was not the empirical observable particle itself, but rather the Higgs field, the invisible quantum field in motion that produces the particles.[59] All known matter is in motion and all motion is matter/energy. 'Matter is movement and movement is matter.'[60] It is a real kinetic process of materialisation and 'indeterminate performance'. The criteria of performative (process or kinetic) new materialism, which distinguish it from other new materialisms are threefold: (i) matter is pedetic; (ii) an iterative, ongoing, indeterminate process; and (iii) relational and immanently self-caused.[61]

[57] Braidotti and Hlavajova (n 17) 277; Dolphijn and Tuin, *New Materialism: Interviews & Cartographies* (n 14) 44.

[58] Nail (n 21); Nail (n 8); For a short introduction to the concepts, see Nail (n 45); see, eg, Philippopoulos-Mihalopoulos (n 8); Käll (n 5).

[59] Nail (n 8) 52–62.

[60] T Nail and T Kim, 'An Interview with Thomas Nail' (2023) 2 *Mobility Humanities* 104.

[61] While this field of new materialism aligns with, for example, Hohmann's more general view of new materialism it eschews, at the same time, the opening to vitalism. Thus, performative new materialism focuses on physicality and stresses the entanglement and intra-action of all matter. Matter is not characterised as vital or lively but in motion. J Hohmann, 'Diffuse Subjects and Dispersed

Pedesis is defined as '[...] the motion of semi-autonomous self-transport: the motion of the foot to walk, to run, to leap, to dance unpredictable'.[62] It implies that all matter is in motion and that it is 'continuous with its previous position', but its new move is indeterminate. Pedesis is inherent to the motion of matter. Matter's pedetic nature is explained by its relation to other motions making it indeterminate but not random or probabilistic, as 'position only occurs in relation to momentum'. The influence of matter and its response to motions, both self and others, and the contingency make it 'capable of producing emergent metastable states' over time. Pedesis is a precondition for the curvature of motion or *flow* of matter which are necessary for motion or flows to intersect, and hence to create composites or *folds*. These states appear solid or stable but become turbulent again when entering into new, material relations.[63]

Pedetic motion is an *iterative, ongoing, and indeterminate process* at the smallest quantum level as well as on the largest spatiotemporal scales. It is an open process and cannot be captured by limits and *boundaries* because they are constantly rearticulated.[64] Each iteration is partly novel and unique, yet inseparable from or completely determined by any other. 'Even the always-partly-unique-and-unpredictable performances of the tiniest "single" electron, thus, serve to reconfigure the "entire" open-whole of the cosmos anew' making performative matter radically entangled.[65]

Furthermore, there is *nothing outside* this *relationality*; there *is* nothing but full relational immanently self-caused matter-in-motion. The relations are always asymmetrical and the approach needs to consider particular material power relations. The relationality is also why Gamble et al view the primary inquiry of performative new materialism as seeking to identify the real conditions of the emergence of different beings. This inquiry is ontological, but not foundational. Rather it is historically relational, facilitated by the appearance of increased material, human-nonhuman entanglement in our current era.[66] It is precisely this increased material entanglement of (the) *lex sportiva* that contributions in this volume help to illuminate via their focus on legal entanglement.[67]

Power: New Materialist Insights and Cautionary Lessons for International Law' (2021) 34 *Leiden Journal of International Law* 585, 592. See especially n 59. Gamble, Hanan and Nail (n 2); Nail and Kim (n 60); Nail (n 8).

[62] Nail (n 8) 72.

[63] ibid 72–74; see also Gamble, Hanan and Nail (n 42).

[64] Gamble, Hanan and Nail (n 42); Nail (n 8) 88–91.

[65] Gamble, Hanan and Nail (n 42); Nail (n 8) 88–91.

[66] Gamble, Hanan and Nail (n 42): 'In other words, it does not aim to identify the absolute or immutable structure of being for ever and all time (being qua being). Rather, it seeks to identify, given a particular historical emergence of which we ourselves are an integral, fully-material part, the real conditions of that emergence.'

[67] Nail (n 8) The idea of matter-in-motion being ontologically primary is supported by contemporary physics research, cosmology and quantum gravity, and neither space nor time seems to preexist to matter-in-motion but rather emerge in and through motion. As Nail puts it: 'In short, kinetic turbulence is at the heart of the cosmic-origins of space-time itself. [...]'.

B. Robinson Islands

> 'There is a crack, a crack in everything
> That's how the light gets in'.
>
> – Leonard Cohen

Mark James and Guy Osborn in chapter five of this volume allude to the material production of (the) *lex sportiva* by illuminating the regulatory origins of sport (rules and governing bodies) in nineteenth and twentieth century Europe, not least the United Kingdom (particularly London), noting *competition* as a driver for standardisation and the significant 'substantive, procedural, and cultural' influence of Europe on the legal and regulatory frameworks of sport. The influence remains strong today not least since 'so many of the world's major ISFs, including the IOC, [are] established, located in, and operating from European jurisdictions [...]'.[68] The historical account points to the '*conditions of the appearance*' of sports governance and (the) *lex sportiva* in Europe. Much like Robinson in Defoe's *Robinson Crusoe* (1719) only 'appears first on his island under the more primary threefold natural-human-social metabolic process',[69] so it becomes clear that sports governance and (the) *lex sportiva* only appear first in Europe through material processes.

Taking a historical materialist approach, Collins explains that what distinguished British sports in the 1750s from the rural antecedents was not only the rules of play but also their ability to systematically and regularly generate revenue.[70] Already in the 1750s, sports were becoming commodities: an emerging entertainment industry. Britain's centrality to the birth of modern sport, recognised by James and Osborn, Collins suggests, cannot be separated from the emerging capitalist economy or from the profit-driven aristocratic landowners' agriculture. Sport went from recreational pleasure to a metaphor and reflection of everyday life in a capitalist society. Before the commercialisation of sport in the eighteenth century, the idea of common rules, as we know them, governing sport did not exist. Collins writes that

> [t]he introduction of the codes of rules [...] for all major contests were a direct consequence of the commercial development of sport. This itself was an extension of the way in which the law in the eighteenth century was itself acquiring new significance.[71]

Britain's move away from religious and monarchical authority to an impersonal rule of law based on *property rights* and formal equality can be seen as entangled with the development of early sports regulation as the rules for boxing (1743) and cricket (1744). Broughton's boxing rules from 1734 with the aim of

[68] Mark James and Guy Osborn, in chapter five of this volume.
[69] See Nail (n 2) 178–97.
[70] T Collins, *Sport in Capitalist Society: A Short History* (Routledge, 2013) 2.
[71] ibid 6–7.

facilitating an uncertainty of outcome in competitions were designed under the imperative of profit – enabling legitimate gambling.[72]

Now, a lot has happened with sport and capitalism since the eighteenth century. However, these historical material conditions remain intertwined with contemporary *lex sportiva*. The current regime is not insulated from the material conditions and this is clearly evidenced when James and Osborn explore the production of the regulation on ambush marketing in the wake of the Olympic Games in Sydney 2000. The authors trace how in (the) *lex sportiva* and *lex Olympica*, specifically the Olympic Charter and the Host City Contracts (HCCs), Anglo-European legal thinking and notions of intellectual property, with theoretical and philosophical underpinnings in the work of John Locke and Jeremy Bentham, conjoin with ambush marketing techniques, *physical locations* (Olympic venues and routes), and not least with capital; the International Olympic Committee's (IOC) commercial and economic interests, and its revenue streams to co-produce an Olympic law[73] ('a super intellectual property right') in the host state.

From a performative new materialist perspective, all of the instances mentioned above are produced by a continuous multiplicity of the *flow* of matter or a kinetic ongoing iterative and indeterminate process of materialisation or becoming/formation. Flows are the invisible material conditions of all of the empirical realities on every scale, including but not limited to, Olympic law, *lex sportiva*, society and nature. Flow does not, however, explain the perceived discreteness around us. For this we need the concept of *fold*. A fold is like an eddy or whirlpool in the flows of being. Folds are the foundation of kinetic structures. Here the fold is understood as the foundation of the structures of (the) *lex sportiva* as a regime in motion.[74] When folds are conjoined it is possible to say that the folds cause an entity. However, to say that folds cause an entity is a shortcut for a more lengthy description of the 'kinetic components' of the metastability.[75]

Ambush marketing can, for example, be conceived as being made up of a multiplicity of material flows and folds comprising of, for example, objectives (increasing profit and brand awareness, and generating psychological effects in humans), techniques (impinging on physical spaces reserved for someone other

[72] ibid 1–13; For the role of competition as a power (an abstract impersonal form of domination) under capitalist arrangements, see S Mau, '"The Mute Compulsion of Economic Relations": Towards a Marxist Theory of the Abstract and Impersonal Power of Capital' (2021) 29 *Historical Materialism* 3.

[73] Mark James and Guy Osborn in chapter five of this volume, defines this as '[…] the body of national laws that is forced into existence by a privately constituted transnational organisation, the IOC […]'.

[74] However, a fold is nothing other than a flow, flowing over itself, responding to itself in a cycle. In other words, the fold is a loop or junction of flows. Flows and folds are, so to speak, what produces the world all the way up and all the way down. Nail (n 8).

[75] ibid.

than the ambusher), effects (creating spatial and temporal event zones in the physical environment).[76] You might object that this is selecting the best or most desirable example. However, even if we consider Bentham's and Locke's work underlying intellectual property law, it is comprised of material flows and folds. Bentham and Locke were humans who are, as Davies puts it, 'an assemblage of symbiotic and autopoietic processes and is, moreover, not only a being but a becoming, an ongoing process of constitution from quite different materials'.[77] With the conceptual framework utilised here, it translates into the view of humans beings as continuities: flows, folds, ordered in fields of circulating matter in motion through which flows of matter are reproduced and transformed.[78]

What is described in the chapter as 'sustained interactions' between normative and legal orders influencing law is, from the materialist perspective advocated here, derived from a wide range of human-nonhuman agencies or intra-acting[79] material flows and folds. James and Osborn's transnationalised process of the creation of Olympic Law from (the) *lex Olympica* in the form of diffusion and transplantation thus becomes an excellent example of the controlled reproduction and redirection of collective material movement across a certain limited field.[80] The production of Olympic law, which is apparent in the chapter, is not abstract, static, immaterial, exclusively human, or autonomous, although it may be reified into such a form, but rather it emerges from a multiplicity of material flows and folds ordered in a field of circulation – Olympic law.

The principal contractual legal framework enabling the Olympic Games, the HCC returns in Yuliya Chernykh's chapter which charts European legal influence on the structure and content of the HCC, *lex Olympica*, and *lex sportiva*. Chernykh states,

> [o]ver time and as the IOC's revenues from media rights increased significantly, the contractual arrangement became more sophisticated. The precision and detail in contractual arrangements grew in tandem with the growth of the Olympic Games and the institutionalisation of the IOC.[81]

Chernykh thus captures how flows of capital and the sporting events in themselves generate the conditions for the creation of metastable folds or the norms of the HCCs. The norms of the HCCs could be understood as the result of

[76] See ibid 14–18.

[77] M Davies, *Ecolaw: Legality, Life, and the Normativity of Nature* (Routledge, 2022) 8.

[78] Nail (n 45) 189–90.

[79] K Barad, *Meeting the Universe Halfway: Quantum Physics and the Entanglement of Matter and Meaning* (Duke University Press, 2007) 125–28. http://ebookcentral.proquest.com/lib/umeaub-ebooks/detail.action?docID=1169310>. Intra-action is the co-constitutive process, where ontological inseparability is not only recognised but foundational and contrasted with common interaction. Whereas interaction assumes that there are separate individual agencies that come before interaction, intra-action signifies the mutual constitution of the entangled agencies which do not precede but emerge through their intra-action.

[80] See Mark James and Guy Osborn in chapter five of this volume, Table 5.1.

[81] Yuliya Chernykh in chapter four in this volume.

human deliberation and acculturation. However, shifting the view of the human to the posthuman means that the latter is in itself a product of various folds, organs/bodies but also norms (legal, social, of subjectivity, more-than-human, capitalist).[82] When the entanglement of matter and meaning is taken seriously, the norms and the European contract law concepts (such as good faith and liquidated damages) that permeate the HCCs become as material as a physical trumpet, see section II.[83] If the HCC's potentially legitimising material effect on what has been described as a '[...] travelling totalitarian state that pitched up in host city every couple of years and subjected the population, especially the poor and racially oppressed, to police state measures'[84] is added to the destructive impact of mega-sporting events on the environment involving destroyed ecosystems, a massive 'carbon footprint', and other long-lasting environmental impacts; the material shaping of the HCCs and the material effects become hard to deny.[85]

Rusa Agafonova's chapter focuses on the capacity of EU competition law to affect the 'Swiss based sports ecosystem', its autonomy, and governance by studying the complex interaction between different legal components. The ecosystem works, in my reading of the author's text, as a metaphor. However, I suggest that it is possible to take it seriously, if not literally. The ecosystem is, just as ecology, an apt metaphor for a new materialist approach which aims to bring relations rather than separations to the fore. Similar to ecology it alludes to diversity, mutuality, porous boundaries, and importantly, movement.[86] From the new materialist perspective the term ecosystem would signal the 'system' embeddedness in material ecologies characterised by (human and nonhuman) agency. Agency here does not require human consciousness but rather a material-kinetic relation or responsiveness.[87] As an example, one of the main reasons (besides the revenue redistribution by the IOC in the wake of the growth of the Olympic Games), according to Chappelet, for the emergence of a sports ecosystem in Switzerland is found in the encounter between the IOC founder, Pierre de Coubertin, and Switzerland. Coubertin made many visits to Switzerland and throughout his life

[82] F Johns, 'Norms' in Braidotti, Jones and Klumbytė (n 23).

[83] ibid 18.

[84] Collins (n 70) 124–25. In the preparation for the 2016 Olympic Games (and 2014 football World Cup) in Brazil, an estimated 1.5 million Brazilians were removed from their homes because of the building of new stadiums.

[85] See Thorpe, Brice and Clark (n 10) From a new materialist perspective, researchers McDonald and Sterling explored the connection between polluted water and the 2016 Olympic Games in Rio de Janeiro, and argued that the media coverage of polluted waterways in Brazil and the impact on athletes, tourists, etc was entirely anthropocentric: MG McDonald and J Sterling, 'Feminist New Materialisms and the Troubled Waters of the 2016 Rio de Janeiro Olympic and Paralympic Games' in J Newman H Thorpe and D Andrews (eds), *Sport, Physical Culture and the Moving Body: Materialisms, Technologies, and Ecologies* (Rutgers University Press, 2020).

[86] Davies (n 3) 58.

[87] Nail (n 2) 132. Self-consciousness found in all matter emerges when it swerves and responds to itself.

remained strongly attached to the country.[88] Coubertin was in particular touched by the material folds in the Swiss landscape, sensing and sensed by the geographical location by lac Leman. His choice of Lausanne as the permanent IOC base was shaped by his vision of a 'modern Olympia on the shores of a Swiss lake'.[89] The founder of the IOC even launched an architecture competition to this end; the winners' design displayed an Olympia on the shores of lac Leman. Thus, just as the Olympic hub has had a strong (not least economic) impact on Switzerland, so it would seem that Switzerland's materiality and a material vision also affected the emergence of the Olympic hub.[90]

Extending this line of thought you could say that *lex sportiva's* Swiss roots are dependent on the waters of lac Leman.[91] Viewing the place as regulator and rule generator, and nonhuman agency as 'constraints, enablers, and co-creators of formal laws, place laws, and governance mechanisms'[92] have served to re-think legal pluralism.[93] Bartel describes place not only as co-producing state and other laws but its own legal order comprising of unique biophysical and social features of constraints of place which may interact, conflict and co-generate other legal orders, including scientific laws. Although sport is allegedly pushing the boundaries of what is humanly possible, gravity and other 'chemical and physical laws control human behaviour'. Furthermore, it co-creates space and place. The place law which is co-created controls in turn 'human behaviours, through material, biophysical, and social factors, and ecological, geomorphological and cultural features, of places'.[94] Extended to the biophysical, legal plurality proliferates and (kinetic-) material processes co-producing the normative are foregrounded.[95]

Mislav Mataija's chapter explores how the notion of proportionality in EU law is translated into the notion of good governance in (the) *lex sportiva*. In my reading, the chapter illuminates how these notions are materially produced. First, in relation to the development of the notion of good governance in sport, the author draws our attention to its origin in corporate governance 'driven [...] by the emergence of commercialisation culture in sport organisations' with the key objective being economic efficiency and not, as one might perhaps think, 'rising awareness of the public role of sporting bodies'. To the author, 'Corporate governance and, by extension, "good governance" is

[88] J-L Chappelet, 'Switzerland's Century-Long Rise as the Hub of Global Sport Administration' (2021) 38 *The International Journal of the History of Sport* 569, 570.

[89] ibid 571 and 583.

[90] ibid.

[91] In a very direct sense, humans working in the sports governing bodies (SGB) get a large part of their drinking water from the lake.

[92] R Bartel, 'Place-Speaking: Attending to the Relational, Material and Governance Messages of Silent Spring' (2018) 184 *The Geographical Journal* 64, 70.

[93] ibid.

[94] Bartel (n 92).

[95] Davies (n 77) 90.

primarily targeted at increasing market value by improving the internal functioning of the organisation and making it accountable to shareholders.'[96] The notion of good governance in sport as interpreted by the author can thus be conceived of as a fold of various notions produced by material flows. While the quotes above sheds light on the material production of the notion of good governance, it also alludes to it 'being not a neutral nor inevitable measure of progress' but rather one associated with capitalist modernity and thus questions its effects.[97]

Second, in relation to the application of EU law's proportionality test to sport, the author shows how folds of good governance and proportionality are intimately and importantly connected as 'competition and internal market enforcement often turns on issues that form part of the "good governance" toolkit'.[98] Mataija states that 'From the EU's perspective, linking good governance with autonomy is perhaps understandable: EU policy-makers want to achieve a measure of progress without too much heavy lifting, relatively risk-free and in the absence of a clear legislative competence'.[99] The intra-action and inclusion of a good governance fold in proportionality leads to the 'proceduralisation of proportionality' – a complicated field of circulation which has the capacity for the application of the principle of proportionality in a sporting context. At the same time, it contributes to covering up the governance of sports governing bodies (SGBs) in a 'layer of credibility', in turn contributing to reifying their 'legal and political autonomy'. In doing so there is a risk of it being overinclusive, occluding necessary measures against '[c]orruption, doping, human rights violations, improper treatment of individual athletes, exclusion of competitors'.[100]

Jan Exner's chapter also departs from the principle of proportionality in EU law and in the European Convention on Human Rights (ECHR). The chapter's focus is on how the EU and the Council of Europe (CoE) affected the 'transnational law-making process resulting' in the World Anti-Doping Code (WADC) 2021. More specifically, he examines how and to what extent the comments of the institutions' representatives in the consultation process shaped the assessment of the proportionality concerning the length of ineligibility periods. The world anti-doping regime comes across as a salient example of the legal entanglement of (the) *lex sportiva* with EU law and the ECHR.[101]

The anti-doping field allows us to trace, perhaps more easily than other fields, the material flows contributing to its production. Through the chapter we can see how the material factors for the comments (the meaningful statements) in the consultation process are made possible by (prohibited) substances

[96] Mislav Mataija, in chapter eight of this volume.
[97] Jones (n 2) 38.
[98] Mislav Mataija, in chapter eight of this volume.
[99] ibid 22.
[100] ibid.
[101] Jan Exner, in chapter seven of this volume.

(cocaine, heroin, tetrahydrocannabinol (THC)), their ingestion, use or possession, and stimulating effects on athletic performance, as well as processes put in place to control (testing, whereabouts information) athletes' bodies and several other conditions. However, from the new materialist perspective advocated here, the material conditions are not simply the generative supporting background. The point is not simply, as Barad makes clear, that there are important material factors in addition to discursive ones. Rather, the discursive practices *are* 'specific material (re)configurings of the world through which the determination of boundaries, properties, and meanings is differentially enacted'.[102] The WADC 2021 can in itself not be abstracted from the invention of the historical condition of alphabet language, distribution of paper, printing press, literacy, data, and social contingency that made the Code possible, as well as the various processes shaping the Code.[103] In other words, the Code cannot be abstracted from the casual intra-actions, flows and folds. The meaning in the comments is thus not the words themselves 'but the ongoing performance *of* the world in its differential dance of intelligibility and unintelligibility'.[104] Through the material-discursive aggregate, flows and folds of the review process contribute to regional stability of motion, a discreteness in the form of the WADC 2021. However, the whole process is only one of a continual infinite sum of matter-in-motion and its relations can thus be redistributed. Read through a new materialist lens, the chapter illuminates the possibility of a material-kinetic historical analysis of the 2021 WADC.

A challenge which informed the conference in Umeå that preceded this volume is captured by the preliminary question: '[…] if not the EU, who will rein in the various abuses and corruption in the sporting world?'[105] Johan Lindholm takes on this question and provides three 'complementary explanations' for certain legal entanglements pertaining to the institutional centre of (the) *lex sportiva*. Building on his biography of the 'foremost authoritative interpreter of *lex sportiva* and main contributor',[106] the chapter contains a case study on the place of the principle of legality in the jurisprudence of the Court of Arbitration for Sport (CAS).[107] Lindholm first brings our attention to the public law principle of legality by tracing its genealogy. In particular, he shows that the principle intra-acts with different understandings of the rule of law. The principle of legality and the rule of law '[…] are deeply intertwined and legality can be understood as a subset of the rule of law, its formal element'.[108] The principle of legality and rule of law are connected to sovereignty, democracy, freedom, and liberty.

[102] Barad (n 79) 145–53.
[103] Nail (n 45) 187.
[104] Barad (n 79) 145–53.
[105] Mislav Mataija, in chapter eight of this volume.
[106] Johan Lindholm, in chapter three of this volume.
[107] See ibid.
[108] ibid.

Furthermore, the origins explain why it '[...] maps closely to a Westphalian understanding of law, law making and legal orders'[109] and functions to limit the exercise of power by government and public entities and not private actors.

After tracing the deeper roots of the principle of legality, the author shows how it is folded into (the) *lex sportiva* in various areas (quasi-penal disciplinary matters and beyond) through the CAS jurisprudence, thereby becoming a legal principle that traverses the formal public/private binary. However, it is also pointed out that the principle might only be one of many public law principles performing this move.[110] From my perspective, the chapter shows how aggregate flows or normativity at the limits of a field (public law), can move on entering into another field of circulation (*lex sportiva*) via another set of folds (CAS jurisprudence). The public law field 'leaks' flow. As stated above, it is a complicated and manifold process producing a folded system where what resides inside and outside is relative. There are no absolute inclusions and exclusions. Furthermore, the legal flows and folds cannot be severed from the historical and material-kinetic conditions of the principle of legality, rule of law, or CAS arbitrators. This applies even for less obvious conditions such as neuronal processing that escapes consciousness but is essential for it to function according to recent research in neuroscience and cognitive psychology.[111]

The chapter then turns to the different theoretical frameworks offering various complementary and non-exclusive explanations of connection of public and private law at the CAS. It becomes clear that the emergence of the principle of legality in *lex sportiva* is perhaps not very different from other norms that '[...] emerge from the thick textures of history, from narratives that circulate between different lives and coalesce into nomoi or normative worlds – shared and inhabited in the way that myths and narratives are shared among members of a communities'.[112] Just as the Greeks did not create their law (nomos) out of nothing but themselves, CAS arbitrators did not create legality in (the) *lex sportiva ex nihilo*, although it might appear that way, as form.[113] Ultimately it was produced from the material-kinetic flows.[114]

Aurélie Villanueva sets out to '[...] show that the EU is developing a societal narrative which has the potential to counterbalance the hyper-commodification of sport'. Villanueva '[...] investigates whether EU law relates to the notion of sport beyond the market and whether it connects the notion of sport to other

[109] ibid 6.

[110] See A Duval, 'Seamstress of Transnational Law: How the Court of Arbitration for Sport Weaves the Lex Sportiva' in N Krisch (ed), *Entangled Legalities Beyond the State*, 1st edn (Cambridge University Press, 2021).

[111] See KN Hayles, 'The Cognitive Nonconcious and the New Materialisms' in S Ellenzweig and JH Zammito (eds), *The New Politics of Materialism: History, Philosophy, Science* (Routledge, Taylor & Francis Group, 2017) 182.

[112] Davies (n 24).

[113] Nail (n 2) 143–47.

[114] Davies (n 3).

notions such as society, cohesion or identity'.[115] The author demonstrates the co-production of a narrative recognising the importance of the social dimension of sport in and through EU policy documents, European Court of Justice case law and secondary EU law. The author concludes that 'EU law grasps sports through its competence to regulate markets but also participates in de-commodifying sport by recognising its societal role'.[116] By drawing into the discussion the ongoing process of 'hyper-commodification' of sport, that is the 'quantitative explosion in the value of sports […] and the broader, intensive commodification of secondary, non-play aspects of the game',[117] the chapter makes it possible for us to see that *lex sportiva* is entangled with a range of commodities.[118]

The commodities (be it the football player, the club, the stadium, the game, etc) might *appear* as individual objects but they are in short: 'only relatively or regionally discrete, like a chain of volcanic islands on a vast ocean. Below the reflective, shining surface of the water are the continual material volcanic processes from which these relatively discrete island emerge'. Marx shows us these material kinetic conditions by which commodities (in *Capital*) and atoms (in *The Difference Between the Democritean and Epicurean Philosophy of Nature*) emerge.[119] Conversely, and in line with what has been stated above, in legal theory the subject is the 'atom' because '[e]very legal relation is a relation between subjects'.[120] Thus, regardless of whether we speak of atoms, commodities and subjects of *lex sportiva* there must be material flows, folds which circulate across a field of co-producing relations, for these 'cells' *to appear*. Appearance is a fundamentally relational process as seen above. Furthermore, the sporting commodities are not passive or inert units of discrete matter for subjective sensation or consumption by humans, as might be obvious to anyone watching a sporting event. Rather, the commodities, the legal subjects and the atoms, are active and passive groups of sensuous objects – of folds – that '[…] form non-anthropocentric assemblages of objects with their own collective agency'.[121]

European legal entanglement of (the) *lex sportiva* have indeed '[…] coalesced around the intersection of sport, competition law, and the fundamental freedoms'.[122] However, this is far from a complete picture. Christopher Flanagan touches on legal entanglements which until now have been largely unexplored territory.

[115] Aurélie Villanueva, in chapter nine of this volume.

[116] ibid.

[117] AJ Walsh and R Giulianotti, 'This Sporting Mammon: A Normative Critique of the Commodification of Sport' (2001) 28 *Journal of the Philosophy of Sport* 53, 55.

[118] See C Miéville, 'The Commodity-Form Theory of International Law' in S Marks (ed), *International Law on the Left*, 1st edn (Cambridge University Press, 2008); E Bronislavovich Pashukanis, *The General Theory of Law & Marxism* (Transaction Publishers, 2002).

[119] Nail (n 2) 49.

[120] Pashukanis (n 118) 109.

[121] Nail (n 2) 59–76 and 137–38.

[122] Christopher Flanagan, in chapter six of this volume.

Focusing on the *Fédération Internationale de Football Association* (FIFA) Regulations, the chapter draws on a broad concept of regulation according to which the latter involves three capacities: (i) standard setting; (ii) information gathering; and (iii) behaviour modification. Flanagan concludes that '[…] FIFA, and indeed most SGBs' are bestowed with the capacities and perform a general regulatory function.[123] Duval has shown that the FIFA Regulations on the Status and Transfer of Players (RSTP) are an emblematic example of legal entanglement involving a constellation of bodies, commonly categorised, legal, social, political, and even digital, public or private, in co-production and re-production of an institutional framework affecting and affected by the standard setting capacity of FIFA.[124] From the perspective advocated here, the bodies are intra-acting with the global market of international football transfers (a multibillion-USD transnational industry) and thus, in short, composed by flows of capital, but also by various (human and nonhuman) flows that in turn affect the market. For example, when SARS-CoV-2, so to speak, jumped the species barrier, the international football transfer market and FIFA's Regulations were affected.[125]

Second, regarding the capacity of FIFA and the RSTP to modify the behaviour of its subjects, professional football players, it is obvious that by determining the status of players, the players' eligibility to participate in organised football, and the players' transfer between clubs belonging to different associations have a wide array of material, not only economic, effects for the players but also beyond.

Third, and perhaps less obviously, through FIFA's information gathering capacity (its Transfer Matching System, FIFA Regulations are intertwined with material conditions because the gathered information is intrinsically material.[126] Similar to 'value', information, data or knowledge are not born *ex nihilo*. Treating information, data or knowledge as separable products to the materialities needed to produce them, separate from 'sites of production, transformation and distribution', implies a 'dematerialisation' undergirded in the division of mind and matter and entangled with commodification and advanced capitalism.[127] In summary, against this background, it is indeed, as Flanagan notes, '[…]

[123] ibid.

[124] A Duval, 'The FIFA Regulations on the Status and Transfer of Players: Transnational Law-Making in the Shadow of Bosman' in A Duval and B Van Rompuy (eds), *The Legacy of Bosman* (TMC Asser Press, 2016).

[125] E García Silvero, 'FIFA Global Transfer Report 2021' (FIFA) 3; M Koopmans and others, 'Origins of SARS-CoV-2: Window Is Closing for Key Scientific Studies' (2021) 596 *Nature*; M Ruiz-Aravena and others, 'Ecology, Evolution and Spillover of Coronaviruses from Bats' (2022) 20 *Nature Reviews Microbiology* 299: '[T]hese [coronavirus] pathogens cannot cause outbreaks in humans unless the conditions for spillover and onward transmission are met. The risk of spillover depends on the level of human exposure, which is increasingly influenced by habitat deterioration and encroachment into wild area'.

[126] 'Contrary to the popular understanding, there's nothing ideal or immaterial about it. Information only exists where there's a material substrate of matter and energy to store, transmit, and process. Information is part of a material world. 'Wark cited in Käll. Käll (n 10) 57.

[127] Käll (n 2) 59–76; For a discussion of devalourisation, see Nail (n 2) 77–99.

illusory to think of FIFA's regulatory functions as being wholly divisible from its commercial functions; there is no neat delineation, the two are intertwined'.[128]

The author concludes by posing the question, who regulates the regulators, the EU or football itself? The answer is football for the most part in the shadow of EU law. However, applying a new materialist lens to the chapter helps us see that perhaps the picture is even more complex. The capacity to regulate is co-produced by a multiplicity of material flows and folds with more or less effect on governance. What, then, does this mean as concerns the urgent questions of responsibility, accountability, and ethics?[129] Let us return to this question in the concluding remarks.

Questions pertaining to responsibility, accountability and ethics or more specifically to the (un)reconciliation of fairness (safety) and exclusion/inclusion in sport policy and (the) *lex sportiva* haunts Audrey Boisgontier's chapter.[130] The chapter differs from the previous chapters. Not only does it engage with the binaries: public/private, law/non-law, state/non-state, etc, but it also includes questions pertaining to the fundamental structuring principle of sport, according to which there is a female category and male category in sport. Only women are eligible to participate in the former and only men in the latter (although there are of course exceptions to this structure).[131] Boisgontier explores the potential for the European Court of Human Rights (ECtHR) to shape *lex sportiva* 'as a more inclusive framework' via the ECHR through the case of the athlete Caster Semenya.[132] Although the Caster Semenya case pertains to the World Athletics Differences of Sex Development (DSD) Regulations concerning the eligibility of athletes with variations or differences in sexual development or 'intersex athletes' to participate in athletic events, the case as well as the chapter is embedded in a discourse pertaining to the question of exclusion/inclusion of transwomen in the female category of sports, more general discourses surrounding 'trans' and the question of whether sex is binary and what is a woman.[133]

By providing a historical account of the control of female bodies in Olympic sports and the DSD Regulations and then shifting the focus on to how ECHR's principles in the case of Caster Semenya before the ECtHR could shape (the) *lex sportiva* and the governance of athletics, the chapter shows, in my view, just how inescapable the kinetic-material conditions of transnational sports law

[128] Christopher Flanagan, in chapter six of this volume.

[129] Duval (n 110) 287.

[130] See, eg, J Pike, 'Safety, Fairness, and Inclusion: Transgender Athletes and the Essence of Rugby' (2021) 48 *Journal of the Philosophy of Sport* 155; E Linghede, L Purdy and N Barker-Ruchti, 'Glitching Trans* Athletes: Possibilities for Research and Practice in Sports Coaching' (2022) 11 *Sports Coaching Review* 64.

[131] See E Linghede, 'The Promise of Glitching Bodies in Sport: A Posthumanist Exploration of an Intersex Phenomenon' (2018) 10 *Qualitative Research in Sport, Exercise and Health* 570.

[132] Audrey Boisgontier, in chapter 11 of this volume.

[133] See, eg, M Imbrisevic and others, 'When Ideology Trumps Science: A Response to the Canadian Centre for Ethics in Sport?S Review on Transwomen Athletes in the Female Category' (2022) 11 *Idrottsforum – Nordic Sports Science Forum* 1.

are. Starting with the emergence of the male-female dualism in Olympic sports at the turn of the twentieth century, hinting at its origins in ancient Olympic Games in Greece, and the subsequent gender verification or sex testing regimes, it becomes clear throughout the chapter how the DSD Regulations are a field or ordered web of folds such as SGBs (for example, World Athletics, the IOC and the CAS); formal legal institutions (such as the Swiss Federal Tribunal and ECtHR); European human rights law (principles such as the prohibition of torture and the right to respect for private life); Swiss and Monegasque law; sport rules (such as the World Athletics' Constitution and Rules and the Olympic Charter); non-governmental organisations (Human Rights Watch); but also of histories of 'nude parades', gynaecological examinations, chromosomal tests, control, current gender norms, biological characteristics, blood samples, cultural presumptions, testosterone, international medical ethics, race, class, nationality, the bodies of athletes Dutee Chand and Caster Semenya, sciences and ideologies and the entangled discourse(s) referenced above. When considered in detail, each and every one of these fields is in turn composed of various material flows and folds, the materially entangled nature of *lex sportiva* becomes apparent. By engaging with the intersex phenomenon, itself a fold produced by a multiplicity of intra-acting flows, which has been used by some to challenge binaries such as man/woman, sex/gender, and nature/culture, the chapter makes us see not just added important material factors, but the material-discursive nature of (the) *lex sportiva*.[134]

IV. POSTHUMAN SPORTS LAW: A NEW MATERIALIST CRITICAL RESEARCH AGENDA

If the contributions in this volume bathed (the) *lex sportiva* in light in the sense that, through the examination of European legal entanglement, they lent themselves to a new materialist reading and extended an invitation to fuse the impure concept of *lex sportiva* with (new) materialist insights; the reader might ask to what avail? Do we need a material, concrete, constantly becoming, relational, and entangled understanding of *lex sportiva*? Do we need a materialist theory of or approach to *lex sportiva*? Do we need a *posthuman sports law*? Can we not be content with the perspective of the 'law' as a human product of the social? While this volume demonstrates that the impure *lex sportiva* deserves to be explored further, I also believe that a new materialist theory could complement the impure approach in order to reveal:

> [...] one of *laws* greatest tricks: the dissimulation of its matter is both convincing and necessary, for otherwise the law could not claim access to that cudgel of cudgels, impartial, blind, objective justice. And so the myth goes. In that way, law has

[134] Linghede (n 131).

managed to dissimulate the fact that it is material through and through. That the law is not just the text, the decision, even the courtroom. Law is the pavement, the traffic light, the hood in the shopping mall, the veil in the school, the cell in Guantanamo, the seating arrangement at a meeting, the risotto at the restaurant. [...] *Materiality is steeped in law just as law is steeped in materiality.* Yet, the law manages to dissimulate itself as ruptured, absent, immaterial and so on (emphasis added).[135]

Lex sportiva is part of the material everything that is connected to everything else.[136] If we want to understand the transnational legal regime of sports in practice and the governance of global sports in reality, it is, in this age of movement and under the conditions of pervasive material human and nonhuman entanglement, important that we traverse the inside and outside distinctions – often upheld in sports law and legal scholarship in general.[137] Only by taking a critical materialist perspective can we fully understand how the production of the transnational legal and regulatory regime of sports is shaped. Building on the impure concept of (the) *lex sportiva*, I have tried to show that viewing the material in this volume through a new materialist lens could raise new and interesting questions such as why should we *ex ante* exclude important materialities from sports law inquiries that have a normative effect? What happens if we consider agency more broadly than human consciousness in the production of *lex sportiva*? How does matter become important in the context of transnational sports law? How do place and space shape instances of *lex sportiva*, say in the context of mega-sporting events or the laws of game? What role does nonhuman subjects, such as horses or the environment, play in (the) *lex sportiva*?[138] What is the relationship between *lex sportiva* and the new turn in code-is-law perspectives or the *lex cryptographica* in the context of football transfers of players? Enquiring into questions like these could contribute to prolonging the research agenda associated with the impure perspective in a posthuman direction. The question remains, what does this mean in terms of human responsibility and the call for strict scrutiny of the legal entanglements of (the) *lex sportiva*?[139] If agency is layered or distributed among (material) flows and folds as suggested, then who, or *what*, is responsible for the effects of global sports governance and which ethico-political commitments should we envision in this context? New materialists and posthumanist scholars have made various suggestions with regard to ethics.[140]

I will settle on two final points: The first is that the performative new materialist perspective advocated here and its ontological primacy of entangled or

[135] A Philippopoulos-Mihalopoulos, 'Critical Autopoiesis and the Materiality of Law' (2014) 27 *International Journal for the Semiotics of Law – Revue internationale de Sémiotique juridique* 389, 410.

[136] See Davies (n 77).

[137] See Käll (n 2).

[138] See ibid; Käll (n 5) 117–41.

[139] Duval (n 110) 287.

[140] See Stenseke Arup (n 6) 121–27, for a short overview.

intra-acting matter-in-motion is not, in short, a move to escape human responsibility. The extreme heat stress or material flows and folds cannot be blamed for the death of migrant workers building the FIFA World Cup 2022 in the Qatari desert, although it obviously contributed to the disaster and can help us understand it.[141] If anything, it signals that we find ourselves in an era where the world is both increasingly mobile and humans are entangled with and (particularly the rich minority) co-producing the world we inhabit, and this needs to be taken seriously in the context of sports law.

Second, whereas the realisation of entangled material reality may induce a notion of human responsibility or a normative horizon for a global governance of sport, it certainly does not dictate exactly how we should play the game. In other words, it does not automatically provide a normative vision for sport to counter inequalities and oppression in our anthropocentric 'deeply hierarchical and capitalist [sports] world'.[142] To this end we need a vision for the governance of sport. However, it is only when the social form of motion of (the) *lex sportiva* is fully uncovered that it can be collectively reorganised – a posthuman transnational sports law.[143] Let us therefore transport ourselves from the contributions of this volume bathed in light to the parts of transnational legal regimes of sport still shrouded in darkness where we can expect that the material processes tend to be less transparent.[144] There is a need for critical (new) materialist agenda and a first step in this direction could be an engagement largely omitted in the chapters of this book, including this one, but alluded to in the introduction to the volume in chapter one: the (neo-)colonial dimension as the basis of the material (re)production of *lex sportiva.*

[141] A Duval, 'How Qatar's Migrant Workers Became FIFA's Problem: A Transnational Struggle for Responsibility' (2021) 12 *Transnational Legal Theory* 473.

[142] Nail (n 9).

[143] Nail (n 2) 199.

[144] K Marx, B Fowkes and D Fernbach, *Capital: A Critique of Political Economy* (Penguin Books in association with New Left Review, 1981) 170; see Nail (n 2) 186.

Index

www.ingramcontent.com/pod-product-compliance
Ingram Content Group UK Ltd.
Pitfield, Milton Keynes, MK11 3LW, UK
UKHW020240290926
15470UKWH00002B/651

9 781509 971442